The Origins of
African American Literature,
1680–1865

The Origins of African American Literature, 1680–1865

Dickson D. Bruce Jr.

University Press of Virginia
Charlottesville and London

The University Press of Virginia
© 2001 by the Rector and Visitors of the University of Virginia
All rights reserved
Printed in the United States of America
First published 2001

⊗ The paper used in this publication meets the minimum requirements
of the American National Standard for Information Sciences—Permanence
of Paper for Printed Library Materials, ANSI Z39.48-1984.

Library of Congress Cataloging-in-Publication Data

Bruce, Dickson D., 1946–
The origins of African American literature, 1680–1865 / Dickson D. Bruce Jr.
p.   cm.
Includes bibliographical references and index.
ISBN 0-8139-2066-3 (cloth : alk. paper) — ISBN 0-8139-2067-1 (pbk. : alk. paper)

1. American literature—African American authors—History and criticism.
2. American literature—Colonial period, ca. 1600–1775—History and criticism.
3. American literature—Revolutionary period, 1775–1783—History and criticism. 4. American literature—19th century—History and criticism. 5. American literature—1783–1850—History and criticism. 6. Slaves' writings, American
—History and criticism. 7. African Americans—Intellectual life. 8. African
Americans in literature. 9. Slavery in literature. 10. Slaves in literature. I. Title.

PS153.N5 B78 2001
810.9'896073—dc21
2001001877

TO EMILY AND JUSTIN

Contents

Contents

Preface

IN TRYING TO UNDERSTAND the origins of African American literature, I have taken what many may find to be an unusual approach. For one thing, this study is something other than a survey of major African American authors and their works, although, of course, they occupy center stage. Rather, it is an effort to investigate the historical conditions for an African American literary enterprise. It is an effort to understand why and how black women and men came to do the literary work they did, as well as why, during its more than a century of early development, such work took the various shapes it did.

This study is also unusual in that its focus reaches well beyond the careers of African American writers and their works. It locates the origins of African American literature in a historical context that includes, among other things, African and American oral traditions, European conventions, American race relations, and political activism. Examining a broad array of works by white as well as black authors, I found the origins of African American literature to be in a process in which black and white writers collaborated in the creation of what I call an "African American literary presence." This involved developing a voice and a persona imbued with authority and standing, taking a place in larger realms of discourse in American society. Such a presence began to evolve even before there were African American writers, and it played a major role in American cultural history from colonial times to emancipation and beyond.

At the center of this process was the question of authority. We are accustomed to thinking of the African American voice as historically an excluded voice, a silenced voice. In the period surveyed here this was not the case. By no later than 1680, as a wealth of evidence indicates, some

English and American audiences—black and white—had come to vest a "black" voice with a special authority that was the product of its very blackness. The modes of authority would change, of course, as would the significance of an African American voice in the larger American context. But the authoritative presence would remain a significant part of literary and cultural life.

Most important to understanding the nature of that authoritative voice, I suggest here, is an examination of the kinds of communities in which it could be asserted, what I sometimes refer to as "discursive worlds." This has meant, above all, an approach to literary activity focusing less on texts than on the webs of interaction among African Americans and between black and white Americans that encouraged literary endeavor and provided for the discursive realms within which it took place.

As we shall see, such interactions and the exchanges they entailed were present from an early time. In chapter 1, for example, I show how traditions for an African American voice were shaped during the colonial era by English literary conventions, African and African American oral traditions, religious developments involving blacks and whites alike, and ambiguities in race relations, all interacting to create new literary forms and possibilities. And as we shall also see, the notion of "interaction" is crucial. As the evidence indicates, Africans, African Americans, British writers, and Anglo-American activists really did collaborate, sometimes quite intentionally, to create a credible black voice and to assert the authoritative possibilities for that voice in contexts far more diverse than one might expect.

A similar approach governs subsequent chapters. Chapter 2, in some ways a linchpin for this study, documents the significance of African American voices to both the Revolutionary cause and the early years of American nation-building. It was during this era that a distinctive African American literary persona began to emerge—apparent initially, and most influentially, in the career of Phillis Wheatley—embodying tendencies in African American voice and authority that had only begun to take shape in earlier times, establishing patterns that would remain important for almost another hundred years. It was also during this era, in the works of both black and white writers, that a distinctively African American critique of the larger society began to enter into the realm of public discourse.

Both these themes—the development of an authoritative black persona and the emergence of a distinctive black perspective on events— guide much of what comes later in the book, though, again, in differing contexts. These include, in chapters 3 and 4, contexts framed by intensifying discrimination, even movements for deportation, during the first three decades of the nineteenth century and, in chapters 5 through 8, contexts created by the rise of immediatist abolition. Though differing markedly, and posing distinctive sets of demands, each of these contexts called forth a quest for black authority—for an authoritative literary persona and a distinctive black perspective—in which a broad array of influences were brought to bear and a wide range of discursive interactions helped shape the personae and perspectives that ultimately emerged. This quest could entail the evangelical interactions, with their powerful celebrations of a pious black voice, that appeared early in the nineteenth century. It could entail the investigations of an African identity prompted by exclusionist movements occurring at about the same time. And it could entail the biracial experiments in literary activism inaugurated by the creation of the *Liberator* in the early 1830s.

The approach taken here, then, to the study of the origins of African American literature is one that investigates, above all, its sources and locates those sources in the changing historical milieu within which literary activity took place. Certainly, this approach is not intended to slight the specifically literary traditions in which African American literary activity became involved, whether those that influenced its development or those it helped to create. One of the focuses of this study is, in fact, the emergence of ideas of a specifically African American literary tradition— widely acknowledged—that began fairly early in the nineteenth century. Such traditions were part of that changing historical milieu. My approach might be described as essentially rhetorical, focusing as it does above all on the purposes of African American writing, on the ways in which writers sought to fulfill those purposes, and on the reasons why they may have believed that certain strategies made sense.

Again, many readers may find this approach unusual in its characterization of African American literature's origins and its insistence on a historically authoritative African American voice. This study may also seem unusual because it presents the claim that such an authoritative voice did play a major role in the continuing social, cultural, and political processes that shaped the American nation. The authoritative voice not only gave African American writers a role in shaping debates over issues of color, slavery, and racial oppression, as one might expect. It also did much to focus American thinking on more general issues of public discourse, including processes of democratization and the nature of the public realm, from at least the middle of the eighteenth century. Focusing on modes of inclusion rather than exclusion may seem strange where the history of African American literature is concerned, but it yields evidence giving that literature a public role and significance that has rarely been noted before. It also helps to highlight and explain the anxieties that literature created beginning by no later than the Revolutionary era. These anxieties would increase throughout the first two-thirds of the nineteenth century.

There is one other sense, however, in which the approach herein to the history of African American letters might seem unusual, even disconcerting. This too grows out of its essentially historical, and rhetorical, focuses. Although I have examined a great number of texts, more than could ever be cited or discussed in the pages to follow, this is far from being, and was never intended to be, a survey of African American authors and their works. Because I focus on the discursive settings within which an African—or African American—voice played its part, the discussion tends to be as much sociological as literary. The concern is, again, to identify those processes and communities in which an African American voice could emerge and in which its creators could feel that there was an audience for it. This means, for one thing, that while textual analyses are important, they tend to be framed by discussions of context, by a focus on the changing historical milieu within which writing took place, rather than on individual works as such.

The nature of this focus is most apparent in chapter 7, in treatments of those authors and works that have attracted the most scholarly attention in our own time—Frederick Douglass's *Narrative*, for instance, Harriet Jacobs's *Incidents in the Life of a Slave Girl*, Martin Delany's *Blake*—but that are put in a somewhat different framework here. The prominence of these works must be acknowledged; their importance was, and is, undeniable. Nevertheless, the focus here is much more on how these works and their creators participated in the particular discursive worlds that both shaped and were shaped by them and on what we can learn from them about those worlds.

Such an approach also accounts for what may seem to be the disproportionate attention given to several writers who I contend played an often underestimated role in helping to shape the discursive worlds in which African American literature took shape—the relatively anonymous storytellers of the eighteenth century, Phillis Wheatley in the Revolutionary era, Sarah Forten in the early years of abolition. Each helped create patterns of expression and authority that even the most prominent writers—a Douglass or a Jacobs—would continue to use, and to build on, as they created what in our own time are regarded as the major works of early African American literary history. Their role as innovators in the development of an African American literary presence gives them a place in this study that they have not often achieved in other treatments of African American literary tradition. Again, this is not to dismiss the importance of some of their now better-known contemporaries and successors. It is, rather, to give the clearest shape to a delineation of those discursive communities that I argue did most to lay the groundwork for the literary traditions whose development this study explores.

The origins of African American literature lay in a dynamic set of processes involving questions of exclusion and inclusion, authority and autonomy, national identity, republicanism, and democracy. They thus provide remarkable insight into the shaping of the American republic and to the formative influences on American public life. Those processes are the subject of this book.

Acknowledgments

I AM GRATEFUL to a number of people for help in writing this book.

Much of the research was done at the University of California, Irvine, with the help of UCI's interlibrary loan staff. Their assistance in locating and obtaining materials was invaluable. Some research did, however, have to be done at other repositories, including the Historical Society of Pennsylvania, the Library Company of Philadelphia (special thanks to Phil Lapsansky), the Boston Public Library, the Houghton Library at Harvard University, the Library of Congress, the Moorland-Spingarn Research Center at Howard University, the Beinecke Library at Yale University, the Bancroft Library in Berkeley, and the Schomburg Center for Research in Black Culture of the New York Public Library. I received excellent assistance at all of these.

I also appreciate the financial support that made my research possible. Grants from the School of Humanities and the Program in African-American Studies at UCI funded much of the research-related travel. I am also grateful for an opportunity to spend a month as scholar-in-residence at the École des Hautes Études en Sciences Sociales, where ideas developed in America underwent some tough scrutiny and where I was also afforded an ideal environment for putting this study in relatively final form.

Several individuals read and commented on portions of this study in one form or another. I appreciate the thoughts, encouragement, and suggestions provided by Robert Hall, Graham Hodges, Emma Lapsansky, George Price, Rita Roberts, David Waldstreicher, and Henry Wonham. I owe particular thanks to James Brewer Stewart, who got involved

Acknowledgments

in this project at an early stage, read the whole thing in more than one version, and offered both unfailing support and invaluable criticism.

Finally, my thanks to the two anonymous readers for the University Press of Virginia and to Richard Holway, the Press's history and social sciences editor, for helping this study become a book.

The Origins of
African American Literature,
1680–1865

1

Background to an
African American Literature,
1680–1760

⚬⚬⚬

To UNDERSTAND THE ORIGINS of African American letters, it is necessary first to understand the framework within which a black literary
enterprise could develop. This framework, antedating the first known
publications by African American writers, was the product of complex
issues of voice and authority, appropriation and attribution in colonial
America and metropolitan Britain. Such issues grew out of the tendencies and ambiguities of race relations in the seventeenth and eighteenth
centuries, as well as the tensions and tendencies in understandings of
color, similarity, and difference during the first 150 years of British settlement in mainland North America. All these developments, taken together, created the kinds of possibilities and constraints that defined how
African Americans sought to influence the larger society or to use writing
to establish a place for themselves in it.

I

The British colonies on the North American mainland presented an
uncertain, shifting picture for people brought from Africa and for their
descendants. The history of colonial race relations was neither static nor
monolithic. At various times and in various places, Africans in North
America faced systems of slavery and freedom that were both oppressive
and permeable, often at the same time. They were encouraged to think
of themselves as part of a larger American colonial society but as people
expected to remain at that society's margins.

The Origins of African American Literature

The complexities of colonial race relations as they developed over time are becoming increasingly understood. The debate over the status of the first Africans to arrive in British North America remains heated, as does the debate over their place in a colonial cultural order. Tendencies and practices were often contradictory and unstable. On the one hand, even before colonization, as the work of Winthrop Jordan and others has made known, the English had developed thoroughgoing ideas of an African distinctiveness and inferiority, drawing on preconceptions rooted in images of blackness and on behavioral and physical differences between the two peoples. A sizable body of travel literature, written by English adventurers and traders who visited the African continent, was widely read in England prior to North American settlement and was well known in the colonies after that. With few exceptions, it offered a strikingly negative portrayal of Africans and their ways of life. Africans were described as a brutal and ugly people, filthy and licentious. The influential North African known as Leo Africanus, whose portrayals of sub-Saharan peoples were familiar to English readers by 1600, wrote that "by nature they are a vile and base people" and declared Africans to "observe no certain order of living nor of lawes," a description English visitors generally tended to confirm. John Hawkins, the first important English slave trader, spoke in the 1560s particularly of the basic dishonesty of "the Negro (in which nation is seldome or never found truth)," and he and others told stories of African treachery giving substance to such a charge. Such concrete views were supplemented by a scientific thought that questioned African humanity in significant ways, not to mention a biblical thinking that, drawing on the story of Noah, described black Africans as the descendants of Noah's son Ham, cursed as a result of his own indiscretions to a state of permanent and eternal servitude.[1]

Such ideas were among the powerful forces pushing toward differentiation and, ultimately, exclusion of Africans from colonial societies beginning early in the era of English colonization, no more than half a decade after their first recorded arrival, in Virginia in 1619. Though their status was uncertain, they began to be set apart from the white population in a variety of ways by as early as the mid-1620s. Over the next few decades, increasing differentiation was to characterize colonial American societies. The fixing of slave status was the most visible proof of this process. Appropriate legislation appeared obliquely as early as 1641 in Massa-chusetts and more clearly during the 1660s in Virginia and Maryland.[2]

Nevertheless, countertendencies existed, and to many of those caught up in the system the outcome of processes of differentiation and subor-dination was far from inevitable. There were a variety of reasons for this ambiguity. One was that there were ambiguities in relationships be-tween African and English settlers during and even after the first century of the American colonial period. Africans themselves appear to have ar-rived in America with varying expectations and varying approaches to American conditions, helping to create some of the colonial ambiguities. Some of the earliest arrivals appear to have been relatively familiar with Europeans and with European society. Ira Berlin has suggested of the early-seventeenth-century "charter generation" of Africans in the colonies that many came from a Creole world that had itself been tak-ing shape in European outposts, first in Africa and later in the Western Hemisphere, since the late fifteenth century. Brought to mainland North America, they knew the kinds of societies they were entering. Isolated neither by language nor by significant cultural differences, they sought to make a place for themselves within emerging colonial societies.[3]

Many succeeded. The famous case of Anthony Johnson, likely such an individual, showed that it was possible for an African, like a European, to move from servant to prosperous landowner in seventeenth-century Virginia. Johnson was not alone. Others in Virginia, Creole or not, also moved from servitude to freedom and even prosperity. This was the case elsewhere too. In seventeenth-century New York and New England there were at least a few black property holders who, by their station, demon-strated a measure of permeability in colonial systems.[4]

Another reason for ambiguity was that modes of exclusion varied in British colonial societies. Segregation and discrimination appear to have been haphazard in the seventeenth century. In New England, as Robert Twombley and Robert Moore have shown, blacks and whites appear to have been treated equally before the law, and in all the colonies, courts were open to, and used by, everyone, including African slaves. In all the colonies as well, social contacts between blacks and whites, especially outside the elite, were frequent and extensive, as were economic rela-tions, particularly those involving free people of color and nongentry whites. They appear to have been conducted on relatively equal terms. Even interracial marriage, if uncommon, was not unknown. Late-seventeenth and early-eighteenth-century legislation outlawing the practice was significant for what it said about both the occurrence of such marriages and opposition to them. It is also worth noting that as late as 1699 some white Virginians presented a petition urging repeal of that colony's legislation.[5]

Thus, through much of the seventeenth century relations between blacks and whites remained conflicted and not wholly clear in British North America. The signs of utter exclusion and even degradation were present as all the colonies moved toward the institutionalization of African slavery. Nevertheless, the movement must not have appeared inexorable because, for a variety of reasons, some people of African origin and descent found ways to move within colonial society, and some English colonists seem to have been perfectly willing to encourage their efforts.

There was certainty and conflict throughout the eighteenth century, though within a context of hardening racial boundaries and hardening structures of enslavement. The legislative efforts that since the 1660s had been intended to fix an equation between "African" and "slave" in the older colonies were accompanied by slave codes defining what form African enslavement was supposed to take. Such codes were intended to ensure white control over Africans in most aspects of life. They regulated the movement of slaves, prohibited, or at least inhibited, slave gatherings, and provided for dealing with runaways. They gave whites in general patrolling and disciplinary powers to keep slaves in check. And, of course, whites were given leave to control slaves by means of the most brutal physical treatment.[6]

The importance of color to the equation was emphasized by the extent to which, early in the eighteenth century, restrictions came to be put on free people as well. Laws excluded their testimony in court, especially in the South. In several colonies, free blacks suffered punitive taxation and were even prohibited from owning property. In a visible sign of exclusion, it was during the early eighteenth century in Virginia, and elsewhere, that blacks lost the right to vote, a right presumably exercised in earlier times. This was necessary, Virginia's governor, William Gooch, said in 1723, to "make the free-Negros sensible that a distinction ought

to be made between their offspring and the Descendants of an Englishman, with whom they are never to be Accounted Equal."[7]

Here, too, countertendencies remained. Some were the result of differences in demographics or differences in time and place. In the northern colonies, the proportion of blacks to whites remained relatively small,
with the percentage of blacks in the population ranging from about 4
percent in Massachusetts to about 15 percent in New York. For the most
part, blacks and whites lived and worked in close proximity to each other,
in the same household or on the same farm. In New England, a few
slaves were also involved in the maritime industry—on fishing boats and
whaling ships, in the coastal trade, or even on vessels plying the Atlantic
between America and England—living and working, though enslaved,
in a diverse and at least somewhat less bounded social environment.
There remained a handful of black property holders, some with fairly
substantial holdings, and a few black owners of small businesses. Such
people faced severe discrimination, but their presence at least challenged
the clarity of any equation between color and slavery or servitude.[8]

If the South, with its plantation society, offered greater constraints
and less diversity, possibilities for autonomy and for achievement were
not entirely absent. In Charleston, for example, slaves were generally allowed to till small plots of land for their own purposes, which allowed
them to dominate the town's public market by midcentury and gave
some a fair measure of economic independence. The emergence of a
class of skilled workers and tradesmen also led to some economic possibilities for Charleston's black population. The involvement of some
slaves in coastal and overland transport had an effect in South Carolina
that was similar to that in New England. Possibilities for buying freedom, whether by slave merchants or skilled workers, further challenged
the monolithic equation of slavery and color even in the deepest of
southern colonies.[9]

Possibilities for economic autonomy were to some extent matched by
those for cultural autonomy. Though not always directly challenging discrimination, these possibilities nevertheless helped maintain modes of
independent action that made white control somewhat less pervasive,
and invasive, than it sought to be. Forms of cultural autonomy included,
most visibly, the ways in which people used, modified, or lost elements
from the African cultural traditions that many brought with them. In

the South, especially in the plantation districts of the lower South, African elements were strong and visible, reinforced by a significant reliance on African importation for the slave workforce and by the relative isolation of much of the slave population from European influences. In both North and South Carolina, for instance, the persistence of an African consciousness was evidenced by a persistence in the use of African names. Adaptations of such West African–derived festivals as John Koonering provided an important moment each year in the lives of plantation slaves. Even the linguistic distance between masters and slaves appears to have increased during the eighteenth century, pointing toward the existence of a relatively autonomous cultural world despite the continuing oppressiveness of plantation slavery.[10]

Further north, possibilities for cultural autonomy were more complicated. Acculturation was great during the seventeenth century and well into the eighteenth. Because there was little importation directly from Africa, and because of the nature of contacts between blacks and whites, there was a lack of cultural distance between the groups mirroring the lack of physical distance. It was only beginning in the 1740s that an influx of people from Africa began to create an enlarged African influence on the black communities of the North. This growing African presence led in some ways to an impulse for a greater cultural autonomy, although it was an impulse that took shape within a social framework of continuing contact with European-dominated settings and institutions.[11]

There were many indications of such impulses, including mid-eighteenth-century attempts in New England and New York to found the kinds of benevolent societies that would be important to urban African American life in the late eighteenth and early nineteenth centuries. More complex, and more widespread, was the development during the mid-eighteenth century in New England of "Negro Election Days," held with white encouragement, in which local blacks chose "kings," "governors," and other officials, individuals who served significant, authoritative roles, adjudicating and punishing a variety of social and even legal offenses committed by members of the community. Elections were accompanied by an array of festivities and represented a complex synthesis of African and English elements. Some aspects, including treating, feasting, and parading, were similar to, and perhaps influenced by, English colonial traditions. Others, including songs and dances taking place on Election Day and activities satirically mocking both black and white leaders clearly reflected African backgrounds. In fact, such satiric mockery was to become an important way, in a variety of arenas, for African Americans both to use and to play with an otherwise over-whelmingly Anglo-American cultural setting. In some parts of New England there were also "Negro Training Days," which, like the Negro Election Days, borrowed from white forms—in this case the militia muster—but, through motley dress and an intentional incompetence, ridiculed white pretensions and even played with white stereotypes of black "limitations."[12]

The Negro Election Days and related activities thus brought at least some measure of community self-assertiveness within a framework created by relationships between whites and blacks in New England society, a framework in which people could demonstrate their independence from total white domination over their lives and activities. Such occasions allowed for at least a semblance of community control and also revealed a people not so awed by Anglo-American society as to be unable to stand back and comment on, even ridicule, the structure of social relationships in which they had to live.

The patterns of race relations framing possibilities for African American autonomy and expression were thus complex in British colonial North America. They were also crucial in developing and shaping traditions of African American thought that would ultimately contribute to the emergence of an African American literature. They provided a necessary precondition for its origin and influenced both the constraints on that literature and the directions in which it would grow. This was because they provided, above all, areas in which African Americans in colonial society could assert their voices in ways they believed could be effective and authoritative in a variety of social and cultural realms.

II

In no area were the ambiguities more important, or more fully developed, than in that of religion. And in no area were there more profound implications for the development of the complex issues of voice and authority, appropriation and attribution, that were to constitute the background for the emergence of African American literature as such.

To see this, it is useful to begin with an example, uncovered by the historian Erik Seeman, of an African American speaker who deliberately sought to assert himself into the realm of colonial public discourse. Speaking before a revivalist "strict congregationalist" audience in 1754, a Connecticut slave named Greenwich offered a critique of slavery, mainly on scriptural grounds, that demonstrated both a sense of possibilities for self-assertion and authority on the speaker's part. As Seeman says, Greenwich's critique showed a strong familiarity with scripture and, along with an autonomy of voice, a knowledge of arguments about slavery that only white people were believed to possess. Greenwich, for example, took on the popular theory that Africans had been condemned to slavery as descendants of Noah's disrespectful son, Ham, while addressing theories that justified the enslavement of people presumptively conquered in war. Based on religion, Greenwich's testimony was an important instance of a slave's perception of possibilities for inserting himself into a debate with more than religious implications, a debate over the nature of slavery and the status of people of African descent in the larger colonial realm.[13]

Greenwich's performance was itself the product of more than a half-century's developments in colonial American religious life. These developments also illustrated the ambiguities in colonial race relations that encouraged perceptions of autonomy and efficacy in the slaves' assertion of a voice in colonial life, pointing toward possibilities for the literary activity to emerge by the second half of the eighteenth century, even before Greenwich's address. These religious developments were themselves the results of efforts, often occurring by fits and starts, to bring Christianity to the slaves.

Despite the Christian purposes often expressed and sometimes pursued in the British colonization of North America, there was very little effort to take Christianity to the enslaved Africans in the colonies during the first century of settlement. In keeping with the ambiguities of the age, many individuals of African descent did seek Christian baptism during the seventeenth century; others, especially those of Creole origin, were already Christians when they arrived. Nevertheless, the conversion of Africans and African Americans to Christianity did not assume any significance until the early years of the eighteenth century, and even then it was a conflicted, highly debated enterprise that reached only a small part of the population. Still, the process was to have enormous cultural and political implications.

Christian outreach efforts took different forms in different places, not unrelated to the demographic and social differences between the regions. Most were carried on under the auspices of the Church of England by the Society for the Propagation of the Gospel in Foreign Parts (SPG), founded in 1701. The society's mission in America was to reach out to the Native Americans and to slaves, and its missionaries began their efforts as early as 1702. In both North and South these missionaries encouraged slaveholders to allow their slaves to attend worship and to receive the kind of preaching and instruction that would lead to conversion and baptism. At least a few missionaries, shocked by the brutality of slavery, sought through teaching and example to encourage better treatment of slaves.[14]

In New England, SPG efforts were less important than those of the Congregational Church, dating to the first half of the seventeenth century. As early as 1693 Cotton Mather organized a Society of Negroes, chiefly made up of slaves who had been permitted by their owners to meet for worship and instruction. In 1706, Mather even included in *The Negro Christianized*—an early argument for slave conversion—a catechism intended especially for slaves. Such formal activity was fairly scattered and had limited impact, but it was supplemented by household and family worship, which usually included household slaves as well as white servants and members of the family. Through daily prayer and Saturday and Sunday evening Bible readings, instruction, and prayer, many slaves were exposed to Christian teaching, and some were converted.[15]

In the mid-eighteenth century these kinds of efforts, in the South and the North alike, were boosted by the colonial revivals that made up the Great Awakening, the context within which Greenwich's strictures on slavery took shape. In some places the Awakening opened slaveholders' hearts to the mission to the slaves, improving the possibilities for instruction and conversion. More importantly, blacks, both slave and free, attended the services of such leading revivalists as Jonathan Edwards and George Whitefield, who reported success among their black auditors. Samuel Davies, working mainly in Virginia, claimed especial success among the people of African descent both in conversion and in dedication to Christian teachings.[16]

Throughout the colonial period, even with the force of the Great Awakening, the number of black Christians remained quite low. The proportion of slaves converted was minuscule in the Southern colonies and represented only a small part of the population even in New England. Slaveowner opposition to conversion was strong and often effective throughout the era, especially in the South, and one should not discount the resistance of slaves themselves to the Christian mission. Some of this resistance was practical. In colonial Charleston, for example, many slaves decided that religious services interfered with the more important business of market day, always held on Sundays. At the same time, there remained some loyalties to African religious traditions, as to other elements of African cultures, loyalties that competed with and often exceeded any appeal Christianity might have, inhibiting the influence of Christianity in African American communities.[17]

Still, for an understanding of the development of African American thought and literature, the significance of the story of Christian conversion goes beyond matters of numbers and variation and includes both the structures of color and condition it reveals and the possibilities it opened up for African Americans themselves.

One significant element of the story was the very presence of debate and conflict among whites over the question of conversion. Such divisions emphasized, at the simplest level, the extent to which slavery was not a wholly monolithic system and that there was, at least potentially, room for maneuvering and even self-assertion within the system. This was shown in the responses of at least some slaves to the debate, especially from early in the colonial period, over whether conversion and baptism might imply freedom for the Christian, over whether Christians could, in fact, be held as slaves. The roots of this debate antedated European colonization in the Western Hemisphere, but the debate itself was revitalized by the development of colonial slave systems throughout the seventeenth century and well into the eighteenth. It was also a major source for slaveowners' opposition to conversion.

The debate also provided important evidence that at least some slaves, well before even Greenwich's time, were familiar with the main sources of division in the European societies into which they were brought. This was the case when, in 1655, the Virginia slave Elizabeth Key sued for freedom on the ground that, among other things, she was a baptized

Christian. In 1667 another Virginia slave, Fernando, also based a suit for freedom on the grounds of his Christian faith. Fernando's suit was dismissed, and the results of Key's were far from clear, at least on this matter, but the important thing is what both suits show that Fernando and Key knew about their society and what they thought might underlie a reasonable course of action in it.[18]

And they were not alone. The idea that conversion might bring freedom was widely known among slaves and continued to be documented until at least the 1750s. Late-seventeenth-century legislation in Virginia, Massachusetts, and Maryland provided that, as Virginia's 1667 law stated, "baptisme doth not alter the condition of the person as to his bondage or Freedom." Such legislation attests not only to the power of slaveholder concerns but also to the extent to which slaves themselves were helping to reinforce those concerns, aware of and attempting to use ambiguities in the system.[19]

Such events and continuing traditions indicate, at an intellectual level, processes similar to those that characterized social and economic life, based on both a familiarity with and an effort to maneuver within main currents of British colonial life. Religious missionary activities encouraged such a process in other ways as well, ways relating closely to the issues of African American autonomy and authority seen elsewhere in colonial societies. These issues laid the groundwork for the kind of literary activity that would emerge by the mid-eighteenth century.

Missionary activities among African and African American slaves created, above all, an interplay of ideas of equality and subordination in the promulgation of meaning of Christian conversion. From the earliest days of missionary activity the missionaries walked a fine line. To reluctant slaveholders these clergymen justified their efforts by arguing that Christianizing slaves would produce a more docile, obedient servile class, one prepared to obey their masters from a sense of obligation and Christian duty. As early as 1680 one of the earliest proponents of a mission to the slaves, the Anglican minister Morgan Godwyn, assured slaveholders that this was the case, noting that none of the slaves he had baptized had become "less diligent after *Baptism,* than they ever were before." Eight decades later the Virginia planter Robert Carter Nicholas, a champion of missionary activity, similarly urged that "by making them good Christians they would necessarily become better servants" because of religion's "probable & direct Tendency to reform their Manners." From Godwyn on, few missionaries departed from a vision that saw in slave conversion a support for bondage, a vision guiding the Christian message they addressed to all those slaves they were able to reach.[20]

In addressing the slaves, always in company with slaveowners, the missionaries reinforced such a message, urging the propriety of absolute obedience, developing a patriarchal Christianity in which slavery itself was of divine ordinance. "Some he hath made *Masters* and *Mistresses*, for taking Care of their Children, and others that belong to them," the noted Thomas Bacon told a Maryland congregation in the 1740s. "Some he hath made *Servants* and *Slaves*, to assist and work for the *Masters* and *Mistresses* that provide for them." Such remarks, intended to placate slaves and slaveholders alike, gave Christian sanction to relationships of separation and subordination on which the slave system rested.[21]

The problem was that the missionaries could not assert their case without acknowledging at least the spiritual equality of all human beings. Godwyn defended his own efforts in part based on his view "of the *Right* which our *Negro's* have, and may justly claim to the exercise of *Religion*," a right arising simply from "their being *Men*." Beyond that, he denied anything like innate racial inequality, referring his readers to history to point out that "*Cesar's* account of the Ancient *Britains*, is not such as should make us proud." He rejected any views of Africans that saw them as fit only for enslavement. Cotton Mather made a similar point, writing of Africans, "They are *Barbarous*. But so were our own *Ancestors*." Godwyn went a step further, looking to an ancient time when "*Africa* was once famous for both Arts and Arms," rivaling Rome as a seat of empire, whatever its present condition might be. He noted as well Africans who had figured in biblical times, including the Queen of Sheba and such African fathers of the church as St. Cyprian and Augustine of Hippo.[22]

Such a message ultimately did infiltrate the missionaries' messages to the slaves themselves, though couched in a more conservative language. Benjamin Fawcett, counseling a religion of obedience in his 1756 *Compassionate Address to the Christian Negroes in Virginia*, nevertheless quoted from the book of Acts to advise his audience of slaves and slaveholders that God "hath made of one Blood all Nations of Men" and that "God is No Respecter of Persons." The message was hardly without egalitarian implications. During the Great Awakening the prime force for slave conversion, George Whitefield, though he never failed to preach obedience to the slaves and viewed conversion as the best precaution against slave rebellion, nevertheless proclaimed spiritual equality not only to slaveholders but to the slaves themselves, urging that all were united in the church, including, as he put it, "even *you despised Negroes.*"[23]

The logical conclusion of such views, of course, was to challenge the very fabric of slavery itself, despite the intentions of Godwyn and, later, Whitefield. This was made apparent even during Godwyn's time by those pioneer opponents of the institution, the Pennsylvania Quakers. In one early exhortation, from 1693, a group of Philadelphia Quakers proclaimed that "*Negroes, Blacks,* and *Taunies* are a real part of Mankind, for whom Christ hath shed his precious Blood, and are capable of Salvation, as well as *White Men.*" Linking outward with inward liberty, they rejected the enslavement of all people, anticipating arguments that would become increasingly common over the next century, especially among Friends. As John Woolman wrote in 1754, slavery became indefensible when one recognized, as the Bible proclaimed, "that all Nations are of one Blood," despite the efforts of such clergymen as Fawcett to draw another conclusion.[24]

Slaveholders, in their opposition to Christian conversion, acknowledged the egalitarian tendencies in the missionaries' efforts. The famous comment of a South Carolina woman who opposed Francis Le Jau's efforts was one example of this: "Is it possible any of my slaves should go to heaven, & must I see them there?" Another of Le Jau's opponents resolved "never to come to the Holy Table while slaves are Recd. there." Godwyn, who reported being challenged by West Indian slaveholders, complained virulently that if "those black Dogs" should be made Christians, they should also "be like us."[25]

There is no reason why at least the small minority of slaves and free people exposed to Christianity should not have been aware both of the egalitarian tendencies in the Christian message and of the debate and discussion that lay behind them. Confrontations between ministers and slaveholders giving rise to such remarks were far from rare, as Le Jau, Godwyn, and others made clear. They were probably far from private as well. Moreover, on at least a few spectacular occasions the debate broke out into the open in ways that fully involved the slaves themselves. This was the case, for instance, when the South Carolina planter Hugh Bryan, deeply affected by Whitefield, felt compelled not only to encourage Christianization among his own slaves but also, before he was forced to recant under community pressure, to prophesy black liberation.[26]

The Bryant case was, of course, unusual. Taken together, however, all these controversies and confrontations can only have helped subvert any naturalization of the slave system, as Greenwich's remarks make plain. But the ambiguities in the religious setting were to have still further implications, pointing toward those arenas beyond the slave community in which slaves and other people of color could act in ways that were both autonomous and authoritative.

Perhaps the most important aspect of those arenas, so far as an African American literary enterprise was to be concerned, was education. Throughout the colonies there was a general conviction on the part of those who sought to convert slaves to Christianity that right belief required real understanding and that understanding would be achieved only through education and the diffusion of at least a basic literacy. Samuel Davies, for example, made this a central part of his message, for example, when he suggested to slaveholders that they "encourage your Negroes to learn to read, and give them all the Assistance in your Power." Using spelling books, psalters, and Bibles, those who sought to reach an unchurched African population also sought to build the kind of intellectual foundation upon which, in their view, religion had to rest.[27]

In much of colonial America these efforts were led mainly by the missionaries of the Society for the Propagation of the Gospel. In New England, similar kinds of efforts were carried on not only formally but through family life and especially the family worship, which was expected to include slaves. Here, too, not only religious principles but also the means of understanding them were part of the process even if, in keeping with a vision that saw conversion as support for slavery, the focus was usually on obedience and duty. Nevertheless, for some slaves education was an essential element in their religious development, a fact that carried implications of its own.[28]

Education was at least as much an object of debate among whites as was conversion, just as staunchly opposed by many slaveholders, just as strongly defended by those who sought to bring Christianity to people of African descent. In South Carolina, for instance, the Anglican leader

Alexander Garden founded a school for blacks in 1743, and the school continued to operate despite colonial legislation passed in 1740 prohibiting teaching slaves to write. But even if this debate, too, must have helped to reinforce evidences of a divided white society, it also reinforced other tendencies in processes of religious conversion that countered an entire subordination of Africans in America and even encouraged perceptions of a possible black autonomy and authority.[29]

The training and education of Africans, and particularly of slaves, must be understood in the context of shifting seventeenth- and eighteenth-century attitudes toward the education of those outside the elite. The Virginia governor William Berkeley showed one side of such attitudes in his well-known 1671 remark that "I thank God *there are no free schools* nor *printing,* and I hope we shall not have these hundred years; for *learning* has brought disobedience, and heresy, and sects into the world." As the historian Richard Brown has shown, such views remained alive through the eighteenth century. Even as some, including missionaries in the South, sought to extend education and learning throughout society, there were those favoring a stable social hierarchy who saw only danger when the blessings of learning were extended to society's "meaner sort," white as well as black.[30]

Within this context, and as education applied to slaves and other people of color, learning could contribute to that weakening of boundaries in regard to religious communion that raised so many issues in other contexts. Although the children of slave masters and mistresses might not join slave children in classrooms, missionaries urged poorer white parents to send their children to the schools that were being set up for slaves. Compounding the problems associated with the education of society's "lower orders," such schools also created a setting of social and intellectual equality directly at odds with the emerging racial order of colonial America. Not surprisingly, slaveowners in both North and South objected to such joint schools, much to the distress of missionaries and others interested in educational reform.[31]

The concerns behind such opposition were likely enhanced, moreover, by an at least occasional reliance on black teachers in schools of religious instruction. As early as 1714 in New York, Elias Neau, a French merchant working under the auspices of the Society for the Propagation of the Gospel, was being assisted by literate blacks in his efforts to encourage slave literacy. In South Carolina in 1743 the society actually purchased two young men, ages fourteen and fifteen, specifically for the purpose of training them as teachers in Alexander Garden's school. The effort bore fruit, as one of them continued to teach until his death, and the school's demise, in 1764. In Virginia in the 1760s Jonathan Boucher reported that in his own educational efforts he relied on literate slaves, operating fairly independently, to try to instruct others "in their respective Neighbourhoods." Samuel Davies had encouraged a similar kind of plan.[32]

Literate slaves not only had intellectual authority as teachers. As the case of Greenwich shows, they could also move toward the realization of the slaveholders' worst fears by interpreting for themselves the Scripture and its application to their lives and conditions. Claims to a religious voice, including claims of authority and autonomy, became especially strong as Africans also came increasingly to see themselves as part of the process by which Christianity was spread. Such claims were asserted fairly early by black converts, even before Greenwich's address. They informed, for example, a letter a Virginia slave addressed to the bishop of London in 1723, pleading for freedom and Christian instruction. And it was an authority other blacks accepted. In 1710 Francis Le Jau reported from South Carolina that one of his students, "the best Scholar of all the Negroes in my Parish," had developed, from his own readings, an apocalyptic vision that had widely influenced many of the slaves in the surrounding neighborhood. Le Jau was more worried than pleased and did his best to squelch the man's influence; nonetheless, at least one Christian slave was viewed by other slaves as having the authority to deliver the message of religious truth.[33]

Such figures only paved the way for a man like Greenwich at midcentury, and he was likely joined by many others during his time. Blacks attended the services of such noted revivalists as Whitefield, Jonathan Edwards, and Samuel Davies and played an active role. In the heat of the revival meetings, many blacks, as well as women and children, broke down old barriers of exclusion and subordination to proclaim the gospel, not only to other slaves but to all in attendance, even to great crowds.[34] There is much to indicate their impact. A measure of that impact may be seen in the objections that antirevivalists raised to their very presence, as well as the significance they attached to that presence. In the early 1740s one conservative New Englander complained that in the revivals blacks had "become (as they phrase it) Exhorters," able to speak before mixed audiences and to receive a hearing, even to claim a title, in the setting of religious services. Another was outraged upon hearing his own servant preaching in what he said were "the very phrases of Mr. Whitefield." Such angry reactions indicate that for the speakers and their audiences alike, those exhorters had claimed a religious authority that transcended lines of color, at least in the heat of a revival service. As Susan Juster has suggested, they had taken a place of their own in that community of language that the revivals, with their emphasis on preaching, sought to put at the core of Christian life.[35]

Thus, if one should be careful not to overestimate the impact of Christianity on African Americans in the colonial era, one should also be careful not to underestimate Christianity's cultural importance. It allowed for the possibility of an entrance by black people into an intellectual setting, a realm of thought, and a world of skills that might otherwise have been defined as exclusively white. Giving a place to the black voice, it challenged any definition of intellectuality and intellectual authority based on color. Providing for at least one kind of community in which a black voice could be heard, it placed at least a measure of such authority in the hands of people of African descent, even slaves. And, of course, it created a subset, however small, of literate slaves, providing an essential underpinning for the emergence of an African American literary life.

III

Such possibilities were most visible in regard to religion, but they may have arisen more generally in the larger world of debates over slavery and color that began to take shape in the late seventeenth and eighteenth centuries. If such debates were not as strong during the colonial era as they would be later, they were present nonetheless. The colonial period saw an emerging antislavery position that was rooted in religion but was evolving in ways that drew on a variety of intellectual currents of the day. It was a position that, anticipating Greenwich's remarks, both shaped and was shaped by an assertive African American voice.

Much of early antislavery was, again, rooted in those doctrines of spiritual unity that John Woolman had put forward in 1754, citing the biblical doctrine that God had made all nations "of one blood." Woolman's position was itself rooted in that early Quaker tradition of antislavery going back to the late seventeenth century. The earliest English Quaker antislavery proponent, Friends founder George Fox, was only among the first to apply the biblical affirmation Woolman had cited. The refrain was echoed by virtually all the major opponents of slavery in the colonies in the eighteenth century, from Samuel Sewall in his 1700 book *The Selling of Joseph* through Woolman and beyond.

Arguments for human unity underlay but were not the only terms in which debate was couched. The sinfulness of the slave trade itself was denounced in the earliest Quaker protests and echoed thereafter. A 1688 Quaker petition, for example, decried slavery in part on the ground that "such negers are brought hither against their will and consent, and that many of them are stolen." To the crime of kidnapping was added the equal horror of taking individuals from their families. The 1688 petition viewed this in terms of the sin it created, since slavery meant committing "adultery, in others, separating wives from their husbands and giving them to others." Sewall declared in 1700 that "it is likewise most lamentable to think, how in taking Negros out of *Africa,* and selling them here, That which God has joyned together men do boldly rend asunder; Men from their Country, Husbands from their Wives, Parents from their Children."[36]

Africans in America knew and contributed to this last argument, as evidence from the period makes plain. In New England, particularly, where most slaves were in close and almost constant contact with their masters' families, this contact often involved an exchange of stories and reminiscences, an exchange in which slaves spoke as much as they listened, filling audiences with accounts of their own lives and experiences, including their memories of life before slavery, in Africa.[37]

The stories often struck a bitter note. As some slaves recounted their lives, they told of the horrors of kidnappings in Africa and the condemnation of innocent men, women, and children to enslavement. They told of how they, or their parents, as they went about their daily activities, had been grabbed by slavers on the prowl for innocent victims. Above all, they evoked the sufferings felt by husbands and wives separated from each other forever, about the terrible separations of brothers from sisters, children from parents. Jinny Cole, for example, claiming to be the daughter of "a king in Congo," recalled how, at about age twelve, she was out with playmates when the children "were pounced upon by a party of villains whose skins were white, but whose hearts were black as the prince of Ethiopians." They were taken aboard a slave ship, and, "Jin" remembered, "we nebber see our mudders any more." Jinny Cole became a slave in Deerfield, Massachusetts. Chloe Spear similarly described how, as a young child, she and her playmates had been seized and carried aboard ship. As the recorder of her memoir put it, one could learn "from her own lips" how she and her companions had been torn forever from "the fond embraces of their parents and brothers and sisters."[38]

Such stories were not without effect. The nineteenth-century abolitionist Elizabeth Buffum Chace, born in 1806, recalled her own father's eighteenth-century conversion to antislavery as a result of listening, while a little boy, to an ex-slave named Pedro telling "tales of the sufferings of the slaves, of their capture in Africa, the miseries of the slave-ship, and of his own adventures in the escape of his family." Such testimony, more than any other factor, made slavery detestable to this pioneering abolitionist. Thus, even in the colonial period the stories of slaves themselves had come to play an important role in white antislavery thinking.[39]

These oral testimonies also became part of more formal early debates over slavery. This was certainly the case for the great Quaker abolitionist Anthony Benezet, who in several antislavery tracts beginning in the 1760s related the firsthand account of "a poor *Negroe*, not long since brought from *Guinea*." According to Benezet, the man had been kidnapped on his way to a spring to fetch water for his sick children, immediately carried away from his homeland, and transported to America. As Benezet said, it was a story that could be heard many times by those who took the time to listen, and it made a powerful case against the institution of slavery. Benezet acknowledged its influence on him, and some later abolition figures also acknowledged the influence that such tales heard in childhood had had upon their own adult antislavery convictions.[40]

But the presence of such stories in antislavery literature and among slaves themselves was revealing in other ways. The historian William Piersen suggested that these were tales that, even during the colonial era, assumed legendary status among the slaves, told as true, even firsthand narratives by many slaves, though likely based on the actual experiences of very few. Kidnapping, especially by whites, was a relatively rare event in the actual procuring of slavery's victims from Africa. In this sense the stories may have been most important for the way they dramatized a view among slaves themselves of their enslavement as a matter of theft, an illegitimate taking of any of the institution's victims from their lives and relations. Such stories conveyed a sense of every slave's vulnerability to an arbitrary system, a sense driven home for many in the colonial period and after by the reality of the separation of slave families by a domestic trade that was also well established.[41]

Whatever their function, the stories' significance, and their place in both black and white traditions suggests a kind of dual awareness of issues surrounding slavery, notably in New England but perhaps elsewhere as well. It also suggests the sort of community outside religion in which a black speaker could achieve both influence and encouragement. Through the stories, whites learned from slaves something of what slavery could mean to an individual entrapped in it. At the same time, evidences of the power of such tales over whites—evidences found, for example, in the behavior of a man like Elizabeth Chace's father—helped to encourage the diffusion of those stories among slave storytellers, encouraged by their apparent impact.

This dual awareness also suggests a role for slave testimony in the formation of one of the most important trends in eighteenth-century antislavery, the emergence of an ethic founded on sentimentality as a basis for condemnation of the institution. Founded on an ideal of empathy and compassion as bases for moral action, an ideal that began to emerge influentially in Anglo-American thought in the early years of the eighteenth century, this ethic looked toward an antislavery position emphasizing a sympathetic imagining of what it would be like to be a slave, on the terrible pains, emotional as well as physical, such an experience entailed.[42]

As slaves told their stories they gave content to such an ethic. They helped their attentive white audiences understand the meaning of emotional pain as such, and they were apparently effective. The first recorded versions of such tales indicate both the centrality of emotional pain to the stories and how impressive those pains were to the audience. The emotional core of enslavement was to become increasingly apparent in literary, antislavery renditions of the slave experience, as when Nathaniel

Appleton wrote in 1767 of "those poor children who are dragg'd from their mother's arms, and never taste the sweets of liberty."[43]

Thus, the debate over slavery was never just a debate among white Europeans. Although their receptiveness to the slaves' testimony may well have resulted from the kinds of changes many historians have noted in accounting for the rise of antislavery, slaves themselves seem to have given content to the antislavery cause.

Here, then, was an important area of authority for African Americans caught up in slavery, an authority growing out of the lived experiences of those who could tell about slavery's brutal core. The shape it took in the development of an antislavery argument suggests that by the eighteenth century at least some whites and blacks, and not just Greenwich, had come to recognize a role for slaves in the debates and discussions of color and slavery in British North America.

Other developments in the Anglo-American world similarly suggest such an understanding, particularly developments in the emergence of a black voice in Anglo-American letters and in the complex representations that voice was to take. To be sure, until the closing years of the eighteenth century England would produce no writer of African descent comparable to a Juan Latino in sixteenth-century Spain or the scholars Anton Wilhelm Amo and Jacobus Elisa Johannes Capitein in eighteenth-century Germany and Holland. Nevertheless, the black voice would emerge with increasing strength in English letters through the period. This emergence would provide a framework for the process of mutual reinforcement that both shaped slave tales and made them effective. It would have much to do with the development of a distinctively African American literary presence as the colonial period drew to a close.[44]

The black voice in English literature goes back, at the very latest, to the end of the sixteenth century and the beginning of the seventeenth, to the masques of Ben Jonson or the plays of Shakespeare. Africans had resided in England since about the mid-sixteenth century; some masque performances even involved black performers. Even in the early seventeenth century a few dramatic and literary representations took on issues of color and difference, breaking from much of the travel literature by asserting, as did Jonson's "Masques of Blackness and Beauty," the humanity and even nobility of Africans. However, the important black voices in

21

the English debate over slavery date to the end of the seventeenth century and the works of writers who began to confront the subject directly.[45]

A pioneering effort in this regard was Thomas Tryon's *Friendly Advice to the Gentlemen Planters of the East and West Indies*, published in 1684. As David Bryon Davis has noted, Tryon was a radical in many ways, and though he never quite condemned the slave system as such, advocating mainly reform and amelioration in the treatment of slaves, he nonetheless denounced much about the system, in ways that looked forward to a more thoroughly antislavery case. Among British writers, Tryon was one of the first, as Davis says, to condemn the separation of families brought on by the trade, and he was also one of the first to put his protests in the voice of a slave. Tryon had spent some time in Barbados. His work, he said, was based on his own experiences, and his slave speaker offers what are presented as firsthand arguments against the cruelties of slavery and of the ideas of color on which it was based.[46]

Tryon's slave spokesman develops his arguments in a frank, outspoken debate with his own master, and much of the focus of the debate is on the hypocrisy of Christian slaveowners who denied their slaves access to the gospel and to Christian baptism. In the course of the debate, however, the slave also uses his position to undermine any slaveholder claims to Christian virtue. Asking his own master, for example, about the demands of Christian duty, and learning that the Gospel of Christ requires, among other things, "To *fear the Lord* that created all things" and "To *be Merciful*, and do unto all men, as we would be done unto," Tryon's slave says, "I cannot but also much wonder and admire that you *Christians* live and walk so wide from, and *contrary* unto all those undeniable Truths, and holy Rules, so that what you preach with your *Tongues*, you pull down with your *Hands*." Decrying such hypocrisy, Tryon's slave describes slaveowners as an abusive class, asking rhetorically, "Do you not oppress us at your pleasure, *beat, whip, over-labour*, and *half-starve us*," adding, "Nor do our tender *Children*, and dear *Wives* escape your violence." He declares, "Your Houses are cemented with *Blood*, and all your *Dainties* and your *Riches* are accompanied with the dolorous Complaints, Sighs and Groans of your poor Vassals."[47]

Most importantly, however, Tryon portrays a dialogue in which a slave's words could have some effect on the master. Although, as Davis has emphasized, at least part of Tryon's story involves a reconciliation on the slave's part with his own status, the master, with whom he will have to deal, is also presented as a changed man. The slaveowner is shown to realize, as a result of this dialogue, that there is no way to reconcile the standard, brutal treatment of slaves "to the Doctrine of our holy and harmly Christian Religion," and he is shown to recognize as well that he and his fellows are creating a world in which a man, "how hard soever he uses his Slaves, is counted a *brave Husband*, and a *good Christian*, too," so long as he is forcing his slaves to produce "vast Quantities of *Sugar*."[48]

Tryon's *Friendly Advice* set up a complex structure of authority involving a slave and master, a representative African and the world of white readers, and helped reveal what was at stake when a slave assumed any authority at all. In his perception of the hypocrisy of slaveholder society Tryon's spokesman has a better sense of that society than does the master, despite the master's standing as a full member in the social order. Moreover, Tryon clearly put the slave in the role of teacher, and the master, in that of pupil. In this regard, Tryon's dialogue helps to illuminate issues of color and authority that were to continue to take shape in the literary assertions of a black voice in the seventeenth and eighteenth centuries, issues paralleling those in social and cultural realms.

While it might be possible to interpret what appears to be such an obvious role reversal as that created by Tryon as a kind of pointedly liminal expression, designed to bring home the truth of Tryon's concerns about English Christian hypocrisy, especially in its slaveholding regions, there is much more to the dialogue than that. Tryon appears to have been genuinely concerned about what was occurring on the English plantations; his portrayal of their horrible brutality rings true. And, Tryon's dialogue seems to say, no one can better testify to that brutality than one who has lived it. Whether Tryon learned from life is hard to say; his dialogue certainly invites readers to believe that he did and to see such a lesson as both possible and important.

Tryon's dialogue also helps to suggest, further, how uncertain connections were between color and authority in the final two decades of the seventeenth century. The form of the dialogue is itself revealing. With a long history in Western tradition, and especially in Christian evangelism, the dialogue, as Virginia Cox has suggested, betrays a self-consciousness about communication, a self-consciousness about authority, that, in the case of Tryon's work, paralleled the more pervasive instability of race relations in the early period of British colonial slavery. It is noteworthy that Tryon's 1684 work was anticipated in form by such an effort as John Eliot's 1671 *Indian Dialogues*, intended as a guide for missionaries to the Native Americans but putting the arguments for Christianity in the mouth of a Native American convert. Eliot was self-conscious about his use of the dialogue form. Recognizing a need to teach former "pagans" how to communicate in English Christian terms, and to prove the possibility of their doing so, Elliot asked rhetorically, "What way more familiar than by way of dialogues?" There may be no reason to believe that Tryon knew of Eliot's work, but there is reason to suggest that his use of the dialogue embodied the same needs and ambiguities that motivated Eliot to turn to the form as a way of representing the possibilities for communicating across gaps of religion and, by implication, color. It was also a way of indicating, wittingly or not, that connections between color and authority were not wholly fixed.[49]

Tryon's work was well known, circulating in America as well as in England, but it was no match for Aphra Behn's 1688 work *Oroonoko*, a novel popular not only in itself but as adapted for the stage by such playwrights as Thomas Southerne. Behn apparently had spent some time in Surinam, where her story was set, and claimed to have been "an eye-witness to a great part" of the story, using a first-person narrative voice that often put her on the scene of the events her novel recounted.[50]

The story tells of a "Coramantien" African prince, Oroonoko, who had both courage and intellect and was educated in European ways, and of his beautiful Imoinda. Both are condemned to slavery, Imoinda because of her dedication to virtue, and Oroonoko, in a way consistent with oral traditions of kidnapping, through the perfidy of a British sea captain. Much of the story takes place after the reunion of the two, fortuitously, on a plantation in the New World. Oroonoko's cultivation and noble bearing are immediately apparent to all, including his new owner, and like Tryon, Behn uses Oroonoko's story and his words to condemn, by contrast, the hypocrisies of Christian civilization. The story is ultimately a tragic one. Frustrated in his desires for freedom for himself, Imoinda, and their unborn child, Oroonoko, now called Caesar, leads a rebellion that results in his capture and, again because of white treachery, a cruel beating. Desperate, he ultimately kills Imoinda and tries to kill himself. Before he can die, he stoically suffers a cruel execution, dismembered alive.

Much in *Oroonoko* looked toward the sentimental antislavery of the following century, especially the fundamental role in the story played by the devotion between Imoinda and Oroonoko and the pains of their separation. But it might also be noted that Behn's title character was, first and foremost, a man of honor who by his own courage and forthrightness put to shame the Europeans with whom he had to live. Given the framework of more than a century of travel literature preceding Behn's work, a literature stressing the innate perfidy of Africans, her portrayal of Oroonoko as a man of honor in a world of perfidious Europeans becomes all the more remarkable.

Whether Behn actually knew an Oroonoko is harder to say, although colonial societies certainly had their share of slaves of noble background and demeanor, and enslaved Coramantee warrior princes had a special reputation in the Caribbean for courage and defiance. The brave endurance of long, torturous executions by those accused of rebellion was legendary. Even in less spectacular settings the presence of such figures was notable. Anticipating the virtuous characterization of Imoinda was a queen John Josselyn described after a 1638 visit to Massachusetts, who under pressure from her owner, Samuel Maverick, to breed with a young manservant refused to do so and was thus, upon Maverick's command, taken by force. According to Josselyn, to whom she turned for assistance, her nobility was widely recognized by other slaves, and he observed in them "a very humble and dutiful garb" toward her. She was only one of a number of noble slaves from the era who, like Oroonoko, were distinguished by their resentment of white authority and their rage toward white power. Both the legendary status of such figures and the sympathy they inspired paved the way for the credibility Jinny Cole received for her recollections of life as a daughter of "a king of the Congo."[51]

Behn thus used an African voice against oppression, if not against slavery, that was far from incredible. Having a basis perhaps in her own experiences and certainly in elements of Anglo-African and colonial American traditions, Behn's work vested authority and honor in an African speaker, moving from life to a literary representation of a black voice speaking against slavery.

Subsequently, through the eighteenth century, similar figures continued to appear in English letters. Some, like the beautiful Yarico, were fictional. Appearing originally in 1711 as an Indian maiden, by 1738, in a poetic version of her much-told tale, she was reincarnated as "A *Negro* Virgin" of "well proportion'd limbs and sprightly eyes" who came upon a white sailor, Inkle, shipwrecked and in desperate straits on her native shore. She nurses him back to health, to which he responds with professions of gratitude and devotion, and she becomes his devoted lover and the mother of his child, only to be betrayed by him and, consistent with other traditions of kidnapping, sold into slavery upon the arrival of an English ship. In a poetic epistle to her betrayer, she condemns him for his "barbarity to me," reminding him that she herself saved him from "some *Barbarian's* knife," calling to mind the irony imbuing Tryon's condemnation of a Christian master by a presumably heathen slave. And she contrasts her own hope of heaven, learned from a Christian priest, with the doom Inkle is almost certain to face.[52]

Others appear to have combined fact with literary creation. In 1734 Thomas Bluett published the memoirs of Ayuba Suleiman Diallo, whom Bluett called Job ben Solomon, a Muslim African merchant who, like many, had been kidnapped into slavery by a treacherous British sea captain and shipped to Maryland. His status and literacy in Arabic becoming known to the philanthropist James Oglethorpe, he was sent to England, where he learned English and "had the Honour to be sent for by most of the Gentry" of the area around London and even by the royal family. Ransomed from slavery, he was eventually returned to his Gambia family and freedom in his Gambia homeland.[53]

As was the case with the fictional Oroonoko, Job's character as well as his experience spoke against slavery and African inequality, although he was described as having hair that was "long, black, and curled, being very different from that of the Negroes commonly brought from Africa." According to Bluett, Job was a man of remarkably good "natural Parts," distinguished by the "Acuteness of his Genius" and by his learning, including his knowledge of the "Alcoran" and even of "the historical Part of our Bible." Able to converse capably with the English elite, he spoke volumes against the institutions and ideas underlying African oppression.[54]

In such characters as Oroonoko, Yarico, and, to a lesser extent, Job ben Solomon one sees at least something of the influence of romanticism, or at least exoticism, in English representations of Africa and Africans. A fashion for the exotic grew during the eighteenth century. By midcentury it had become a staple of the emerging antislavery cause, serving as a counterimagery to the older, largely negative presentations of Africa and Africans found in older traders' and travelers' accounts. James Grainger, in his lengthy 1764 poem *The Sugar-Cane*, built on this counterimagery when he urged the "planter" to "let humanity prevail." The slave, he wrote, may have been a prince in his own land: "The richest silks, from where the Indus rolls, / His limbs invested in their gorgeous pleats." Such exotic imagery, widely present during the period, probably also contributed to the images a story like Jinny Cole's conjured up.[55]

Exoticism was not, however, essential to an effective black literary voice. There was little about Tryon's slave speaker that was exotic. Nor was there much that was exotic about one of the more striking antislavery speakers of the period, Moses Bon Sàam, a Jamaican slave rebel whose harangue to his followers was reported in a magazine called *The Prompter* in 1734 and republished in the *London Magazine* and the *Gentleman's Magazine* in 1735. Represented as an actual speech, though the critic Thomas Krise has written that it was probably the rendering of a white British abolitionist, it was also very much in the tradition of *Oroonoko*, being the remarks of a slave exposed to European education and well versed in the more contemporaneous eighteenth-century ideals of natural rights. The speech also, in the tradition of Tryon's *Friendly Advice*, turns traditional categories upside down, but it goes even beyond Tryon on occasion, as when Moses declares, "What wild imaginary Superiority of Dignity has their sickly *Whiteness* to boast of, when compar'd with our Majestic Glossiness!" His knowledge of the Bible shows him that the man for whom whites named him was "the happy *Deliverer* of a *Nation! A Nation, chosen* and *belov'd* by *God!* From just such a *Slavery* as That which You, and your Forefathers have *groaned* under." Proposing to seize the land, he even finds a ground in European history for his hopes, reminding his followers that even such a traditionally weak nation as the Dutch were only "a Hundred Years past . . . *White Slaves* to a Monarch, who *now* calls them His *Brothers*." Based on such evidence, Moses concludes, "Assure yourselves, your Enemies will *embrace* you, in spite of your *Colour*, when they foresee *Destruction* in your *Anger*; but *Ease*, and *Security*, in your *Friendship*."[56]

That such remarks could be presented as taken from life, whatever their actual origin, showed still further the extent to which a black voice could be credibly presented as inserting itself in the debate over slavery emerging in the British arena. In this case it was a voice that not only challenged slavery but also helped to confirm the strongest slaveholder fears about the education of slaves. As printed in the *Gentleman's Magazine*, the speech was prefaced with the warning, taken from Horace, "This is a *Black*, beware of him good Countrymen."[57]

Interestingly, as Krise reports, the speech also inspired a response, this time in the putative voice of a free man of color, formerly a slave but now himself a planter, defending slavery and rejecting Moses Bon Sàam's efforts on behalf of the slaves. *The Speech of Mr John Talbot Campo-bell* presented a European-educated writer well-versed in the literature of slavery who told of being kidnapped from West Africa but who, unlike many, received great advantages in his Jamaica home. According to Campo-bell, the Maroons had no chance of success and should desist from rebellion. Moreover, the planters, given their place in the empire, could do little to end slavery even if they wished to. Krise has pointed out that *The Speech of Mr John Talbot Campo-bell*, published in 1736, was not actually that of a black speaker but was written by the white West Indian Robert Robertson. It represented, as Krise says, no less than the speech of Moses Bon Sàam or even Job ben Solomon's memoir, an act of "white ventriloquy" intended to define an African subject in English terms and, in this case, to turn the black voice against itself. In doing so, however, the speech nonetheless conceded the possibility of an authoritative black voice and even presented the possibility of credible black participation in the increasingly heated debate over slavery. More tellingly, that Robertson found a black voice useful, even necessary, may show how important that voice had become in literary terms to the antislavery cause and, hence, how much incipient champions of the institution felt a need to respond to it, mobilizing a black voice of their own.[58]

Ventriloquy or not, then, there is much to suggest the presence in the eighteenth century of a body of people in England and America who were both receptive to and concerned about the role of a black voice in public affairs. In this the literary realm closely paralleled the social in ways that illuminate both. On the one hand, it was significant that the voice itself was black. Difference as such and especially the putative associations with blackness mattered in all situations, whether literary or social. That the slave Tryon created was a supposed inferior who was able to teach his master morality was an important element in Tryon's dialogue. So was the fact that slaves, in reality and in literature, could tell stories of European perfidy and betrayal. If, for example, Thomas Haskell is right to base the emergence of antislavery in a growing devotion to contractual understandings of social relations, then such stories clearly put English betrayers in a terrible light. But more significantly, that such stories could be told by blacks, who were presumably inferior to the English in matters of morality, made English failure seem all the more notable. As a commentator said of an African prince whose tale of betrayal was widely circulated in the mid-eighteenth century, the events must have "filled his Mind at once with as black Thoughts" of his white betrayers, "and with better Foundation" than too many English commentators "affect to have for those of his Country with very little Cause." The black voice, expressed and evoked, became an instrument of social criticism, telling a tale and exposing hypocrisy at the same time, precisely because it was black.[59]

At the same time, the fact of an audience for such a voice does correspond to the lack of complete stability in race relations through much of the eighteenth century. As David S. Shields has pointed out, literary enterprise (including storytelling) and community formation were closely connected in England and America, and both were problematic on grounds going well beyond color. If difference was important in the development of an authoritative black voice, its assertion nevertheless gave rise to possibilities for inclusion in literary and social realms that went along with those uncertainties about community and color found in other areas of colonial life. That such figures as Job ben Solomon achieved a kind of celebrity status during their time in the English world helps to confirm some of these possibilities.[60]

One should be very careful not to exaggerate this openness. There is nothing to suggest a wide-open public literary sphere in which whites and blacks mingled as literary equals. But there is much to suggest a small community of readers and writers—or, better, a set of communities—attracted to the force a black voice could have. And at least a few pieces, such as Robertson's, indicate that such communities were large enough and visible enough to provoke attention and concern. When one puts the possibilities—social, religious, and literary—together, one begins to get a much clearer picture of the kinds of foundations upon which the earliest African American writing as such rested, the kinds of "discursive worlds" that gave it shape and encouragement, and some of the key ideas and thrusts put forward in the literature as well.

IV

There is no direct evidence indicating why the first African Americans decided to engage in literary activity or why they wrote as they did, but the foregoing considerations seem to apply, to one degree or another, to their earliest productions, dating from the mid-eighteenth century. A perception of an audience for their productions, perhaps founded as much on social as on purely literary inducements, clearly led the earliest writers to make their efforts. At the same time, even the most exotic literary precedents further illuminate important aspects of the ways in which these early efforts must have been received and possibilities for mutual reinforcement between writers and their audiences. Such possibilities cohere with what evidence there is about the earliest efforts at literary production among Americans of African descent.

To the extent that an assertive black voice in the eighteenth century was connected, in part, to areas of uncertainty and even flexibility in race relations, it is not surprising that the earliest African American literary work appeared in the northern mainland colonies and in New England. The contacts across lines of color tended to be greater there than elsewhere. Such conditions were visible, for example, in the life of America's first known writer of African descent, albeit an unpublished one, Lucy Terry. Terry's only surviving poem, "Bars Fight," written in 1746, did not appear in print until 1893, in a work of local history. But as her late-nineteenth-century biographer, George Sheldon, suggested, it and other works probably circulated informally in her hometown of Deerfield, Massachusetts. Such manuscript circulation was common practice in colonial letters. That it survived at all provides useful evidence for understanding the emergence and development of African American literature.[61]

Terry was born about 1730. She was brought to Rhode Island from Africa as a child and subsequently taken as a slave to Deerfield. In 1735 she was baptized into the Christian faith; she later married a free man of color and subsequently became free herself. In her years in Deerfield, in keeping with the possibilities of the era, she became famous as a story-teller and raconteur among her New England neighbors. Her house, Sheldon wrote, became a "place of resort" among Deerfield's young people. Her poem, written when she was about sixteen years old and probably read to her responsive audience, was a brief account of a Native American attack on Deerfield in which several of her fellow townsmen were killed. The poem begins:

> August, 'twas the twenty-fifth,
> Seventeen hundred forty-six,
> The Indians did in ambush lay,
> Some very valient men to slay
> Samuel Allen like a hero fout,
> And though he was so brave and bold,
> His face no more shall we behold.

It is not, most critics agree, a great poem, but its importance lies less in its poetic virtues than in what it says about Lucy Terry and about literary creation as such.[62]

As the critic Frances Foster says, "Bars Fight" shows Lucy Terry to have been a young woman enmeshed in the popular cultural life of her community. For one thing, it shows her to have been like many young women of her era who sought to capture exciting events in poetic form. This would seem a minor point, but given the dynamics of the period, it shows Terry's sense that she was not wholly outside the discursive community of her time. In addition, while the poem was not a particularly assertive act on Terry's part, and while it certainly bore no overt relation to developing dialogues on slavery and color, it still is important evidence of Terry's confidence in her ability to express herself and her ideas to an audience, not solely black, who were willing to pay attention. That the poem was preserved even among whites indicates that her assessment of the situation was far from inaccurate.[63]

"Bars Fight" is thus important not only for what it says as a poem but also for what it says about Terry and her sense of what she could say and of the kind of public role she could have in her New England world. Her perceptions were of a kind that would have served almost as a precondition for literary effort in a color-structured world. She continued to have such perceptions; hence her continuing activity as storyteller and, apparently, community poet.

At the same time, like other figures of her era, and despite the character of "Bars Fight," Terry almost certainly appreciated the unique authority her African ancestry brought. For one thing, she probably played her part in developing antislavery sentiments. Her reminiscences cohered with those of other African-born blacks, the view being generally accepted in Deerfield that she had been stolen from Africa.[64]

Terry's later life was to show the complexities of her place in New England's discursive community, as she and her family had to confront more directly the facts of discrimination in post-Revolutionary America. In one instance, she and her husband were forced to defend a land claim threatened by one of their neighbors, a threat in which color apparently played an important role. In another, she had to address the denial of admission of her son to Williams College, again on grounds of color. It is a measure of her place in New England's verbal community that in both instances she received what was apparently a respectful hearing from the appropriate authorities. It is a measure of the complexities of that place, however, that while she successfully defended her family's land claims in court, she was unable to persuade the Williams trustees to reverse their decision against her son.[65]

Terry's "Bars Fight" reveals much about the milieu in which an African American writer could find a place within the British North American discursive world. The same may be said of the first known published work said to come from the hand of an African American writer, Briton Hammon's autobiographical pamphlet, *A Narrative of the Uncommon Sufferings, and Surprising Deliverance of Briton Hammon, a Negro Man, — Servant to General Winslow, of Marshfield, in New England; Who Returned to Boston, after Having Been Absent Almost*

Thirteen Years. Unlike Terry, Hammon did not write *Narrative* entirely by himself but dictated it to an anonymous, apparently white amanuensis. Although historians and critics have generally assigned primary responsibility for it to Hammon, it may have greater significance as one of the first American works within that tradition of memoirs and sketches that had begun to appear in England about three decades earlier. It was primarily religious and didactic in purpose and far from openly against slavery: the piece concludes with Hammon's expression of love and gratitude to his master. The *Narrative* may be best understood as a landmark in the development of an African American literature primarily in terms of its creators' attempt to develop a credible autobiographical voice, one which appeared, at least, to be unmediated by its white reporter. That it appeared at all indicates an awareness on the part of its publisher, and perhaps Hammon himself, of a potential audience for such a voice.[66]

But what is perhaps most important about Hammon's *Narrative* is the extent to which it represents a first example of a larger process that would characterize the creation of African American literature until well into the nineteenth century. This was a process of collaboration and mutual reinforcement that made authorship as such less important than authority and credibility, as white and black writers alike worked to develop forms of representation that would appear to describe convincingly a perspective that was credibly and identifiably black primarily by evoking experiences only people of African descent could have.

Hammon's was an exciting story. A slave, Hammon, with his master's permission, shipped out of Plymouth in 1747. He went first to Jamaica and then to the Florida Keys, where, shipwrecked, he and other members of the crew were attacked by Native Americans. Many of the crewmen were killed; Hammon himself was taken prisoner. He escaped to a Spanish schooner, only to again be made a captive, this time by the Spanish, and taken to Havana. In Havana he was confined in a dungeon for four years, despite continuing efforts to escape. Finally, however, he did make his way out of Spanish captivity. Ordered to serve as a chair carrier for the Spanish bishop on a tour of the countryside, Hammon, no longer confined, fled to a British ship docked in Havana, where he received refuge from the captain, who refused to deliver to the Spanish "any Englishmen under English Colours." He was quickly taken to Jamaica and then engaged for three months aboard a British warship; after being wounded in battle, he went on to London. Fortuitously meeting with his old master there, he was able to return to his Massachusetts home.[67]

Several things stand out in Briton Hammon's narrative. Most remarkable, on the surface, is its failure to criticize the slave system. John Sekora is probably right that its publishers saw it as a token of reassurance for white readers concerned about problems of subordination and deference in eighteenth-century Boston. If so, it represents one more indication of the uncertainties surrounding public discourse, a troublesome black voice, and race relations during Hammon's time. In any event, Hammon was represented as fairly comfortable with slavery, describing his relationship with the man he called his "good old master" in glowing terms. Still more remarkable is that according to his narrative, he actually sought out his "good old master" in London, returning to his former status in New England eagerly and happily. As William Andrews has noted, a word like *captivity* in Hammon's narrative applies to his condition in Florida and Havana, not in New England. Massachusetts was his "native land." In a brief introductory epistle titled "To the Reader," he was made to note, without protest, that his own "capacities and condition of life are very low," urging his readers to make allowances for him as they read his work.[68]

On the other hand, there is much in the narrative that reveals an awareness of ongoing traditions and debates on issues of color and condition, making it something more than the straightforward relating of "matters of fact" that Hammon declares it to be in his opening remarks and more, too, than a defense of the existing order. Some elements in Hammon's narrative are particularly striking when read within the framework of the kinds of discussions that had long been going on over issues of color, and they are even more striking when those discussions are put within the framework of ongoing traditions in the African American community. In particular, however much Hammon's amanuensis may have tried to use the text to support a Bostonian system of subordination and deference, the black voice put forward as Hammon's is like so many others in offering an implicit commentary on that very system, a commentary created by virtue of Hammon's very blackness.

First, it is possible to see in Hammon's acknowledgment of his low "capacities and condition" a play on more general ambiguities about a black voice in colonial America. Color, as John Sekora has noted, was not the only issue at stake. Shortly before Hammon's narrative appeared, his publisher had printed a white-authored captivity narrative in which its author asked for indulgence on grounds of youth. Nevertheless, when Hammon's narrative is read in its historical context, even his opening epistle showed a recognition of the kinds of criticisms whites had voiced among themselves when blacks appeared to speak authoritatively in areas of religion, for example, or in the schools and a willingness to proceed within that framework of ongoing discussion and debate. More than Terry, perhaps, Hammon framed his entrance into an American discursive community with a self-awareness that made his work both a claim to and a comment on that same rhetorical world.[69]

Hammon's *Narrative* did something similar by its use of religion, presenting Hammon as a competent, even eloquent member of the larger Christian community, and one whose experiences could have exemplary importance for all Christians. His whole account is devoted to a "deliverance" he himself refers to as "providential," and he likens himself to the biblical David, saved, as Hammon says quoting without attribution 1 Samuel 17:37, "out of the paw of the lion and out of the paw of the bear." In this he was drawing on the long history of what James Hartman has called "providence tales" in English literature, including a lengthy tradition of "sea deliverance" tales and the specifically New England Native American captivity narratives, which recount providential escapes from savage captors. Creating for himself the persona of the Christian delivered from savagery—Native American and Catholic—Hammon occupied precisely the authoritative place in New England's Christian society that had been asserted no less strongly by those who took on the exhorter's role in New England's spectacular revivals. Like Greenwich, Hammon demonstrated a biblical knowledge to back it up, a knowledge further demonstrated in the conclusion of his narrative, praising his deliverance with an unacknowledged quotation from the book of Psalms.[70]

Hammon's place in the larger discursive community was also asserted by creating a narrative based clearly on those English literary genres that for at least two centuries had done much to fix English ideas of the relation of color to civilization. Hammon was cast very much in the mold of a British sea adventurer, a character not unlike a John Hawkins or a Richard Jobson, well known through the English fictions and memoirs that had preceded Hammon's work. Such characters had typically included accounts of derring-do in primitive lands, of captivity and escape, of danger and release, as English adventurers pitted themselves against the "savages" who peopled newly discovered lands. Like Hammon, these were travelers facing danger in exotic locales and savage environments.

Cast in this mold, Hammon was also cast in contrast to "savage" peoples. Thus his narrative both drew on and undermined motifs of difference in earlier literary traditions. At one level, the contrast between Hammon and the natives of Florida, described as "worse" even than the lion and bear from whom David had been delivered, is reminiscent of episodes in Aphra Behn's Surinam, in which Oroonoko was placed in contrast with native peoples whom Behn described as spectacularly primitive in customs and behavior, whose very savagery put the African Oroonoko more on a plane with the narrator, as she accompanied him among them, than at the level of the people they encountered.

But, again, Hammon never claimed nobility; if anything, it was his drawing on the language of the adventurer that did most to undermine the motifs of difference that had influenced, and continued to influence, Anglo-American thinking about matters of civilization and color. In the tale of his captivity Hammon is in every way the Englishman—his name signifying his identity—whose place in English society, as "servant," is ultimately the contingent matter of condition rather than the permanent stain of untranscendible, eternal difference. In the account of his encounter with the natives of Florida Hammon's persona is no different from any other English adventurer's in remote, uncivilized places. Like any of them, Hammon is an Englishman who finds himself in an un-English world facing the dangers it poses. That such a presentation should seem credible is confirmed by the British captain who shelters him in Havana, treating him as an Englishman "under English colours." As Hammon was inserted into a set of traditions that had both supported and condemned the color line in British letters, it was in ways that supported the believability of a black voice within those traditions and spoke to them, and much more, by the very credibility that voice was made to achieve.

The key elements in Hammon's narrative are unlikely to have been fortuitous. His references are too pointed to indicate otherwise, and the issues raised are too clearly tied to well-established African American readings of the debates over color and slavery going on at the time. These were visible in everything from Greenwich's sermon to the kind of play with European forms and customs visible in such practices as Negro Election Day. Whatever the role and purposes of Hammon's amanuensis, there is a black literary presence in Hammon's autobiography founded in practices that had long been rooted in African American discourse as well as in the kinds of literary sources upon which much of the discussion was based.

Briton Hammon was not the only African American literary figure to come upon the scene in 1760. He was joined by the apparently unrelated Jupiter Hammon, a Long Island slave who at the end of the year published a broadside poem entitled "An Evening Thought," which praised the hope and meaning of salvation. Jupiter Hammon was American-born, a skilled tradesman, and perhaps a preacher as well. He apparently occupied a privileged place in the household of the Henry Lloyd family, his owners, even handling some of the family's small financial matters. Although his work and life were to be significantly affected by the American Revolution, and his more important writings and pieces were to appear in the 1780s, his first published poem, like Briton Hammon's memoir or Lucy Terry's unpublished piece, further illuminates the context within which an African American literature began to develop.[71]

Like Lucy Terry's poem, Jupiter Hammon's "Evening Thought" contains no specific references to issues of color or slavery. Certainly, it reveals his familiarity with Christian ideas, particularly Wesleyan versions emphasizing free and universal grace. It also reveals his familiarity with the form of the English hymn as developed by such writers as Isaac Watts and the Wesleys since the early eighteenth century. When Hammon wrote, for example,

> Salvation comes by Jesus Christ alone,
> The only Son of God;
> Redemption now to every one,
> That love his holy Word

he used precisely the kind of structure anyone familiar with English hymnody would have found familiar. Although the history of the poem is not really clear, Hammon was almost certainly able to get it published because of the effectiveness with which he captured familiar forms and ideas, as well as the recognition he had received from others, white and black, within his community.[72]

Thus, like Lucy Terry and Briton Hammon, Jupiter Hammon was drawing on the popular currents of his time, and like them, he was making his own place in society in terms of those currents. Moreover, if there is little or nothing openly challenging to the existing order in Jupiter Hammon's early poem, implicitly, and within the context of continuing discussion and debate, it was quite assertive. Like Briton Hammon's use of familiar religious forms and his demonstration of Bible fluency, "Evening Thought" was a demonstration of Jupiter Hammon's religious capacity at a time when such a capacity remained an open question. In addition, it was a demonstration of such a capacity, in form and tone, that put the writer well within the religious mainstream, showing his ability to use the forms of poets and hymn writers whose influence was already widely felt in the culture. It is impossible to ascribe motives to Hammon's first poetic composition, but given the literary currents of his age, not to mention the social currents represented by Greenwich, Lucy Terry, and others, it is difficult not to see the important literary and cultural claims embodied in the work.

This earliest African American writing was certainly too scanty to serve as the basis for any very far-reaching conclusions about a body of work that was to become more voluminous and more visible in the Revolutionary era. But clearly, those who wrote these initial works had developed a sense of an American racial structure in which they could claim a place — even if held in bondage — and, in the case of Briton and Jupiter Hammon at least, of a context in which there was an audience for their efforts. Certainly, the debate over slavery had created the appearance of an audience, and at least a few antislavery advocates had made clear their own sense of the importance of a black speaker who could both relate the experiences of slavery and even advocate its abolition. Such a step provided an important precondition for, and background to, the more visible African American letters that were soon to appear on the American scene.

2

The Age of Revolution,
1760–1800

❧

THE WORLD IN WHICH Lucy Terry, Jupiter Hammon, and Briton Hammon created the initial writing by African Americans was to undergo drastic change almost as soon as the works of the last two, at least, had seen the light of day. The instability in relations between Britain and the American colonies following the 1763 conclusion of the Seven Years' War powerfully affected race relations, especially slavery. As instability culminated in warfare and American independence, these events, too, affected both the possibilities for continuing literary creation and the character of the work black writers produced.

Issues of color and slavery were never entirely in the background during the turmoil of the events leading up to the Revolutionary War, the conflict itself, and its aftermath. To some extent these issues were raised and kept alive by slaves themselves. Networks among slaves rapidly spread information about the unsettled political condition of the colonies, and many sought to take advantage of the situation. In various parts of the colonies slave resistance increased significantly during the tumultuous years beginning in the 1760s; as disagreement moved toward warfare, resistance also seems to have increased.[1]

The eager response to Lord Dunmore's 1775 Virginia proclamation offering freedom to slaves who would join the British side was symptomatic of the kind of practical impact Revolutionary events had on slaves and on the state of slavery even at the outset of the war. Virginia slaves, some wearing banners proclaiming "Liberty for Negroes," flocked to the British cause. The response was great enough that, revealing something of the kind of society that had begun to take shape in colonial Virginia, the *Virginia Gazette* published a letter seeking to dissuade presumably black readers from answering Dunmore's appeal. Slave awareness of the Revolution was great, and the information was widely dispersed, as many worried slaveholders understood.[2]

But everywhere, slaves and slaveholders alike saw significant links between Revolutionary conflicts and the security of the slave system. As Robert Olwell has noted, this conflict showed a less than monolithic white community as its leaders were forced increasingly to choose between British and American sides. Even in Charleston, no less than Virginia, slaves believed the Revolution pointed toward their own freedom; they were often outspoken in their belief, even to the point of confronting their masters, as Southern newspapers reported with alarm. As an equally alarmed Jamaican observer, Edward Long, noted, the contagion of colonial divisiveness, encouraged by imprudent policies, could spread rapidly, as "even our very Negroes turn politicians."[3]

That everyone was so fully aware of such links was in part the product of the extent to which both slavery and color were brought into focus by Revolutionary ideas. In the pamphlet wars preceding the Revolution itself a number of writers had asserted notions of human equality that crossed lines of color, such as James Otis's famous statement in his 1764 address "The Rights of the British Colonies" that "the colonists are by the law of nature freeborn, as indeed all men are, white or black." As the conflict became increasingly heated, black writers began to enter the lists themselves, giving increased notoriety to the links between slavery, color, and the Revolutionary cause and illuminating the kinds of complex relationships that both stimulated and constrained their efforts.[4]

I

Pride of place in an emerging black literary rhetoric of Revolution and equality goes to Phillis Wheatley. A controversial figure herself, she also mobilized the controversies of the Revolutionary period into a framework that emphasized the roles a black writer could play as well as the forces such a writer had to address. Moreover, she had a self-consciousness about herself as a writer, and her role in the discussions around her, that was revealing of more general issues about the role of a black voice in the Revolutionary debate.

Wheatley was born in Africa about 1753 and brought to Boston's slave market in 1761, a year after Briton Hammon and Jupiter Hammon published their initial works. Like many subjected to New England's slave system, she entered into a white household, where she was exposed to family worship and an education superior to that of most slaves and to that of most young white women as well. Her talents noted by the Wheatley family and their friends, she was early encouraged in her education. Her beginnings as a writer were reminiscent of Lucy Terry's two decades earlier. Her first known poem, composed in 1766 and published by a white sponsor in a Rhode Island newspaper a year later, was about the survival of two men caught in a vicious storm off Cape Cod; she had overheard the story while serving at table and rendered it in verse shortly thereafter. Presenting this and other early efforts to an audience composed of her master's family and friends, Wheatley, like Terry, became the center of a small group attracted to her gifts.[5]

A measure of such an approach to poetry continued throughout her early career. Many of her poems were local in both orientation and publication; a large number were elegies, commemorating the deaths of fellow Bostonians and apparently written at the request of families. Aimed chiefly at a local audience, these undoubtedly helped to build her place within the Boston community. Nevertheless, within about three years of her first publication Wheatley found herself a celebrity, chiefly as a result of a broadside she composed in 1770 upon the death of George Whitefield. Elegiac and thus within the framework of the kind of works Wheatley often wrote, its range, in terms of both subject and impact, included the entire British Atlantic world.[6]

The poem celebrated Whitefield for his "eloquence refin'd" and his willingness "To cross the great Atlantic's wat'ry road / To see *America's* distress'd abode." It also celebrated the steps toward a Christian inclusiveness, across lines of color, that Whitefield's revival had produced. "Take HIM, my dear AMERICANS, he said, / Be your complaints in his kind bosom laid: / Take HIM, ye *Africans*, he longs for you," Wheatley rendered Whitefield's message. In its initial version the poem concluded in part with a tribute to the countess of Huntingdon, who had been a patron of Whitefield's and was soon to be a patron of Wheatley's as well.[7]

The poem is important for an understanding of Wheatley's career in several respects. First, it achieved a large audience for her, and relatively quickly. Within a few months the poem had gone through six editions in New York, Philadelphia, and her own city of Boston, as well as two London editions.[8]

A second respect is the inclusiveness it both expressed and represented. Clearly identified as being from the pen of a "Servant Girl" who had been "but 9 years in this Country from Africa," it placed Wheatley as a poet within the large group of her contemporaries who offered tribute to Whitefield, a group that with her participation immediately crossed lines of color. The poem almost immediately also put her within a larger discursive world. As Julian Mason and David Grimsted have shown, a kind of female evangelical network, including Phillis Wheatley's mistress Susannah, had formed in the wake of Whitefield's preaching in both England and America. This was to provide an early community of support. Especially important was the network's most visible figure, the very countess of Huntingdon who had been such a staunch supporter of Whitefield's work and to whom Wheatley had paid tribute in her poem.[9]

The countess had already shown her openness to an African-born writer, James Albert Ukawsaw Gronniosaw, whose narrative had been published with a dedication to her in 1770. The narrative was itself an important document pointing toward themes of inclusiveness Wheatley pursued in her Whitefield poem, while drawing on older traditions of kidnapping tales and representations of African nobility. It took Gronniosaw from his happy life as the grandson of an African king through the travails of slavery in America to his life as a persevering Christian.[10]

As Gronniosaw—or his amanuensis, Hannah More—told his tale, it was roughly similar to Briton Hammon's in taking the form of a providence tale, describing how Gronniosaw was rescued from a series of trials by the power of God. Where it differed from Hammon's was in the extent to which those trials and tests grew mainly out of Gronniosaw's status as slave and servant. More than Hammon's work, that is, Gronniosaw's explored the kinds of linkages between color, status, and religious hopes that Wheatley had set forth in her poem, with less of the self-reflection Wheatley's poem implied.

Wheatley appears to have known Gronniosaw, and this may have encouraged her to believe that it would be useful to gain the countess's support. She apparently did not feel that her color would hurt her in the effort. With Susannah's support, Wheatley sent her Whitefield poem to the countess. Combining humility with self-assertion, she suggested that "The Tongues of the learned, are insufficient, much less the pen of an untutored African, to paint in lively characters, the excellencies of this Citizen of Zion," a reinforcement of the evocation of her status that introduced the poem, seeking to add to whatever interest the poem itself might have excited by humbly but clearly making the author a part of her work. That the countess arranged for the first publication of Wheatley's *Poems* is proof of the significance of the network and the identity it helped the poet create.[11]

The countess's support of Wheatley (and her support of Gronniosaw) was also of a piece with those religious and cultural developments that had begun to have significance for African American letters even before Wheatley's birth. Considering the poem's introductory remarks and its rapid prominence, the work's success reemphasizes the existence of an audience for a figure like Wheatley and a message of Christian equality that, informed by both religious and antislavery impulses, took on special significance because it came from a black writer. In this it fit into the kind of framework that Whitefield had helped to create and that had also given a distinctive place to Jupiter Hammon and Greenwich a short time earlier.[12]

The principles visible in the Whitefield poem and in its publication and publicity informed virtually all of Wheatley's career during the roughly seven years when she was most active, from about 1767 to about 1774. That career and those principles were, however, given much broader scope by the events going on around her. Wheatley came of age even as slavery was becoming increasingly controversial in Revolutionary Boston. In one of the very first years of her budding career, 1767, the Massachusetts General Court debated an antislavery measure. Whether or not Wheatley was aware of the debate, she had begun to think about links between the kinds of Revolutionary ideals inspiring antislavery New Englanders and her own place as a poet.[13]

A 1768 poem entitled "America," written when Wheatley was about fifteen though not published during her lifetime, shows her already trying to sort out the issues in the growing conflict between Britain and America. While it does not forcefully address issues of slavery as such, it still anticipates her approach to the Whitefield poem by asserting a place for Africans in the discussion, declaring, "Thy Power, O Liberty, makes strong the weak / And (wond'rous instinct) Ethiopians speak." Equating the empowering of her own voice with the undermining of old structures, Wheatley offered a sense of her own poetic career as the product of her marginality, presented with at least a hint of irony, combining that marginality with the possibilities for authoritative comment that her special standing within Boston society could create.[14]

Several of Wheatley's early poems echo "America" in portraying such a stance. In "An Address to the Deist," dated 1767, Wheatley sought to rescue her "addressee" from unbelief in a way that similarly called attention to her marginal position in society and her assertion of, in this case, a religious authority, as she began by asking rhetorically, if the deist were to learn truth, "Must Ethiopians be employ'd for you?" In her more famous but still very early poem "To the University of Cambridge, in New England," also written in 1767, she condemned the dissipation of Harvard's undergraduates, urging repentance, while reminding them that "an *Ethiop*" was the one warning them away from sin.[15]

Her lines are at once simple and fairly complex, given Wheatley's position. At one level asserting her own identity, they assert her perceptiveness and her ability to comment on the world around her. Somewhat more deeply, and ironically, they allowed her, from her own marginal position, to see the failure in others that others failed to see in themselves. They set her, as an observer, on a level higher than those she addressed, including those Harvard students who, roughly her own age, supposedly represented the cream of Boston society.

Wheatley's words and her stance help to illuminate the background to what by the early 1770s would be a more open debate over relationships between color and slavery, on the one side, and Revolutionary rhetoric, on the other. There were many issues involved, including the revolutionaries' frequent and well-known invocation of "slavery" as a description of their own sense of thralldom to an increasingly tyrannical British crown. But for Wheatley—and for others—the facts of color and slavery as such were more critical than concerns about colonial relations with England.

The position Wheatley had staked out was one increasingly linked to Revolutionary events by a number of people. Such a position may have underlain, for instance, the 1770 evocation of the martyred Crispus Attucks, whose name was signed to an otherwise anonymous letter, intended for newspaper publication, threatening Massachusetts Governor Thomas Hutchinson with retribution for the Boston Massacre, in which Attucks had been killed. John Adams, defender of the British soldiers, recorded the letter in his diary in 1773. For Wheatley, exploiting this linkage involved, by the early 1770s, asserting herself more directly in the Revolutionary cause. As early as 1770 she showed an awareness of the developing crisis by composing a poem in tribute to young Christopher Seider (whose name she spelled "Snider"), an eleven-year-old boy killed by a Tory sympathizer at a patriotic demonstration. In 1773 she revised her Whitefield poem to make more direct an expression of hope for freedom. In a poem most likely from 1772 or 1773, addressed to the earl of Dartmouth, she evoked her own love of freedom in a Revolutionary context.[16]

More pointedly, in a later work, produced after war had broken out, she wrote in tribute to General David Wooster, killed in battle. Reversing an older convention, and indicative of her sense that she was part of a larger Revolutionary discursive world, she briefly adopted Wooster's voice. Doing so, she asked that America be kept "ever virtuous, brave, and free," but added:

> how, presumptuous shall we hope to find
> Divine acceptance with th' Almighty mind—
> While yet (O deed ungenerous!) they disgrace
> And hold in bondage Afric's blameless race![17]

In 1774 Wheatley issued her most outspoken condemnation of slavery, in her well-known letter to the Native American minister Samson Occom, himself a protégé of the New England evangelical circle. The letter was subsequently published in several New England newspapers. She referred to the "natural rights" of people of African descent, pointing to the "Love of Freedom" that fired "every human breast," and almost tauntingly suggested that "by the Leave of our modern Egyptians I will assert, that the same Principle lives in us." The openness with which she condemned American hypocrisy, as well as the aggressively ironic language in which she did so, built fairly directly on her earlier approaches to her role as a poet in a color-conscious America even as it showed her confidence that she would find an audience within that same American society.[18]

There was much to encourage a set of perceptions such as Wheatley's. Her own career continued to assure her of an audience, and she continued to work toward building that audience, enhancing her contacts with the Boston elite, contacts she had had since the beginning of her career. Her childhood in the Wheatley household had put her in touch with the kinds of civic figures who ultimately supported her poetic ambitions, and she cultivated these relationships further. Early in the Revolutionary conflict she not only wrote a tribute to General George Washington but also made her work and reputation known to him, even making a point of trying to meet him personally. The poem did her no harm; it even appeared in the *Virginia Gazette*. Her elegies, a substantial part of her poetic work, gave her entrée into the lives of others in Boston's elite. In at least some of her poetic works, for example, a 1769 elegy on the life of the influential minister Joseph Sewall, she made clear her own personal relationship with the person about whom she was writing.[19]

And build support she did. When her volume of poetry finally appeared in Boston, it was accompanied by ringing endorsements from some of Boston's leading citizens. Their endorsements were important. Certainly, as so many scholars have said, it served to answer doubts about her having even written the material attributed to her. From the beginning there was skepticism about the ability of an African girl to write any kind of poetry; hence the presence of extensive authenticating material in her 1773 published volume of poetry, including the testimonials of some of Boston's leading citizens that she was the author of the book. Hence, too, the frontispiece portrait, included at the insistence of the countess of Huntingdon and intended to demonstrate the poet's appearance.[20]

But the basic issue went beyond authentication. In her own preface to her volume of poetry, preceding the endorsement of her white patrons, she made clear that the publication of her work was "at the Importunity of many of her best, and most generous Friends," acknowledging not only their authentication of her abilities but also their role in bringing her work before the public, their apparent desire, as Walt Nott has suggested, to give her a place within Boston's most recognizable, elite discursive community. This was a community far beyond the scope of her early network of evangelical support, and it testified to her visibility in Boston's literary world. Even by the time of her trip to England she was sufficiently well known that the Boston papers took note of her sailing. By the time of her return she was sufficiently acknowledged to be a member of the larger literary realm to engage in a poetical exchange with "a gentleman of the navy" in one of Boston's literary periodicals, the *Royal American Magazine*. Her 1774 letter to Samson Occom, with its attendant publicity, was proof that Wheatley had no difficulty assuming the presence of a public interested in what she had to contribute to the discussion she had reason to believe was swirling around her.[21]

But, again, hers was not a membership that simply transcended color. There is more than a measure of truth in Joanne Pope Melish's emphasis on the element of curiosity in the reception Wheatley received. She was the exception whose very exceptionalism made her interesting. David Grimsted has quoted a French observer who described Wheatley as "one of the strangest creatures in the country, and perhaps in the whole world." But such comments were not incompatible with the position Wheatley appears to have sought, and received, in Boston's elite community of discourse. As her career shows, what was crucial for Wheatley was not only what her color prevented but also what it made possible: a celebrity and a moral authority in the public sphere that gave her an apparent voice among people of influence on a range of important issues.[22]

Still, curiosity cannot explain all of the recognition Wheatley received in the early 1770s, especially as Revolutionary fervor increased in intensity and as more people thought about relationships between Revolutionary ideals, color, and slavery. The debate over slavery itself remained lively throughout these years. In 1772, just as she began to speak most forthrightly on slavery, there was renewed debate in the Massachusetts General Court on the propriety of slavery. The institution was not abolished, but the legislative discussion provided renewed evidence of the unsettled character of slavery during the period and of the value of raising the issue for further debate. It also helped keep interest in someone like Wheatley strong even as it encouraged her to speak forcefully on the issues of the day.

In addition, the specific issue of the black voice, including Wheatley's, was being broached more openly as Wheatley herself moved more clearly toward a Revolutionary stance. At the heart of much of American anger over British policies from the 1760s to the outbreak of war was the crucial issue of consent, of the right of the American colonists to approve imperial measures, especially taxation, aimed at colonial populations. The issue of consent also entered strongly into emerging discussions of slavery. As early as 1764 James Otis had raised the issue directly, arguing that Africans, no less than the colonists, had not entered voluntarily into that state of society in which they found themselves, on this issue attacking American slavery and British tyranny on the same philosophical ground.

Such an approach to the issue of slavery was to become the object of still more heated debate as Wheatley was reaching her prime and Revolutionary arguments were moving toward Revolutionary War. When Harvard focused its 1773 commencement debate on the subject of slavery as such, the issue of consent figured prominently in the discussion. Slavery's opponent, arguing from the position that Africans and Europeans were equal in their capacities, also argued that the degree of subordination slavery entailed, without the consent of those subjected to it, was contrary to the law of nature and hence indefensible. The institution's defender brought together issues of capacity and right in ways that showed the kind of challenge Wheatley represented in the Revolutionary age. He wondered, "Who ever thought the consent of a child, an ideot, or a madman necessary to his subordination," concluding that "every whit as immaterial is the consent of these miserable Africans, whose real character seems to be a compound of the three last mentioned," a view that looked back far into Anglo-American history. His opponent responded with not only a defense of African capabilities but an assertion, anticipating Wheatley's letter to Occom, of the "strong sense of Liberty implanted in the heart of every son of Adam," both of which extended to rights for which Americans were contending, including that of consent, across lines of color.[23]

Here, then, were both opposition and audience in Wheatley's Revolutionary Boston; if one represented a challenge to be overcome, the other represented a source for continuing support and authority. Fortunately, others were prepared to make the same points Harvard's opponent to slavery had made. Most direct was Samuel Hopkins, an early supporter of Wheatley's, in his well-known 1776 Dialogue Concerning the Slavery of Africans. Answering a widespread argument for slavery—that slaves were in general satisfied with their condition—Hopkins asserted that he could not accept such a position "till they have declared it themselves, having had opportunity for due deliberation, and being in circumstances to act freely, without the least constraint." Though not wholly inclusive in his views of people of African descent, Hopkins was apparently sincere in his words, since he had himself approached a slave to raise just such a question and learned from what he heard.[24]

More implicitly, there were also literary and political representations of a black speaker who served to dramatize the possibilities Wheatley represented in life and whose popularity similarly showed the presence of the kind of audience Wheatley's work was intended to reach. Thus, within antislavery, representations of the black voice remained a significant form of antislavery argumentation. Thomas Day's widely read 1773 poem "The Dying Negro," which appeared the same year as Wheatley's collected verse, took the form of a letter from a slave in love with a young white woman who was about to be shipped to the West Indies in order to prevent a marriage. The epistle supposedly was written shortly before the slave stabbed himself to death. Whatever else the poem represented, and there was much in it, it rested on the portrayal of a people who were, no less than Europeans, "reason's sons" and thus worthy of an audience. The radical antislavery revolutionary John Allen, in a brief passage in *The Watchman's Alarm* of 1774, set up a dramatic situation not at all dissimilar to those evoked in Wheatley's poetry and in her letter to Occom when he warned his fellow New Englanders that should they fail to abolish the "vile custom" of slavery, "the oppressed sons of *Africa* may very justly retort this stubborn passage of sacred writ upon you, *Isaiah* lviii.6. *Loose the bands of wickedness, undo the heavy burdens, let the oppressed go free, that ye break every yoke.*"[25]

Thus, as remarks from the Harvard debate suggest, the black voice was both asserted and contested in Revolutionary America. Harvard's proponent of slavery had suggested that there was no place for the African in the debate over slavery, asserting a deficiency of reason, and he was not alone. Edward Long, in his widely read discussion of the Jamaican Francis Williams, who had written a poem in Latin that Long himself published in a proslavery work, used what he described as deficiencies in the poem to question how much one could even expect of an African seeking to work in European forms. Even in the Revolutionary era, moreover, doggerel humor written in dialect appeared to portray vicious images of African Americans and their fitness to join a public realm in which proper English mattered.[26]

Within this framework Wheatley saw even her own work become an object of debate, particularly after the publication of her collected poems in 1773. The proslavery writer Richard Nisbet, in his influential *Slavery Not Forbidden by Scripture*, from that same year, took account of her popularity by dismissing her having written "a few silly poems" as proving nothing about the capacity of Africans for freedom and equality. Bernard Romans, in an elaborate 1775 defense of slavery, recognized the accomplishments of "the Phyllis of Boston" but, describing her as "the *Phoenix* of her race," wrote that he could "bring at least twenty well known instances of the contrary effect of education on this sable generation."[27]

Other responses, however, reflected the kind of supportive audience she had come to expect. Upon its initial publication in England her work was reviewed widely in the leading periodicals, the reviews noting the special distinction brought by her color and condition. An English poet in 1774 verified Wheatley's place in the larger discursive community, the special status her color gave her, and the case she made for racial equality. "Alexis" asked rhetorically, "Why stand amaz'd at Afric's muse," answering, "One God our genius did infuse; / Our coulour's nature's law." Wheatley proved, Alexis wrote, that "'tis learning forms the mid, / Else reason's but a dream." Within the context of American debate the important antislavery leader Benjamin Rush cited her work on behalf of both human equality and the case against the institution—the very citation to which Nisbet had felt constrained to reply.[28]

But perhaps the most important factor indicating the context for the kinds of perceptions Wheatley had was the extent to which similar perceptions appeared to be more or less widely shared by other African Americans seeking to join the debate during the Revolutionary era. The pioneering poet Jupiter Hammon, who, with his owner, fled Long Island for Hartford during the Revolution, seems to have maintained a career as a preacher and writer. The self-consciousness implicit in his 1760 poem "An Evening Thought" became far more explicit in his works from the Revolutionary era. Hammon portrayed a world in which the black writer could, and should, play a distinctive role, and he acknowledged the importance of Wheatley herself in this in a 1778 poem of his own, "An Address to Miss Phillis Wheatley, Ethiopian Poetess." The poem consists of twenty-one four-line stanzas, all but one followed by a biblical citation, some of it a gloss on Wheatley's "On Being Brought from Africa to America," in which she had expressed gratitude to God for the possibility of her Christian life. The allusions Hammon developed could be quite subtle. In a verse making the clearest reference to Wheatley's poem, Hammon wrote:

> Thou hast left the heathen shore;
> Thro' mercy of the Lord,
> Among the heathen live no more,
> Come magnify thy God,

suggesting not only a knowledge of Wheatley's famous poetic line "'Twas mercy brought me from my *Pagan* land" but also her characterization of her white American contemporaries in the letter to Occom as "our modern Egyptians," another pagan people from whom Wheatley and others needed to separate themselves from. Thus, Hammon's poem shows his own sense of the kind of role Wheatley herself was trying to create, as well as his sense of what such a role entailed.[29]

So, too, does a sermon Hammon preached, apparently during the Revolution. In "An Evening's Improvement" Hammon noted the possible objections of those who might say, "What can we expect from an unlearned Ethiopian." As he had done in the Wheatley poem, but more explicitly here, he responded by inundating the reader with a flood of biblical passages proving his erudition, at least so far as the Scripture was concerned. He began his exhortation, moreover, by noting the encouragement he had received to deliver it from his "superiors, gentlemen," similarly claiming his achievement of an influential audience prepared to hear his views.[30]

More striking here, however, is a poem Hammon must have written about this same time, which he attached to the sermon at the time of its publication. Labeled "A Dialogue Entitled the Kind Master and the Dutiful Servant," the poem looks back to the tradition begun by Tryon by dramatizing an open and candid discussion between a master and a slave. The poem contains elements of resistance and, even more, elements of human equality. At one level the servant professes, and the master demands, obedience within an existing order based on slavery; at another level the servant asserts the ultimate sovereignty of Christ: "The only safety that I see / Is Jesus's holy word." For the servant, religious authority transcends the temporal, and servants and masters alike are subject to it.

But here more than anywhere in Hammon's writing a central concern is authority as such, particularly the authority he could have as a Christian, though a slave. The poem has thirty stanzas. In the first twenty-three the voices of master and servant alternate; stanzas 24–30 are all in the voice of the servant, specifically identified as "your friend call'd Hammon," who warns, "You cannot to your God attend, / And serve the God of Mammon." Seizing the last word, Hammon used his dialogue to dramatize the possibilities for authority that Wheatley had claimed—and he, Greenwich, and others had earlier claimed as well—under the auspices of evangelical religion. In this Hammon helped to carry forward an important tie between religious foundations for an African American authority on which Wheatley herself had drawn and the larger concerns that also had come to inform Wheatley's work in particular.[31]

Hammon's references to Revolutionary ideology tended to be oblique, although in his "Dialogue" he did refer to the disruptions brought on by the war. Other writers were more direct in creating ties between their own place as speakers and the issues of Revolution. The ex-slave Caesar Sarter, in a well-known 1774 open letter published in a Massachusetts newspaper, offered a catalogue of slavery's evils, noting the "absurdity of your exertions for liberty, while you have slaves." Sarter asked, in a style very similar to Wheatley's, that his words "not be less noticed for coming from an African." Young Lemuel Haynes, prior to his days of prominence as a New England minister, wrote two pieces at the outset of the Revolution that were indicative of a similar attitude. In his poem celebrating the colonial victory at Lexington—a battle in which he apparently fought— he stressed his identity as "a young Mollatto" who could nonetheless offer his account of current events, much as Lucy Terry had done three decades earlier.[32]

There were, thus, many attempts by Wheatley's contemporaries to enter Revolutionary debates. Haynes himself wrote a 1776 sermon mobilizing Revolutionary ideas, and other familiar themes, in opposition to slavery. Although it was to remain in manuscript, he apparently wanted to have it published, thus joining the era's pamphlet wars on behalf of

Revolutionary ideals and their fulfillment. Near the close of the war a writer identifying himself as "a Black Whig" and "a fellow citizen, though a descendant of Africa," addressed his fellow South Carolinians; saying little about slavery, he urged an American realization of its Revolutionary cause by demanding full independence from any British presence.[33]

The most distinctive links between the kind of strategies Wheatley began to develop in her work and those of other African American writers appeared in a series of legislative petitions from slaves, mainly in New England, asking for relief from slavery. Three of the earliest were from 1773. The authors were either themselves literate or assisted by others who had received some schooling as slaves. They also took advantage of the larger discussions of slavery and Revolutionary principles that had been occurring in the colonies for the preceding decade and followed the debates addressing the issue of slavery that had occurred in the Massachusetts General Court in 1772.

All of the petitions drew on the larger context of Revolutionary pamphleteering and reveal a similar sense of a world in which there was both a need to assert a black voice and a possibility for doing so. Although none succeeded in generating renewed debate within the assembly, much less the abolition of slavery, at least two entered into the contemporary pamphlet wars surrounding the topic. Moreover, as Amy Elizabeth Winans has shown, their efforts were widely disseminated as part of more general efforts to further the Revolutionary cause. The first petition, from January 1773, itself published in pamphlet form, carried an endorsement from a white writer who styled himself "A Lover of True Liberty," connecting the petition with the Revolutionary issues of patriotism and natural. The pamphleteer John Allen moved from dramatization to reality by appending the second, from April, to an edition of his *Oration Upon the Beauties of Liberty*, one of the most widely read sermons of the early 1770s. Finally, the authors of one of the petitions submitted it to the governor and legislature along with a revision of James Swan's 1772 *Disuasion to Great Britain*, which attacked the slave trade in Revolutionary terms. Tellingly reversing the usual pattern of white sponsorship, however, in this case the petitioners themselves had persuaded Swan to undertake his revision, making more apparent the connection between the Revolutionary cause and theirs. These were writers who, like Wheatley, had come to see opportunities in a world of Revolutionary turmoil. [34]

The petitions themselves, while framed in a language different from Wheatley's, show the kinds of conventions in both substance and voice that were coming to characterize a black voice. The earliest, signed only "Felix," though representing "many slaves, living in the Town of Boston," was the least forceful, a "humble petition," but one that still drew on antislavery traditions that had been developing throughout the eighteenth century, as well as on the more recent language of the Revolution. It decried a world in which "We have no Property! We have no Wives! No Children!" but asserted, nevertheless, that "we have a Father in Heaven, and we are determined, as far as his Grace shall enable us, and as far as our degraded contemptuous Life will admit, to keep all his Commandments." The petitioners pledged their continuing obedience to their masters so long as they remained enslaved but still asked relief from "their unhappy state and condition."[35]

The next two petitions, from April and June, were far franker in tying antislavery and Revolutionary ideals together. Echoing Wheatley, the April petitioners asserted that "the divine spirit of freedom, seems to fire every humane breast on this continent," and asserted slavery's incompatibility with such a spirit. Directly confronting patriot ideals, they contrasted the character of New England slavery with that of slavery elsewhere in the hemisphere, claiming, with barely veiled sarcasm, that "even the Spaniards, who have not those sublime ideas of freedom that English men have, are conscious that they have the right to all the services of their fellowmen, we mean the Africans," who had more right to the fruits of their labors. The petition concluded with a request for relief, which "as men, we have a natural right to," and even suggested, as a response to those whites who felt a free black population could never be a part of white Massachusetts, that once freed, the petitioners would devote themselves to earning sufficient funds to transport themselves to "some part of the coast of Africa."[36]

Those petitioning in June similarly asserted their "naturel right to be free" and, picking up on another key Revolutionary theme, also their right "to injoy such property as they may acquire by their industry, or by another means not detrimental to their fellow men." Like their predecessors, moreover, they accompanied their request for freedom with an indictment of America's Revolutionary hypocrisy, noting their condition as slaves "within the bowels of a free Country."[37]

Petitioning continued throughout the war, becoming even stronger in tone. Two additional Massachusetts petitions, from 1774 and 1777, the latter of which led to a bill "for preventing the Practice of holding Persons in Slavery," rested their cases on a claim to natural rights, both showing a debt to earlier petitioners by declaring their origins with "a Great Number of Blackes detained in a State of slavery in the Bowels of a free & Christian Country." Other New England petitions drew on similar ideas, if often in different language. A New Hampshire petition of 1779 drew directly on Revolutionary ideology in asserting that "freedom is an inherent right of the human species, not to be surrendered, but by consent, for the sake of social life." The petitioners' indictment of white America continued to stress the hypocrisy of Christian, Revolutionary America in the face of their own claims to human equality and human rights: "Here we feel a just equality," they wrote, "we know that the God of nature made us free."[38]

By the early 1770s, then, black writers, aware of their standing in colonial society, especially in New England, began to cultivate a fairly well defined stance toward that society, building on the ambivalences over color and status around them and creating strategies within those ambivalences to gain a hearing for themselves. Such tendencies reinforce the sense that, looking back to debates over natural rights, African Americans helped inaugurate the democratization of voice in the political realm that Gordon Wood and others have recognized as one of the more radical legacies of the Revolution. Though not alone, Wheatley and her contemporaries were among the earliest of those "without doors" to assert themselves forcefully into the Revolutionary community of discourse. They were also among the first to find a place in that community. That they remained there, and that their presence caused such anxiety, is testimony to the kind of unsettling of relationships between voice, status, and authority the Revolution helped create.[39]

Such an effort to create effective strategies also informed their use of linkages between Revolutionary ideals and their own position and concerns. It informed other aspects of the work they produced as well. It is possible to see within the context of a developing antislavery tradition a set of widely used themes and images that by the early 1770s provided an important focus for what black writers were trying to do.

In crucial ways the chief underlying principle in this emerging set of conventions drew on one of the more critical themes of the Revolutionary era, namely, corruption. It was a theme that brought together many issues in the Revolutionary setting. At its heart was a belief in the corruptibility of any individual, with corruption liable to come from a position of excessive power, an overweening desire for excessive wealth, or the degeneracy caused by excessive luxury. From the mid-1760s, British policies that Revolutionary leaders found objectionable were explained as resulting from corruption of the British leadership, a corruption the Revolution itself was intended to oppose.[40]

Within the body of antislavery traditions and developing African American writing the chief exemplars of corruption were different but pointed no less to the corrupt motives of those whose actions stood condemned. African American writers appealed, as well, to the very purposes of the revolutionaries, asserting, with varying degrees of subtlety, that under the influence of slavery and its attendant evils the Revolution itself stood liable to corruption, a liability of which African American observers were aware.

Such a focus was implicit in the kinds of indictments of Revolutionary hypocrisy that figured in so many documents from the period, as when several groups of petitioners described themselves as being "detained in a State of slavery in the Bowels of a free & Christian Country." That slavery served as an indictment of Revolutionary commitment was hardly difficult to see; that it showed bad faith toward slaves little different from what, according to revolutionaries, Britain was showing toward the colonies was hard to miss.

As such an indictment appeared, however, it was linked to other representations of slavery, some having roots from before the Revolutionary era. The 1774 Massachusetts petition connected its condemnation of American hypocrisy with images of the petitioners themselves "stolen from the bosoms of our tender Parents" by the African slave trade and "dragged from our mothers Breest" by the domestic system. Linking the indictment of American Revolutionary corruption with their own experiences, the petitioners could put themselves on precisely the same footing colonial writers were assuming in their verbal attacks on British tyranny.

And, again, there was much to encourage their pursuit of such representations because the message was one that had broad currency in the antislavery world. The British radical Thomas Day, though he ultimately supported the American cause, linked a concatenation of issues in his own 1773 indictment of an increasingly revolutionary American people. He wrote that "for them the Negro is dragged from his cottage, and his plantane shade; — by them the fury of African tyrants is stimulated by pernicious gold; the rights of nature are invaded; and European faith becomes infamous throughout the globe." And yet, Day added, in a way many others appreciated, "these are the men whose clamours for liberty and independence are heard across the Atlantic ocean!" Nathaniel Appleton had anticipated Day when he wrote in 1767 that "all mankind have laughed at our pretensions to any just sentiments of Liberty, or even humanity." Such words involved more than an awareness of contradiction; they involved a sense that slavery could prevent the realization of those virtues for which revolutionaries were claiming to contend.[41]

Thus, in citing the corruption of the Revolution black writers played on a charge that was far from theirs alone. By putting such sentiments in their own words, however, linking them with violations of ideals for humane behavior, black writers provided a more distinct perspective on how pretentious those "pretensions" were. Here were commentators who had firsthand knowledge of American corruption, whose experiences validated the charges they made. The value of such a validation was acknowledged implicitly by Allen when he accompanied his brief for independence with a slave petition and even more by Thomas Day, whose indictment of American pretensions helped introduce his "Dying Negro," the tragic tale rendered in the voice of a persecuted slave.

The same may be said in regard to ideas of natural rights. At one level one may understand the assertion of natural rights one finds in Wheatley, or Sarter, or the petitions as a joining in with a tradition of ideas and arguments going back to James Otis. At another level the kinds of assertions one finds in those works and documents served as a reply to the contrary ideas also current in the colonial world, embodied, for example, in the Harvard debater's evocation of African inferiority, which he linked with notions of due subordination of inferiors in even a free social order.

In the Harvard debate, slavery's opponent found a refutation for such contentions in the "strong sense of Liberty implanted in the heart of every son of Adam." African American writers helped to stress both the value and the validity of such a response. Wheatley's open letter to Occom had verified the "Love of Freedom" in African as well as English breasts. The New Hampshire petitioners of 1779 had specifically stressed the significance and credibility of their own testimony to the debate itself, writing, "We feel a just equality," and "we know that the God of nature made us free." The notion expressed here, that love of freedom implied a claim to freedom—consistent with the most radical trends in American Revolutionary ideas—was to take on increasing importance in the debate over slavery as the eighteenth century drew to a close. It was to provide a powerful framework for the shaping of an African American voice as well.

But perhaps no emerging convention in this critical era was more revealing of the interplay between an African American voice and Revolutionary ideas than the extent to which black writers helped to include Africa as a motif in Revolutionary debates. The authors of the 1774 Massachusetts petition described not only how slaves had been stolen from their parents but also how they had been taken from their homeland, a "popolous Pleasant and plentiful contry." Caesar Sarter similarly referred to Africa as "a land of ignorance" but also "a land of comparative innocence—and a land that flows, as it were, with Milk and Honey." It was an imagery Wheatley had used as well. The poem to Dartmouth portrays her own kidnapping and the "pangs excruciating" her parents must have felt at her loss. She directly cited the authority of that experience in determining her own feelings about slavery and her hope that "others may never feel tyrannic sway." In the Dartmouth poem she implied an idyllic setting in what was "*Afric's* fancy'd happy seat." In her poetic exchange with the "gentleman in the navy" she offered her own visions of Africa, describing how "With native grace in spring's luxuriant reign, / Smiles the gay mead, and Eden blooms again." She wrote of Africa's "soil spontaneous," which "yields exhaustless stores."[42]

In the specific imagery they used these writers looked back to a clear set of sources that presented similarly idyllic views of Africa. Their imagery had roots in the oral traditions of kidnapping and betrayal in which storytellers evoked the idyllic Africa from which they had been stolen. It also had roots that went back to *Oroonoko*, if not before, almost certainly reinforced by the works of Anthony Benezet and his admirers. Beginning in the early 1760s, Benezet, who had been influenced by what he learned from slaves, also presented extracts from the travelers' literature that had been taking shape throughout the mid-seventeenth century to create an almost idyllic picture of Africa and Africans, the continent being "fruitful and in many places well improved," with a land that "yields all year round a fresh supply of food." As Benezet wrote, "But little clothing is requisite, by reason of the continual warmth of the climate, the necessaries of life are much easier procured in most parts of Africa than in our more northern climes." As for the people, they "appear, generally speaking, to be an industrious, humane, sociable people, whose capacities are naturally as enlarged and as open to improvement as those of the Europeans."[43]

Such images, synthesizing a range of literary and oral traditions, widely informed Revolutionary American arguments in opposition to slavery, as when Nathaniel Appleton noted in 1767 the incompatibility of slavery with Revolutionary ideals but also suggested, anticipating Wheatley's later mention of "Afric's blameless race," that slavery was particularly base. It was aimed, he said, at "an harmless people" who, "but for the interruption from white people might enjoy all the sweets of a rural life, being bless'd with a fine fruitful soil, which yields with small labour all the necessaries of life." Given the currency of such imagery, it is not surprising that Wheatley and others turned to it and, giving it the imprimatur of experience, took it to the larger Revolutionary community in which they played a role.[44]

Such imagery took on added importance, however, in the Revolutionary climate. In a time when the language of corruption was rife, the image of a pristine Africa was of a piece with tendencies toward a golden-age primitivism informing the thinking of at least some Revolutionary figures. Offering a world in which the corrupting force of greed and materialism appeared to be absent, an idyllic Africa really did appear to be the organic community underlying republican ideals. The imagery of its historical corruption by Europeans still further allowed for an African American experience uniquely suited to provide a perspective on Revolutionary affairs.

It was perhaps this potential Africanizing of Revolutionary ideas that also encouraged a renewed stress among some whites on a counterimagery of African barbarism. A measure of the strength of such imagery is its role in the Harvard debates. Slavery in America was defended in part by its contrast to supposed conditions in Africa, where all men and women faced "an entire subjection to the tyrannizing power of lust and subjection." The proslavery speaker asserted "the superiority of a slave in this country, in point of condition, to a natural inhabitant of *Africa*." [45]

Such negative imagery became even more widely diffused as the Revolution proceeded. It became a cliché in the celebration of Americans rights to contrast British traditions, of which these were a part, with the despotisms of Asia, parts of Europe, and especially Africa. Praising British institutions, while condemning their corruption, one pamphleteer wrote in 1775, "In *Africa*, scarce any human beings are to be found but barbarians, tyrants, and slaves: all equally remote from the true dignity of human nature and from a well-regulated state of society."[46]

Given such views, the importance of the imagery Wheatley and others were helping to put forward lay, at one level, in the ways it allowed them to contrast their own memories with the secondhand visions of Harvard debaters and Revolutionary pamphleteers. But at another level it gave Africa and their own background a place within the Revolutionary milieu. As all evoked an idyll interrupted by corrupt Europeans, they could still further undermine the claims to superiority on which rested not simply a proslavery argument but the sense of an American virtue compatible with slaveholding as well.

And, above all, they could do so specifically as black writers. Such a stance was at least implicit in the words of the 1779 New Hampshire petitioners as, at one point, they described the tearing of children from families and how, because of avarice, the children were "seized, imprisoned, and transported from their native country, where (though ignorance and unchristianity prevailed) they were born free, to a country where (though knowledge, Christianity and freedom are their boast) they are compelled and their posterity to drag on their lives in miserable servitude."[47]

The stance behind such an ironic juxtaposition of a truly free and unchristian Africa with a professedly free and Christian America was that of the observer whose very experiences punctured the adjectives so sarcastically employed. As Rafia Zafar has noted, Phillis Wheatley had been even more pointedly sarcastic in a letter written a few years earlier to the London merchant John Thornton. The letter discussed her possible participation in a plan created by the New England ministers Samuel Hopkins and Ezra Stiles to send two African-born young men — Bristol Yamma and John Quamine — back to Africa as missionaries. Asked if she could join in such a venture, Wheatley, playing on popular imagery, suggested "how like a Barbarian Shoud I look to the Natives" should she actually seek to live among people in Africa. Her very identification as a black writer allowed her to satirize popular negative imagery in a way that evoked a larger, developing tradition of African American voice as well.[48]

II

The framework Wheatley and her contemporaries helped to create was to provide a foundation for the subsequent elaboration and enrichment of an African American voice through the end of the eighteenth century. Its development was further shaped and refined by the issues of an emerging American republic, including the continuing issue of American slavery. The debates over slavery begun during the Revolution continued strong at its end, symbolized to some extent by Thomas Jefferson's tormented reflections in his influential post-Revolutionary *Notes on the State of Virginia*. Unable to shake a belief in African American inferiority, particularly in regard to "reason," he was convinced that "the real distinctions which nature has made" made for an incompatibility such that blacks and whites could never live together in the United States, at least not in a state of equality. Emancipation, he feared, would lead to racial warfare. And, he famously predicted, "the Almighty has no attribute which can take side with us in such a conflict." Outside the Deep South the discomforts raised by Revolutionary arguments continued to be strong. Almost everywhere north of Maryland slavery was put on a course of extinction, however gradual, by the century's end. Even in Jefferson's Virginia, where slavery was never really seriously threatened, there was enough discussion to make it appear, at least, that the institution was vulnerable to abolition.[49]

This sense of vulnerability was to be enhanced not only by the continuing work of Revolutionary ideals but also by the events in the nearby slave society of Haiti, where revolution broke out in 1793. Under the leadership of Toussaint L'Ouverture and other men of African descent, the revolution showed how powerfully slaves themselves could act against the institution, and with a violence that made Jefferson's concerns seem all the more pressing. This revolution, as has often been noted, had an immediate and enormous impact on American thinking, although for reasons that are only partly clear its role in African American letters, as such, was to be less immediate, deferred until after the eighteenth century's end.

Still, much antislavery thinking remained rooted in the ideals of Revolution or in older themes of sentimentalism. Much also grew out of the reorientation of American Protestantism that began to take shape by the end of the eighteenth century, especially by the growth of evangelicalism as it was embodied in Methodist and even Baptist church organizations. There is much to debate about the links between evangelicalism and antislavery. It is clear that for many evangelicals the stress they placed on experience and community posed the same kinds of dilemmas with regard to slavery and color that Revolutionary ideology posed for many white patriots. The evangelical denominations attracted great numbers of black converts and in some places lived up to their ideals by significantly closing the social distance between black and white church members. If most others quickly made their peace with slavery and especially with distinctions based on color, there was still, in the South as well as in the North, a significant minority of whites as well as blacks who practiced Christian fellowship and strongly rejected slavery at least until the century's end, and in some cases beyond.

At the same time, outside the South the terms of race relations changed radically between the end of the Revolution and the opening of the nineteenth century. The abolition of slavery, however gradual in most states, led to the creation of sizable, relatively diverse free Negro communities, especially in northern cities. Within these communities a variety of factors helped to encourage sources for further literary activity and developments. By the end of the century, Boston, New York, and Philadelphia, for example, saw the creation of schools for black children, some under white auspices, some under the leadership of free people of color. African American leaders began in earnest to develop organizations devoted to mutual help and assistance, as well as to agitate for fairer treatment. Church organizations began to take shape not only among free people in the North but also among free people and slaves alike in the South. All of these organizations and activities helped provide the setting for an independent leadership within African American communities and for addressing the world outside those communities as well.

Because of this shifting context, the issue of the possibility of an authoritative black voice was joined and discussed more fully and more openly in the closing years of the eighteenth century than previously, even during the Revolution. Representations of such a voice were both more varied and more loaded than they had ever been before; black and white commentators alike brought up the significance of such representations in ways that had only been anticipated by Wheatley, her predecessors, and her contemporaries.

In the earliest years of the republic blacks and whites alike frequently stressed that there was a place for a black voice in the American public life. In a 1794 address the antislavery minister Theodore Dwight echoed Samuel Hopkins's earlier response to proslavery arguments asserting the happiness of slaves under their masters by asking rhetorically, "Have the slaves been asked the question?" Dwight himself published several poems evoking the voice of the slave, praying for release. And he was only one of many antislavery writers to do so.[50]

But the significance of such voices had come under increasing discussion throughout the United States. One indication of the nature of this discussion was the continuing emergence of black literary celebrities during the closing years of the eighteenth century. Afro-British writers, including Olaudah Equiano, Ignatius Sancho, and Ottabah Cugoano, became well-known figures on both sides of the Atlantic. In addition, Phillis Wheatley's reputation continued to grow and be discussed during the closing years of the century. To many of those opposed to slavery, the legacy of Wheatley's work was significant. Antislavery writers and orators in England and America not only cited Wheatley's life and career as evidence against slavery and on behalf of human equality but also quoted from her works. David Grimsted suggests that so influential was her example that the Virginia planter "Bob" Carter, who had been so deeply moved when he read her poetry as a teenager, may well have been led to emancipate his slaves as a result.[51]

No less significant, even after her death Wheatley remained a presence in American literary life, as Walt Nott has shown. An early indication of this was the marking of her death by an obituary in the *Boston Magazine* that described her as "known to the literary world by her celebrated miscellaneous Poems." More fitting, given that world, was the inclusion in that same issue of an "Elegy on the Death of a late celebrated Poetess," signed by one "Horatio." The elegy paid tribute to Wheatley, to her poetry, and to a sensibility deeper than the color of her skin. The magazine also referred Horatio's readers back to an earlier page where it had printed what may have been Wheatley's final poem, an elegy to an infant boy. The poem was itself accompanied by a proposal for a new volume of her work.[52]

This recognition, with its implications for membership in the new nation's literary community, probably had much to do with Thomas Jefferson's famous dismissal of Wheatley's poetry, as part of his reflections in the *Notes on the State of Virginia*, as "beneath the dignity of criticism," echoing Richard Nisbet's 1773 remarks. As Nott has said, Jefferson's need to address Wheatley's achievement—he was similarly negative about Ignatius Sancho's efforts—was a measure of the kind of anxiety a black voice could create, an indication that such a voice as Wheatley's had to be dismissed because it could not be ignored.[53]

Still, as Wheatley's case shows, the hallmark of the period was contestation, not dismissal. Jefferson's remarks, as such, were quickly challenged. This was done, for example, as a part of an antislavery chapter, much focused on Jefferson, in Gilbert Imlay's 1797 *Topographical Description of the Western Territory of North America*. Citing Jefferson's comment, Imlay quoted one of Wheatley's early poems, asking his readers to compare "her genius and Mr. Jefferson's judgement." Imlay added, "I should be glad to be informed what white upon this continent has written more beautiful lines."[54]

Perhaps even more revealing was a poetic tribute to Wheatley published about the same time in the *New-York Magazine*. The poem was signed "Matilda" but was probably written, Eugene Huddleston suggested, by a male writer with aspirations of his own for a place in the nation's emerging "Republic of Letters." Indicating, first, that Wheatley remained a member of what was understood to be the sphere of public discourse, the poem also took a swipe at Jefferson by declaring that Wheatley's achievement proved the "mental pow'r" of the race.[55]

Wheatley's is not the only case to which such considerations apply. Her continuing celebrity also points to a developing tradition for African and African American celebrities within a larger world, almost as though a small canon were beginning to be established. Wheatley was cited most often, but others also appeared. An anonymous 1795 New Hampshire pamphlet, *Tyrannical Libertymen*, brought up the case of Job ben Solomon, concluding, "The story might now be told, that a tear would be no unnatural effect."[56]

As this embryonic process of canon formation indicates, the growth of the African American literary enterprise during this era was complex and complicated. It was not simply a matter of black writers beginning to write, and in ever greater numbers, although this is part of the story. It was also a matter, going back even before Briton Hammon and Phillis Wheatley, of creating forms and conventions that seemed to provide, within a discursive world, a basis for a distinctively black intervention into the public sphere. This necessarily collaborative effort was much of what was involved in the development of the earliest African American literature.

At one level, this development involved the emergence of fairly clear conventions, some looking back to the colonial period. These conventions involved both thematic elements and assertions of authority. In regard to slavery, and to color, most carried forward traditions and forms developed even before the Revolution, including petitions and other attempts to bring about relief from a system based on odious distinctions of color. One of the most widely noted, from a Massachusetts woman named Belinda, was submitted to the General Court in 1783. Belinda's owner had fled Massachusetts during the Revolution, and after fifty years' enslavement Belinda had been left destitute. She asked the General Court for an allowance from the abandoned estate, which was granted, if never fully paid.[57]

The petition itself was a virtual catalog of the developing conventions of antislavery, especially black-authored antislavery, written by an amanuensis clearly familiar with its forms. It contrasted an idyllic African life with the dangers brought by slavers, describing how in her childhood Belinda had "enjoyed the fragrance of her native groves," not realizing "that Europeans placed their happiness in the yellow dust, which she carelessly marked with her infant footsteps." It told how, by an "armed band of white men," she was "ravished from the bosom of her country, from the arms of her friends, while the advanced age of her parents, rendering them unfit for servitude, cruelly separated her from them for ever."[58]

Whatever the mixed practical results of the petition, it was not to lie buried in the legislative archives. When, after several years of nonpayment, Belinda again memorialized the Massachusetts assembly, the petition reemerged, printed in 1787 in Mathew Carey's widely circulated magazine, the *American Museum*. Carey published the petition without comment but followed it immediately with an unsigned "Address to the Heart, on the Subject of American Slavery," which evokes, in different words, images used in Belinda's petition, describing an African father "reclining in the arms of balmy rest," watching the "gambols" of his children, preparing for a feast. But then "a cloud rises in the west. The journey of the whirlwind is not more rapid in its progress." The idyll is about to be replaced by a scene of burning villages, the festive song by "the shrieks of the dying victims."[59]

Belinda's amanuensis remains unknown, but she or he clearly saw value in using the primitivist conventions that Wheatley and others had also drawn on. This was so much so that one modern critic has cited an earlier, English fictional text as a source for the petition. More likely, however, the petition, which was real, drew on conventions that were widely distributed, rooted in the lengthy traditions of antislavery discourse, written and spoken, as Vincent Carretta has said. The juxtaposition created by Carey, whether intentional or not, also helps to illuminate the way in which Belinda's petition both gained credibility from its reliance on those conventions and lent further credibility to them through its apparent basis in experience. This was a foundation the petition itself built on as, not with total accuracy, it evoked the captured Belinda's "agony, which many of her country's children have felt, but which none have ever described." By so inscribing Belinda's memories, as the petition purported to do, Belinda's amanuensis, and the editor Carey, reemphasized the distinctive authority to be claimed by one who had lived through the experiences Belinda's petition recounted.[60]

Belinda's petition became widely known and probably helped lay the groundwork for a late-eighteenth century explosion in literature evoking a black voice to make what was essentially a sentimental case against slavery. Suggesting the kind of reciprocal influences this literature involved, James Gronniosaw's amanuensis, Hannah More, for example, wrote several such pieces. Like many, she called on both sentimental and oral traditions to imagine and represent the anguish caused by slavery. One may also note, as at least one bit of evidence for reciprocity, the 1791 publication of a poem called "Monimba" in the *Massachusetts Magazine*. The poem, looking well back into tradition, recounts the kidnapping of a young African mother who, faced with "horrid slav'ry's death like weight," chose to leep from the slave ship to a "watry grave" and thus escape "the madd'ning sons of blood." The poem was signed "Belinda."[61]

Works such as Belinda's petition, however, only began to explore the possibilities for a black voice pursued in the late eighteenth century. No less revealing of the directions such a voice could take is the still more widely circulated exchange between the black scientist Benjamin Banneker and his correspondent Thomas Jefferson, initiated by Banneker in 1791. Along with a copy of his almanac, Banneker sent a letter acknowledging membership in "a race of Beings" who "have long been considered rather as brutish than human, and Scarcely capable of mental endowments." He referred to Jefferson as "a man far less inflexible in Sentiments of this nature, than many others," and thus as one who could be enlisted in the effort "to eradicate that train of absurd and false ideas and opinions which so generally prevail with respect to us."[62]

Banneker's letter was an effort to open a dialogue — in a sense like Jupiter Hammon adopting a model that had been around for a while — here with one of America's most prominent slaveholders but ostensibly a troubled one. Although there is no reason to assume that he was familiar with the dialogue tradition, there is much to suggest that he had the same sources of encouragement that lay behind Hammon's efforts, and Wheatley's as well. Like them, he had already gained an audience, even before his approach to Jefferson. That his work was an eloquent denial of such ideas as Jefferson's on black inferiority had been widely asserted by his Maryland supporters for several years. James McHenry, a former student of Benjamin Rush's and a prominent figure in Maryland politics, who described Banneker as "my black friend," suggested that even most whites given Banneker's chances for education would remain his intellectual inferiors. To an extent, that is, Banneker had already begun an effective dialogue before he decided to participate in it himself. Jefferson was at least open enough to reply, and what he said, incidentally, would have been far from discouraging to Banneker and his supporters. He received the almanac and acknowledged its significance "against the doubts which have been entertained" against people of African descent, although, as Annette Gordon-Reed has noted, Jefferson remained convinced enough of his own views to suggest that someone had assisted Banneker in the work.[63]

The Banneker-Jefferson correspondence thus traveled a step farther along the road Belinda's petition had taken, opening up a dialogue, or at least the possibility of a dialogue, across lines of color. Following the scenario Hammon had set up in his "Dialogue," Banneker sought to use the authority conferred by his own identity and achievements to offer a compelling answer to the kinds of speculations Jefferson had pursued.

If the dialogue Banneker sought to create had at least imaginative precedents in tradition, it also had parallels beginning in Banneker's own time. In 1790 in New York a newspaper debate was begun after one "Rusticus" wrote a piece asserting black inferiority. He was answered by "Africanus," who described himself as black and denied the truth of what Rusticus had written. That a black voice could be persuasive was also something many antislavery figures continued to document, as Woolman and Benezet had in earlier times. William Roscoe, who would become an important English antislavery figure in the closing years of the eighteenth century, dated his "awakening" to conversations with a black man. Still more important was the case of Warner Mifflin, an elite Virginian induced to free his slaves and to become active against the institution itself. In a pamphlet describing the change he told of how, as a teenager, he had been in the fields with his father's slaves and one asked "whether I thought it could be right, that they should be toiling to raise me, and I sent to school, and by and by their children must do so for mine also." Mifflin reported that as a result of the remark, he "determined never to be a slaveholder," a resolution he carried out.[64]

Such accounts were accompanied by a renewal, in literary form, of the kinds of pieces that had been developed earlier by such figures as Thomas Tryon and Jupiter Hammon, the imagined dialogue between master and slave. One fairly early example is a dialogue between the captured African Itanoko and his white friend Ferdinand in the French writer Joseph LaVallée's remarkable "The Negro Equalled by Few Europeans," a translation of which appeared serially in Carey's *American Museum* in 1791. Asserting that "the liberty of man is an inalienable right, which can neither be bought nor sold," Itanoko powerfully convinces young Ferdinand, son of the ship captain who had betrayed him into slavery, of the hypocrisy and perfidy of the European, slaveholding world.[65]

The longest lived and most widely noticed was, however, the debate printed in the popular schoolbook compiled by Caleb Bingham, *The Columbian Orator*. This was the "Dialogue Between a Master And Slave," which was later to have great influence on Frederick Douglass. Intended, like all the book's selections, to inspire pupils with "the ardour of eloquence, and the love of virtue," the dialogue clearly put the articulate slave and his arguments against slavery into the mainstream of American rhetoric. The dialogue virtually dramatized Dwight's question, for in it the master, confronting a runaway, essentially asks what a well-treated slave could want. The slave replies, "Since you condescend to talk with me, as man to man, I will reply," and offers a series of arguments against the institution, founded in his own experiences—his kidnapping, the likening of slavery to theft, and the love of freedom common to all. Like Mifflin's slave, but more immediately, he persuades the master of the evil of the institution, the master grants the slave his freedom on the spot.[66]

It would be difficult to say that all these dialogues constituted a tradition going back to Tryon and Hammon, at least in the sense of there being any internal evidence that each of the writers had knowledge of and drew on the works of the others. Rather, the re-creations of the form show what, in the opinion many people in the late eighteenth century, the black speaker could do, the authority that a black speaker could have, and the role that the black speaker, as such, could play in the mounting debates over slavery in the new American nation, something Banneker appeared to show as well.

And, again, the proof of the power of such voices may lie most clearly in the efforts to undermine them. Thomas Jefferson's dismissal of Wheatley's poetry was only one example of such efforts. Jefferson, however, found himself vulnerable to attack in the 1790s for his willingness to pay attention to Banneker, described by William Loughton Smith and Oliver Wolcott, two of Jefferson's most ardent foes, as the "negro Benjamin" and "the *reputed* author of an Almanac which was either dedicated to or sent, with some complimentary epistle, to his brother author, our philosopher." Here, at least, the idea of exchanging ideas with a black author was presented as essentially unthinkable.[67]

A more subtle attempt at undermining such a voice as Banneker's was the growing popularity, in magazines and elsewhere, of dialect-speaking blacks, whose very dialect portrayed their inability to engage in rational public debate. In jest books and elsewhere the presentation of such characters placed blacks at the margin of reasonable discourse, bringing together connotations of status, language, color, inferiority.[68]

Hugh Henry Brackenridge's 1792 novel, *Modern Chivalry*, provided only one example of such an effort, but it went straight to the heart of the issue raised by Banneker, not to mention that raised by Smith and Wolcott. In one episode, a Maryland planter in possession of a "petrified mocassin" is invited to address the "Philosophical Society." Acknowledging his slave "Cuff" as the discoverer of the moccasin, the planter defers, encouraging the society to admit Cuff and to give him the honor of delivering the address. Brackenridge had great fun burlesquing contemporary scientific discussions of the origins of difference in color. He also had great fun burlesquing Cuff's efforts at scientific speech and his master's encouragement of those efforts. According to Cuff, his master had told him, "You be a filasafa, Cuff, fo' sartan: Getta ready, and go dis city, and make grate peech for shentima filasafa." The parallels with Banneker's case are uncanny, as Brackenridge's dialect sought to undermine something very like the process Banneker had lived through and employed in his efforts to open the dialogue with Jefferson.[69]

To be sure, dialect was not always connected solely to purposes of burlesque. Take, for example, the frequently reprinted story of the slave who, offered a chance to be buried beside his master, refused, saying that if "de devil come looking for massa in de dark, he might take away poor negar man in mistake," a story that was itself part of African American tradition, as well as magazine humor. There were, moreover, a number of overtly antislavery pieces in which dialect was used in ways that replicated the stance Wheatley had helped create, stressing difference and using difference as the foundation for a distinctive moral authority. One told of a slave accused of stealing a knife and a corkscrew, whose master demanded that he be whipped. The slave demanded the same treatment for his master: "He know very well poor Tom be tolen from his old fadder and mudder; de knife and the cork-screw have neder." The charge was dismissed. Still, the negative implications of dialect were great enough that the pioneering black leader Prince Hall, toward the close of the century, appears to have sought to disarm dialect as an evidence of African American capabilities. Representing the words of an unlettered West Indian who, looking through a telescope, saw "de clipsey," Hall used the example to emphasize that condition in and of itself was far from conclusive evidence of the wisdom of any individual.[70]

But one of the most telling examples of the anxiety a black voice could create in the late eighteenth century was an odd piece purportedly by one "Adahoonzou, King of Dahomey," that was published in several American newspapers during the same time and reprinted in the *New York Weekly Magazine* in 1792. This piece, regarding the African slave trade, put into words a common defense of it, arguing that Africans would continue to fight even if there were no trade to supply and asserting that captives taken in war would simply be put to death without the alternative of a slavery into which they could be sold. According to the "king," such captives and others sent to the Europeans could only say, "White men will not kill us, and we may even avoid punishment, by serving our new masters with fidelity." It may be that at least one of slavery's defenders could find the need to vest authority in a black voice, as well as a white one, to support his cause; it may be that the emergence of black voices endowed with authority posed a challenge that itself needed to be answered.[71]

Thus, the issues and contestations of authority apparent in regard to black voices since the Revolutionary era looked back to the emergence of strong figures such as Wheatley and, for many, the petitioners who had taken advantage of the Revolutionary context to argue strongly against slavery and exclusion. This Revolutionary pattern continued to develop during the era of the early republic. It continued to create openings in the realm of public discourse, unsettling relationships between voice, status, and authority.

What was true in the secular realm was also true in the realm of religion. The closing years of the eighteenth century saw a great expansion of Christianity generally, and especially among American slaves and free people of color conversion and even church membership reaching unprecedented levels. The status of black Christians within the churches, however, could vary greatly and was important evidence of the hold of "color" on most white Americans and, in the South, of slavery as well. As the number of black converts grew, white Christians made steady efforts to curtail black rights and black participation in church congregations to ensure that if blacks were to be considered church members, they would not have the same rights and privileges as whites.[72]

Still, the story itself was not without variation. The message of inclusiveness, of community, was strong in evangelical Christianity, and in many parts of the United States there were genuine tendencies toward an inclusiveness that transcended lines of color, narrowing social gaps and giving to black Christians a place of some visibility in Christian congregations. Particularly in sparsely settled areas, even of the South, lines of color occasionally loosened under the impact of experiential religion and strongly held beliefs, producing at least an approximation of equality in individual congregations.[73]

What one sees with regard to congregations was also true of the much more difficult issue of black religious authority, particularly the development of a black ministry. In the fervor of evangelical services, as had happened during the Great Awakening, black exhorters arose to preach to whites and blacks alike; dedicated converts returned to their plantations prepared to continue in the effort to convert others. In the late eighteenth century, however, these works were even more positively encouraged, the roles of such black preachers more fully institutionalized than in the past. Such prominent religious leaders as Richard Allen, Absalom Jones, George Liele, Andrew Bryan, and Lemuel Haynes all began their careers during the heated expansion of an inclusive Christianity in the closing years of the eighteenth century.[74]

Here, too, the patterns illustrate the possibilities for a black voice within a larger community of discourse. Certainly, at least some of the country's white religious ministers, proponents of black church membership, expected black ministers to deal primarily with black congregations, serving, as had been the case during the work of the Society for the Propagation of the Gospel, as liaisons between the churches and black, especially slave, communities. The white Methodist bishop Francis Asbury at least implied such a view when, after hearing a talented slave ex-horter in Delaware, he concluded "that it appears as if the Lord was preparing him for peculiar usefulness to the people of his own colour. Let the Lord choose his own instruments, and send by whom he will." The black minister George Liele took the same position, describing his call, while in Georgia, to instruct people "of my own colour in the word of God."[75]

But again, the possibilities for black ministers were not everywhere defined wholly along lines of color, either for the preachers themselves or for white congregations. Well into the 1790s, black Christians self-consciously sought to make their abilities and their knowledge known to white audiences as well as black; white congregations returned encouragement and support. Jupiter Hammon preached to mixed congregations and throughout his career received endorsement from whites and blacks alike. Such figures as George Liele and John Chavis were strongly encouraged by white congregations for whom they preached, despite Liele's account of his call. Richard Allen in the early days of his itineracy preached mainly to white congregations in Pennsylvania.[76]

The situation was not a simple one. Black preachers were always on dangerous or at least uncomfortable ground, North and South. There were cases of open persecution of the sort that faced an Andrew Bryan, whipped and beaten in the early years of his career for his attempts to spread the gospel. Where persecution was not so open, there was still the kind of separation and subordination that led Richard Allen and Absalom Jones by the early 1790s to begin to think seriously about the creation of a black church independent of white control.[77]

Still, in all these contexts the possibility of an authoritative black voice remained real. This could include a ministry chiefly to black congregants, but one with possibilities for independence of expression and organization within the context of a white-dominated Christian America. It could include the kind of low-level, subtle ministry across lines of color dramatized in the dialogues of Tryon and Hammon, as black Christians brought religion to their masters. Richard Allen performed such a service on the plantation where he lived as a young, enslaved convert.[78]

It could also extend outward, and into the literary realm. Accounts of the lives of such black Christians as John Marrant and Boston King were published in Britain and in the United States for their exemplary importance to white as well as black readers. Similar themes were distilled down to brief sketches, published on both sides of the Atlantic, of "pious Negroes" whose lives could serve as examples to all.

In most cases, these works, too, emphasized the distinctive power of the black voice. In Marrant's case issues of color were somewhat muted, at least in the most common edition of his narrative, edited by the some-time Huntingdonian William Aldridge, but this was unusual. As Ellen Eslinger has noted, the late-eighteenth-century evangelical emphasis on separateness and humility helped to reinforce a role for those whose faith persisted in the face of the worst of obstacles. No one epitomized such a role more than American slaves. When John Rippon introduced some of George Liele's letters to white Baptist readers by noting that a brief mention of Liele had "produced an earnest desire to know the circumstances" of Liele's career and "the *character* of this poor but successful minister of Christ," he caught at least some of the special interest a black saint could create.[79]

III

Where it was acknowledged, then, the black voice continued to make its place in America both within specific communities of discourse and as a result of its distinctive character. The result was to magnify the kinds of themes and positions associated with the black speaker from the time of Wheatley and her contemporaries, if not before. By early in the post-Revolutionary period there was a fairly well established tradition for the content of an African American literary production as well as a distinctive stance within the emerging republic of letters. At the center was the tense confrontation between assertions of egalitarian ideals and assertions stressing, in a variety of ways, the distinctive position of the black observer within the American setting.

In asserting a human equality the black speaker usually drew on a variety of traditions. One of those traditions was the assertion of human unity that emphasized the intellectual and emotional equality of people of African descent. A letter purportedly from a West Indian in the 1789 *American Museum* played on such themes. Signed by "a free negro" and sponsored for publication by the New York Manumission Society, it questioned the significance of color. Virtually quoting Shylock's famous speech from *The Merchant of Venice*, it asked, "Has not a negro eyes? has not a negro hands, organs, dimensions, senses, affections, passions?" A little over a decade later, in 1800, the businessman James Forten did the same thing in a letter that was connected with the petition Absalom Jones had sent to the United States Congress in 1799. The letter was written to the Massachusetts congressman George Thatcher, who had presented the petition to the House of Representatives. In his letter Forten picked up on the same language that had inspired the West Indian writer, but in a particularly revealing way, when he noted, "Though our faces are black, yet we are men; and though many among us cannot write, yet we have all the feelings and passions of men." Much as Hall had done with his evocation of dialect, Forten challenged traditional modes for evaluating possibilities of speaking authoritatively even as he asserted, through his knowledge and the allusive character of his words, his own claim on an ability to do so.[80]

In making his point the way he did Forten was already showing the strength of at least one convention in the assertion of human unity. Not only had he been preceded by the piece in the *American Museum*, but other writers had used language quite similar to his. The English novelist Anna Maria Mackenzie, for example, in her 1793 *Slavery; or, the Times* had her black hero declare, "Do not the same beams enlighten, the same passions inform, the same principles animate us?"[81]

The language of the Revolution also remained important. Such language was particularly critical to the legislative petitions that continued to go forward through the end of the century. Absalom Jones, the Philadelphia minister, drew heavily on such language in a petition to the United States Congress he drafted and circulated in Philadelphia in 1799, a petition presented, though ultimately defeated, the following year. The petition was a protest against the federal fugitive slave law of 1793, a law that had heavily affected black Philadelphians, not only fugitives who had sought refuge but free people who under pretext of law had been kidnapped and sold into slavery. The petition referred to the "natural right to liberty" that the petitioners could claim, a liberty that extended to protection of their persons and property, as well as to a securing of their right to petition for relief from oppressive laws.[82]

In asserting natural rights and human equality these writers continued to point toward an American hypocrisy, revealed by slavery. The theme had survived the Revolution because slavery had survived the Revolution. Its use in a black-voiced document had, as in earlier times, the tendency both to create an ironic perspective on contemporary events and to claim for the black speaker a unique authority to convey that perspective.

How this theme could be carried forward into the era of the early republic was especially evident in a 1788 series of essays signed by one "Othello" and published in Carey's *American Museum*. Othello's identity has never been established. In the early nineteenth century Henri Grégoire identified him as black; others have suggested that he was likely a white abolitionist or a politician. Crucial, however, was not Othello's color but, again, what he represented, as his essays serve as evidence of what many felt a black writer could contribute to the America discussion.[83]

Writing, "Blush, ye revolted colonies, for having apostatized from your principles," Othello described the horrors of the slave trade in familiar terms, while asking, "Will such a practice stand the scrutiny of this great rule of moral government?" Othello went back to the same language of corruption so common in Revolutionary times and applied it to the new republic, and he assigned slavery to an "insatiable, avaricious desire to accumulate riches, cooperating with a spirit of luxury and injustice." The indictments went forward, all intended to reveal a baseness at the heart of a slave-owning society, one that Othello, by virtue of his identity, was well positioned to see. It was perhaps for this reason that Carey published Othello's remarks immediately after a condemnation of the slave trade by the British abolitionist Granville Sharp.[84]

The stance taken by Othello, combining a philosophy of natural rights with a recognition of the failings of the slave-owning American republic, found other modes of expression. More than baseness, for example, Othello's indictment also implied a loss of Revolutionary principles, and here, too, the black voice could use its own position to point up American failings. A short time after Othello's essays appeared in the *American Museum*, the magazine published the letter from the West Indian "free negro" in support of human equality. In addition to paraphrasing Shakespeare, the author reviewed recent history. "I hear Europeans exalted," it said, "as the martyrs of public liberty, the saviours of their country, and the deliverers of mankind." But, he said, "when a generous negro is animated by the same passion, which ennobled them—when he feels the wrongs of his countrymen as deeply, and attempts to avenge them as boldly—I see him treated by those same Europeans, as the most execrable of mankind."[85]

In keeping with the kind of place that a black voice had to come to occupy, moreover, was the juxtaposition Matthew Carey also created for the "free negro"'s essay. He placed it immediately after a report of a speech made by William Pinckney, a Maryland legislator, in support of a bill before the state assembly intended to liberalize the laws of private emancipation. Pinckney also saw slavery as a contradiction to American principles. "Call not Maryland a land of liberty," he declared. "Let us figure, to ourselves, for a moment," he continued, "one of these unhappy victims, more informed than the rest, pleading, at the bar of this house, the cause of himself and his fellow sufferers." Pinckney went on to offer, based on his imagination, what such an "orator of nature" might say, stressing a need for justice and, no less, a need to "vindicate your public councils from the imputation of cruelty, and the stigma of causeless, unprovoked oppression." The relationship set up between the two pieces, intended or not, was, again, one of mutual reinforcement, even mutual authentication. The "free negro" helped emphasize the veracity of Pinckney's imagined address even as Pinckney helped prepare the way for an acknowledgment of the relevance of what the "free negro" had to say. Both worked to identify the black voice with a critique of America's failing to live up to American principles.[86]

Many of these same considerations applied in the realm of religion. At the heart of a black religious discourse in the late eighteenth century were a series of biblical assurances of human unity and of religious hope. Many black Christians, for example, took hope in the biblical assurance that "God is no respecter of persons" (Acts 10:34), or, as Prince Hall paraphrased it, "God hath no respect of persons." The passage proclaimed not only the universality of the Gospel but, as a group of Philadelphians wrote in 1789, an "encouragement for us of the African race" that they were the equal of any people, in the sight of God.[87]

This commonly cited passage was powerfully supplemented by a second biblical assurance that also figured frequently in work from the period, a verse proclaiming that God "hath made of one blood all nations of men for to dwell on all the face of the earth, and hath determined the times before appointed, and the bounds of their habitation" (Acts 17:26). The phrase had figured in antislavery pieces since the colonial period, and it continued to appear in texts in the upcoming decades.

But taken together, the passages provided an important background for one of the more common modes of African American self-reference during the era, that of membership in the African *nation*. Wheatley had used the term in her correspondence, writing in 1772, for example, of her pleasure at the progress of Christianity among "so many of my Nation, Seeking with eagerness the way to true felicity." In his 1799 petition, Absalom Jones decried "the oppression and violence which so great a number of like colour and national descent are subject to." The connotations of such a word allowed precisely the kind of stance Wheatley and others had sought to take, a stance stressing their common humanity with all the "nations" of the earth, while still noting the distinctive position of their own "nation" in relation to that of Anglo-America.[88]

In this, such writers as Wheatley and Jones indicated an important point about the language of nationhood and African American identity taking shape in the late eighteenth century. The use of such language did not originate with them. Most significantly, the South Carolina Anglican Alexander Garden had referred in 1740 to blacks constituting "a Nation within a Nation," a characterization that would not die with him.[89]

But the terminology became all the more important later in the century. Issues of inclusiveness and exclusiveness had been taking shape in American thinking since the Revolutionary period. Some scholars have argued that just as British definitions of an *English* nation were becoming increasingly exclusive to the British Isles prior to the Revolution, at least some Americans were creating more exclusive concepts of nationhood for themselves after the Revolution. Peter Onuf, for example, has called attention to Thomas Jefferson's belief, reinforcing his general sense of "natural distinctions," that blacks in America constituted a separate, "captive nation," one that probably deserved freedom but also must remain distinct from an American "nation" with its own "national characteristics." For Jefferson, as Onuf says, national identity implied homogeneity.[90]

Whether one can see black writers setting up a counterdiscourse, it is clear that their use of the term *nation* and its linkages within the antislavery framework to biblical ideas raised questions about any Jeffersonian assumptions of what a national identity should entail. Here, too, one sees a thematic expression of the kind of stance toward American society taken by Wheatley and carried forward by Othello and others. For them, *nation* meant not merely a matter of difference but a way of talking about that interplay of similarity and difference upon which a black public voice could rest.

Such an emphasis was still further enhanced by a third passage, which appeared very often and clearly went back to Wheatley as well. In her response to Hopkins and Stiles regarding their missionary venture in Africa, Wheatley had expressed the biblical hope, from Psalms 68:31, that with enough effort, "Ethiopia Shall Soon Stretch forth her hands Unto God." The passage was to gain increasing currency during the closing years of the eighteenth century, connected not to hopes for extensive conversion but for a much greater future. Prince Hall, in a 1792 address, tied the passage to his own hopes for a brighter future for African Americans in Boston. In the wake of the Haitian revolution he saw a still more profound way in which Ethiopia had begun to "stretch forth her hand, from a sink of slavery to freedom and equality." Here was a sense of the power of providence in the history of African Americans that had great implications for the future.[91]

The role of divine providence in the lives and histories of people of African descent was one of the more striking themes in African American–based literature during the late eighteenth century. At one level it involved a continuation of the tradition inaugurated by Briton Hammon's narrative, and even more by James Gronniosaw's, a documentation of the role of providence in the preservation of one's life and the advancement of one's purposes. A series of narratives published in England and America about such figures as John Marrant, Boston King, Ottabah Cugoano, and Olaudah Equiano followed Briton Hammon in displaying the hand of providence in guiding their subjects and enabling them to survive in the world. Marrant, for example, drew on the same models of Native American captivity that Briton Hammon had used in showing how God had preserved him in the hands of "savages," going beyond Hammon to give an account of his success in bringing many of those savages to conversion.

At another was the further exploration of the role of providence in the continuing mystery of enslavement. Some of what appeared in this era harked back to Wheatley's "On Being Brought from Africa to America." Jupiter Hammon's "Winter Piece," an address delivered in 1782, fairly echoed Wheatley, as well as his own poem in tribute to her, in suggesting that "God in his wise providence" had permitted Africans "to be brought from their native place to a christian land," using such an idea to encourage "christian families" to feel the responsibility to educate their servants but urging patience in the hope for freedom as well. In his famous 1787 "Address to the Negroes in the State of New York," Hammon similarly invoked the hand of providence in the hope for freedom, telling his audience, "If God designs to set us free, he will do it, in his own time, and way."[92]

Hammon's "Address" was widely known, having been printed and circulated initially by the influential Pennsylvania Abolition Society and ultimately going through at least three editions. The title page placed the sermon directly in the mainstream of a literature of human unity and equality, quoting the passage from Acts assuring the reader that "God is no respecter of persons," and built on Hammon's earlier "Dialogue" by asserting the necessity of good behavior, as well as obedience, within the system of slavery, but with an ultimate obedience to God. Still, the epigraph guided much that Hammon said, as he noted, for instance, that "there are but two places where all go after death, black and white, rich and poor; those places are Heaven and Hell." He also moved closer to the mainstream of Revolutionary rhetoric when, denying an interest in freedom for himself—chiefly, he said, on account of his age—he added, "I should be glad if others, especially the young negroes, were to be free." He said, with an irony that looked back to the petitions of the Revolutionary years, "that liberty is a great thing we may know from our own feelings, and we may judge so from the conduct of the white people, in the late war." If Hammon's address was no clarion call for freedom, it was still a testimony to human equality and an evocation of providential possibilities and hope for the future.[93]

The tradition in which Hammon spoke was well established by the time he made his speech. When the Philadelphia freedman Cyrus Bustill addressed a group of slaves in the same year, he, like Hammon, reminded his audience more than once that "God is no Respecter of Persons" while urging both obedience within slavery and God's promise of freedom for all. With roots in a theology that both indicted slavery and saw God's hand in everything, this was no apology for slavery but, rather, an effort to fit both the present condition and future hopes of African Americans within the context of an argument for human unity and a positive connection between the African "nation" and God. The idea was familiar enough that the Philadelphian Joseph Sansom, the white antislavery author of a long work entitled *Poetical Epistle to the Enslaved Africans, in the Character of an Ancient Negro*, was far from speaking for whites alone when he published his work in 1790, creating a fictional voice that sounded very much like Hammon's or Bustill's in counseling others to

> Think not to right yourselves—let God arise,
> Fit you for freedom, and then make you free,
> As he design'd his creature MAN to be.[94]

There were caveats. The English poet William Cowper in 1793 published his widely reprinted poem "The Negro's Complaint," in which his speaker directly questioned:

> Is there one who reigns on high?
> Has he bid you buy and sell us,
> Speaking from his throne the sky?

Cowper's speaker answered no, and so it was for a young William Hamilton, destined to be one of New York's key African American leaders by the early nineteenth century. Writing to the Federalist statesman and antislavery figure John Jay in 1796, Hamilton found Cowper's "Negro's Complaint" satisfactory to speak for him; he quoted directly from it and added his own assent to Cowper's conclusion: "Has God appointed us as their slaves? I answer No." Such sentiments were to become increasingly common in the years after Hamilton's note.[95]

For the most part, however, the invocation of providence remained an important element in African American rhetoric. It was but a short step from the kind of general invocation found in Hammon or Bustill to versions of the more pointed one Wheatley had anticipated when she referred to American slaveholders as "our modern Egyptians." A Virginia slave purportedly wrote a poem in 1790 lamenting his condition and praying,

> When will the sun of freedom rise?
> When will a Moses for us stand,
> And free us all from Pharaoh's hand?

That the slavery of Africans in America could be analogous to that of the Israelites in Egypt and betoken the same relationship with God was a point that reinforced precisely the kind of stand that Wheatley had taken and that allowed figures like Hammon and Bustill to counsel patience and hope at the same time.[96]

These kinds of ideas were especially important to the Boston Masonic leader Prince Hall, a tradesman, activist, and founder of the first black Masonic lodge, in Boston in 1775. Hall was widely known in Boston and the Atlantic world. He was generally recognized as a spokesman for the city's African American population; his activities, as well as those of the lodge, were well reported in the Boston papers. When the prominent Boston minister Jeremy Belknap was asked in 1795 by the Virginian St. George Tucker about the "harmony" between blacks and whites in Boston, he cited a comment he had solicited several years earlier from Hall as his authority for claiming that relationships were generally good.[97]

Hall's record of activism was also lengthy and well known. He composed one of the Revolutionary petitions to the Massachusetts General Court in 1777. He composed another in 1787, this time requesting support for a venture to establish a colony of freed people on the west coast of Africa. In 1788 he led another petition campaign protesting the kidnapping of three freemen who had been sold into slavery. The petition was printed in the *American Museum*, along with petitions from other Bostonians. Together, the petitions resulted in the release of the victims and contributed to legislation in Massachusetts intended to guard against future abductions.[98]

As a Mason, Hall was particularly concerned with the ancient pedigree of African peoples. In his 1792 address he emphasized the African origins of important figures from the ancient past—of Ebedmelech, a "blackman" who had saved the prophet Jeremiah "from the jaws of death," and Tertullian and Cyprian, fathers of the Christian church. In doing so he looked back to ideas reaching at least to Morgan Godwyn, suggesting a perhaps underground tradition that extended back through the eighteenth century and that had been further developed in the lodge itself by John Marrant in a 1789 sermon. Marrant had noted that "ancient history will produce some of the Africans who were truly good, wise, and learned men, and as eloquent as any other nation whatever, though at present many of them in slavery."[99]

But within the developing framework of African American writing Hall went a step further. Tracing a direct line of descent for Masonry from Solomon, "our Grand Master," Hall found a special provenance for black Masonry, recounting how Solomon "was not asham'd to take the Queen of Sheba by the hand, and lead her into his court, at the hour of high twelve, and there converse with her on points of masonry (for if ever there was a female mason in the world she was one)." Despite the recognition he received generally, Hall had long struggled fruitlessly for acceptance by white Masons at the time of this address; his words reflected his struggles. At the same time, his words looked beyond those struggles to place white color-consciousness within biblical reproach. The same may be said of his brief reference to the story from the book of Numbers of Aaron and Miriam, punished for their objection to Moses's marriage to "an Ethiopian woman." The lesson, as Hall noted, was that "he that despises a black man for his colour, reproacheth his Maker, and he hath resented it," as God's punishment of Miriam revealed.[100]

Hall's excursus into biblical history was only a part of a larger emphasis in many presentations by African and African American voices of themes of moral superiority. These were themes that cohered closely with the tradition of asserting and demonstrating a superior stance toward the American world, such as Wheatley did, even as a teenager, in her ironic comments on the Boston of her day, and Othello and the "free negro" did in their comments on American ideals. In religion this usually entailed demonstrations that blacks were more pious than whites around them, a notion implicit in Richard Allen's claim, for example, to have been the one to take religion and prayer into the house of his master. James Gronniosaw in his earlier exemplary narrative had similarly contrasted pious slaves with impious masters, as when, describing his own youth, he offered an account of an old man beaten for criticizing his mistress's swearing. The Afro-English writer Ottabah Cugoano offered a variation on the theme when he talked about the customs of his own African homeland, noting that his people had kept "a sabbath every seventh day, more strictly than Christians generally do."[101]

There was much to encourage such a perception, and much to reinforce the stance such writers took. Certainly, the persecution many black religious figures underwent contributed to this. Whites and blacks alike appear to have recognized the clear parallels between the sufferings of these late-eighteenth century figures and earlier generations of martyrs for the church. Andrew Bryan, among the most publicly persecuted of black Christians, was reported to have told his persecutors when he was undergoing a beating for his religious activities "that he rejoiced not only to be whipped, but *would freely suffer death for the cause of Jesus Christ,*" powerfully impressing whites and blacks alike.[102]

John Marrant's narrative offered a similar portrayal of piety and persecution. Its most common editions, edited by William Aldridge, tended to ignore issues of color in favor of those of religion. In an edition of his own, however, Marrant inserted material that reintroduced a prophetic black persona, recounting the suffering he and some of his slave congregants had undergone when he sought to carry his message to a South Carolina plantation. Caught in a service, "men, women, and children were stript naked and tied, their feet to a stake, their hands to the arm of a tree, and so severely flogg'd that the blood ran from their backs and sides to the floor." Marrant confronted master and mistress, threatening them with God's vengeance—a vengeance apparently realized when the cruel mistress died of a violent fever only two months later. One can only speculate why Aldridge chose not to use the passage. But one can be more certain that for Marrant it helped to emphasize the peculiarly prophetic role a black Christian could play in the Atlantic world.[103]

Such tales of suffering and persecution, together with the evocation of providence, the sense of African Americans' superior piety, and the tales of black Christians' martyrdom, all pointed toward the way a black voice implicitly and explicitly represented both an addition to the discussion of issues of race and color and a mode for questioning the pretensions of the larger Anglo-American society. By the end of the century such a role for the black voice was to become increasingly common. The strength and even sincerity of white piety were called into question by the experiences of an Andrew Bryan. The history taught by Prince Hall and the authoritative religious voices and examples of Richard Allen or James Gronniosaw undermined any notion that whites were somehow destined to lead American Christianity, as did the evocations of providence by Jupiter Hammon and Cyrus Bustill.

Many of these themes came together in the 1794 pamphlet published by Absalom Jones and Richard Allen, A *Narrative of the Proceedings of the Black People During the Late Awful Calamity in Philadelphia, in the Year 1793*. The calamity was a yellow fever epidemic, during which the city's black Christians performed major services for the white sick and dying. They did so with the encouragement of Benjamin Rush, who assured Allen that blacks were not susceptible to the disease. Since Rush turned out to be wrong, many blacks also became sick and lost their lives. As the epidemic subsided, Mathew Carey wrote an attack on the city's black community, accusing them of profiting from their services. Jones and Allen's pamphlet, written in reply, detailed the sacrifices they and their coworkers had made.[104]

They also attached three brief "addresses" to the pamphlet, one "to those who keep Slaves, and approve of the Practice," another "To the People of Colour," and a third "to the Friends of Him who hath no Helper," intended for their white supporters. All three built heavily on themes of religious authority as those had come to be developed into a black persona. Their address to the people of color echoed the words of Hammon, Bustill, Sansom, and others who had counseled patience and trust in God. Jones and Allen referred to the authority of their own experiences in preaching as they did; their own bouts of impatience had left them "in darkness and perplexity."[105]

In addressing both friends and foes among the whites, they drew no less heavily on ideas of providence and, especially, the precedent of the Israelites. Addressing their friends, they described theirs as a "more than Egyptian bondage." To their foes they warned "how hateful slavery is in the sight of that God, who hath destroyed kings and princes, for their oppression of the poor slaves." Taking note of defenses of slavery on grounds of the inferiority of the slaves, they asked, "Would you not suppose the Israelites to be utterly unfit for freedom, and that it was impossible for them to attain to any degree of excellence?"[106]

Finally, they drew heavily on imagery connected with notions of an equal if not superior capacity for piety in black Christians. Taking the high ground, they expressed their own purposes as ministers "that we may all forgive you, as we wish to be forgiven." Reenacting the same dialogue Banneker had initiated and others had continued to dramatize, Jones and Allen worked within what was becoming a well-established framework of conventions and traditions, helping to mold an identifiably black voice in the early republic.[107]

That people of African descent could be so exemplary was even more strongly supported in works by writers, white and black, who, building on past traditions, created representations of Africans and African Americans directly contrasting with a white world they presented as given to perfidy and greed. Such a point was most visible in a late-eighteenth-century revival of interest in the heroic, enslaved African nobleman, of the sort earlier embodied in Aphra Behn's Oroonoko, as a literary type. The representation of African nobility enslaved could take many forms. Frequently printed as true was the story of a young African prince who, sent by his father to London, was seized by the ship's captain and sold into slavery in the West Indies. He was released and sent to London, where he attended a performance of a theatrical version of Oroonoko. The experience "so strongly affected the young prince, that he was forced to retire at the end of the fourth act." Here was a story whose motifs of feeling, African virtue, and white perfidy were put in such a pithy form that its numerous parallels could be easily assumed and built on in a wide range of ways.[108]

One of the more elaborate and popular accounts along these lines was John Stedman's 1796 Narrative of a Five Years' Expedition Against the Revolted Negroes of Surinam, which was widely read in both Europe and America. Combining tales of military adventure with natural history and horrific portrayals of the treatment of slaves in the Dutch colony, strikingly illustrated with drawings by William Blake, the book also reported Stedman's conversations with unhappy slaves themselves, testifying to the suffering and sorrow slavery had brought them. Among these conversations he reported an encounter with an old slave, son of a king, who told him the familiar tale of European betrayal and kidnapping, extending the credibility such accounts had already attained to his own work.[109]

At the book's center, however, and responsible for much of its popularity, was its account of Stedman's own relationship with the beautiful Joanna, a young enslaved mulatta whose beauty enchanted him and whom he represented in the book as his wife—a not entirely accurate version of the actual relationship, as Mary Louise Pratt has shown. Stedman described Joanna as nobility enslaved, the child of a European father and a mother whose parents "were most distinguished people on the coast of Africa." The realization that such a young women could be "exposed to every rude blast without protection" was a revelation, claimed Stedman. He intended it to be a revelation for his readers as well, though he also expected them to be versed in the earlier tradition of a black-voiced opposition to slavery, including, as Werner Sollors has noted, the tales of Inkle and Yarico. Only those who had sided with "Incle" rather than the "much-injured *Yarico*," Stedman wrote, could fail to appreciate the case that Joanna, by her very existence, made against slavery.[110]

But Joanna's words were no less eloquent testimony than her life. Reporting that he offered her the opportunity to accompany him to Europe, and away from Guianese slavery, Stedman also described her refusal, made because of the difficulties it would cause him. Still, she professed her devotion to him, saying, "Though a slave, I have a soul, I hope, not inferior to that of an European; and blush not to avow the regard I retain for you." When, the following day, he brought her an expensive present, she returned it to the merchant and returned the money to Stedman, not wanting to compromise whatever "good opinion" he might have of her "disinterested disposition." Stedman concluded, "Such was the language of a slave," the implications of which were clear.[111]

Such images of an African nobility were themselves framed within the discussion and debate over slavery and color in which they had their place. The kinds of negative images of Africa that had dominated the accounts of travelers and slave traders since the fifteenth century appeared even in the late eighteenth, standing in contrast to the reevaluations offered by Benezet and Wesley and the idyllic images Wheatley and her contemporaries had put forward. In the particularly virulent writings of Robert Norris, for example, Africa was again presented as a place of savagery, barbarism, and filth. He told stories of brutal executions and human sacrifices, describing, for example, a king's palace approached by a path "paved with *human skulls*." He directly took on the notion of a nobility, writing that even the use of words such as *king* or *general* or *palace* could be no more than a convenience of language. "I may hope it will be deemed a very excusable burlesque," he wrote, "to dignify a brutal barbarian with the title of *king*."[112]

Thus, when antislavery writers either in fiction or from experience evoked the kinds of images they did, they were answering, at least implicitly, a continuing tradition of negative ideas. Perhaps the most notable example of this was the widely published *Narrative* of Olaudah Equiano, which appeared in England in 1789 and in the United States within the next two years, going through several editions. Equiano's was an extremely rich narrative; it was also deeply rooted in the traditions contributing to antislavery writing by the end of the eighteenth century.[113]

In many ways Equiano's *Narrative* was an elaborate gloss on developing conventions, which is not surprising if, as Vincent Carretta has suggested, Equiano was American- rather than African-born. In his narrative Equiano described himself as the kidnapped son of a chief who was deeply aware of the world into which he had been spirited. A devout Christian, he, like Briton Hammon, saw the hand of providence in the events he recounted. The Africa he described owed nothing to Norris, as Equiano drew on primitivist traditions, particularly on the works of Benezet, to describe Africa as a land "where nature is prodigal of her favors." There were slaves, he admitted, "but how different was their condition from that of the slaves in the West-Indies," he said, responding to proslavery contentions of American benevolence. As Equiano traced his story, he was in every way the enslaved man of nobility. Exploiting the ironic stance Wheatley had developed, in episode after episode Equiano made clear his moral superiority to his captors, to those who continued to hold him in thrall.[114]

The same may be said of an American narrative from the very end of the century, that of Venture Smith, dictated to an amanuensis and published in 1798. Smith was a popular local figure from New England, famous in part for his great physical size and strength, who had traveled from slavery to prosperity. Like Marrant's, Smith's narrative was offered as an exemplary account of a man's life, but his color was itself an important part of the story. His white editor, Elisha Niles, suggested that the reader might see in Smith "a Franklin and a Washington in a state of nature, or rather in a state of slavery." Smith could certainly be an example to the growing free black population. As Robert Desrochers has said, he could also have an exemplary role that went beyond the free black community, especially in an early republic that many perceived to be in a state of decline. Niles wrote that "some white people would not find themselves degraded by imitating such an example."[115]

Smith was wholly in the mold of captured African nobility. His father, he said, was a "Prince of the Tribe of the Dukandarra," and Smith went on to tell a tale of warfare and betrayal very close to those of his literary peers. In contrast to Norris's dismissive picture of an African nobility, Smith described his father as a man of enormous honor, "a man of remarkable strength and resolution, affable, kind and gentle, ruling with equity and moderation." The horrors Norris described had no place in Smith's father's kingdom. Smith himself was an exemplar of virtue in his life, a life that never wholly ceased to be threatened by continuing white treachery, usually treachery out of greed. Bringing to life a literary model, Smith also localized it by portraying his own rise as a successful landowner and businessman, in ways that both preserved the nobility and removed the exoticism from his story and his career.[116]

The overall effect of such figures as Smith and Equiano was to undermine the kind of dichotomy between savagery and civilization that Norris and his predecessors had made central to their work and to help keep alive, and further ground, primitivist traditions. That slavery itself represented a challenge to that dichotomy became an increasingly important theme in antislavery writing generally toward the close of the century. When the white minister Samuel Miller declared in an address before the New York Manumission Society in 1797—an address widely diffused by virtue of its reprinting in the *Columbian Orator*—"OH AFRICA! Thou loud proclaimer of the rapacity, the treachery, and cruelty of civilized man!" he was only one of many to see slavery as providing such a test. "The Negro Boy," a late-eighteenth-century poem that was also rendered as a popular song in 1796, described how, as a result of the "thirst of Gold" in England and America, "man turns a savage to his kind and blood and rapine mark his way." The singer himself took on the role of repentant betrayer in this recounting of a young boy stolen from his parents and sold away from his home.[117]

This reversal of categories was to play an important role in antislavery writing and in the works of black writers themselves. White and black opponents alike drew an obvious lesson from the slave trade in particular, a practice distinguished by nothing so much as its brutality. The repentant slave trader John Newton stressed the vulnerability of women seized for the trade who were "exposed to the wanton rudeness of white savages." Equiano, also described the brutal scene aboard a slaver: "The white people looked and acted, as I thought, in so savage a manner; for I had never seen among any people such instances of brutal cruelty." Earlier, Othello had described slave traders as "a savage enemy," and the slave trade as a cruel moment when family members were "barbarously snatched" from each other forever.[118]

It may be because such conventions were so strong, incidentally, that one must note the relative absence of evocations of Haiti and the Haitian revolution even as its impact grew on American thinking. Certainly, such an egalitarian as Abraham Bishop would seek to draw parallels between the Haitian revolutionaries and the American heroes of 1776, and, as David Gellman has shown, other white editors sought to represent Toussaint L'Ouverture in statesmanlike ways. Nevertheless, the kind of black-voiced revolutionary who had much earlier spoken from Jamaica was notably absent from the literature, and black writers ignored Haiti altogether, however much, as Douglas Egerton has demonstrated, its example was taken up in the popular consciousness of slaves in the South. While one can only speculate on this literary absence, the most likely explanation is that the reports and events from Haiti, conforming, as they did, to frightening Jeffersonian images of racial warfare, simply could not be squared with dominating traditions of primitivism and innocence, especially as those helped to relativize developing nationalist tendencies in America.[119]

In any event, such a background to the relativizing of "savagery" and "civilization" itself gave a strong experiential base, and still stronger connotations, to the historical accounts that denied any endemic white claims to superiority. In a manner harking back to Cotton Mather, Equiano admonished, "Let the polished and haughty European recollect that *his* ancestors were once, like the Africans, uncivilized and barbarous." John Marrant, in his 1789 address to the Boston Masons, reminded them that "we shall not find a nation on earth but has at some

period or other of their existence been in slavery." And the arguments jus-
tifying the practice had, he noted, remained unchanged. In 580 Saint
Gregory had seen a group of young British slaves brought to Rome for
sale: "Gregory (sighing) said, alas! For grief, that such fair faces should
be under the power of the prince of darkness, and that such bodies
should have their souls void of the grace of God." But Britons had been
condemned to slave coffles—the pope's sighs notwithstanding—at a time
when, as Marrant's address had shown, the African fathers of the church
had already made their contributions to the creation of a Christian
civilization.[120]

Here, then, was to be a major thrust in the developing literature of
antislavery, and one in which a black voice could make a unique statement. Standing significantly outside the American system, the black
speaker could represent the individual who, by his very marginality,
could perceive with peculiar clarity the pretensions of whites shown well.
When Venture Smith, recounting an incident of white treachery in an
American court, could write that the outcome, "whatever it may be
called in a Christian land, would in my native country have been
branded as a crime equal to highway robbery," while noting that his ad-
versary "was a *white gentleman,* and I a *poor African,* therefore it was *all
right, and good enough for the black dog,*" he not only drew on a tradition
for indicting the selective justice of a color-conscious America, he not
only appealed to a body of imagery that was steadily developing around
him, but worked toward the creation of a distinctively black-voiced indictment of the world in which he lived.[121]

3

Literary Identity
in the New Nation,
1800–1816

OVER THE FIRST TWO DECADES of the nineteenth century the situations facing African American writers differed in important ways from those of the Revolutionary period. The result was heightened efforts to create a distinctive African American voice within a context in which black-voiced indictments or commentaries on American affairs continued to have significance. These efforts themselves continued to build on modes of self-assertion and identity that went back to the colonial period while incorporating new elements and new concerns in African American life.

The first decade of the nineteenth century presented reasons for both optimism and pessimism on issues of slavery and color. Most important, New Jersey's Act for the Gradual Abolition of Slavery, of 1804, had put slavery itself on the road to extinction everywhere in the North. From the perspective of many African American leaders, the capstone was the 1807 federal legislation to close the African slave trade on 1 January 1808 as the United States joined Britain in putting a legal end, at least, to what many early antislavery advocates saw as the most nefarious feature of the system.

At the same time, free Negro communities continued to grow throughout the North and elsewhere. The process of institution building begun in the late eighteenth century itself became more intensive. African American churches, though not to become wholly independent denominations until the second decade of the century, grew significantly during the first decade, developing a growing number of important leaders. In New York, Philadelphia, Washington, and even Charleston important steps were taken toward developing African American educational institutions, some with white leadership, others created and sponsored by African Americans themselves. Of no less significance was the founding of a spate of mutual benefit societies in almost all of America's major cities between 1800 and 1810, with more to come in the ensuing decades. These societies served a variety of functions for their members, including providing insurance to assist the families of the deceased, but also served as centers for communal and even literary activity, as well as settings for the emergence of a self-conscious urban elite. In schools, churches, and voluntary associations many saw grounds for the growth of a community that ultimately could become part of the larger society, proving itself in the context of the American world.[1]

Such developments could easily be taken as signs of progress and of hope for the future. Surveying the scene in 1813, one African American observer declared that much that had taken place in America during the early years of the century demonstrated that "the land in which we live gives us the opportunity rapidly to advance the prosperity of liberty" and that diligence and dedication alone were necessary for that opportunity to grow. He was not alone in offering such an assessment.[2]

Not all signs were so positive, however. Even as slavery was seen as at least on its way to ending in the North, there was much to indicate its still firmer hold on the states of the South. Flexibility in the upper South was giving way to stricter controls, especially in the wake of Haiti and then of a rebellion plot led by a slave named Gabriel, a plot uncovered in Richmond, Virginia, in 1800. The slaveholding regimes wanted to forestall the occurrence of such events in the future. Free people of color suffered new disabilities, and restrictive legislation made manumission more difficult and less common after the enthusiasms of the Revolutionary era had waned. On the eve of the abolition of the slave trade, importation reached significant levels: the number of slaves imported in the decade before closure was virtually double that of the preceding decade. The domestic trade continued without abatement.[3]

In some areas there were real losses. Even in the North, as free black communities grew there were more restrictions placed on free people themselves. In many areas there was a severe curtailing of economic opportunities; disfranchisement was debated and enacted in Ohio, New Jersey, Maryland, and Kentucky. Blacks and antislavery whites built schools, but blacks were denied, and continued to be denied, access to public institutions in New York, Philadelphia, and elsewhere. In the area of religion losses were severe. For one thing, the major bodies made an increasingly public peace with slavery and the color line, although among white church figures a few antislavery advocates remained. A few black leaders continued to make something of a mark, but even the limited flexibility of the late eighteenth century clearly had become a thing of the past. The evangelical response to slavery, especially in the South, increasingly became defined within the context of the institution itself—in devotion to the mission to the slaves, in the encouragement of "Christian" treatment of the enslaved. Talented black clergy were to be confined to ministering to "those of their own color"; older possibilities for an authority that transcended distinctions were increasingly constrained as a result of social pressures, largely originating from within the churches themselves.[4]

Finally, as a number of scholars have stressed, the tendencies toward an exclusivist white national identity that had been apparent in the 1780s and 1790s would develop still further in the early years of the nineteenth century. Although the nature of the public sphere remained contested, the contestation was increasingly a debate among white men, as blacks and others were increasingly defined as being outside the public realm. Disfranchisement and growing discrimination were important measures of this process. So were national rhetorics asserting that America's community of public discourse should be the exclusive property of whites.[5]

I

Claims to authority thus became more complex during the first decades of the nineteenth century. The audience had in a sense changed, especially in religion but more generally as well. The possibility for authority was more challenged, or—more threateningly—dismissed, during the era, whether this was marked by stricter subordination according to color in the churches or by disfranchisement in the political arena, however limited the influence of black political activity in the past. In the realms of literature and language such efforts were marked in a variety of ways. One was a still more vicious use of dialect, especially as race came even at this early date to be bound up in partisan politics. Although there had been such efforts in the 1790s, the early years of the nineteenth century saw a real growth in dialect forms. David Waldstreicher has shown that even in New England, Federalists and Republicans sought to discredit each other by ascribing black support to the opposing side, using fake documents written in dialect as evidence. Rejecting any propriety in a black role in public life—treating even the possibility of such a role as ridiculous—these documents showed an America moving more confidently than ever before toward a white national political identity.[6]

Still, there remains evidence for an alternative discursive community taking a critical perspective on emerging forms of white American nationalism. This community, including both blacks and whites, was one for which issues of slavery and color provided important touchstones for thinking about an American nation. It was a community for which slavery continued to be a blot on the nation, and discrimination a serious concern.

Evidence for this lies in the authority for a black voice throughout the era, and in several realms of public discourse, even if this authority was to become more problematic during the first decade of the nineteenth century. The bases for its claims were, however, to become more elaborate and self-conscious, tied to changing currents affecting issues of identity itself, issues involving what it meant to be an African living in a changing America.

Approaches to issues of identity and authority took shape gradually over the first two decades of the nineteenth century, bringing together forms and conventions that had been developing since the colonial period, with concerns growing out of changing conditions African Americans had to confront. Certainly, there remained a continuing assertion that the black voice could, and should, provide a unique perspective on American events, especially in regard to issues of slavery and color. This assertion was to guide both the rhetorical purposes and the thematic thrusts of black writers during the period. Both are evident, for example, in a key document from 1813, James Forten's *Letters from a Man of Colour*. Forten's letters were written in opposition to a bill before the Pennsylvania legislature intended to prohibit the entry of free people of color into the state. The legislation had widespread support among white Philadelphians—and significant opposition as well—and the wealthy Forten sought to use his own standing in the city, where he had received great respect, to counter the sentiment that had led to its being proposed.[7]

Like many who spoke out against slavery and discrimination, Forten began by holding the proposed legislation up to the fundamental principles of the American republic, as embodied in the Declaration of Independence and, even more, in the traditions of Pennsylvania, which he treated as a traditional haven for "the African race." His indictment of the legislation demonstrated his own understanding of American principles: he described its provisions as "characteristic of European despotism," and he described those empowered to enforce the law as having a power akin to "tyranny or oppression." Defending the character of free people of color, he had much to say about the character of whites as well. Noting the drunkenness with which many celebrated the Fourth of July, especially, he said, "Is it not wonderful that the day set apart for the festival of liberty should be abused by the advocates of freedom, in endeavoring to sully what they profess to adore," not only by their drunkenness but also by their custom on that day of abusing and harassing people of color.[8]

The ironies of the situation were clear to Forten. "My God, what a situation is his," Forten said of the free man of color. "It has been left for Pennsylvania, to raise her ponderous arm against the liberties of the black, whose greatest boast has been, that he resided in a State where Civil Liberty, and sacred Justice were administered alike to all." These were not the only ironies Forten could see. Returning to the Shakespearean language of his 1800 letter to George Thatcher, Forten again asked rhetorically, "Are we not sustained by the same power, supported by the same food, hurt by the same wounds, wounded by the same wrongs, pleased with the same delights and propagated by the same means?" From here he could raise real questions about Anglo-American pretensions to a unique claim on civilization, as he asked, "Where is the bosom that does not heave a sigh for his fall, unless it be callous to every sentiment of humanity and mercy?"[9]

His conclusion, again echoing the letter to Thatcher, placed him within the context of the standards he had set forth. "My feelings are acute," he wrote, "and I have ventured to express them without intending either accusation or insult to anyone. An appeal to the heart is my intention, and if I have failed, it is my great misfortune not to have had a power of sufficient eloquence to convince." Continuing in the same vein, Forten suggested, "I trust the eloquence of nature will succeed," again linking honesty, right feeling, and virtue in a way that also supported the case against a callous white America in which the legislation Forten opposed would be seriously considered.[10]

On this occasion the legislation did not pass in Pennsylvania, although such laws existed elsewhere, and there were to be subsequent efforts even in Pennsylvania to enact "immigration" restrictions into law. But what one sees in Forten's *Letters* is a continuing assertion of an ability to take a place in public debates and to offer one's own experiences, and those of other African Americans, as a distinctive validation for one's views.[11]

In literature too this sense of a uniquely authenticating black voice continued to play an important role in discussions of race and slavery. Such an earlier work along these lines as William Cowper's 1788 poem "The Negro's Complaint," first published in the 1793 *Gentleman's Magazine* and quoted thereafter by William Hamilton and others in opposition to slavery, maintained its popularity for apparently encapsulating, from the slave's point of view, the horrors of slavery. In 1806, for example, the editors of the *Virginia Religious Magazine,* published at Lexington, saw fit to print the poem, along with a laudatory tribute to Cowper. No less significant was the way Benjamin F. Prentiss, a New Englander, both used and authenticated the voice Cowper represented in the odd purported autobiography of an ex-slave named Boyrereau Brinch in 1810. At one point Brinch, thinking of his own situation, calls to mind Cowper's piece, in toto, as a fair representation of his own feelings and perceptions.[12]

To the extent that networks of mutual reinforcement and authentication remained an important element in shaping African American literature, then, it is worth nothing that the late-eighteenth-century explosion in literature evoking a black voice continued to define a frame after 1800 in which both racial rhetoric and black writing could evolve.

The process was visible in a number of works. The converted former slave trader Thomas Branagan, whose work was strongly supported by such black Philadelphians as Richard Allen, cited the importance of his own experiences with slavery, including not only what he saw but also what he heard—the "complaints and prayers" of those who suffered under bondage —as a force in producing his transformation. He recounted the process in his first work on slavery, A *Preliminary Essay on the Oppression of the Exiled Sons of Africa*, published in Philadelphia in 1804. Even as he wrote, Branagan said, he could "see the wounds and tears of these unhappy victims to the sordid avarice, and infernal cruelty of their oppressors," and he could hear their words, spoken in familiar tones. "Thou hast made us rational creatures," he could hear them say. "Our misery therefore is intolerable." And he recounted the feelings that had often struck an antislavery chord, as when he imagined the slaves lamenting that "often, with sorrowful hearts and weeping eyes, do we recollect our once happy, though homely, abodes; our near and dear relations; our waterbrooks; our rosy bowers, our vernal groves, our shady woods, and scented meadows." In two long poems, *Avenia* from 1805 and *The Penitential Tyrant* from 1807, Branagan even tried to follow Cowper's example and render those complaints in verse. But however he wrote, it was the grounding in experience that gave imprimatur to his work, and as Allen's support suggests, Branagan's work entered into a discursive world including blacks and whites alike, where it could continue to reinforce widely shared themes and images.[13]

Benjamin Prentiss's purported autobiography of Boyrereau Brinch was one of the most remarkable efforts to create an efficacious black voice during this period. Prentiss assured his audience that the work was taken down from Brinch and that he, as editor, had sought mainly to clean up the English and put Brinch's often random recollections into a "regular chain." Nevertheless, the narrative was in most ways a compendium of earlier works, repeating stories others had told. Prentiss quoted Cowper and drew on motifs that harkened back to Aphra Behn and "Inkle and Yarico," to such earlier autobiographies as those of Equiano and Venture Smith, and to African American oral traditions. It told of treacherous sea captains, of children, including Brinch, kidnapped and lost to their families, of merciless slave traders, of Africans of noble birth and bearing, and of Europeans without scruples of faith. It told of a Brinch who, against all odds, sought to do for himself and his family as much as the constraints of slavery and color would allow. Emphasizing the physical horrors of slavery, the narrative was a testimony not only to Prentiss's sense of the power of a black voice such as Brinch's for making the antislavery case he sought to create but, again, to those processes of tradition building that had come to characterize the shaping of a black voice.[14]

Given this continuing role for a black voice, it is not surprising that there were many thematic continuities in its evocation by black and white writers alike. As Branagan and Prentiss make clear, the barbarism and brutality of separation from an African home and family, and the pain it caused, continued to provide one of the most telling indictments of slavery and the slave trade. This was a theme peculiarly susceptible to a black-voiced work, whether narrative, poetic, or testimonial. John Teasman, the pioneering black principal of New York's African Free School and one of the key leaders of the city's free black community, helped to indicate what appeared to be the continuing thematic power of this motif in an 1811 address celebrating the state legislature's approval of the official incorporation of the New York African Society for Mutual Relief, one of the most important organizations of that type founded during the era. Teasman himself had played a major role in the efforts for incorporation, visiting Albany and meeting with legislators on the society's behalf. His address offered some insight into the kinds of arguments that he believed had carried the day. In particular, he told how legislators were moved as they contemplated "the sacrifices and miseries occasioned by the slave trade and slavery," as they were encouraged to conceive "how hard it must be to be dragged from our native land, from every thing near and dear, from a land flowing with milk and honey, into a strange land, there to be degraded and sorely oppressed." From Teasman's point of view it was no wonder that the theme continued to play a role in African American literary efforts.[15]

Equally important in the eyes of many for what it said about the institution was the degradation slavery entailed for the slaves. The great Vermont minister Lemuel Haynes made such a characterization a focus of his own indictment of slavery, delivered in an 1801 sermon titled *The Nature and Importance of True Republicanism*, decrying an institution in which slaves "have been taught to view themselves a rank of beings far below others, which has suppressed, in a degree, every principle of manhood." Haynes was especially effective in relating slavery's degrading power to the concerns of all Americans, using it as an exemplar of the effects of despotism and the need for vigilance over that "heaven-born liberty wherewith Christ hath made us free."[16]

Haynes was ideally placed to make such a point. The son of a black father and a white mother, in 1801 he was in the early stages of a career serving largely white congregations in New England. Learned, theologically sophisticated, and an effective member of New England's conservative ministry, Haynes only rarely spoke out on issues of slavery and color. Creating what was as nearly as possible a color-blind career in early-nineteenth-century America, Haynes made his mark more for his theological rigidity—and staunch Federalism—than for anything having to do with his African background. Nevertheless, as his works from the Revolutionary era make clear, he was well aware of the significance of his color and never really lost sight of it over the course of his long career. He had to know, and his audience had to appreciate, that by his presence in front of them—and beyond, given the dissemination of his sermons in pamphlet form—he proved the truth of his words, and the falsity of those ideas connecting color and inferiority that underlay alternative views of a degraded African race.[17]

A language claiming natural rights for Africans as well as Europeans, anger over the denial of such rights, and the ways in which an African American complaint could make clear the message such a denial sent to the world all remained a part of an African American rhetoric in the early nineteenth century. Thus, one may note a letter from one black Philadelphian to the English evangelical activist Dorothy Ripley in which the writer said that "while the nations of Europe are contending to catch the draught [of liberty], the African is forbidden to lift up his head towards it." He declared, "Every man has a right to his liberty, and we must by ties of nature come under the title of men." Describing the frustration of one's own desires for freedom continued to deny white American pretensions and to condemn white American hypocrisy at the same time.[18]

Finally, an African condemnation of Christian hypocrisy, going back to Morgan Godwyn and Thomas Tryon, if not before, remained important in the early years of the nineteenth century. Prentiss's Boyrereau Brinch took the traditional approach by describing how, "in the 16th year of my age, I was borne away from native innocence, ease and luxury, into captivity, by a christian people, who preach humility, charity, and benevolence." Prentiss made the thrust of Brinch's remark especially clear as he had him exclaim, "Father! forgive them for they know not what they do."[19]

Issues of Christian hypocrisy became more compelling in those same years, however, as a result of developments within the churches themselves, especially the kind of drawing of the color line for congregations and ministers alike that occurred in evangelical organizations after about 1800. Christine Heyrman points out the toughening of standards for, and increasing restrictions on, black ministers in the slaveholding South in the first decade of the nineteenth century. Outside the South the segregated pew became firmly entrenched during this decade.[20]

The result was both an adaptation to and an indictment of white-led American Protestantism. The creation of primarily black congregations, a process inaugurated at the end of the preceding century, continued apace as hopeful black ministers began to define themselves in terms of their hopes for service to a black Christian community. Much of this process is evident in the 1810 autobiography of the Methodist George White. Certainly, White drew heavily on earlier traditions. Though set wholly in the United States, the autobiography evokes the tragedy of family separation as White recalls being taken in infancy from his mother. He tells of growing up in a slavery that, following a period of treatment better "than is usual in this land of human oppression and barbarity," was marked by incessant cruelty and pain. The narrative also traces the workings of providence, as White recounts his own conversion and God's inspiration for his master's decision to will him free, despite the heirs' opposition.[21]

The autobiography focuses more, however, on White's extremely difficult struggle to be accepted as a minister in the Methodist Church, a struggle that took place within what was mainly a black setting, his main opposition coming mainly from black clergy (an opposition he never really explains). Moving away from issues of slavery and color for much of the work, White focuses on the possibilities and constraints within a black religious community, a life in terms of which he increasingly understood himself and his work. And ultimately he justified his own career by noting that the fate of black Christians, "being my own blood, lay near my own heart," driving him to spread the gospel in New York as well as in Virginia, where he preached frequently to slave congregations.[22]

The inward turning found in White's narrative was, however, only one dimension of issues of religious authority as they began to take shape in the early nineteenth century. No less crucial was the way the emergence of black religious institutions could be interpreted within more traditional frameworks of color and authority. As black religious organizations emerged during this period, relations between black congregations and white parent bodies were difficult and oppressive. Early black church leaders, including Richard Allen and Absalom Jones, fought running battles with white church leaders, who demanded extensive control over black congregational affairs, including the rights to preach and conduct services. Desires for autonomy, coupled with the important role an independent black church could play in growing communities of free people of color, began to build in the 1790s, providing an important stimulus for a separate African American religious life.[23]

Within this framework there were important notes of white Christian hypocrisy in the very creation of such churches. As Will Gravely has noted, the story of the origins of Philadelphia's black churches in the forcible removal of Richard Allen and Absalom Jones from their seats at the city's predominantly white St. George's Methodist Church was to assume mythic proportions as those churches grew in the early nineteenth century. The story, whose details, including its dates, became increasingly controversial, involved Jones's and Allen's kneeling for prayer in an area newly reserved for whites in a church they had attended and served for several years. Pulled roughly to his feet in the midst of prayer, Jones asked only to be allowed to finish. White trustees continued to try to force him to move, and he, Allen, and other black members left the church, never to return. Although, as Gary Nash has emphasized, these black Methodists had considered withdrawing prior to the incident, the St. George's story quickly began to serve as a founding legend for the most visible and significant black institutions of the era. Placing the origins of those institutions directly in a framework of unchristian white behavior made them, by their very existence, not only evidence of black courage and faith but also the kind of living indictment of white Christianity's shortcomings that John Marrant, Andrew Bryan, and even Boyrereau Brinch had represented for years.[24]

Thus, separation itself became a form of commentary in the legend of the churches' founding that on the one hand encouraged a more autonomous group identity but on the other hand pointed to an autonomy understood within longer traditions of public discourse. Many of the themes of this emerging perspective were captured in the works of an African American minister and writer named John Jea. Although published in England, these works focused mainly on American issues and events, Jea having grown up a slave in New York. Like Equiano a generation earlier, Jea did much to mobilize existing traditions for narrative purposes. Although, John Saillant has suggested, there is much internal evidence for Jea's having been American-born, Jea's narrative begins by describing how he was stolen with his family from Africa. Like Marrant, he tells of a master who was opposed to the conversion of slaves and persecuted the Christians among them. Picking up on themes used by Prentiss and others, Jea also tells how his master's behavior taught him to hate Christians and "to look upon them as devils." Still, Jea was converted in his teens, and though he was to experience great hardships, including the execution of his wife for the murder of their child, he would embark on a highly successful career as a missionary in America and abroad.[25]

There is much that is notable in Jea's narrative. Certainly, his miraculous account of attaining literacy, so effectively discussed and tied to tradition by Henry Louis Gates Jr., helps to emphasize the importance of literacy as such, as well as the moral significance of literacy, in an America increasingly hostile to black aspiration. According to Jea, his literacy was not the product of effort or stealth but came on him suddenly as a gift from God, who taught him "to read in one night, in about fifteen minutes."[26]

No less important, however, is the extent to which issues of black identity, autonomy, and moral force informed Jea's work. Again, one may note Jea's use of traditional motifs expressing such ideas, particularly as motifs of black faith and white hypocrisy framed the whole of his narrative. But they are elaborated and reinforced still more fully in a small collection of hymns he wrote and appended to his narrative. While drawing on the forms of contemporary revival hymnody, Jea incorporated autobiographical elements, and in ways that captured motifs from his narrative and from African American tradition. In one, for example, he describes the kidnapping of his family from Africa, their subjection to slavery, and their being told by their enslavers "that we had not a soul." The hymn goes on to praise a God who proved the slavers wrong. In another, he tells how Christ "nail'd my tyrants to his cross, / And bought my liberty." Invoking themes of providence, freedom, slavery, and retribution, Jea helped to point toward an autonomously black religious community that, by its very existence, expressed both black religious achievement and an indictment of white Christianity.[27]

Such themes came to be embodied in the institutions as such. As African Americans began to build independent religious institutions, these churches could be presented as perfect examples of the kinds of things black men and women could do if given the chance. Dorothy Ripley, the English evangelical, recorded how such a lesson could be learned as a result of her visit to Richard Allen's church in 1803—though she would become embroiled in controversy as a result of Allen's enforcement of Methodist rules preventing her, as a woman, from addressing the body. Prentiss's Boyrereau Brinch, addressing his white readership, urged the same reaction on them as he exclaimed, "Do you not see some geniuses burst forth and rise above the tyranny and oppression they are under, and stand as monuments of admiration." "Go," he said, "to the African churches, in the cities of New York and Philadelphia, see the devout attachment to the religion of their Savior. Hear the pathetic and persuasive eloquence of their preachers, and then answer my inquiries." John Teasman, whose own efforts at institution building were notable, made a similar point, saying that arguments for African inferiority were confounded by the churches and asking rhetorically, "Is not divinity embraced with as much devotion? Does not the pulpit exhibit as pure christianity and with as much imagination?" Religious character, as these figures verified, authenticated the abilities of Africans in American society. Autonomy enhanced the power of the argument rather than serving to remove African Americans from the public realm.[28]

Something similar may be said about continuing processes of canon formation involving African American letters. Literary history fit well within such a framework of testimony to African achievement, with its implicit indictment of prejudice. The tradition that African American writers had begun to create also represented a growing tradition of independent literary work. The Philadelphia abolitionist John Parrish illustrated both the process and its significance when, in 1806, he republished James Forten's 1800 letter to Massachusetts Congressman George

Thatcher, originally written to thank the congressman for his assistance in seeking to put the 1799 petition effort of Absalom Jones before the U.S. House of Representatives. On the one hand, Parrish gave the letter the kind of historicity that was essential in canon formation. On the other, he used the achievement of eloquence the letter represented to demonstrate that Forten, by the quality of his correspondence, could lay claim to a place in the world of public discourse. "Taken from the author's own handwriting," Parrish assured his readers, the letter demonstrated that Forten "is not only a man of talents, but of feeling and gratitude," qualities important in any public man of the era.[29]

That lessons could be learned from such achievements as Forten's received still more widely noted testimony in Henri Grégoire's influential *Enquiry Concerning the Intellectual and Moral Faculties, and Literature of Negroes*, published in France in 1808 and in the United States, in English translation, in 1810. Focusing on well-known figures, including Amo, Capitein, Wheatley, Banneker, and Equiano, as well as the perhaps apocryphal Othello, Grégoire used their accomplishments as primary evidence against ideas of African inferiority, offering severe strictures on those who held to such ideas regardless of evidence. His indictments of Thomas Jefferson, whose support he had initially sought for his work, were especially strong; about the noted passage in the *Notes on the State of Virginia* attacking Sancho and Wheatley he wrote: "To support his opinion it was not enough to undervalue the talents of two negro writers: it was necessary to establish by argument and by a multitude of facts, that if the situation and circumstances of blacks be the same [as for whites], the former can never rival the latter," a contention Grégoire set out to remedy in his book.[30]

Both Sancho and Wheatley, especially the latter, received extensive discussion in Grégoire's book. Noting Wheatley's popularity, Grégoire also praised her ability, characterizing Jefferson's condemnation of her poetry as nothing more than an assertion, to which, he suggested, "it is sufficient to oppose a contrary assertion." But the strongest argument against Jefferson's view, and in favor of his own, lay in the poetry itself, he believed, and he made his case by quoting briefly from Wheatley's "On Being Brought from Africa to America" and printing three other poems of hers in full.[31]

Wheatley, as Grégoire indicated, remained the capstone of the African American tradition. When Joseph LaVallée's novel *The Negro Equalled by Few Europeans* was republished in 1801 in Philadelphia, its two volumes also included a printing of Wheatley's *Poems on Various Subjects*, not only using Wheatley's work to authenticate LaVallée's fictional, powerfully articulate African character but also tying her career in with the case against European hypocrisy at the heart of the novel.[32]

An anonymous New England writer using the name "Philanthropos" similarly drew lessons from Wheatley's work and career, and did so in the black-voiced framework that had taken shape in the years following the American Revolution. Presenting an "artless narrative" in the voice of "an hapless African" named Zaama, Philanthropos at least obliquely addressed Thomas Jefferson's strictures, and with a bit of irony, by noting that Wheatley "was a woman of extraordinary genius, even for an American!" The career of Banneker was similarly brought to account, again evoking Jefferson, in the suggestion voiced by Zaama that such figures might be exceptional, "but are not those examples sufficient to found our claim to rationality, and convince the world that we are not merely capable of being made 'hewers of wood and drawers of water'?" Zaama concluded by voicing the same perceptions of American hypocrisy others had advanced, saying of slaveholding, "If Christianity be a name without reality, and tolerates such injustice, I desire not the title of Christian." He added, "If 'Republicanism means any thing or nothing,' away with your political professions—Let me return to Africa, and live under a despotism, without tyranny—a royal government without slavery!"[33]

Still, nothing contributed more to the framework of an African American canon and to the fixing of important conventions within that canon than the emergence early in the nineteenth century of what was arguably the first African American–initiated literary genre in the early republic, the short-lived but significant series of addresses beginning in January 1808 commemorating the abolition of the slave trade by the United States and Britain. These addresses were the centerpieces of daylong ceremonies, especially in New York, Philadelphia, and (usually on 14 July) Boston, marked by parading, anthems, and specially composed hymns and poems, all giving thanks for the ending of the trade. Such celebrations continued for several years in all three cities, ending only as white harassment in some places and a pessimistic sense that the law was being only halfheartedly enforced led to their discontinuation.[34]

At one level, as several scholars have noted, these addresses and their occasions reflected the forces for black autonomy visible in the founding of churches and other African American institutions at the time. Setting symbolic dates apart from the July Fourth celebrations of white Americans, for example, African Americans used the celebrations to make a distinct claim on public space, a claim that represented both an alternative to and a comment on the burgeoning white nationalism of the era.[35]

At the same time, the addresses also demonstrated how firmly a canon had evolved around certain conventions for an African American voice, particularly for the black literary community's public representation of itself to itself and to the larger world. They showed how much of a consensus had been created among members of that community on issues of identity and self-definition within the American world.

The addresses tended to draw heavily on the African American literary forms that had preceded them. Most described the horrors of the trade, its sundering of families, its tearing of people from their homelands. A youthful Peter Williams Jr., nineteen or twenty years old and a recent graduate of John Teasman's African School, in an 1808 New York address that marked the beginning of what was would be an outstanding public career, proclaimed, "Oh Africa, Africa! to what horrid inhumanities have thy shores been witness; thy shores which were once the garden of the world, the seat of almost paradisiacal joys." He conjured up the scene in ports as the enslaved were "separated without regard to the ties of blood or friendship: husband from wife; parent from child; brother from sister; friend from friend." And he urged his hearers to "see the parting tear, rolling down their fallen cheeks: hear the parting sigh, die on their quivering lips." Absalom Jones in his 1808 Philadelphia oration similarly spoke of "the anguish which has taken place when parents have been torn from their children, and children from their parents, and conveyed, with their hands and feet bound in fetters, on board of ships prepared to receive them." Drawing on the same idyllic traditions as did Williams,

Jones contrasted the terrible toil to which slaves were subjected with "the habits of ease which they derived from the natural fertility of their own country."[36]

Other themes were similarly familiar: orators characterized the trade as a gross violation of humanity, citing the familiar passages from Acts, assuring their audiences that God was "no respecter of persons" and had "made of one blood all nations of men." Moreover, as the quotations from Acts often implied, the key theme in virtually every oration was that of providence. While those dedicated men and women who had worked in America and England for the abolition of the trade certainly deserved to be praised, it was God who had acted to bring about its end. As Henry Sipkins—who had introduced Peter Williams the preceding year and, being about the same age as Williams, was himself a recent graduate of Teasman's school—declared in an 1809 address, "In commiseration to our state thou didst inspire, by the dictates of humanity, men who became the vigilant exterminators of that commerce which has much depopulated the land of our nativity." More than one orator concluded from the events the commemorations celebrated that here, more than ever, was a sign that Ethiopia would soon stretch forth her hands to God, and hymnists composing works for the occasions made the same point. Robert Sidney proclaimed in 1809:

> God has shown his gracious power;
> He has stopt the horrid traffic,
> That your country's bosom tore.[37]

Thus, the key motifs of the addresses quickly achieved a formulaic quality and spread rapidly. Young Russell Parrott, in his early twenties, delivered several orations in Philadelphia beginning in 1812. A printer and already an emerging civic leader, Parrott described the horrors of kidnapping and the terrors of "the pestilential dungeon" of the slave ship. Reduced to slavery, the victims, "unused to a laborious life, (for, in the native land of our fathers, nature seems to have scattered plenty with a luxuriant hand)," were condemned to lives of pain and brutality. Parrott too went on to pursue themes of human unity and equality even as he assured his audience of the hopes portended to peoples of Africa and America by the ending of the trade.[38]

The nature of the addresses commemorating the end of the slave trade suggests, again, the near consensus among speakers and their audiences regarding what it was most important to say in the fights over slavery and color. The addresses themselves suggest the kind of intellectual network and tradition that had come to shape that consensus. That such figures as Williams, Sipkins, and Parrott, young as they were, could so quickly create a formula for discussion of the slave trade's end suggests how pervasive its key themes and motifs must have been in the discourses of the schools, churches, and societies. The ideas they used and the ways they expressed those ideas must have been fairly familiar to them by the time they composed their speeches, on the heels of the slave trade's abolition, again demonstrating that the process had been under way for some time.

Perhaps one measure of this consensus can be seen, not in the address of a black speaker, but in the oration delivered for an 1808 celebration in Boston at the request of members of the African Meeting House by the well-known white minister Jedidiah Morse. Focusing heavily on issues of education and moral reform, issues that had long concerned him, Morse, who had been active within Boston's black community, molded his address according to the kinds of conventions that Williams and Jones had already drawn on and others would continue to use. Like them, he urged his audience to "imagine the arrival of a *slave ship*, on the African coast," and the horrors it portended, the separations of families, the removal of men, women, and children from their homes. He admitted the "reproach to the Christian name and profession" the trade itself entailed. Going on to celebrate the workings of providence and the hope for the future, Morse also tied his condemnation of the trade to themes that recognized the distinct perspective tradition would have taught him his audience brought to the subject, as he noted the long history of a trade maintained "by the countenance and authority (I blush while I declare it) of *Christian* nations!" In his address, then, Morse was no less connected to the network of tradition than were Williams and Jones, Sipkins and Parrott, showing, again, the breadth of that network and its significance in early American thought.[39]

But there was another dimension to the addresses that was of special importance, and it too fit within the context of developing traditions. This was their significance as orations. They were rarely confined to the occasions of their delivery, and they were understood to have greater purpose than the celebration of the slave trade's abolition. Many of the addresses were published as pamphlets, which in itself shows an interest in achieving a wider audience. Russell Parrott, for example, sent two copies of one of his own efforts to the wealthy Philadelphia philanthropist Roberts Vaux in the hope of further publicizing his achievement.[40]

William Hamilton offered a clear expression of why such publicity was important in an 1809 address to the New York African Society when he held up a pamphlet that had been made of the 1808 oration by Peter Williams Jr., which included Henry Sipkins's introduction. According to Hamilton, the two pieces taken together represented a remarkable achievement. Of Sipkins's introduction Hamilton said: "The address or frontispiece to the work is a flow of tasteful language, that would do credit to the best writers." Turning to Williams's oration, Hamilton noted that it "is not a run of eccentric vagaries, not now a sudden gust of passionate exclamation, and then as sudden calm and an inertness of expression, but a close adherence to the plane of the subject in hand, a warm and animating description of interesting scenes, together with an easy graceful style."[41]

Here one can see Hamilton working to maintain a place for African Americans within the realm of public discourse, as Parrish had sought to do for Forten a few years earlier. Hamilton clearly knew the standards for refined speech, and as Parrish had done for Forten, he made much of the ability of two young black men, who normally would have been excluded from the realms of public discourse, to meet those standards.[42]

Finally, and no less revealing given his purposes, Hamilton actually began his tribute to Sipkins and Williams with an invocation of Phillis Wheatley's career and achievements, putting the two young men in a context of recognized literary accomplishment that, taken as a whole, looked toward a clear conclusion. "If we continue to produce specimens like these," said Hamilton, "we shall soon put our enemies to the blush; abashed and confounded they shall quit the field, and no longer urge their superiority of souls."[43]

Hamilton was sufficiently attuned both to the realm of public discourse and to traditions of African American voice to make a case within the framework of each. The printing of the addresses, moreover, had clearly moved them into a broad realm of public discourse, that defined by the larger realm of printed publication and distribution rather than the essentially contained audience of the celebration itself. The printing was done with great self-consciousness. Like Wheatley and her successors, the publishers of these addresses provided an appendix to their pamphlet, focusing mainly on Williams's oration. "Having understood that some persons doubt my being the author of this Oration," Williams included testimonies from such figures as the Episcopal bishop of New York authenticating his role. As had been the case for Wheatley, such endorsements not only validated Williams's authorship in the face of skepticism but also proved the awareness of Williams himself, as well as his claims on the public sphere, in the larger world of cultural leadership.[44]

Within this framework it was not difficult for Hamilton to move, a year later, from Williams's oration, along with Sipkins's prefatory address, to validate the claims to human equality of everyone of African descent. He described the resulting pamphlet as "a specimen of African genius," adding, "African I term it because in the position that the present argument is offered, it makes no kind of difference whether the man is born in Africa, Asia, Europe or America, so long as he is proginized from African parents." At one level Hamilton may have been moving toward a position celebrating an African "racial identity," even a kind of nationalism. As Gary Nash has emphasized, although there were many precedents for an "African" identity going back to the Revolutionary era, its assertion by African Americans would become increasingly common in the early nineteenth century. Most institutions created by blacks, for example, chose to use the word *African* in their titles as a way of defining both their character and their distinctiveness. In drawing on such language, Hamilton was reinforcing the kind of collective statement of identity made by the very occurrence of the commemorative occasions. No less significant, however, is the way in which, citing the "position" of the "present argument," he saw in the addresses a tacit reply to assertions of African inferiority. If the degraded slave could be taken as "representative" of African potential, why, Hamilton asked, should this not be true for Williams and Sipkins. The very quality of their remarks should "confound" the prejudiced, providing, Hamilton suggested, the most irrefutable argument on behalf of human equality and natural rights.[45]

Again, at least one aspect of a unique African voice lay in this function of validation. Using the addresses as evidence against denials of racial equality, Hamilton evinced an understanding of their significance that was compatible with Wheatley's understanding of her work, Equiano's of his, and the appreciative use of a black voice by everyone from William Cowper and Othello to Thomas Branagan, Benjamin Prentiss, and Philanthropos. The "African," speaking for the African, had an irreplaceable role to play and provided the most relevant evidence on issues of slavery and color.

II

Still, the slave-trade addresses revealed only one dimension of this issue of validation, and even narratives and antislavery fictions told only part of the story. Through the early years of the nineteenth century the relevant issues of African American validation and African American voice remained highly complex and problematic, impossible for many people to ignore but not always tied to any particular point of view.

This was especially true in regard to the religious realm, where changes were taking place rapidly on a variety of fronts, where questions of color and status were becoming more troubling than they had ever been before. Even as the religious situation had become more complex, understanding the significance of an African American voice to the religious context had become more difficult. This was most notable in the emergence among white evangelicals of a black literary voice designed to cohere with the early-nineteenth-century accommodation of evangelicalism to slavery.

Such a voice was to play an important role in furthering a religious orientation that abjured any effort to end the institution in favor of a focus on a mission to the slaves, bringing a conversion through which the black Christian found both fulfillment in religion and peace with enslavement. Adapting earlier traditions of African piety, black voices were created that still more openly testified to the acceptability of such a course. In 1803, for example, the *Massachusetts Missionary Magazine* published a poem by a white South Carolinian allegedly converting into verse words "taken from the mouth of an African servant." The poem represented the servant's joy in faith and concluded, in its penultimate stanza:

Here, slavery! thy soften'd chain
And yoke I gladly bear;
Thy burdens yield no grief nor pain,
Thy toils demand no tear.

Slavery's gift of contentment was validated by the slave's purported expression of faith.[46]

A more elaborate example of such a voice was that created in 1808 by the South Carolina Baptist minister and planter Edmund Botsford. A longtime champion of the mission to the slaves, Botsford had led churches with significant black memberships since the 1780s. He was also a strong defender of the slavery's compatibility with an evangelical faith. In 1808 Botsford published a work entitled *Sambo and Toney: A Dialogue in Three Parts*, a popular piece that went through several editions. The story is set on a plantation and focuses on the efforts of Sambo, a Christian slave, to bring his friend, the irreligious Toney, to salvation. Botsford, who favored the use of converted slaves as plantation ministers, created in Sambo the perfect representation of what he thought such a figure should be like. Not only is Sambo an eloquent spokesman for Christianity but he persuades Toney that one of the real virtues of conversion is that those who find religion become "good and faithful servants," at peace with themselves and with their place in the world.[47]

In fantasizing a religious proslavery dialogue Botsford was joined by the evangelical Episcopal priest William Meade, of Virginia. Meade appended a piece "by a gentleman of our own Country" to his 1813 edition of Thomas Bacon's 1749 sermons to Maryland slaves. His gentleman went beyond Botsford, to some extent, creating, as Thomas Tryon had done more than a century earlier, a dialogue between a slave and a slaveholder. Unlike Tryon's, however, this dialogue raised no issues about the mistreatment of slaves. Its overall message was summarized in words given to a slave who had learned that his "great master in Heaven sees me, and that I am serving him when I am serving my master."[48]

No doubt there was a fair amount of anxiety in these dialogues, for many black Christians continued to connect their faith with freedom. This was true of John Jea. It was also true of a Kentucky slave, ultimately expelled from her church, who, as Stephen Aron reports, told her mistress that Christians never kept slaves and that "thousands" of whites were "wallowing in Hell for their treatment of Negroes." At one level, then, these writers saw the need to create a reassuring black voice to counter an all too real black voice that many of their slaveholding readers might have encountered.[49]

As they did so, however, they also reflected issues of authority and status, authentication and validation, that had long been taking shape for black voices. For one thing, whether in a quest for credibility or simply as testimony to the power of developing traditions, these dialogues drew on older motifs of exemplary piety. They even drew on those of African American spiritual autobiography to make the case for slave Christianity. In one noteworthy passage the slave in Meade's dialogue recounts his effort to attain biblical literacy, describing the Bible itself as a gift from God and his literacy as the product of God's assistance. The words suggest a tradition of black testimony informing an array of religious expressions.[50]

No less striking are the egalitarian emphases in these works. In *Sambo and Toney* Botsford sometimes tries to make clear that despite Sambo's persuasiveness, religious authority lies with a white regular ministry. A slave he calls Fanny praises the local minister for having "been one good man for true"; she notes that "all the black people love him too much, he talk so plain we poor black people understand most every word he say." But Botsford does not always maintain such clear lines. He makes one slave, Uncle Davy, a prime agent in opening the master's heart "for let the minister come and preach to we black people." And Sambo makes a speech that potentially, at least, raises issues of color and status, although Botsford probably intended it to assure slaveholding readers that slaves need see no incompatibility between their condition and evangelical teachings of Christian community. When, at an early stage, Toney objects to Sambo's urging him to attend meetings by arguing that "the minister never preach to we black people," Sambo responds that "the minister preach to every body," that "the word of the Lord speak to every body alike, white people, black people, rich man, poor man, old man and young man, and it say, repent every one of you." Meade's author makes a similar point when one of his slaveowning characters reminds another, "Great and small, black and white, master and slave, shall stand together before the judgement seat of CHRIST."[51]

For all their proslavery intent, these dialogues help reveal the place an African American voice had assumed in discussions of color and slavery, here in a religious setting. By seeking validation for a mission to the slaves, finding a voice such as the one they created for slave spokesmen to be necessary, these writers, no less than their antislavery counterparts, found themselves granting at least some unique authority to those they hoped to suppress, representing the black voice as the only one that could give a distinctive authentication to the position they hoped to portray. It is almost as if Meade's dialogue were intended to provide a black authentication for the position Bacon had put forward more than six decades earlier.[52]

As works by Botsford and Meade also show, the patterns of black authority and even the conventions of black expression had become fairly pervasive by the first years of the nineteenth century. These writers' inability to leave a black voice out of the discussion of slavery and religion was striking, whatever role they hoped that voice would assume. The implications of this inability are still more apparent in another work from the period—an 1816 piece by Meade entitled "A True Account of a Pious Negro"—as well as in at least one response to it. Constructed as a story of an acquaintanceship between a clergyman and a slave convert, Meade's account offers a similarly ambiguous picture of a slaveowning Christianity. Even more than Botsford, Meade stresses his recognition "that neither the colour of his body, nor the condition of his present life, could prevent him from being my brother in our common father." Although one editor who reprinted the piece suggested that there was also the lesson "that religion, and that only, will make a man content and comfortable in the lowest situation," he recognized Meade's message of brotherhood and, even more than Meade, emphasized the power of the example for those readers whose "great and superior advantages" may still leave them "far from being equal to what seems to have been the case with this poor but virtuous negro." Echoing "pious Negro" motifs from earlier times, the concessions inherent in such remarks are no less significant than the proslavery, or at least not altogether antislavery, thrust in much of the account.[53]

The ambiguities apparent in this body of evangelical writing provide an important framework for an attempt during these years to reassert a ministerial authority for blacks along more egalitarian lines, a framework that also built on the kinds of institutional bases that had been taking shape during the first decade of the century. This was Daniel Coker's *Dialogue Between a Virginian and an African Minister*, published in 1810, when Coker was teaching at the African School in Baltimore and only a few years before he embarked on what was to be a controversial career in the African Methodist Episcopal Church. The dialogue is rich in references, both overt and implied, to the larger traditions of African American literature. Strikingly, given the reliance of many early African American narratives on white amanuenses—from Briton Hammon's in 1760 through Venture Smith's in 1798, as well as, ostensibly, Boyrereau Brinch's from the same year as Coker's dialogue—Coker created a dramatic situation in which the dialogue is recorded by a friend of the fictional minister, one "Mr. C.," presumably Coker himself. It represents an assertion of authority over the black voice that accords well with the kinds of statements that had already begun to appear in the orations commemorating the slave trade.[54]

In the dialogue Coker set up a situation in which a Virginia slaveowner seeks out a visiting black minister known for his statements on behalf of equal rights. The minister, a free man, is a knowledgeable, professional man of the cloth, and the dialogue takes place on a sociable plane, as though between equals. As it proceeds, the Virginian offers a litany of arguments in support of slavery—legal, historical, political, and especially scriptural—revealing, as Ira Berlin has said, the extent to which a fully developed proslavery position was beginning to develop, not to mention Coker's own awareness of it. The minister, who possesses a superior knowledge of the conditions of slavery, a greater sense of the institution's brutal underpinnings, and a superior command of the very scriptures to which the Virginian so often has recourse, demolishes the arguments one by one. At one point the minister even teaches the Virginian how to use a concordance so that the slaveholder can get his scriptural citations straight. Although it is hard to know whether Coker had read any of the black-voiced, proslavery literature that had begun to appear earlier in the decade, he did much to turn that literature on its head, putting black religious authority to antislavery purposes. He also gave his minister a highly effective voice: by the end of the dialogue, harking back to the form as it appeared in such sources as *The Columbian Orator*, the Virginian acknowledges his obligation to offer freedom to those he holds as slaves.[55]

Coker's reassertion of ministerial authority drew on traditions of validation going back to Thomas Tryon and, paradoxically, carried forward by Botsford and Meade that demonstrated the possibility of a black religious authoritative presence from whom whites could learn. It also drew on ideals of achievement found in Wheatley and brought forward by Hamilton and others in celebrating the orations of a Peter Williams Jr. or the abilities of a Henry Sipkins, as Coker's minister speaks with knowledge, sophistication, and civility, meeting the highest standards of public and private discourse. Thus, here was a minister of African descent who, by virtue of both background and training, had much to teach a slaveholder, and Coker dramatized a scene going back to the imaginings of Samuel Hopkins and Theodore Dwight, representing the Virginian as a man incapable of ignoring the African minister's ability, much as Hamilton only a year earlier had suggested that the abilities of a Williams or a Sipkins would confound anyone who sought to build a society based on ideas of superiority and inferiority founded upon color. That Coker chose to identify his minister as "African," moreover, tied the dialogue still more closely to the trends Hamilton too had stressed.

But as Coker asserted the possibility of authority, he picked up more fully on that theme of distinctiveness underlying a celebration of black achievement in the context of American life. His dialogue is followed by a set of appendixes consisting mainly of three lists: of "African ministers," of "African churches," and of men "who have given proofs of talents," all, revealingly, through an ability to offer skillful sermons and addresses. These lists lend credibility to the persona Coker presents in his *Dialogue*, showing the basis in reality for his literary creation. The lists are preceded by a quotation from 1 Peter 2:9–10: "But ye are a chosen generation, a royal priesthood, and an holy nation, a peculiar people." Here Coker was drawing on a position implicit in the already long tradition of black indictments of white American and Christian hypocrisy, as well as in the ministerial figure employed in his *Dialogue*. Identifying the hand of providence in the emergence of African American men of distinction, Coker located the source for their authority, even religious superiority, in a direct relationship between God and people of African descent.[56]

Motifs of superior piety and dedication to principles had long appeared in African American literature, especially where the African voice had been used, by whites and blacks alike, as a vehicle for social criticism; these motifs remained current in Coker's own time. Prentiss, for example, had Boyrereau Brinch, even as he celebrated the achievements of black churches in America's cities, suggest to his white readers that they not only view those churches but also "behold your ministers of the gospel," implying that they might suffer by the comparison.[57]

With Coker, however, there was a move in a slightly different direction. For earlier writers, as for Prentiss, the roots of an African moral superiority lay primarily in the sufferings Africans had endured and the authority that pain and exclusion could bring to the oppressed. Still, there had long been elements of a belief in a chosen peoplehood in analogies to the enslaved Israelites that had appeared early in thinking about African slavery. Phillis Wheatley's reference to "our modern Egyptians" was an early case in point. Coker's direct invocation of that status and his tying of it to African American institutional and literary achievements opened at least some new possibilities for thinking about issues of authority, voice, and self-definition as these intersected with questions of color and status in the early nineteenth century.[58]

These possibilities were explored in a variety of ways during the period. The continuing use of Israelite analogies represented one. Absalom Jones had likened the travails of American slaves to those of ancient Israel in an 1808 Thanksgiving address. In an address from that same year to the African Society of Boston, Prince Saunders, then a teacher at the city's African School, also built on the analogy, recounting, "When Joseph speaks of himself as coming down to Egypt, he saith, *I was stolen and brought down here and sold.* So, many Africans may use the same language, or similar expressions—I was brought to America and sold." The selling of both, he argued, was the culmination of the progress of sin "in the hearts of the children of men," revealed in the intransigence of Pharaoh toward the emancipation of the Hebrew slaves and in the clinging to slavery by white Americans as well. The evocation of chosen peoplehood in Saunders's words and its implications regarding those who kept slaves provided an important foundation for thinking about what it meant to be an African in America, for defining a presence in a slave-holding world.[59]

Such an exploration probably also lay behind an emerging historiography from the period, one that continued to confound categories of "savagery" and "civilization" by pointing to a European past with a history of "barbarism" worse than that often ascribed to Africa. One may see elements of such efforts in the primitivism and irony found in works from Behn's *Oroonoko*, through Wheatley's poems, to Branagan's *Avenia* and beyond. It was the sort of view inscribed in Russell Parrott's 1812 address commemorating the abolition of the slave trade, where he described the slave trader in Africa who "uses every art that vice can devise, or savages can execute, to accomplish his horrid purpose." Grégoire had made a similar point when he charged that since the beginning of the slave trade, "Europe, which calls herself christian and civilized, tortures without pity, and without remorse, the people of Africa and America, whom she calls savage and barbarian."[60]

During the early nineteenth century, however, such a perspective would be given still more historical specificity in an emerging body of images of the history of the slave trade found in the orations commemorating that trade's abolition. Henry Sipkins in 1809 looked back to the exploits of John Hawkins in the 1550s to find images of human depravity and baseness "from the sight of which human nature revolts with terror." Peter Williams Jr. saw the roots of the trade's horrors in the actions of Columbus himself, whose greed had led, first, to the "enslaving of the harmless aborigines," laying the foundation for an African trade that would embody the worst in human nature and the beginning of a history that would show the depths to which Europeans could sink. Such accounts gave a new historical dimension to the traditional indictments of a slave trade and slavery that in themselves confounded categories through their attendant horrors that would, as John Teasman said in 1811, "cause barbarous cruelty to shudder and turn pale," even as they also suggest the historical lessons Teasman must have been offering to such students as Williams and Sipkins in the New York school.[61]

Also apparent here, in somewhat skeletal form, was a view of history that by itself placed Europeans on one side of a moral divide and Africans on another. Again building on images dating back to Oroonoko, and well-inscribed in African American tradition, young Henry Sipkins gave these a historical reading when he described the exploits of John Hawkins, who initially sought to obtain slave captives through violence. Then, "finding the slaves purchased at too dear a price, being often at the expense of many lives," Hawkins began to resort to methods of guile and corruption, instilling in Africans "a spirit of avarice, and love of luxury" that he could manipulate to his own benefit. Such plans worked, Sipkins said, because of the nature of the victims: "The harmless Africans, who had ever been strangers to the arts of deceptions, became an easy prey to European wiles." Here were, at least implicitly, two contrasting histories revealing the basic characters of two very different peoples, the one with traditions of greed and treachery, the other with those of innocence and honesty. Whether Sipkins knew he was reversing types the actual Hawkins had portrayed, he certainly was using primitivist images to assert a historically based moral superiority on which to stand in relation to the society he addressed.[62]

As had been the case earlier, it is likely testimony to the strength of such conventions that despite their presence elsewhere among both white and black Americans, violent revolutionary motifs remained conspicuously absent in the works of black writers and even among white antislavery figures during this period. As before, this was a striking omission, since through those years Haiti had remained an important topic on the American scene. It influenced white fears, as well as, in some places, a black revolutionary consciousness. In terms of both the plot it represented and the white response it evoked, Gabriel's Rebellion of 1800 also showed the impact of both Haitian events and an underground revolutionary tradition among people of African descent in America.[63]

Again, the absence is striking, especially since in some ways such sentiments fit in well with other motifs in the construction of an African American voice. Abraham Bishop and the "free negro," for example, had earlier illustrated how slave revolutionaries could help expose American hypocrisy. The same was shown in the words of an accused conspirator brought to trial in conjunction with an 1804 plot. He told the court, "I have nothing more to offer than what General Washington had to offer had he been taken by the British and put on trial." That his words were reported and publicized by the antislavery English traveler Robert Sutcliffe, writing in 1812, enhanced their significance as a comment on his prosecutors' hypocrisy.[64]

That very significance emphasizes, even more, the general neglect of such sentiments during this period among black writers and their allies. Again, the concerns of savagery and civilization were major themes, and conventions of innocence and betrayal, which did not quite square with Haitian violence, continued to be used to express those concerns. Thus, one of the few pieces actually to use Haitian motifs, Thomas Branagan's *Avenia*, simply merged Haitian events with traditions of African nobility — naming an African prince Louverture — to recount a tale of resistance and warfare on the African coast. Ultimately, however, Branagan's tale turned into a more typical indictment of American hypocrisy and personal tragedy, his beautiful young heroine driven to suicide by her enslavement.

This same relativistic concern also helps to account for the continuing development of traditions grounding histories of savagery and civilization in the more distant past. In the 1780s John Marrant, looking back to Morgan Godwyn and Cotton Mather, had recounted how the label "natural slaves" had once been applied to medieval Britons; even Equiano had reminded Anglo-American readers of an ancestry once "uncivilized and barbarous." The motif remained alive into the new century. Grégoire had drawn on it, not surprisingly, in noting, in a way that echoed Marrant, that present condition was no measure of capacity for future achievement. Otherwise, he said, "the descendants of the ancient Germans, Helvetians, Batavians and Gauls, would be still barbarians." An even more elaborate version of the same theme appeared in an extended refutation by one "Humanitas" of the "Ham" argument, published in Kentucky in 1805. Suggesting that the Britons and Gauls were no less descendants of Ham and no less under the "curse of Canaan" than were Africans, he also showed how "British Canaanites" had been enslaved since ancient times, a history providing the same justification for slavery as that to which "African Canaanites" had been subjected, as well.[65]

Efforts to confront issues of authority and color could build on such continuing traditions. Undercutting any arguments for exclusion built on easy categories such as "savagery" and "civilization," these traditions also created a space within which yet another presentation of history could find sources for support. This presentation of history justified an African presence in the Western world by virtue of an ancient pedigree as noble as, if not nobler than, that claimed by its current leaders.

Since the colonial period, and through the eighteenth century, a variety of authors had sought to establish an ancient pedigree for people of African descent, referring, as Prince Hall did, to the African provenance of such Old Testament figures as the Queen of Sheba, or, moving a bit forward, to the African origins of certain church fathers. Others cast the net more widely. Olaudah Equiano, for instance, talking about the customs of his African forebears, compared them to those of the ancient Israelites, suggesting his ancestors' descent, like the Jews', from Abraham himself. Prentiss showed both his familiarity with the tradition and his understanding of its significance as he had Boyrereau Brinch suggest something very similar, noting oral histories among his people "which traced the origin of that people to the days of Noah," adding that "Ziphia the high priest in our language, I understand to be Jethro, the priest of Midian, who went and lived in a foreign land, and who was father in law to Moses." Such stories may not have been without foundation since, as H. Z. Hirschberg found, reports of "Judaized Negroes" in the western Sudan and as far south as Futa, in modern Guinea, appeared in the accounts of Arab travelers dating to the Middle Ages. In any event, such words not only placed Brinch in the same religious constellation as that of his readers but gave him an ancestral place in it that was stronger than most of them could claim.[66]

Others, however, had begun to speculate on a slightly different pedigree for the descendants of Africans in America, one that went to the roots of the society in which they had come to live. The New Yorker William Miller, in his 1810 address in the African Church in New York, suggested that "ancient history, as well as holy writ, informs us of the national greatness of our progenitors. That the inhabitants of Africa are descended from the ancient inhabitants of Egypt, a people once famous for science of every description, is a truth verified by a number of writers." There were many lessons Miller could draw from the story, but clearly, it was a story that was consistent with the notions Coker and others had also put forward. Far from being outcasts from the unfolding of history, Africans had laid civilization's very foundations, achieving a greatness upon which all the world had depended for its future growth and development. The irony of exclusion and the hypocrisy at its base became, in these terms, undeniable.[67]

By the time Miller offered his suggestion, the history on which it was based had begun to receive some currency. Its most important source was in the writing of Constantin François de Chaseboeuf, comte de Volney, whose most important work on the topic, *The Ruins*, appeared in an American edition in 1802. Volney, who had begun his studies of Egypt in the 1780s, had made much of the African origins of Egyptian civilization, and he had anticipated the irony Miller emphasized in his speech. Paraphrasing the Greek historian Herodotus, Volney wrote that a "race of men now rejected from society for their *sable skin and frizzled hair*, founded, on the study of the laws of nature, those civil and religious systems which still govern the universe." Volney was to be the main influence in the development of such a view prior to Miller's address, although his views were seconded by such important scholars, also French, as Vivant Denon, who had led the Napoleonic scientific expeditions into Egypt in 1798 and was well enough known in the United States to have been elected to the American Academy of Arts in 1801.[68]

The idea was to become even more fully established for a large audience in 1810, the year of Miller's address, by Henri Grégoire, drawing on Volney and others. Paraphrasing Volney, Grégoire wrote that "to the black race, now slaves, we are indebted for the arts, sciences, and even for speech." Even in the works of such figures as the proslavery Edward Long he found African character described as "very analogous to that of the ancient Egyptians," giving further testimony to the possibility he, Miller, and others had begun to draw from his predecessors.[69]

Although, as Bruce Dain has emphasized, the idea would gain a more systematic exposition in African American writing toward the end of the 1820s, the ensuing decade saw some further use of it as a way of continuing to think about the Anglo-American and African pasts. This is particularly notable in remarks by William Hamilton, contained in an 1815 address commemorating the abolition of the slave trade. The address focused heavily on issues of savagery and civilization. Relativizing a host of connections between color, religion, civilization, and slavery, Hamilton began by noting that "some nations have painted their devil in the complexion of a white man." The phrase goes back at least to a piece by the English writer Thomas Map that appeared in the United States in the *Columbian Magazine* in 1788 challenging late-eighteenth-century exclusivist notions of national identity. Map wrote, "To a fair faced *white*, a negro is an object of disgust; and yet, strange to tell! the negroes represent the *devil* himself as being *white*."[70]

Hamilton, however, took the meaning of the phrase a step further. Following Grégoire, who had also suggested "that different tribes, presenting the devil in the most unfavorable colour, paint him white," Hamilton entered into the historical framework Sipkins had developed a few years earlier. "View the history of the slave trade," said Hamilton, "and then answer the question, could they have made choice of a better likeness to have drawn from?" He reinforced the comparative histories of cruel and kindly peoples. But he elaborated still further on African history as such, noting, "Africa has a long, and in some parts, a proud account to give of herself. She can boast of her antiquity, of her philosophers, her artists, her statesmen, her generals; of her curiosities, her magnificent cities, her stupendous buildings, and of her once widespread commerce," focusing on the greatness of Egypt to give a concrete history to his account.[71]

Hamilton even provided an account of Egyptian history that replicated what had traditionally been offered for Africa in general. "Egypt was anciently settled by an honest, industrious, peaceable and well-disposed people," who created a society in which "they were all rich alike, for that one common storehouse clothed and fed them," he wrote, and he went on to describe how "they lived in peace and quietness, until a wicked nation entered and laid waste their country." There was more than one such invasion, and the peaceful people of Egypt ultimately "sought an asylum in the interior." Thus, "those inhabitants that occupy the country from the tropic of Cancer to the cape of Good Hope were originally from Egypt," and they continued to practice the peaceable ways of their ancestors. Combining the emerging ideas of an Egyptian background with more traditional primitivist notions, Hamilton created a historical account that fully paralleled, as he himself emphasized, the history of Africa since the arrival of the Portuguese, "the first traders in African blood and sinews," and those Europeans who had followed in their wake.[72]

A similar if more clearly biblical case for the ancient significance of Africans was developed by Jacob Oson, a Connecticut minister and schoolmaster, in an address delivered in both New Haven and New York two years after Hamilton's. Modifying the Volneyan tradition somewhat —though he seems to have been aware of it—Oson argued that all Africans were descended from Ham. Then he used the story of African Egypt to show how empires could rise and fall, how even the greatest of nations could be brought low—clearly a lesson from which the proud Americans could learn. Nevertheless, Oson found much to celebrate in the Egyptian past. Citing Josephus as his primary source, he told how Abraham had taken science to Egypt, whence it had spread to Greece and, thence, to Western civilization. Like Hamilton combining motifs of primitivism with those of ancient greatness, Oson said, "Was there ever a land more fertile than that of our ancestors? History informs us that the arts and sciences sprang from thence; and that they were a very mighty and powerful nation." Their fall was a lesson; it also provided a basis for hope of a future restoration, as well as a denial of a European monopoly on history.[73]

This, too, Oson considered an important point, and he moved beyond ancient Egypt to make it. "Africa is not silent in history," Oson said, "[or] literary characters," and he mentioned several, focusing mainly on the fathers of the church, as others had before him, while also noting the warriors and poets, "Hannibal and Asdrubel, Terence and his competitors."[74]

The mention of Terence, it should be noted, further emphasizes the existence of a tradition beginning to connect African American writers to a canonical past, as well as the self-consciousness with which that tradition was maintained. The poet Terence, a Carthaginian-born Roman slave of the second century B.C.E. who received his freedom and achieved literary fame, had figured in thinking about African American writing since at least the time of Phillis Wheatley, who in "To Mæcenas" had cited Terence as a literary ancestor. But Terence also had been an object of controversy. Jefferson, for instance, had mentioned him in his *Notes on the State of Virginia* as an example of ability in a slave, but he had used that example as a way of further denigrating people of African descent. Asserting that Terence and other noted slave poets of the ancient world "were of the race of whites," Jefferson argued that their work showed more accomplishment than anything Wheatley or her contemporaries had produced. Jefferson's critics, noted by Grégoire, took him to task for this—although Grégoire himself considered Terence "of Arabian descent"—as part of a debate entered by black writers as well. A member of the New York African Society, in an 1815 address to the group, quoted Jefferson on this point, asserting: "This very Terence that holds so conspicuous a place in the list of learned slaves, was an African, as we learn from his biography." And he used Jefferson's argument to make a still more ironic point about the prejudice that Jefferson's remarks revealed. Noting how many of the slaves Jefferson mentioned had served as teachers in Roman households, the speaker asked, "Should an African of our day possess the philosophy of Newton, the logic of Locke, or the learning and piety of Porteus, would he be honoured with the tuition of his young master? Let those of our colour that have made progress in literature, answer this question."[75]

The ancient world could, or at least should, provide a pedigree for the role of Africans in the modern. That it could do so was widely implied, and as the New York African Society speaker seems to have understood, those instances when it did not revealed either the blindness or the anxiety of those who failed to take it seriously. But no less important is the extent to which this evocation of the past evoked an authorial stance that built on the kind of historical notions of distinction and superiority contained in Coker's evocations of chosen peoplehood or on the comparative histories advanced by Sipkins, Hamilton, and Grégoire. It evoked a kind authority built on the "peculiarity" of those whom history and providence had shown to be special, whose witness had set them apart from much that was in the world.

In keeping with such notions of both achievement and distinctiveness, such providential ideas were to become quite pervasive in African American thinking during the early nineteenth century. They even influenced the kind of institution building that was taking place within African American society as the creators of those institutions came to represent themselves and their purposes. Such ideas had informed, for example, earlier Masonic references to ancient biblical precedents for African achievement or, especially, the way that, building on the paradigm created by the legendary use of Richard Allen and Absalom Jones's martyrdom at St. George's Church, builders of a black church viewed themselves and their enterprise, combining ideas of chosen peoplehood, providence, and an indictment of white oppressiveness. Thus, at the founding of the African Methodist Episcopal denomination in January 1816 Daniel Coker gave a stirring address in which he declared that "the Jews in

Babylon were held against their will. So were our brethren," character-izing in such words the overbearing leadership of white Methodist or-ganizations and the sufferings of black Christians under their rule. Reinvoking notions of providence, Coker saw the creation of an inde-pendent church as a time when God was "opening the door for you to enjoy all that you could wish," denouncing his more timid brethren for not leaping to respond to God's offer. The *Doctrines and Discipline of the African Methodist Episcopal Church*, published in 1817, embodied Coker's perspective, describing the churches prior to independence as being "in bondage to white preachers," a bondage that the founding of the organization had brought to an end. Echoing the motifs of "peculi-arity" that Coker had put forth in his *Dialogue*, such language connected the organization itself with the providential ideas Coker and others had begun to express.[76]

Here, then, was a language of African American voice and identity growing out of, but also building on, elements in that realm of public dis-course that had helped give birth to and shape that voice for some time. Rooted in religion, history, and tradition, it brought together issues of inclusion and autonomy, achievement and authority, in ways that rein-forced the kind of distinctive stance toward society pioneered by Wheat-ley and others of her time. It was a language that entered into modes of representation and self-representation, into institution building, and into an understanding of history and the American nation.

It was also a language that entered into some of the most ambitious projects of institution building on the part of African Americans, those fo-cusing on emigration and colonization outside the United States. Even prior to 1800, colonization had developed something of a history among white and black Americans alike. Whites, drawing on Jeffersonian no-tions of racial fear and national identity, saw colonization as a way of get-ting rid of an anomalous, potentially troublesome population. Such figures as Ferdinando Fairfax and St. George Tucker in Virginia, along with William Thornton in New England, proposed colonization schemes during the final years of the eighteenth century. But many African Americans, too, were thinking about colonization, and had been for some time. As early as 1773 one group of slave petitioners in Massa-chusetts had asked not only for emancipation but also for funds "to trans-port ourselves to some part of the coast of Africa, where we propose a settlement"; they proposed something like a colonization venture, albeit on a fairly small scale.[77]

More serious efforts among African Americans began to take shape in the late 1780s, again in New England, under the auspices of such groups as the African Union Society of Newport, Rhode Island, the African Society of Providence, and Prince Hall's African Masonic Lodge in Boston. These groups, like the 1773 Massachusetts petitioners, based their cases primarily on their pessimistic assessments about an American future and their hopes for a better one in Africa. The Masons, for example, cited the "very disagreeable and disadvantageous circumstances" likely to exist "so long as we and our children live in America," petitioning the Massachusetts legislature for funds "to return to Africa." Both groups combined such motivations with missionary purposes. The Masons hoped to be "the means of inlightening and civilizing these nations now sunk in ignorance and barbarity"; the Newport group would similarly enlighten an Africa trapped in "darkness and barbarity." Both attached their missions to an effort at nation building. The Masons described plans to gather a group that "shall form themselves into a civil society, united by a political constitution in which they shall agree," as the basis for their colonizing enterprise. They planned to develop an agricultural base, which they would use to "lay a happy foundation for a friendly and lasting connection between that country and the United States of America." The Newport group espoused similar hopes, implying, at least, an international relation linking them to American and English commercial networks.[78]

In many ways these procolonization documents cohered with other themes in African American literary traditions. The use of irony was important; so, in subtle ways, were notions of missionary purpose and nation-building. Although they did not entirely break from idyllic visions of Africa itself—the Masons spoke of returning to "our native country," whose "warm climate is much more natural and agreable to us"—the colonizationists reinforced ideals of ministerial authority transcending lines of color, as they stressed their ability to carry the gospel to genuinely foreign parts. As they outlined their more nationalistic plans, they also reasserted their ability to live up to the standards of American republicanism, as well as their ability to build a republic from the bottom up, without white assistance, in the absence of white oppression and exclusion. Their plans were not very different from what some white Americans were posing as a basis for their own national destiny, linking national purpose to commerce and participation in a larger "world" order. One white South Carolina nationalist of the same era, for example, proclaimed that commerce would bring the United States its "turn to figure on the face of the earth, and in the annals of the world." Commercial hopes, national identity, and international standing were firmly linked by the time these groups sought to turn those ideas to purposes of their own.[79]

In this era of post-Revolutionary fervor such plans received only mixed support. A group of Philadelphians contacted by the Newport organization responded, pointedly, that "with regard to the emigration to Africa you mention, we have little to communicate on that head, apprehending every pious man is a good citizen of the whole world," and they declined to get involved. Moreover, none of the groups succeeded in creating a colony on the African coast. One, the Providence society, did send a delegate to the British settlement in Sierra Leone in 1794, but the scheme failed, primarily because adequate financial support was lacking.[80]

The period after 1810, however, saw a significant revival of interest in colonization under the leadership of the sea captain and merchant Paul Cuffe, whose work evoked a positive response from African Americans in New England, Philadelphia, New York, and elsewhere. It also illustrated African American thinking about issues of identity, authority, and color during the period.

Cuffe was born in 1759, his father an African-born freedman, his mother a member of the Wampanoag nation. He went to sea as a teenager and embarked on his career as a shipowner in the early 1780s. His political consciousness also developed quickly. Refusing during the Revolution to pay taxes while he was deprived of the rights of citizenship, he was one of a group of Massachusetts blacks to petition the legislature in 1780 for a redress of grievances, citing both the lack of representation for black people in Massachusetts political life and the services of black people to the American Revolutionary cause.[81]

Cuffe showed an interest in African colonization as early as 1808, when he began to collaborate with members of the African Institution in England—the group responsible for developing Sierra Leone as a colony for freedmen and freedwomen—and with Quaker merchants from Philadelphia toward creating a colonization project of his own. Although his plans were disrupted by the War of 1812, he sailed several times on a triangular route between America, England, and West Africa, and in 1815 he succeeded in taking a party of thirty-eight emigrants from Philadelphia and New Bedford to the Sierra Leone colony. It was to be his only successful colonizing voyage. He continued his organizational efforts in the America but made no further trips.[82]

Cuffe's thinking about colonization put him in the tradition developed by the Boston Masons and the Rhode Island groups several decades earlier. A man of wealth because of his successful shipping business, Cuffe developed ideas about colonization that merged genuine commercial interests in Africa with a search for independence and equality through the legitimizing power of trade. Cuffe summarized his ideas in an 1811 letter to a key British supporter, William Allen, writing that when the colonists were "able to carry on commerce, I see no reason why they may not become a nation, to be numbered among the historians' nations of the world."[83]

Such words help to indicate the complexity of Cuffe's colonizationist thought, the ways in which he drew on and synthesized an array of traditional sources, using them to create a kind of national identity on which he could build. Like his predecessors, Cuffe brought evangelical impulses to his colonization project; he also connected his project with traditional providential hopes, suggesting that if the colonists remained faithful to their purpose, he could foresee the day when "Ethiopia" should "stretch out her hand unto God." At the same time, those impulses informed the more contemporarily defined notion of nation-building, which was influenced by strains found not only in projects that had preceded his but also in those ideas put forward by such figures as the exuberant South Carolina nationalist whose celebration of commerce so clearly anticipated Cuffe's own. Meeting with colonists in Sierra Leone, Cuffe advised them to use religious gatherings to discuss the colony's affairs and to "keep a record" of the proceedings "in order that they may be left for the benefit of the young and rising generation." In this, Cuffe was thinking, in a slightly different way, of a "historians' nation." Along with Jefferson and other American contemporaries, Cuffe liked the "dreams of the future better than the history of the past," to use Jefferson's words, and stressed national possibilities based less on a common heritage than on common effort and a view toward the future. He envisioned an African nation beginning its history at the moment of its founding while creating a past on which each succeeding generation could build.[84]

What made Cuffe unique in relation to both his African American predecessors and his contemporaries was the way he linked African nationality with trade by looking toward the creation of a commercial network of Africans living in Africa and elsewhere. One important part of his project was cultivating the support of influential businessmen, including James Forten, who had little interest in going to Africa but saw the commercial possibilities of Cuffe's endeavors, which were an element in Cuffe's nation-building effort. Elaborating on discussions of African unity, Cuffe described all people of African descent as members of a "dispersed race of Africa," and he claimed that his own loyalties lay with "the whole African family," echoing William Hamilton's slightly earlier evocation of an African identity based less on where one lived than on how one was "proginized." Cuffe thus conceived of African unity in a framework of a historical African diaspora, and he worked toward the creation of an African nation to be realized in diasporan terms. Although the nation he envisioned was to be centered in Africa, the community that would serve as its foundation would include Africans everywhere.[85]

Cuffe showed a strong concern for both the key issues and the basic ideals of nation-building. He was aware of the currents of thought about national identity and nationalism generally in the Atlantic world and of their implications for African Americans. Yet Cuffe was not a derivative thinker. Like his predecessors, he took a developing vocabulary of nationalism and, exploring its relevance to African American needs and possibilities, saw colonization as a possible way to put rhetoric into practice so that "this peopel might rise to be a peopel," as he suggested to Jedidiah Morse.[86]

Cuffe's arguments became a model for contemporary thinking about colonization. One anonymous potential recruit from Providence showed their power when he wrote to Cuffe that his interests had grown out of a concern for "the welfare of our brethren in Africa and all other parts of the earth wheresoever they are scattered." James Forten, toward the end of Cuffe's life, virtually quoted Cuffe when, speaking of the reluctance of many black Philadelphians to join in a colonization scheme, he mused, "My opinion is that they will never become a people until they come out from among the white people."[87]

Cuffe's project and career help to indicate how influential traditions that had been taking shape in regard to African American letters since the time of the Revolution had become. Since the 1780s Cuffe had sought to make himself a public figure, and his efforts to build a colonization venture intensified that quest. This involved not only communicating and meeting with such influential figures as Thomas Clarkson, Jedidiah Morse, and James Forten but also creating a place for himself in the public sphere. A biographical sketch initially entitled "Memoirs of an African Captain" began to circulate as early as 1807 and received widespread distribution during the War of 1812, a war to which Cuffe himself was staunchly opposed. His voyages, as well as the venture itself, received widespread newspaper coverage, especially as his efforts began to gather momentum after about 1811. When he took his small company of colonists to Africa in 1815, the voyage was widely reported, as were his specific plans for the voyage, suggesting, again, an ability to create publicity for himself and his enterprise.[88]

As he had even during the Revolution, he also continued to act the part of a public man, a citizen, with the rights of one. In 1812, when his ship was seized in American waters for illegally carrying British cargo, he went to Washington and met with President James Madison in a successful effort to recover the vessel. In 1813, seeking American permission to get on with his colonization venture despite wartime strictures, Cuffe again went to Washington, where, consulting primarily with Quaker supporters, he presented a petition to Congress requesting support. The petition itself, described as being from "a descendant of Africa," attempted to show how his colonization plan would be of benefit to African Americans and to "bretheren of the African race within their native climate," promoting "the Civilization of Africa" through commerce and education. Familiar in its language, it received a respectful hearing in Congress, though it was ultimately rejected as an unjustifiable exception to wartime policy. But even though the petition was denied, its reception verified the efficacy of Cuffe's public voice, not only in the seriousness with which it was considered but also in its publication at the time in the influential *National Intelligencer* at the request of the paper's sub-scribers.[89]

The recognition Cuffe sought and received helps to indicate, yet again, the realm of national discourse in which African Americans believed their voices could, and should, remain audible. As Cuffe entered into it, "a descendant of Africa," he revealed his familiarity with models combining distinctiveness and a privileged stance toward the American social order. One of the more famous stories about Cuffe—based on an episode recorded in his journal—involves an 1812 encounter he had in New York with two Methodist ministers, who for some reason asked him if he understood English. Sarcastically, he replied, "There was a part I did not understand—viz. That many persons, who profess being en-lightened with the true light, yet had not seen the evil of one brother pro-fessor making merchandize of and holding his brother professor in bondage—this has often felt very trying to me."[90]

Cuffe also found ways to adopt that voice in the presentation of his own sense of mission. In 1812 Cuffe published a short pamphlet on his project, *A Brief Account of the Settlement and Present Situation of the Colony of Sierra Leone, in Africa*, in which he described his plans for a settlement and his dealings with the "natives of Africa," among whom he saw some favorable signs. But he was also deeply concerned about the in-volvement of those peoples in the slave trade, something he hoped his own enterprise would help to bring to an end by providing economic al-ternatives. Still, his words were revealing. Of one people he wrote, "So accustomed are they to wars and slavery that I apprehend it would be a difficult task to convince them of the impropriety of these pernicious practices." Of another he noted that "they themselves were not willing to submit to the bonds of slavery," even though they were deeply involved in the trade, and that, while he had made an effort to convince them of their error, "the prejudice of education had taken too firm hold of their minds to admit of much effect from reason on this subject."[91]

Undoubtedly, Cuffe was reporting what he had seen in Africa, but there is no escaping the double meaning in his words, especially in light of his efforts to press his Methodist query at about this same time. Africans were not the only people of whom the "prejudice of education had taken too firm hold" on the questions of slavery and color, as his query to the Methodists clearly indicated, and the tradition of laying African wars for slaves on the corrupting influence of the European trade had too long a history not to provide an implicit background for Cuffe's indictment of a war-ridden African people. Talking about Africa, Cuffe drew on a set of implicit references to his own country that had worked primarily to undermine the civilized pretensions of a slaveholding society. Commercial in its focus and diasporan in its definition, Cuffe's nation-building project was no less influenced by an authorial stance whose assertions of a special perspective had long characterized an African American voice.

Cuffe's venture and his arguments and efforts on its behalf show how broad the realm of possibilities could be within an emerging African American literary identity. Developed to protest slavery and discrimination in America, it could be turned to more assertive purposes, even to purposes of nation-building, serving as a framework for asserting a national distinctiveness and a national purpose that built on the moral high ground African American writers had long been able to use in their works. Cuffe never quite came right out and said it, but he was able to create a colonizationist movement that essentially ignored the Jeffersonian arguments of incompatibility while using the kind of moral self-identity, in distinction to the white American world, that had become increasingly important in African American rhetoric during the second decade of the nineteenth century.

Cuffe's career also provides a background for understanding what was to become a key issue in the development of African American thought and writing in the upcoming decade and a half. Cuffe's colonization venture died with him, but the debate and discussion over colonization itself was to become increasingly heated in the United States, among African Americans in particular. This was due to the founding in 1816, the year before Cuffe died, of the American Colonization Society under the leadership of white Americans with varying levels of sympathy for the cause of human equality and for people of African descent as well. The challenge this organization posed and the framework within which that challenge was addressed were to dominate African American writing until at least the mid-1830s.

4

The Era of Colonization,
1816–1828

AFTER THE TIME OF THE American Revolution nothing spurred thinking about issues of African American literary activity, of African American voice and authority, like the creation and activities of the American Colonization Society, including its program of encouraging African American emigration to Africa. Operationalizing notions of a white American national identity, though led by white Americans whose motives varied widely, the society from the outset had tense and complex relationships with African Americans, especially with the free people of color at whom much of its program was aimed. Even though many had been drawn to Cuffe's program and to those of his predecessors, a sizable number of black people, both slave and free, viewed the society with favor or, at the very least, believed that its program offered possibilities for personal achievement in Africa that were unlikely to be realized in the United States. Even more black people, however, viewed the society with horror and spoke out strongly against its aims and purposes.

There was much in the early rhetoric of the colonization society and in the character of its founders to encourage both reactions. The founders themselves came from differing backgrounds and brought different purposes to their work. One of the most visible, and the man long identified with the creation of the society, was the Reverend Robert Finley, of New Jersey, a deeply religious man who was no less deeply troubled by the effects of slavery on American society. Viewing slavery as a national sin and impelled by missionary ideals, he believed that the evils inaugurated by those who had brought Africans to America could only be repaired through a project of repatriation and the gift of the gospel to Africa, which was what his colonization plan proposed.[1]

Finley's approach to colonization synthesized ideas from such earlier white figures as St. George Tucker and Ferdinando Fairfax, as well as Jeffersonian notions of national identity, with those of Paul Cuffe, his predecessors, and his admirers. The possibilities of realizing a black nation through the work of African Americans were important to Finley. He urged that sending to Africa a body of migrants who were familiar with the civilization of America and with Christianity could be a means for realizing Africa's potential. "With what joy would she view them," he wrote in his seminal *Thoughts on the Colonization of Free Blacks* in 1816, "improved in arts, in civilization and in knowledge of the true God. She would forget her sorrows, her wounds would be healed, and she would bless the hands of her benefactors." Africa would take its place among the nations of the world.[2]

At the same time, Finley predicated his sense of the need for colonization on a vision of the future that owed much to Thomas Jefferson's view that black and white peoples in America could not live together in a state of freedom and equality. Though he saw signs of progress among the free people of color in the North, he concluded that "the friends of man will strive in vain to raise them to a proper level, while they remain among us. They will be kept down, on the one side by prejudice, too deep rooted to be eradicated, on the other, by the recollection of former inferiority, and despair of ever assuming an equal standing in society." The only solution was to "remove them. Place them by themselves in some climate, congenial with their color and constitutions," by which he meant Africa.[3]

Other figures in the colonization society shared one or both of Finley's aims. Ideas of incompatibility dominated much of the earliest colonization rhetoric, though a democratic language stressing possibilities of self-government and nation-building, along with an emphasis on missionary purposes and possibilities, was important as well. Many who cooperated with Finley shared his essentially antislavery beliefs; others were attracted to the venture, especially in the South—where such figures as Virginian Charles Fenton Mercer were at least as important as Finley in the creation of the society—simply because if it were successful, it would provide for a way of getting a "troublesome" free black population out of the way.[4]

The aims of the American Colonization Society built on and even magnified issues of authority and color that had long figured in the development of African American thought and letters, as Finley and many of his colleagues understood. For them, it was always important to stress that any plan for colonizing the free people of color in the United States was a plan to be undertaken with their consent. It was not to be a project of forced deportation but, rather, one of voluntary emigration, however subtly coerced, chosen by the migrants themselves.

I

The relationship of this concern to issues of color and authority became apparent virtually from the moment of the society's founding. The society was incorporated on 28 December 1816, electing officers and issuing a memorial to Congress over the name of Bushrod Washington, nephew of George Washington and a Supreme Court justice, the society's first president. Within days the Washington *National Intelligencer*, which favored the society and its program, published a "Counter-Memorial proposed to be submitted to Congress on behalf of the free people of colour of the District of Columbia," in which it set forth arguments against the society's plans, in ways that directly looked to issues of color, consent, and national identity.[5]

The countermemorial was purportedly written by a group of "free people of colour, resident in the district of Columbia, born in the United States, and of parents born there also." Building on older traditions that rejected Jeffersonian tendencies toward an exclusionary national identity, the countermemorial also moved in new directions, stimulated by the discussion of colonization, to consider African American claims on a place in the American nation. The "memorialists" said that "they would rather die than quit their native country" and pledged to "cling to this their native soil whilst they have breath and be buried where their fathers before them are buried."

The motif was to be repeated often in the coming years. In some sense playing on Jeffersonian notions of homogeneity as the basis for national identity, the countermemorialists based homogeneity on history and human unity, both of which should transcend the racialist tendencies in

Jeffersonian and white colonizationist views. The "memorialists" also took a somewhat less than favorable view of Africa as "a country inhabited only by savages and wild beasts."[6]

But even more important were issues of consent. Here, too, the memorialists asserted an American identity, but one founded on rights as well as on history and experience. The countermemorialists questioned the right of such "arbitrary associations of men" as the society "to decree that your memorialists are miserable." They declared themselves "free men" who "consider themselves in every respect qualified to determine for themselves what is, and what is not, for their own benefit and advantage," concluding "that indeed of all the rights and privileges which they hold under the constitution and laws, they consider the right to determine for themselves whether they be happy or not, by far the most natural, the most precious, and the most inviolable."[7]

It is difficult to know who wrote the countermemorial. In most ways it anticipated other memorials and remonstrances that were soon to emerge from mass meetings of free people of color opposed to the society's plans, even expressing a distrust of the society's assurances that any emigration would be voluntary rather than coerced. In this it suggests at least the author's familiarity with an emerging body of sentiment rejecting the colonizationist plan as well as, undoubtedly, opposition among free people of color in the Washington area. In other ways it went off in very unusual directions. Ridiculing the view on the part of men from Jefferson to Finley that differences in color created a basic incompatibility between peoples of African and European descent, the countermemorial suggested that the real solution to the society's concerns was amalgamation: "In a few generations the odious distinctions of color would pass away." And it could easily occur. "Among your memorialists," said the countermemorial stated, "are very many young men, of industrious and sober habits, of ordinary school education, and of mechanic trades, who would not feel themselves degraded by intermarriages with the whites."[8]

The paper's editor took the piece for a satire, noting that the writer's "object, it is apparent, is to endeavor, by ridicule, to check the progress of the Colonization Plan," and he wanted no one to "mistake for gravity the well-meant irony of our correspondent." If the editor's interpretation is correct, it shows the extent to which consent notions continued to raise complexities in regard to color and status in the United States and how they created, for some, real areas of vulnerability for an enterprise like colonization, which, harking back to Botsford and others, appeared to seek the consent of people of color to their own exclusion from American life.[9]

On the other hand, in suggesting "amalgamation" as a solution to the American color problem the countermemorial may have been, and more likely was, an early, ultimately procolonizationist effort to parody and thus undermine what was already shaping up as a significant body of argument in opposition to the society. Even to acknowledge a role for blacks in the discussion of colonization was to admit them into the realm of public discourse, into the American public sphere. The writer made this clear when he had the memorialists propose a future in which, through "amalgamation," they should become "blended with the great American family." Far from satirizing colonization, that is to say, the author of the countermemorial used the apparent assertion of a black voice into the public realm to challenge such assertions in themselves. The effort was intended to illustrate, in a particularly vivid way, the dangers of not going forward with the colonizationist scheme, while dismissing the interest of Finley and others in securing black consent. That it did so through the bugbear of "amalgamation" drew a connection destined to play a role in antiblack rhetoric through the antebellum period and beyond.

Still, Finley himself continued to see consent as an important element in the colonizationist cause. He wanted to show that colonization really represented the wishes of many free people of color, that he was speaking for them and that they would validate his efforts. By the time the *National Intelligencer* piece appeared, he, along with his coworker Samuel Mills, had already begun to correspond with Paul Cuffe, seeking support and cooperation, which, at the beginning at least, Cuffe seemed willing to give. Also, with Cuffe's encouragement, Finley and Mills soon began to contact those leaders in New York and Philadelphia who had supported Cuffe in the past, including, especially, James Forten. Forten, along with Absalom Jones, Richard Allen, and others, were generally supportive of the idea, although as Gary Nash has shown, they soon learned that they represented a small minority of their constituents.[10]

As Nash has also shown, the response in Philadelphia was stronger than Finley, Forten, or Cuffe expected. At a 15 January 1817 meeting of three thousand people chaired by Forten, at which he, Jones, Richard

Allen, and John Gloucester all spoke in behalf of colonization, the nays had it. Most in the crowd distrusted the motives of white colonizationists and, echoing concerns expressed in the countermemorial, feared that the society planned, not a voluntary scheme of emigration, as Cuffe had proposed, but a compulsory deportation scheme. Far from seeing it as an antislavery measure, they saw it as a plot by slaveholders to rid their own region of a potentially subversive population.[11]

The result was a memorial that strongly condemned both the American Colonization Society and its aims. The memorial's similarity to the Washington "countermemorial" was striking, suggesting, again, that the Washington document had caught themes in circulation even before the society's founding—perhaps in response to other exclusionist efforts— but it nonetheless had great impact on its own. It was to set the tone for African American opposition to colonization over the next two decades.

Acknowledging the racist nationalist implications of the scheme, the Philadelphians described colonization as a measure intended to "exile us from the land of our nativity." Writing that "our ancestors (not of choice) were the first successful cultivators of the wilds of America," they stated: "We, their descendants feel ourselves entitled to participate in the blessings of her luxuriant soil, which their blood and sweat manured." The exile proposed by the society "would not only be cruel, but in direct violation of those principles, which have been the boast of this republic." The society's proposal cast a "stigma" on all free people of color, even as it abandoned them in a hostile environment after generations of exclusion from the mainstream of their own society: "Without arts, without science, without a proper knowledge of government, to cast into the savage wilds of Africa the free people of color, seems to us the circuitous root through which they must return to perpetual bondage." Signed by Forten, Jones, Allen, Gloucester, and others, the memorial declared a unanimous and unreserved opposition to the society and its plans.[12]

Philadelphia was not the only city where vocal opposition developed. In addition, no doubt, to Washington, Richmond was the setting for a large meeting that took a more moderate stance, but one no less skeptical of the enterprise. Recognizing some virtue in colonization itself, the Richmond memorialists urged a project focusing on "the most remote part of the land of our nativity"—suggesting a location on the Missouri River—something they would prefer to "being exiled to a foreign country," and demanded a right to participate in the discussion.[13]

Finley was surprised and troubled enough by these responses to return to Philadelphia to try to rebuild support. He met with leaders and had some sense that he had persuaded them that both separation and colonization offered the best prospects for their future. The result, however, was a mass meeting during the summer that resulted in a longer "Address to the humane and benevolent Inhabitants of the city and county of Philadelphia," reiterating many of the points made in the earlier memorial but also predicting that if slaveholders used colonization as a way of granting manumissions to individual slaves, the result would likely be those the slave trade had wrought on Africa: "Parents will be torn from their children—husbands from their wives—brothers from brothers—and all the heart-rending agonies which were endured by our forefathers when they were dragged into bondage from Africa will be again renewed, and, with increased anguish. The shores of America will, like the sands of Africa, be watered by the tears of those who will be left behind." Again raising issues of consent, they assured their readers that such a plan had not been requested by them. [14]

The problems such objections, and such voices, raised for Finley are illustrated by a brief piece he composed in 1818, a short time before his death, drawing on a long tradition in the development of an African American voice. This was his "Dialogues on the African Colony," set in heaven and involving an imagined discussion on colonization among William Penn, Paul Cuffe, and Absalom Jones, the latter two also recently deceased. Cuffe is represented as the spokesman for colonization and the society, Jones as the opponent, and Penn as an initially neutral participant whom each respects and wishes to persuade. Penn has heard of colonization and is, like the Philadelphia memorialists, deeply concerned that through such a plan, "no further violence or cruelty will be attempted against" people of African descent.[15]

In his representation of Jones, Finley revealed the weight of the language of opposition that had developed in Philadelphia and Richmond during the preceding year. "Jones"'s words draw heavily on the memorials and remonstrances that had appeared earlier. He cites the cruelties of the slave trade and argues that colonization would merely compound them. He notes the progress of the free black communities and asks, "Whence the necessity of their leaving a country to which they have now become attached by long habits, and in which their means of comfortable subsistence and their modes of living are constantly improving?"

Echoing the Richmond memorialists, he suggests that if there must be separation, it should be to some other location within the bounds of the United States, along the Missouri or the Mississippi River.[16]

Significantly, Cuffe speaks for Finley even as Finley draws on Cuffe's thought, as well as his own. In Africa, Cuffe says, "a whole nation would be released and restored to the land of their forefathers." Africa "would be explored and civilized; the institutions of political freedom, and the benign influence of the gospel extended over that most dreary and benighted corner of earth." With such progress, Africa would ultimately "contest the palm of greatness with the other nations of the earth" and achieve the respect of all. This would never happen for people of African descent in the United States, where "their minds are in too depressed a sphere to be reached by the influence of most of those motives that most powerfully operate upon mankind." Only in Africa could freedom and virtue be achieved.[17]

Finley made Cuffe an effective spokesman. Penn, though a great believer in brotherhood, has to concede the truth of much that Cuffe is made to say. "However the good and humane may struggle" to eradicate prejudice in themselves and others, white Americans are unlikely to succeed, Penn says. Rejecting inferiority, he nonetheless is made to feel that for blacks "the wall of partition between them and the whites" will always remain "impassable." More telling, even Jones recognizes the force of colonization arguments, rendered in Cuffe's voice. By the end, both neutral observer and opponent are converted to the society and its cause.[18]

At one level the dialogue shows just how prescient the Washington countermemorialist was. Finley, like many of those who had come before, apparently saw the necessity not simply of black consent to his project but of a black validation for his positions, a validation he sought to achieve by representing his ideas in a black voice, drawing, in this case, on an authentic figure and on a relatively accurate portrayal of a debate blacks themselves had put forward to get his point across. Paradoxically, given Finley's point of view, he, no less than Edmund Botsford a decade earlier, felt the need to portray a black consent to exclusionist policies, to vest a black voice with the very authority his policies would ultimately seek to deny, to maintain a place for the black voice in public deliberation even as he worked toward its ultimate disfranchisement and removal from the American world.[19]

Given the issues at stake, it is also not surprising that one result of the founding of the American Colonization Society, and of the debates it inspired, was the emergence, really for the first time, of questions about who could legitimately speak for the free people of color in the United States and the reinvigoration of questions of credibility so far as a black voice was concerned, especially as public documents opposing the plan continued to appear. In 1819 Philadelphians raised such questions as they attacked the society for publishing an announcement in a local newspaper urging support for the society and claiming sizable black interest in its scheme. Following another large meeting, another remonstrance, signed by Forten and Russell Parrot, was issued rejecting the society and its scheme and suggesting that any black supporters were simply "a few obscure and dissatisfied strangers among us" who wanted chiefly to be made "Presidents, Governors and Principals in Africa," while the sentiment among "the respectable inhabitants of colour" remained decidedly opposed."[20]

The society itself showed its assessment of the significance of such charges by continuing to publicize voices of its own speaking on behalf of the society and its cause. In its 1820 annual report the society presented a letter signed by a number of colonists in Sierra Leone urging Americans to immigrate. "Africa, not America, is your country and your home," the colonists wrote, and they weighed in from experience, albeit in the framework of longstanding conventions, as they drew on primitivist views of an African land of plenty, one that would achieve complete happiness with the arrival of more colonists to bring the gospel—the only thing lacking—to the minds of the native peoples.[21]

The society also continued to try to link itself with the authority of Cuffe. In the same annual report, for instance, it published an extract from Peter Williams's 1818 discourse on Cuffe's death, including the portion in which Cuffe was said to have seen himself as "a member of the whole African family." It did so despite Williams's own somewhat less than enthusiastic view of the society, not to mention Cuffe's very different view of the "African family" from that proffered by Finley and other white colonizationists.[22]

Something similar may be seen in the society's treatment of one of its most noted black converts, Daniel Coker. Coker had written about the special destiny of African Americans in his 1810 *Dialogue Between a*

Virginian and an African Minister; at the founding of the African
Methodist Episcopal Church he had spoken further about a special
African character and destiny. Such tendencies, along with a familiarity
with Cuffe's ideas, may have influenced Coker to begin thinking about
colonization, as did a despair over divisions within the Baltimore African
churches and a series of personal financial reversals. There is also some
evidence that the colonization society sought him out, offering him inducements to come to its assistance. In any event, by the end of the
decade Coker had come to look upon the society's efforts with favor, and
he became an eloquent spokesman for the possibilities the society offered
free people of color for a new life in Africa.[23]

Much of the testimony Coker supplied in support of the society appeared in a journal he began in 1820, when he himself went to West
Africa. The society published the journal almost immediately, identifying Coker as a "Descendant of Africa" and using the journal to try to
demonstrate the support it could achieve from an African American
leader. What would ultimately become the society's own colony at
Liberia was not yet established when Coker went to Africa. Venturing to
Sierra Leone, among the first of the society's emigrants, he was himself
involved in negotiations that led to the acquisition of a territory for future
American migrants. During that same period the society's white com-
missioner, Samuel Crozer, died, and Coker became the society's chief
agent on the ground, a post he retained for several months. Even after his
replacement he continued to be an important figure in Sierra Leone,
where he remained after other Americans had moved on to the new territory, living there until his death in 1835.[24]

Coker seems to have felt, as his earlier writings indicate, a strong af-
fection for Africa. He saw commercial possibilities, as others had, and
claimed something like a spiritual tie with Africans as people. "My soul
cleaves to Africa," he wrote shortly after his arrival, "in such a manner as
to reconcile me to the idea of being separated from my dear friends and
the comforts of a christian land."[25]

But the journal was in keeping, above all, with the missionary purposes often cited by the society as being among its aims, and it presents
a Coker who is fully in accord with those purposes, who sees the enterprise as ultimately under the guidance of providence. Looking out on the
sea as he approaches the African continent, Coker can only think of the

eighteenth chapter of Isaiah, in which the prophet contemplates the land "which is beyond the rivers of Ethiopia" and "a nation scattered and peeled" to ask, "What is God about to do for Africa? Surely something great."[26]

He presented further evidence for such a prophetic vision in the Africans themselves. Visiting a market and seeing that the people "were all nearly naked, both men and women," he is again brought to Isaiah, this time in the twentieth chapter, drawing on complex associations between biblical prophecy and ideas about ancient Africa that had been developing since the close of the eighteenth century. The passage prophesies the reduction of ancient Egypt and Ethiopia by the Assyrians, as those defeated in war would be led away naked and barefoot, falling from their former glory. Even as they fell, however, they could rise again, standing as an example to the world. In the very appearance of the Africans he describes, Coker puts his own hopes within a rhetorical framework that was well known in African American literary traditions.[27]

Coker thus said much to support what at least some society leaders offered in their official rhetoric, undercutting the more negative tendencies—stressed by opponents—in the colonizationist cause. In a letter attached as an appendix to the journal, addressed to a Baltimore friend contemplating emigration, Coker commented on the good native character of the Africans and on the potential of the continent itself. "It is a rich land," the letter reads, "and I do believe it will be a great nation, and a powerful and worthy nation," even if "those who break the way will suffer much." Directly denying the contentions of the Philadelphia memorialists and others, in another appended letter he declared, "We have no reason to fear, for Africa is our home."[28]

For all his apparent nationalism, however, Coker was far from breaking with the society itself, and he was willing to use his pen to validate the society's character. Noting tensions that had developed on shipboard between the colonists and the society's white agents, Coker met with all the men among the colonists and vouched for the agents, saying that one only wanted "a sable skin to make him an African." He also demanded the signing of a pledge of "full confidence in the judgment and sincere friendship of the agents." Over the next couple of years Coker continued to do the work of validation, representing a black voice in favor not only of the society's enterprise but of the organization itself. In one of a series of letters appearing in the society's *Fourth Annual Report*, letters addressed to an audience that was made up, at least ostensibly, of blacks as well as whites, Coker offered positive views of the future for the African colony, and he set forth the opinion, sometimes encouraged, that colonization itself would help bring an end to slavery. But he also concluded, "I am confident of one thing, that for some time we shall need white agents," giving a clear endorsement not only of the society's goals but of its operations. Here, then, was an important black validation of the society, firmer, perhaps, than Finley's imagined speakers in heaven.[29]

II

The American Colonization Society's reliance on black voices is important not only for the ambiguities it helps to emphasize in the colonizationists' aims and purposes but also because of the extent to which it shows how complex issues related to the creation of an African American public presence and a literary persona, intersecting with those of color, authority, and, in this setting, credibility, could become. To some extent, these issues remained rooted in traditions going back to the seventeenth century, building through the era of the Revolution, and carried forward from the earliest days of the American republic. These issues went well beyond colonization as such. The idea of a black voice that could speak directly to the experience of slavery continued to play a role in American letters even as many people were turning to issues of colonization and consent.

The moving force of a contact with slaves as a formative influence on antislavery feeling, for example, remained important even in the difficult era of the 1820s. The southern abolitionist John Rankin, for example, conceded that slavery in the abstract might "wear a tolerable aspect," but "when I bring it near, inspect it closely, and find that it is inflicted on men and women, who possess the same nature and feelings with myself, my sensibility is immediately aroused." The much-cited comment of John Randolph, of Roanoke, who was at least publicly ambivalent about slavery, that the greatest orator he had ever heard was a slave mother whose "rostrum was the auction block" dates from this period.[30]

Traditions of black-voiced protest against slavery also remained vital throughout the period. Such an influential publication as the *Genius of*

Universal Emancipation, which the antislavery Quaker Benjamin Lundy began to publish in Ohio in 1821, was filled with poetry and fictions, representing slave voices bemoaning the cruelties they had to undergo, that offered the kind of indictment of a slave society and its hypocrisies their experiences allowed them a special vision to see. In one of the first, entitled "Soliloquy of Sambo, A Negro Slave," Sambo recounts his pain in order to level an indictment: "Ye white men, your hearts are e'en harder than steel, / You war against reason — to mercy you're foes."[31]

Such poetry was given reality by narratives that substantiated more fictionalized representations. William Grimes, a fugitive from Virginia living and writing in Connecticut ten years after his escape, cast his purposes in terms Rankin would have appreciated when he wrote that one reason for setting out his life story was that "to him who has feeling, the condition of a slave, under any possible circumstances, is painful and unfortunate, and will excite the sympathy of all who have any," long a motive behind antislavery presentations of black personae. And Grimes did tell a terrible story of suffering and betrayal as, once in Connecticut, he was found out, almost remanded to slavery, and forced to use most of what he had been able to accumulate through hard work and industry to purchase his freedom. "Let any one suppose himself a husband and father," Grimes wrote, "possessed of a house, home, and livelihood: a stranger enters that house; before his children and in fair day light, puts the chain on his leg, where it remains till the last cent of his property buys from avarice and cruelty, the remnant of a life, whose best years had been spent in misery! Let any one imagine this, and think what I have felt."[32]

Clearly evoking the power of the black voice to describe the truth of slavery, Grimes validated his indictment of the system through a vivid evocation of the experiences he had undergone. "If it were not for the stripes on my back which were made while I was a slave," he wrote, "I would in my will leave my skin a legacy to the government, desiring that it might be taken off and made into parchment, and then bind the constitution of glorious happy *and free* America." His concluding line reads, "Let the skin of an American slave, bind the charter of American Liberty." As many critics have noted, such lines, linking Grimes's body with his experience and each with his authoritative stance toward slavery, virtually summarized the claims of the black voice in the American discursive world, claims that had been taking shape for decades before Grimes's work appeared.[33]

The claims Grimes represented were to be made a number of times during the second and third decades of the nineteenth century. Lemuel Haynes, as John Saillant has shown, also took advantage of traditions associated with a black-voiced commentary on American affairs to protest not only against slavery but also against the white nationalism that colonization and other trends represented. Examining an 1820 sermon Haynes preached on the rescue of two white accused murderers from the gallows, Saillant shows how Haynes represented his own role as confidante to one of the accused and the moral role it entailed. He did so in a way that stressed his own rightful place in the community of religious and moral discourse the events evoked and his own distinct role as a commentator on that community.[34]

It was in this vein that African American speakers, complementing Grimes and Haynes, continued to demonstrate by their words, deeds, and very presence the hypocrisy of white America and to assert their superior understanding as black observers of American principles. William Hamilton, in an 1827 oration commemorating the abolition of the slave trade, did this, as earlier speakers and writers had done, through an attack specifically aimed at "an ambidexter philosopher" who could assure the world "that all men are created equal and then suggest that some men are not." This was the same Thomas Jefferson, Hamilton reminded his audience, who both kept slaves and told the world "that God hath no attribute to favour the cause of the master in case of an insurrection of the slaves."[35]

Hamilton's invocation of providence reflects the continuing prominence of Jefferson, by now almost the archetypal symbol of American hypocrisy for African Americans in regard to slavery and to their own peculiar destiny to reveal that hypocrisy. Even white minister Thaddeus Harris, speaking in Boston in 1822, similarly cited Jefferson's prediction of divine retribution for slavery. Harris too did so in a way that looked not so much forward to insurrection but to Jefferson's hypocrisy and to the unique way in which a black experience could comment on it.[36]

Thus, traditions of African American ideological critique tended to remain important through the 1820s. Exemplary traditions, especially exemplary religious traditions, also remained alive during this period.

Solomon Bayley's *Narrative,* written by himself but filtered through an English amanuensis, Robert Hurnard, told the familiar story of a Christian slave tested by slavery. Like Grimes, Bayley also was an escaped slave who had been retaken by his owner and forced to purchase his freedom. But as William Andrews has noted, Bayley's lesson was entirely a Christian one, for he felt that in his experiences, from slavery to freedom, the lesson to be learned was "that God is rich in mercy towards sinners of the deepest die."[37]

Nevertheless, exemplary traditions could not be divorced from issues of color and condition even if they were evoked in ways that did not challenge the prevailing order. Elizabeth Ladd's 1824 *Some Account of Lucy Cardwell, a Woman of Colour* used Cardwell's happy death as proof of the scriptural claim "that God is no respecter of persons," but mainly as an "encouragement, more particularly of her own colour" to follow Cardwell's example. Sometimes, however, more subversive versions continued to appear. The *Washington Theological Repertory* in 1821 reported an exemplary story of a slave whose master refused to allow him to attend prayer meetings. "Well, Massa, you sell my liberty?" "I have no objection to that." "Well, Massa, how much?" "Two hundred fifty guineas." It was a large sum, but one the slave worked hard to pay, so important had religion become to him. Here, at least, was a tale that more than implicitly put slavery in a bad light by showing the superior religiosity of one whose piety put both the slaveholder and the system itself to shame. In the process, intentionally or not, it helped to put forward notions of moral superiority that others were advancing in more militant terms.[38]

This theme and an array of other traditions were given a vivid rendering in the story of Abd al-Rahman Ibrahima, known as Abdul Rahaman, a Moslem prince who became a celebrity after being discovered and finally freed from Mississippi slavery in the late 1820s. Abdul Rahaman told of having been taken in battle, kidnapped, and sold into slavery in about 1788. Finally writing an Arabic letter in 1826 seeking contact with his family, Ibrahima was recognized as nobility, freed, and, following a tour of the North to raise funds for his passage, returned to Africa, where he died.

As Ibrahima's biographer Terry Alford has shown, although most of what people learned about the prince was true, it was also colored by exaggeration and tradition. Ibrahima's story of his own noble origins and military career echoed similar tales of enslaved nobility going back to the eighteenth century. Moreover, Ibrahima's tale appeared only shortly after accounts, less well known, of one Omar ibn Said, a Moslem prince turned Christian slave in South Carolina. Unlike Omar, however, Ibrahima deliberately evoked traditions associated with Oroonoko and other exotic types. In his fundraising efforts he often appeared on tour in the dress of a "Moorish prince." Where Omar played on ideas of religious superiority founded in "pious Negro" traditions, Ibrahima stressed the harsher conventions of a black-voiced indictment of American hypocrisy. Once, when asked about his feelings toward Christianity, Ibrahima is said to have replied, "The [New] Testament very good law; you [Christians] no follow it; you greedy after money. [If] you good man, you join the religion. [But] you want more land, more neegurs; you make neegur work hard, make more cotton." Whether on his own or through his amanuenses—and several memoirs of Ibrahima appeared, most not in dialect—Abdul Rahaman illustrated not only the role a black voice was expected to play but also the role of tradition in the construction of that voice.[39]

Many writers thus continued to invest a unique political and religious authority in a black voice, grounding that authority in traditional frameworks of distinct experience and unique perception. They also maintained tradition as they continued to evoke the significance of a lengthy history of literary production, in the process helping to maintain a kind of African American literary canon. Phillis Wheatley's career continued to be of interest to antislavery writers and editors. So did the efforts of other literary figures. In 1822 the *Abolition Intelligencer*, of Kentucky, joined Lundy's *Genius of Universal Emancipation* in publishing selections from Ignatius Sancho's correspondence in order to "furnish instruction to those who doubt the mental strength of the blacks." The *Intelligencer*'s editor, John Finley Crowe, also produced a lengthy series of essays entitled "The surprising influence of Prejudice," intended to expose the irrationality of accusations of African inferiority, citing literary achievements, among other factors, to make his case.[40]

A year earlier, in a *Short History of the African Union Meeting and School-House, erected in Providence (R.I.)*, a member of the meeting, after celebrating its accomplishments, attached an excerpt from the *Providence Gazette* that he had found relevant to his own concerns. This excerpt, like the piece Crowe had published, also focused on issues of inferiority and achievement and also used literary accomplishment as a key form of evidence, in this instance citing the correspondence between Banneker and Jefferson, as well as the achievements of a Haitian official, Baron de Vastey, for support.[41]

The *Short History* is further revealing, however, because it includes an extract from an "English paper" praising the achievements of ancient Africa, claiming that "the Greeks so celebrated for the polish of their taste, were in a state of the greatest ignorance and barbarity; living like beasts upon herbs and acorns, till civilized by colonies from Egypt." Here, too, was a theme that remained vital in thinking about the place of Africans and African Americans in the world order. Lundy's *Genius of Universal Emancipation* had evoked Egyptian history in an 1822 essay directly attacking the views on African inferiority in Jefferson's *Notes on the State of Virginia*. An unnamed New York writer rendered the idea poetically in the same year, celebrating an Africa "where Art and where Science first grew; / Where pyramids tower'd aloft on the view." The place such a history gave to modern people of African descent within the larger "civilized" world remained an important ground for asserting a place within the American public realm.[42]

Such efforts to demonstrate the historical importance of African peoples were given new impetus by new anxieties white Americans were showing about the role of a black voice in the public arena, carrying forward but going beyond traditions initiated in earlier times. This anxiety was revealed in part by the parodic "counter-memorial" from Washington, D.C., that appeared in response to the founding of the American Colonization Society. But the growing white nationalism of the early nineteenth century was finding expression in more than the issue of colonization. As James Brewer Stewart has emphasized, the 1820s represented a time of significant difficulty, much of it in the face of, and probably because of, continuing institutional development among free people of color. One may note, as Graham Hodges has done, the building and subsequent destruction of New York's "African Theater," the focus of at least some resentment for daring to present Shakespeare, in 1822. One may also note, with Stewart, the exclusionist legislation, including New York's 1821 restrictions on black suffrage, throughout the decade as evidence of similar anxieties and resentments.[43]

In the South, such anxieties had the added impetus, never entirely absent, provided by fears of slave unrest. During the 1820s these fears were exacerbated when, in 1822, an insurrectionary plot led by the freeman Denmark Vesey was uncovered in Charleston, South Carolina. This led to a crackdown on those people of African descent who appeared to act too "free" as well as to increasing efforts to enforce restrictions on literacy. But it did not take a specific incident to bring such anxieties into play. Even before Vesey, Virginia's legislature showed its anxiety over issues of voice and authority, about the dangers of black activity in the religious realm, by voting to restrict African American ministers' access to slave congregations. The northern evangelical Jeremiah Evarts, criticizing the legislation, cited the example of Lemuel Haynes to condemn what white Virginians had done, but Virginia's legislators would have thought muzzling Haynes less an unjust than a positive outcome of their efforts.[44]

The anxiety also came through forcefully in what Gary Nash and Shane White have described as an explosion in dialect writing, intended to demean blacks and to dismiss the possibility of an articulate black speaker, that began to be visible during the late 1810s and, even more, during the 1820s. Accompanying a complementary growth in visual caricatures, especially of middle-class blacks, these materials also ridiculed many of the endeavors that were at the center of a black literary culture — the voluntary associations that had sponsored such occasions as the orations celebrating the end of the slave trade, the growing body of black speeches and essays in favor of the abolition of slavery, invariably referred to as "bobalition" in this body of writing. Even Phillis Wheatley's work, so important to antislavery, came in for a dialect parody toward the end of the decade. As Henry Louis Gates Jr. has said, the parody not only revealed a desire to mock but, like the purported countermemorial, showed enough familiarity with the work itself to indicate the author's appreciation for the impact her example might have had in discussions of national identity. Ridiculing speech, these materials also ridiculed as pretentious any efforts by blacks to enter into the American public discourse.[45]

III

Still, as the 1820s went forward, it was the colonization plan and the suspected motives of the American Colonization Society that did most to bring issues of color and authority into focus. Some of this process took place within the society itself. White colonizationists were always of more than one mind, or at least were forced to portray themselves in more than one way, on issues of color and status. In outlining their aims, from the beginning white colonizationists had stressed the character of the free people of color as "alien and outcasts in the midst of the people," as one put it in 1825. They cited statistics of crime and pauperism in an effort to prove that blacks could not become productive members of American society. They offered images of Africans as a people who "have less constitutional sensibility; less foresight; and attach a vastly less value to human life and happiness than christianity and education have taught us to do." Though relating such shortcomings to condition rather than viewing them as innate, these colonizationists nevertheless cited the persistence of those failings as ample evidence of the incompatibility of African and European peoples on a level of equality in a common society.[46]

But colonizationists had already gotten off on the wrong foot with African Americans, and they continued to provoke opposition. Meetings continued to rally African Americans to attack the society. Prominent leaders continued to condemn the scheme. Most notable was a series of letters from the "Colored Baltimorean" William Watkins, a prominent civic leader, attacking the society for its portrayal of African Americans. Watkins's letters, which began to appear by the mid-1820s in Benjamin Lundy's *Genius of Universal Emancipation*, did much to make African American concerns known to a wider antislavery audience.

It is indicative of some colonizationists' awareness of the problem they were creating that they began to turn at least as often to traditions supporting an African American authority as to a language invoking black failings. Motifs of nation-building, pioneered by Cuffe, remained an important part of colonizationist rhetoric into the 1820s and beyond, building on past traditions even as they were adapted to the colonization society's cause. In one essay focusing directly on African American achievements in the fledgling colony a spokesman for the society wrote of his hope that Liberia was "destined to be remembered by future generations in Africa as Jamestown and Plymouth are with us," and, in a familiar way, saw in Liberia the germ of "the promise that 'Ethiopia shall stretch out her hands unto God.'" Such parallels were invoked by other colonizationists. Matthew Carey, in a letter to John H. B. Latrobe, noted the difficulties facing Liberian settlers. He argued that they ultimately had to be seen as similar to those facing the first settlers of Virginia, placing both within a similar paradigm of colonization and nation-building.[47]

White colonizationists also celebrated black achievement in ways long known to antislavery tradition. They told of talented black individuals such as a Bermuda slave who, self-taught, had "made himself master of the first six books of Euclid, has read the writings of Locke, and most of the standard divines of the church of England." They also celebrated talented Africans like the Gambian king Panabouré Forbana, possessed of "an upright heart, an honest mind, and a clear judgment." The society's official journal, the *African Repository*, which began publication in 1825, was the source for, and published, William Cullen Bryant's primitivist tribute to an African chief, capturing themes that had long been common in the development of an African American literary persona. The *Repository* in fact offered a range of fictional voices supporting its cause, from Bryant's African chieftain to a poetic rendering of "The Negroe's Dream," in which a slave was portrayed dreaming of "an African shore, / Where black men can also be free," visualizing "A white man, with look so benign— / Determined—unbending—and yet / So lovely—'twas almost divine" devoted to sending him there. The magazine also joined in celebrating "Abdul Rahahman, the unfortunate Moorish prince," presenting a translation of his memoir in support of his efforts to return to his African home. Ibrahima thus validated both positive African images and the society's aims through his own life and ambitions.[48]

Finally, the *Repository* also became a key source for ideas about ancient African greatness, helping to develop a theme that had begun to appear in African American letters about fifteen years earlier. In its first volume, of 1825–26, the journal published two lengthy pieces on the topic, one signed only "T.R.," the other an extract from a longer piece by T. Edward Bowdich. Both sought, in various ways, to demonstrate the origins of civilization in ancient Egypt and Ethiopia, and both sought to establish that modern sub-Saharan Africans were the descendants of those ancient peoples. Bowdich, for example, focused heavily on modern African beliefs and customs, showing their similarities to those of ancient Egypt and concluding from them a direct line of descent. The message, as "T.R." stressed, could be directly related to the colonizationist enterprise, and in ways that earlier American writers had sought to relate it to the place of black people in America: greatness could appear in the future where it had appeared in the past. "And why may not America, the best and the brightest in this wonderful series of revolution, carry back *by colonies* to Africa, now in barbarism, the blessings which, through ages that are passed, and nations that have perished, were received from her?"[49]

There was, of course, a method behind the society's madness. Not only were white colonizationists of two minds about African Americans but they were caught on the horns of a dilemma, as such an early commentator as the Washington countermemorialist recognized and as later critics would stress. If Africans' descendants were unfit to live in the American republic, how could they reasonably be expected to succeed in building a republican society on the shores of Africa? The society's defenders could hardly deny black capacity even if they had to deny the possibility of black success in the United States. Such a severe moral and logical ambiguity in their position demanded the similarly ambiguous representations in their arguments even as the desire for black support, whatever its basis, required mobilizing themes and images with a clear basis in what appeared to be the African American discourse of the period.

But the real force of tradition and of issues of authority can be seen in the complex ways free people of color themselves continued to create black voices for use in the colonization debate. This process involved not just the ways in which opponents of colonization helped to set the terms of the debate, as Finley's dialogue and other documents made clear. It also involved the contributions of a few people of color who, like Daniel Coker, saw at least some merit in the American Colonization Society and its work.

There was much to encourage black support for the society in the years after its founding, despite the widespread opposition. For one thing, many African Americans continued to evince an interest in colonization of some sort. Early opponents, including those in Richmond, did not dismiss the idea out of hand; they only rejected the society's African proposal, looking for some place in the United States. At the very time when the society was publishing its encomiums to ancient Africa, moreover, there was a movement more clearly centered among black Americans examining the prospects for emigration to Haiti. The movement's origins reached back to the society's early days, to efforts by Prince Saunders, a member of the Haitian government, to encourage such a plan, meeting particularly, as both Cuffe and Finley had done, with Philadelphia's influential black leadership.

Saunders, who earlier had corresponded with Cuffe, presented Haiti as a place of potential richness, though one in need of outside assistance and the virtues that ties with America and American immigration could bring. As Saunders himself understood the possibility of Haitian colonization, however, it was mixed in with the very issues of authority and color that debates surrounding the American Colonization Society had also raised. In a collection of Haitian public documents that he prepared for wide distribution even before his recruiting efforts in Philadelphia, Saunders made much of the documents' importance as evidence of racial equality, noting a widespread charge, leveled in Europe and America, that they "are not written by black Haytians themselves; but that they are either written by Europeans in this country, or by some who *they say*, are employed for that purpose in the public offices of Hayti." Saunders offered his own testimony, upon his honor, "that there is not a single white European at present employed in writing at any of the public offices," that "all are black men, or men of colour."[50]

Saunders's plan never really got off the ground. Saunders himself ended up in some disgrace in both Philadelphia and Haiti. Nevertheless, he received early support from James Forten, Richard Allen, and other inveterate opponents of the American Colonization Society. They appreciated his linking of colonization with real self-determination, as Cuffe had done. That his plan had tapped into a genuine sentiment for emigration was further indicated, moreover, by a subsequent effort beginning in the mid-1820s initiated by the president of Haiti, Jean-Pierre Boyer, who made direct contact with African Americans interested in emigrationist possibilities. Attracting significant American support, especially from Richard Allen (and from within the colonization society as well), the effort also attracted about two thousand emigrants during 1824–25. This effort too was to fail. Most of the emigrants were sharply disappointed by what they found in Haiti—by its people, its government, and its society. Many quickly returned to the United States, followed by more over the next several years. Still, the project showed that an interest was present, a sentiment to be cultivated toward the success of the more ambitious project the American Colonization Society had in mind.[51]

Some of the most significant work in this regard played on pockets of emigrationist sentiment in such southern cities as Richmond and William Watkins's Baltimore, where Daniel Coker had spent much of his career and where he had laid much of the groundwork for a colonizationist appeal. In both cities conditions had been deteriorating since early in the nineteenth century; in both, free black communities existed in an uneasy relationship with a slaveholding society. Emigration at least appeared to be a desirable alternative to existing conditions, and to some, the colonization society appeared a useful vehicle. Responding to such interest, the society focused strong efforts in both cities toward encouraging colonization and cooperation between itself and leading African Americans. As a result, both cities produced visible spokespersons who sought to demonstrate their support for the society and to help create a language that could make the society's work appealing within the framework of both existing and developing traditions of African American discourse.[52]

Perhaps the most revealing effort to develop such a rhetoric took place near the end of 1826, resulting in a "Memorial of the Free People of Colour to the Citizens of Baltimore," which expressed a desire on the part of a group of African Americans to emigrate and urged white support of the society and its efforts. The memorial, which was widely disseminated not only in Baltimore but elsewhere, especially after its almost immediate publication in the *African Repository*, was intended not only to meet its ostensible purpose of raising support but also to provide clear evidence of African American interest in the society and its plans, countering what had been a far more visible opposition.[53]

The memorial was a complex document with a complex history, one that went directly to issues of authority, culture, and validation as these had taken shape since the era of the Revolution. It was, for one thing, the product of several factors, including the apparently genuine interest in colonization on the part of a number of black Baltimoreans. It was the result of discussions held in two large meetings at the very churches whose divisions had driven Daniel Coker to Africa six years earlier. The first was held at the influential Bethel Church on 7 December 1826. There it was approved by those attending and signed by the minister William Cornish, a former assistant to Richard Allen, and Robert Cowley, a teacher. The second meeting was held at the Sharp Street Church. The morning after the Bethel meeting, the minister George McGill had contacted colonization society officials to complain that notice of the Bethel meeting had been inadequate, urging the scheduling of another, several days later, at Sharp Street. Here too the memorial was adopted, signed by the chairman, James Deaver, a ropemaker, and by the freeborn boot- and shoemaker Remus Harvey. The meetings, particularly the one at the Sharp Street Church, were stormy, and the memorial did not escape severe criticism, but the outcome can only reflect the favorable sentiments toward colonization that motivated at least a significant number of those present.[54]

The meetings were not the only evidence of interest. At least a few of those publicly associated with the memorial transformed their sentiments into action: George McGill moved to Liberia in 1827, where he achieved some prominence, serving a few years later as acting agent for the colonization society. Remus Harvey took his family there early in 1828; he became a teacher.[55]

But if the document spoke for people genuinely interested in colonization, other questions of voice were more problematic. In particular, the document's authorship was far from clear. It was also the product of a concerted attempt by two of the colonization society's white leaders, Charles C. Harper and John H. B. Latrobe, working through the "African churches" to demonstrate the black support so often cited in the society's literature. They organized the initial meeting at Bethel to discuss both the general issue of colonization and the memorial itself; they were the officers McGill approached to set up the Sharp Street meeting. And they were chiefly responsible for the memorial's dissemination and publication.[56]

Harper and Latrobe's role created problems, however, and these were widely recognized. Benjamin Lundy reprinted the memorial in his *Genius of Universal Emancipation* as "purporting to be from the people of color in Baltimore," and perhaps indicating his own awareness of the storminess of the debates, he questioned "whether this memorial is, or is not, the voice of the *majority* of our colored people." Several months later he would again describe it as "the memorial *said to be* got up by them." In Philadelphia, continuing the tradition of opposition to the society, three thousand members of the city's African American community gathered on 22 January 1827 specifically to respond to the Baltimore memorial. Led by Jeremiah Gloucester and Richard Allen, the assembly produced a "Remonstrance" of its own, proclaiming that "the views of all should be known, and considered," and condemning the memorial's presentation of "opinions and sentiments entirely erroneous; calculated by their circulation and adoption, materially to injure rather than benefit our brethren in these United States."[57]

Comments by Harper and Latrobe may, however, be most to the point. After the meetings, according to Harper, the memorial underwent some editing, chiefly having to do with "expressions" in which the memorialists "might seem to have speak too harshly of themselves." Such comments indicate the presence of a strong white hand in the memorial's composition. But they also demonstrate the presence of a black hand, one that would not let the document go forward without an intervention into what it said.[58]

There was many illustrations in the memorial of its collaborative character. Certainly, there are concessions to its white audience. Prejudice is described in virtually Jeffersonian terms as "natural" and is not used to indict white colonizationist goals. Whites are absolved of the sin of slavery, blame for which is laid at the feet of the British. At the same time, the memorial put colonization squarely in the emancipationist camp, capturing an emphasis that went back to Cuffe, if not before, and ignoring contrary tendencies in the white colonization movement. African Americans had as much of an influence on the document's silences as they did on its words, on what it did not say as much as what it did. In particular, though it cited the problems facing free people of color, it shied away from the kinds of images of degradation, poverty, and crime to which white colonizationists often referred, focusing more on the lack of opportunities for free people of color and the pessimism such a lack engendered. Regarding the excision of language noted by Harper in which the memorialists appeared to "speak too harshly of themselves," the omitted "expressions" are not too difficult to imagine given the formulas of white colonizationists.

But, above all, the memorial was well within traditions associated with an African American voice. This was particularly true as it juxtaposed the condition of free people of color with the professed values of its white audience. The memorialists described themselves as "surrounded by the freest people and the most republican institutions in the world, yet enjoying none of the immunities of freedom." In using such language, and in their expressions of hope for the kind of society they would build in Africa, where they would prove themselves "republicans after the model of this republic," they showed themselves fully aware of American ideals and purposes and of the meaning of their own exclusion from the institutions of American life.[59]

The memorial thus reveals something of how important a black validating voice remained, even to people who, like Harper and Latrobe, were working hard to get black people out of the United States. The white colonizationists, at least some of them, understood that their program was not without moral ambiguity. They took pains to assure their readers, as well as themselves, of their good intentions. In the introduction to the memorial's publication in the *African Repository*, the journal asserted that "to the hope and belief that we should contribute, essentially, to the improvement and happiness of the free people of colour, by establishing them in a community on the African coast, does the Colonization Society in a great degree owe its existence." In a sense the memorial endorsed that claim, an African American approval for what the society was doing, indicating yet again the kind of validation only an African American voice could provide.[60]

It also demonstrated how well formed traditions for creating such a voice had become, the possibility that by this time there was something of a consensus about what kinds of positions a black speaker would be likely to take. This is shown clearly by the elements of protest and irony that, however well Harper and Latrobe appreciated them, are a part of the document's juxtaposition of black conditions and white values by a promise to carry American, republican institutions to African shores and an assertion of an ability to do so.

Along these lines, it also showed, as Botsford's dialogue and others works had many years before, how difficult it was to put a black voice to the purposes of its own exclusion, which is not surprising, given the contradiction in purposes such an effort implied. Such differences were strongly apparent in the concessions the memorial made to the opponents of colonization. Speaking of the alien status of Africans in America, the memorial described black and white Americans as being united "only by soil and climate," portraying blacks themselves as "natives, and not yet citizens." In the context of the 1820s both phrases were filled with meaning. Among white colonizationists it was a commonplace to describe colonization as repatriation of the African to "his native soil," as in the poetic "Negroe's Dream," published a year before the memorial. In asserting an American nativity and a tie to American soil the memorial denied this major motif in white colonizationist rhetoric, a denial reinforced by the refusal to acknowledge Africa as the only possible destination for emigrants. "The world," it said, "is wide." Confounding the white nationalist ideology behind the society, denying its major tenets while accepting the more practical impulses for emigration, the memorial thus took a position much closer to that of opponents to colonization, who since 1817 had stressed an American nativity and the role of African Americans in the creation of American prosperity and achievement.

The 1826 memorial was not the only attempt by blacks and whites alike to create a procolonization public voice, nor was it alone in the representations of voice and authority it displayed. Over the next year, testimonies to the value of African colonization from black speakers themselves continued to appear, with both white colonizationists and black supporters attaching a special mission to such a testimony. Prompted by the Philadelphia "Remonstrance," in reply to the Baltimore memorial, a group of colonists in Monrovia prepared a rebuttal of their own, which was widely publicized by the society and printed in the *African Repository* at the end of 1827. The colonists praised the liberty they had found in Liberia, which they said had not been present in "our native country." They spoke of their rights, their prosperity, and especially their escape from "that debasing inferiority with which our very colour stamped us in America." They looked forward to building, and felt they were building, "a new Christian empire" that would be an example to the world.[61]

More important, perhaps, were the efforts of Lott Cary, a Richmond Baptist minister who went to Liberia in 1821. Born a slave in Virginia in about 1780, Cary converted to Christianity in 1807 and purchased his freedom in 1813. Profoundly religious, he began to develop an interest in an African mission in 1815, and a series of letters from Sierra Leone colonists published in the Baptists' *Latter Day Luminary* in 1819 furthered his interest in colonization. Despite some apparent distrust of the colonization society's motives, within two years he departed under the society's auspices for Africa.[62]

Cary was a powerful leader among the colonists, and initially, at least, his relationships with the society were far from easy. He had strong conflicts for a time with the society's agent in Liberia, Jehudi Ashmun. In late 1823 and early 1824 Cary led a pair of brief rebellions, seizing arms and a food-storage warehouse, in response to Ashmun's policies, temporarily driving Ashmun away; later, however, he and Ashmun were to work closely together in matters of colonial organization and recruitment.[63]

Always commercially minded, and maintaining relationships with Richmond merchants throughout his Liberian career, Cary wanted very much to encourage immigration to the colony, and he began fairly early to serve as a spokesman for the cause. He wrote back to Virginia encouraging immigration even before his rebellion against Ashmun and the society. By 1825 the same *Latter Day Luminary* that had so influenced his decision to emigrate was publishing material by and about Cary in support of its own procolonization views and missionary purposes, praising his efforts and likening him to the founders of the British colonies in North America. The *African Repository* similarly reported his efforts, publishing letters from him describing such successes as his "conversion of a native African," letters assuring its readers that anyone doing a survey of Monrovia's citizens would discover that "there would not be one found among them that would be willing to return to America, unless you should chance to fall upon one that ought not to walk at large in any place." As John Saillant has discovered, Cary also prepared a lengthy "circular letter" in 1827 that was designed to recruit immigrants and responded specifically to both the Philadelphia "Remonstrance" and the Baltimore memorial.[64]

Cary had great hopes for his circular, sending it to one of his Richmond commercial contacts to arrange for publication in cooperation with their mutual friends in the society. For reasons that remain unclear, the circular did not appear in print; and if Cary had wanted to push the matter, the possibility was closed, since he was killed in an 1828 accident before learning the circular's fate. But his own sense of a role for himself as a spokesman for colonization and of the appropriate nature of an African American voice for colonization is reflected in the character of the document.[65]

Cary aimed his strongest words at the Philadelphians. Claiming the rights of men, they had forgotten that those rights "were lost on that same day, that their ancestors were taken Captives and conveyed into America

—and made Slaves among a strange people." They remained, he said, in captivity. Leaders like Allen, Gloucester, and "Fortune" [Forten] may have achieved a measure of success, but most remained in menial positions, with little hope of improvement, whatever their exertions. And they remained unmindful of the tenacity of a prejudice among whites that was unlikely to disappear, no matter what the accomplishments of individuals of African descent, a prejudice from which Liberia offered freedom and escape. In his indictment of white America, as Marie Tyler McGraw has suggested, Cary was not too far from others in turning the colonization society's rhetoric back on itself.[66]

But his brief rebuke of the Baltimoreans may be more revealing. For them—and, significantly, he accepted their authorship of the memorial —his criticism was succinct. They had memorialized, but most had refused to emigrate. More importantly, in making their concessions to a white audience—asking to be sent away, as he characterized the memorial's message —they had shown a subservience that Cary found appalling. Perhaps because Cary was unaware of the circumstances of the memorial's composition, he could not appreciate the fine line the document had to walk between "voices." But that in itself is important because Cary's strictures help to point to issues raised by the memorial that go beyond those of tradition and validation involved in the development of a black voice as these had taken shape prior to the mid-1820s. Cary's strictures also help reveal the tensions inherent in that voice, from a black as well as a white point of view, as a result of having to meet the demands of at least two audiences, a demand made clear by the genuine ambiguities involved in the colonizationist plan. Issues of independence and authority, as well as color and authority, were also implicated in a document like the Baltimore memorial, something Cary seems to have sensed, if he did not entirely understand its roots. But what he sensed about the need for independence and autonomy was to enter the discussion of African American literature and voice with increasing explicitness at almost the exact moment when Cary's "circular letter" was composed.[67]

The most important step in the direction Cary's letter evoked was the creation during that year of the first black-owned, black-edited newspaper in the United States. This was the *Freedom's Journal*, founded in New York in 1827 and edited by John B. Russwurm and Samuel Cornish. The editors brought strong qualifications to the enterprise. Cornish, who would drop out of the enterprise for reasons of health after only a few months, was born free in Delaware in about 1795. Moving to Philadelphia in 1815, he had become a Presbyterian minister by the end of the decade. He served briefly as a missionary to the slaves in Maryland, then settled as a full-time minister in New York in 1822. He also became a visible opponent of colonization and of the American Colonization Society. His significance as an opponent was acknowledged by the society's officers well before the founding of *Freedom's Journal* both as a result of his activities and because of a lengthy piece he had sent to a New Jersey newspaper excoriating the society, a piece later republished in Lundy's *Genius of Universal Emancipation.* Cornish and Russwurm made a strong anticolonizationist message a major part of their newspaper as well. The apparent efficacy of the anticolonizationist voice Cornish, with Russwurm, put forward in *Freedom's Journal* was enough to cause him difficulty with a few white supporters and prominent Presbyterians in New York.[68]

Russwurm, who continued to edit the *Journal* until its demise in March 1829, was born in Jamaica in 1799 to a white father and a black mother but grew up in Quebec and Maine, where he settled with his father. By 1826 he had already become well known as the first black graduate of a major American college, Bowdoin, where he delivered the commencement address, focusing on the achievements of an independent Haiti and on his hope that the Caribbean nation had "laid the foundation of an Empire that will take a rank with the nations of the earth."[69]

There were several motivations behind the founding of *Freedom's Journal.* Most immediate was the growing racism of the 1820s. Above all, the racism of the New York press, especially the New York editor and politician Mordecai Noah, noted for his scurrilous attacks on New York's free black population, provided an impetus for their effort. But Russwurm and Cornish also singled out the American Colonization Society, at least implicitly, in this regard. "Our vices and our degradation are ever arrayed against us, but our virtues are passed by unnoticed," they said, asking rhetorically, "Is it not very desirable that such should know more of our actual condition, and of our efforts and feelings, that in forming or advocating plans for our amelioration, they may do it more understandingly?"[70]

Certainly, by this time Cornish and Russwurm were not the only ones aware of a need to counter misrepresentations. Only about a month before *Freedom's Journal* began publication, Enoch Lewis, a white Quaker editor, had created the *African Observer,* also to be devoted to correcting false impressions about free people of color. Lasting for about a year, and containing a variety of articles on "the history, ancient and modern of Africa," along with "biographical notices of negroes who have been distinguished for their virtue or abilities," it too was intended to provide an accurate account of "the situation, character, and future prospects of the free coloured population of the United States."[71]

Still, *Freedom's Journal* was the first black-edited, black-controlled periodical in the United States, and in the way Russwurm and Cornish stated their case they also raised directly, for what appears to have been the first time, the question that had been implicit since, especially, the inauguration of the colonization debate, namely, who should control the black voice? They were clear that unless that voice were controlled by black people themselves, black people could never be certain of fair and accurate representation. Though long implicit even in Wheatley's thinking and certainly exacerbated by the colonization debate, here the idea became something of a guiding principle, calling into question the credibility of the kinds of voices that the colonization society had cultivated and on which it had come to rely. Speaking of the need for such a journal as they had created, Cornish and Russwurm wrote, "We wish to plead our own cause. Too long have others spoken for us. Too long has the publick been deceived by misrepresentations, in things which concern us dearly, though in the estimation of some mere trifles" (16 March 1827).

Many people agreed with the *Journal*'s editors about its necessity. As early as July 1827 free people of color in Fredericksburg, Virginia, included toasts to the *Journal* in a July Fourth celebration of New York's emancipation of the remaining slaves in that state. A free Virginian wrote to the paper at about the same time that the appearance of such a paper, "edited by persons of our own colour, and devoted to the interests of our long oppressed and stigmatized race; cannot fail to awaken the liveliest joy and gratitude in every bosom, that is not callous to humanity and virtue"; and he expressed his own assurance that the paper could not "fail to produce a happy effect" (6 July 1827).[72]

The paper drew on a broad array of sources for its content. Given its purposes of self-representation, one function the paper served was to provide a pioneering outlet for African American writers — poets, story writers, and essayists. Nevertheless, the paper also drew freely on the works of white as well as black writers, accuracy rather than authorship being the key to its purposes. It essentially encapsulated the kind of antislavery community that had helped to create an authoritative African American literary presence since before Wheatley's time.

Individual issues of *Freedom's Journal* also covered a broad array of topics, not all of them having to do with problems of color, but these were certainly key to the journal's focus and success. Colonization remained a strong focus. The paper's editorial columns attacked the American Colonization Society, publicizing the anticolonization sentiments of leading African American writers and activists. Within only a couple of months of its creation the *Journal* published an attack on the Baltimore memorial, asserting that many present at one of the meetings had registered a dissent from the document (18 May 1827). In early 1828 the *Journal* published a stinging rebuke of the testimony of the Liberian colonists who had sought to counter the Philadelphia remonstrance. John Russwurm, writing for the paper, suggested that even if many African Americans developed an interest in colonization, "we would not ask the aid of the American Colonization Society to carry us to their land 'flowing with milk and honey'" (25 January 1828).

No less important in the paper's columns were calls to African American readers for social and cultural "improvement." The historian Frederick Cooper rightly noted the paper's significant concentration on concerns about self-help and social improvement, on what the editors saw as a need for blacks to become more "respectable" in their behavior and appearance. According to Cooper, more space was devoted to these kinds of concerns, as well as to related issues such as education and temperance, than to protests against slavery or discrimination or even to the challenge of colonization.[73]

These questions dovetailed in important ways with the kinds of concerns that lay behind issues of authority and self-definition in the American public realm. They informed the kinds of literary issues implicit in the very founding of the *Journal*, encouraging literary culture and literary achievement as part of the effort to improve free black society while also responding to that society's traducers. At the same time, if the editors of *Freedom's Journal* saw the need for a potent black voice, they also elaborated on and even expanded the bases for authority and credibility that had underlain its presentation in the past.

Like many of their predecessors, Russwurm and Cornish sought to establish that people of African descent had already proved their right to a place within the realm of American public life. They published an array of pieces devoted to demonstrating human unity and equality, whether through explorations in biology or in history. A lengthy series of articles in 1828 entitled "On the Varieties of the Human Race" took up biological questions, focusing on the variety of colors characterizing many species, the climatic causes of variation, the mutability of coloration, and color's irrelevance to ability or capacity. Representing the articles not as offering anything new but as a compendium of "long established facts," the author presented a case for human unity that sought to demolish any arguments for the inclusion or exclusion of people from the "human family" on grounds of color (18 April 1828).

Freedom's Journal also drew on traditions stressing the historical importance of ancient Africa, a theme that had remained current in the years leading up to the paper's creation. In December 1828, over two issues, the paper reprinted the 1825 essay by "T.R." celebrating the greatness of ancient Africa, which had initially appeared in the *African Repository* In 1827 it published a poem entitled "Africa," describing the continent as "Land of the wise! where Science broke / Like morning from chaotic deeps." Prior to that, during the spring and summer of 1827, a pair of original essays on the topic also appeared. "The Mutability of Human Affairs," by Russwurm, drew heavily on Volney and condemned the hypocrisy of an American society that treasured ancient African civilization but refused equality to those descended from its creators. The other, signed only by "S.," focused on the subject of "African genealogy," elaborately tracing Africans' connections to the other peoples of the world and surveying ancient history to connect contemporary African peoples with an Egypt that "was once the richest and happiest country in the world; flourishing with plenty, and even learning, before the patriarch Abraham's time" (17 August 1827). Possibly written by the fourteen-year-old James McCune Smith, which the historian Bruce Dain has suggested (the author apologized for any inaccuracies on the ground of being "quite a youth"), the article concluded, similarly, with an indictment of American hypocrisy and, in the tradition of Daniel Coker, with the evocation of God's promise that Ethiopia would again stretch forth her arms (31 August 1827).[74]

Such evocations of an ancient pedigree, with their providential overtones, continued to give foundations to an African American self-definition that could demand a place in the American public realm. So did the continuing indictments of American hypocrisy, giving weight to distinctly black perceptions of the society in which they lived. This, for example, was the theme of a poem called "The Sorrows of Angola," written by "one of the sons of Africa" in response to the American celebration of the "national Jubilee, July 4, 1826," and published in the *Journal*, on 8 June 1827, and elsewhere. The poet wrote:

> While music, bells and cannons peal,
> To hail the festive day,
> The thoughts within my bosom steal,
> Of helpless—Africa!

The *Journal*'s approach to the literary enterprise as such built on this sense of the importance of a black literary voice and its distinctive role in American society. The paper's almost constant encouragement of schools, libraries, and literary societies was understood not only in terms of encouraging respectability but also as an important part of the further integration of black Americans into American public life. The Pittsburgh leader John B. Vashon pointed this out in a letter defending the paper from attack and praising its role in showing black readers that nature had been "beautiful to them as it respects mind," something that could only be done by a paper "conducted by one of their own race" (8 February 1828). About two months later a Boston meeting in support of the *Journal* chaired by the minister Hosea Easton resulted in a resolution of support noting not only the need for a black voice to represent black Americans but also, in the words of the merchant David Walker, one of the paper's local agents, that it helped to remedy what he described as one of the greatest "disadvantages the people of Colour labor under, by the neglect of literature" (25 April 1828).

The *Journal* itself celebrated African American literary achievement in ways that helped to reinforce the kinds of points Vashon and Walker made by documenting the impact black writing had, and could have, on the larger society. Excerpts from Phillis Wheatley's work appeared in the

Journal along with accounts of her life and career. James Forten's 1813 "Letters of a Man of Colour" were reprinted in February and March 1828 specifically to illustrate the role a black writer could play in the battle against the color line. The *Journal* also published a lengthy excerpt focusing on literary achievement from John Finley Crow's series "The Surprising Influence of Prejudice" that had originally appeared in the *Abolition Intelligencer* in 1822.

Something similar may be said about the *Journal*'s efforts to publicize more contemporary literary achievements. When Russwurm published an essay on slavery delivered in 1828 by the twelve- or thirteen-year-old New York student George R. Allen, he appended testimony by white members of the New York Manumission Society attesting to Allen's authorship of the piece, demonstrating the influence the young man's eloquence had had on white ideas about African talents and capabilities (14 March 1829).

It was not uncommon for the *Journal* to stress this kind of testimony when it reprinted works by black authors, often unknown, that had originally appeared in other publications; it confirmed, rather than compromised, the paper's claims to represent an efficacious African American voice to the larger world. In June 1827, for example, Russwurm and Cornish reprinted from the *New Haven Chronicle* a poem by "one of the sons of Africa" in the city, a poem that, the *Chronicle* editorialized, served to prove "that this race, depressed, degraded and trampled upon as they are by the whites, are not entirely brainless, as some seem to suppose." The poem itself was a paraphrase of the noted passage from the Song of Solomon 1:5, but one more in keeping with past concerns of voice and authority than with the kinds of African-centered ideas with which the passage had often been invested, as in Prince Hall's citation of it, for example, at the end of the preceding century. The poem began, "Black, I am, oh! daughters fair, / But my beauty is most rare," going on, however, not to evoke themes of African beauty and identity but instead to provide a black-voiced testimony to the glory of salvation: "Black, by sins defiling flood, / Beauteous wash'd in Jesus' blood" (8 June 1827).

The *Journal* devoted still more attention to the works and career of the North Carolina slave poet George Moses Horton, who began to receive significant public notice in 1828. Horton, born in about 1797, had begun to frequent the area around Chapel Hill and the University of North

Carolina in about 1820. Able to read, he had been egged on by students to present "orations" before them, in a manner not entirely unreminiscent of the treatment accorded "Cuff" in Brackenridge's *Modern Chivalry* —a cruel joke that Horton seems to have recognized as well as anyone. But Horton, who had long enjoyed making poetry, soon began dictating his poems to students and, somewhat in the tradition of Lucy Terry and Jupiter Hammon, as Blyden Jackson has said, became increasingly appreciated for his real ability.[75]

Horton wrote on a wide range of topics. Famously, he provided University of North Carolina students with love poems on request. Like Hammon, he composed religious poems and was deeply influenced by the hymn forms and themes of evangelical Christianity. Celebrating poetry for its own sake, he described how, when he was troubled, "My muse ascends above the cloud / And leaves the noise behind." He also wrote about his own bitterness as a slave in such pieces as "Slavery" and "Liberty and Slavery," in both of which he concluded, here in words taken from "Slavery":

> Then let me hasten to the grave,
> The only refuge for the slave,
> Who mourns for liberty.

The first-person imprimatur Horton's life gave to such lines, however rooted they were in tradition, was to endow them with an impact found not only in their appearance in *Freedom's Journal* but in their influence on antislavery writing for years to come.[76]

Whatever the influence of the poetry itself, moreover, Horton's early career exemplified the significance that could be invested in a black voice of proven literary attainment. For one thing, it helped to verify the *Journal*'s contention that literary achievement would be recognized, for Horton's early work appeared not only in the pages of *Freedom's Journal* but also in local North Carolina papers, including the *Raleigh Register*. It also allowed the paper to play on the possibilities literary achievement should create for overcoming at least some of color's cruel effects, since Horton's emergence inaugurated a campaign, including white champions as well as black, to gain him his freedom. The *Journal* itself editorialized that Horton "is undoubtedly a man of talents, and it seems somewhat hard that they should be buried, as they will be, in a measure, if he is doomed to waste the prime of his days in vile servitude" (12 September 1828). The paper even saw the effort as a kind of test. Announcing the support in Horton's cause of one of its Boston agents, David Walker, the paper added, "We would manifest to our Southern brethren, that were our means equal to our wishes, the footsteps of a slave should not pollute the soil of our common country" (3 October 1828).[77]

Unfortunately, the effort Horton inspired had less than positive results. Apparently, enough money was raised to buy Horton's freedom. Although the offer was refused by James Horton, the poet's owner, the attempt enlisted the participation not only of the *Journal*'s readers but also of such influential whites—and white southerners, to boot—as the president of the University of North Carolina and even the governor of the state in negotiations directed toward Horton's emancipation. The American Colonization Society, believing that Horton hoped to depart for Liberia upon emancipation, also got involved. It sponsored a subsequent effort to raise funds by the sale of Horton's poetry, which was compiled into an 1829 volume, *In Hope of Liberty*, published in North Carolina. That effort also failed. If, however, the final outcome was decidedly mixed—and, ultimately, a powerful lesson in the limitations as well as the potential of black literary achievement—the *Journal*'s campaign showed an optimism and a sense of efficacy that fully cohered with its more general presentation of the black voice in a larger American context.[78]

In the paper's own columns such a view also appears to have underlain the kinds of works it published, as well as its presentation of those works. As had been traditional since Wheatley's time, much that appeared in the *Journal* was intended to emphasize the importance of a distinctive black perspective on issues of color and authority. Its columns followed tradition in presenting, for example, poems and brief pieces capturing the sorrow of the enslaved, expressing a pain in slavery that only a black voice could portray. Horton's poem "Slavery" was one example. Another, which appeared in the Journal on 14 March 1828, perhaps by the New Haven black minister Amos Beman but signed "Africus," described "the tears of a slave," asking,

> Can a land of Christians so pure!
> Let demons of slavery rave!

> Can the angel of mercy endure,
> The pitiful tears of a SLAVE!

And, again, the paper also published similar works by white writers, control rather than authorship being the key to its understanding of independence.[79]

But *Freedom's Journal* also brought new variety to the black voice, investing it with a novel, more subtle significance. For one thing, at a time when "bobalition" satires had been ridiculing the very efforts the *Journal* represented for more than a decade, its editors did not themselves shy away from dialect. In 1829, for example, the paper reprinted from a Massachusetts paper a lengthy dialogue in which a slave named Cuffee reported a series of family disasters to his young master at college. The dialogue was an exemplar of indirection, beginning with the slave's report that the pet crow had died because "he been eat too much carrion" and culminating in the news that "old Missa die of a broken heart; for old Massa he been die two or free days afore; and Missa neber get over that" (14 February 1829).

The *Journal* also published one of the first lengthy pieces of fiction by a black American writer. Like the serial essay on African genealogy, it was signed simply "S." Written specifically for the *Journal*, it may also have been authored by the teenage James McCune Smith. The story, running over four issues in January and February 1828, was entitled "Theresa—A Haytien Tale." It was a romance set during the Haitian war for independence, in the time when, "provoked to madness," the "sons of Africa" in Haiti had "armed themselves against French barbarity" (18 January 1828).

The story, not always easy to follow, recounts the adventures of Theresa, a young Haitian, her sister, and their mother, Madame Paulina, as they seek to flee from their native village, which is threatened by French troops, to the safety of an isolated refuge. The story presents chilling scenes of French destructiveness and cruelty as it follows the women's daring trek through the Haitian countryside. And it evokes noble images of Haitian womanhood in the image of Theresa herself, much of the plot revolving around her solitary efforts to warn the great Haitian general Toussaint L'Ouverture of French plans against him. Her efforts require her to leave her mother and sister and to suffer mightily before she ultimately succeeds in her mission and is reunited with a family she feared she had lost.

Whatever its quality as narrative, "Theresa" represents one of the first attempts to confront the Haitian revolution and perhaps the first attempt by an African American writer to create a black romantic heroine. Its author adapted primitivist imagery to describe a Haiti in places free of the French corrupting influences. Making the form more up-to-date, the author evoked Theresa's feelings for her mother and sister and for her country in ways that were well in line with the familial images of popular nineteenth-century literary emphases on emotional ties and strong, mutual feeling as both appropriate for a well-bred young woman and representative of an ideal virtue. The story also laid claim, in keeping with the *Journal*'s own concerns about respectability, to the ability of women of African descent to conform to the highest American ideals of feminine character. It was an important effort to put literature into the service of the kinds of purposes *Freedom's Journal* had outlined for itself from the beginning, broadening the scope of literary purpose to include the validation of an African American self-definition that, in the *Journal* at least, had been a matter of great importance.

The same may be said of the range of other literary works appearing in the *Journal*. Although historically there had been a close connection between the African American voice and issues of color and oppression, *Freedom's Journal* made at least some attempt to broaden the scope of that voice by broadening its range. Several writers contributed poems on such popular, genteel American themes as the death of the beautiful young woman and even on poetry itself. Several writers published often in the *Journal*, including one who signed herself "Rosa," a poet who for some months helped to bring themes of gentility to the paper's readers before bringing her career to an abrupt and unexplained end. That her contributions had been enjoyed and were certain to be missed is clear from a brief, poetic correspondence the paper published in March 1828 between Rosa and one "Frere," a reader who encouraged her to "take thy harp again" and grace the *Journal*'s pages (21 March 1828). Rosa, however, announced in verse an end to her career, a disillusionment with the effort: "Tho' sweet the airs," she said of her songs, "they now afford, / No magic spell upon mine ear" (16 May 1828). Whatever the sources of

Rosa's disillusionment, her presence, along that of others like her, in the *Journal*'s pages, was evidence of a broadening view of literature and literary achievement, one in keeping with the approach to literary activity proclaimed by the *Journal* from its earliest days.

Freedom's Journal ceased publication in March 1829, in part as a result of financial difficulties, even more because the editor, John Russwurm, abruptly decided to shift his position on the incendiary issue of colonization. In mid-February he published a "Candid Acknowledgment of Error," quickly reprinted in the *African Repository*, in which he declared himself "a decided supporter of the American Colonization Society." He continued to express that view, alienating the *Journal*'s longtime supporters and thus hastening the paper's demise. By the end of the year he was in Liberia, beginning what was to be a successful African career.[80]

Even as *Freedom's Journal* was doing its part for the encouragement of African American writing and an African American literary culture, however, other movements and concerns were developing in thinking about that enterprise itself. At least something of the tenor of these developments was captured in an address delivered in Providence by the minister and *Freedom's Journal* agent Hosea Easton on Thanksgiving Day, 1828. Easton, a member of one of Boston's most influential black families and an important community leader in his own right, used the occasion to denounce the hypocrisy of American injustice, along with a "colonizing craft" that he described as "diabolical," and to urge unity and dedication on the part of the free people of color. In a brief passage he also noted how "God has raised up some able ambassadors of truth among our population; and though they are held in contempt by whites, yet God has caused his light to shine through them, to the great shame of our oppressors." Using literary achievement to highlight American hypocrisy, Easton nonetheless went on to emphasize the lesson that would also be brought home through the story of George Moses Horton, emphasizing that it was the contempt and demeaning treatment that such "ambassadors" could not escape, for all their talent and ability. The mood Easton captured was to become more common in upcoming days.[81]

5

The *Liberator* and the Shaping of African American Tradition, 1829–1832

❦

A PERIOD OF just under four years, beginning roughly in the middle of 1829 and extending into 1832, was critical for African American literary life. These years were marked by powerful challenges to African Americans in many parts of the United States that represented real setbacks. They were also marked by new and influential voices and new and significant developments that affected the course of African American literary traditions.

One challenge derived from the demise of *Freedom's Journal*. For six months, beginning in May 1829, one of the *Journal's* founders, Samuel Cornish, attempted to develop a successor publication, *The Rights of All*. The paper had many of the same concerns as its predecessor, while strongly rejecting John Russwurm's turn to colonization. Cornish again hoped to speak, as he had in *Freedom's Journal*, on behalf of African Americans by creating a paper that would "at all times, give a correct representation of that people, in opposition to the persecuting, slanderous accounts so often presented to the public eye." As its supporters hoped, it would allow for communication among people of color, while reaching out to "our white fellow citizens" and "mankind at large." For all its good intentions, however, *The Rights of All* lasted for only six issues, appearing monthly until it ceased publication in October. Cornish had the same problem securing paying subscribers that had plagued *Freedom's Journal*, and he was ultimately unable to keep it going by himself.[1]

Other ventures on the part of African American journalists were similarly plagued, although many people continued to perceive the need for an independent voice. In 1831, for example, John G. Stewart, of Albany, tried to create a new paper, the *African Sentinel and Journal of Liberty*, on the ground that "there should be *at least* one public JOURNAL, conducted by a coloured man, and devoted to the interests of the coloured population throughout this country." The effort was strongly supported by Benjamin Lundy in the *Genius of Universal Emancipation*, where, drawing on what had become firm traditions, Lundy reprinted extracts accompanied by his own endorsements of Stewart's abilities. Tying authority to history, he urged blacks to support the paper in order to "*shew* to your traducers, beyond the power of contradiction, that the African bosom yet glows with the generous emulation that erst nourished the arts and sciences to maturity in Ethiopia and Egypt, while Asia made less pretensions to knowledge and moral grandeur; Europe was involved in barbarism; and America was unknown to the civilized world." The *African Sentinel*, like *The Rights of All*, only lasted for a few issues, but its purposes and its sources of credibility continued to illustrate the framework within which a black voice was recognized and understood.[2]

The continuing need for a black voice was further brought home at the end of the 1820s by what many people perceived to be an increase in episodes of antiblack activity. Most important in terms of immediate impact was the series of actions in Cincinnati aimed at the repression and exclusion of the city's African American population. In 1804 and 1807 Ohio had passed a series of "Black Laws" designed to discourage free people of color from entering the state, including provisions requiring proof of freedom, the posting of a substantial bond, and a guarantee, attested to by at least two white men, of good behavior. The laws were haphazardly enforced, but in 1829 city officials decided to revitalize them.[3]

Cincinnati's whites showed some division over the decision. There was actually some opposition to the enforcement policy from city newspapers; the Cincinnati Colonization Society, predictably, supported it. At least some whites used the policy as a pretext for taking matters into their own hands and decided to expel the black population forcibly, subjecting African Americans in Cincinnati to an onslaught of mob violence.[4]

The Cincinnati oppression also produced a strong reaction, as many of the city's people of color felt compelled to flee the mob or to escape the proscriptions an enforcement of the Black Laws would entail. Delegates from the city's black community began negotiations for land in

Canada on which Cincinnati refugees could settle, and in the end at least eleven hundred people left the city, some for Canada, others for elsewhere in the United States. The events in Cincinnati were extensively covered by Cornish's short-lived newspaper, in which he suggested that "surely the dark ages of heathenism are returning at least, to Ohio." Despite his opposition to the American Colonization Society, Cornish even published positive accounts of life in Canada for the benefit of those considering emigration.[5]

I

There is much to be said about the events in Cincinnati, much of which obviously has little to do with literature. Nevertheless, those events did lead to thinking about the place of African Americans in the realm of public debate. As people sought to respond to those events, they could see both the need for an effective voice and, as Cornish's words made plain, the continuing relevance of existing traditions of representation to asserting that voice in the public realm. Peter Williams Jr., in a sermon delivered on 4 July 1830 for the benefit of Cincinnati refugees, had little difficulty holding the Ohio oppression up to the light of the Declaration of Independence. He denounced the situation as one in which people of color were "deprived of their inalienable rights, by the very men who so loudly rejoice in the declaration, that 'all men are born free and equal.'" Using the sermon to attack the American Colonization Society, noting that "we are natives of this country," he saw in the virtual expulsion of many free people from Cincinnati precisely the kind of involuntary colonization that the society's opponents had feared from the beginning. A group meeting in Rochester, New York, held specifically to respond to the Ohio outrages attributed them to the malign influences of the slaveholder, declaring, "While boasting of liberty, he tramples on the dearest rights of men and is the greatest robber of it on earth."[6]

But these same developments also led to a heightened focus on the need for a more assertive voice, one result of which was the calling of the First National Negro Convention in 1830. One of the moving spirits in the effort, if not *the* moving spirit, was Hezekiah Grice, a Baltimore tradesman who had earlier been involved in the creation of a society to encourage trade with Liberia. His purposes, which became a substantial

focus of the convention, included creating more discussion of emigration, using the Cincinnati situation as a basis for thinking more about the
possibilities of moving to Canada. It was a small group that came together in Philadelphia during the summer of that year, and opinions regarding emigration were divided, but the meeting resulted in a greater
interest in concerted action, in bringing together key figures from around
the nation to address common concerns in what Grice, as well as others,
saw as a setting of heightened oppression. One of the main achievements
of the meeting was to lay the groundwork for subsequent conventions
that were more national in scope.[7]

The convention of 1830, however small, also revealed its participants'
concern for an effective voice, one that could communicate both for and
to African Americans in a difficult era. In this, the convention was part of
a trend begun with the founding of *Freedom's Journal* and continuing
through Cornish's efforts with *The Rights of All*. Under the leadership of
Richard Allen, the group issued an "Address to the Free People of Colour
of these United States" expressing anxiety about the growing trend of discrimination against free people of color "in several States of the Union,
especially that of Ohio," and, citing the Declaration of Independence,
condemning the outrages. The delegates also roundly condemned the
American Colonization Society and, assuming the stance long occupied
by colonization's foes, predicted the society's likely failure to achieve at
least some of its professed aims in Africa: "Tell it not to barbarians, lest
they refuse to be civilised, and eject our Christian missionaries from
among them," Allen and his colleagues declared, "that in the nineteenth
century of the Christian era, laws have been enacted in some of the states
of this great republic, to compel an unprotected and harmless portion of
our brethren, to leave their homes and seek an asylum in foreign climes."
Following Grice's lead, they urged those who could no longer endure
conditions in the United States to consider Canada as a possible refuge
because of its many similarities to the American homeland, save, of
course, that in Canada "no invidious distinction of colour is recognized."[8]

But in ending with a call for a subsequent, larger gathering to be held
the following year, the delegates also encouraged changes among African
Americans, urging efforts to help blacks in America achieve economic
independence through training and education. "That our mental and

physical qualities have not been more actively engaged in pursuits more lasting is attributable in great measure," they said, "to a want of unity among ourselves," as well as to a willingness to settle for the kinds of menial trades in which so many urban free people of color were engaged.[9]

In language and concern the address of the 1830 convention was but one of many documents that showed the impact of one of the most influential works from the era, *David Walker's Appeal, In Four Articles; Together With A Preamble, to the Coloured Citizens of the World, but In Particular, and Very Expressly, to Those of the United States of America.* The work initially appeared in 1829 and went through three editions, each succeeding edition stronger than its predecessor, prior to Walker's sudden, mysterious death in 1830. The delegates were aware of Walker's work, Grice, for example, having come across it several months prior to the convention. The call for unity, the encouragement of education and ambition, and the condemnation of American hypocrisy all had recently been highlighted for Grice, Allen, and their associates by Walker's *Appeal*.[10]

Since his days as an agent for *Freedom's Journal* Walker had become an increasingly visible figure in Boston's African American community. In 1828 he played a major role in the formation of a new organization, the Massachusetts General Colored Association. In a major address to the group at the end of the year he anticipated the kinds of concerns that Allen's group would express in Philadelphia a year and a half later. In his 1828 address Walker expressed hopes that the Massachusetts General Colored Association would help black people achieve unity not only in Boston but "so far, through the United States of America, as may be practicable and expedient." He was aware of some of the same problems the Philadelphia group noted as well, anticipating some of their more specific arguments. "Now, that we are disunited, is a fact," and a major factor "in keeping us from rising to the scale of reasonable and thinking human beings," Walker said, asking, "Do not two hundred and eight years of very intolerable sufferings teach us the actual necessity of a general unity among us?" Recognizing the presence of "good friends" among the whites, Walker nevertheless argued that only unified, independent action by American people of color could ameliorate the oppression they faced. And recalling traditional ideas of providence, he concluded with his belief "that God has something in reserve for us, which, when he shall have poured it out upon us, will repay us for all our suffering and miseries."[11]

As Walker's biographer Peter Hinks has emphasized, the Massachusetts association was not the only group of its kind created during this period, and Walker's call for unity was part of a trend that was evident in many places and was epitomized in the plans of the 1830 convention at Philadelphia. But Walker's *Appeal* was the most powerful statement of that trend, and its language and conceptualization had major implications for an emerging African American literary culture.[12]

There was much to connect Walker's *Appeal* to past traditions in the literature of African Americans. As Hinks has noted, Walker drew heavily on the ideas of ancient African greatness that had played a part in thinking about African Americans since the opening of the nineteenth century. He also drew heavily on such more recent accounts as those appearing in the *African Repository* and *Freedom's Journal* when he described "the sons of Africa or of Ham, among whom learning originated, and was carried thence into Greece, where it was improved upon and refined." He drew on a still older tradition with a double-edged use of Egyptian history, likening the slavery of Africans in America to that of Israel in Egypt, while declaring that "the condition of the Israelites was better under the Egyptians than ours is under the whites." Echoing earlier generations, he compared the histories of Europe and Africa to relativize the concept of barbarism, saying that European history revealed a people who acted "more like devils than accountable men."[13]

Much of the pamphlet was taken up with Walker's attack on colonization. He quoted copiously from such leading figures in the colonization society as Henry Clay to establish the nefariousness of the organization and its program. In words that echoed the earliest African American memorials against the society, he said, "America is more our country, than it is the whites—we have enriched it with our *blood and tears*. The greatest riches in all America have arisen from our blood and tears."[14]

At the same time, Walker also caught, and built on, the mood Hosea Easton had captured only a short time before, expressing an anger that, if anything, went beyond Easton's. Some of this anger was encapsulated in his powerfully negative view of whites and in his calls for revolutionary violence to overthrow the system. The calls were connected, as implied in his 1828 address, to a strong sense of the power of providence, as well as to an assertion not only of the right but also of the necessity to revolt against oppression. God, he declared to his readers, "will give you a Hannibal, and when the Lord shall have raised him up, and given him to you for your possession, O my suffering brethren! remember the divisions and consequent sufferings of *Carthage* and of *Hayti*."[15]

But most significant was Walker's building on traditions of African American moral superiority going back to Coker, even to Wheatley, achieving a directness that, looking to tradition, went far beyond his predecessors. Some of this was conveyed, as it had been implicitly by earlier writers, in his vision of the comparative histories of Europe and Africa, which led him to conclude that Africans "never were half so avaricious, deceitful and unmerciful as the whites, according to their knowledge." This sense of moral superiority structured virtually all of Walker's *Appeal*, and he built on traditional modes of expression to reinforce it.[16]

At the center of every article making up the *Appeal* was an indictment of American hypocrisy. Continually, Walker set himself up as the black observer who by virtue of his status was positioned to see the hypocrisy of American life, which white Americans (whom he referred to consistently as simply "Americans") were unable to recognize. Recounting that hypocrisy, he pointed to the failure of Americans to live up to the professions of the Declaration of Independence, from which he quoted extensively. And as a dedicated Christian himself, he reserved special venom for the failure of "Americans" to live up to their own professed Christian ideals.

But perhaps Walker's most revealing use of the moral stance he adopted was in his treatment of Thomas Jefferson. The refutation of Jefferson's imprecations on Africans and their descendants in the *Notes on the State of Virginia* was central to Walker's pamphlet. He brought up the *Notes* frequently, condemning Jefferson's characterization of "difference of colour" as "unfortunate," especially Jefferson's statement that "I advance it therefore as a suspicion only" that blacks are "*inferior* to the whites in the endowments both of body and mind." According to Walker, this passage "has in truth injured us more, and has been as great a barrier to our emancipation as any thing that has ever been advanced against us."[17]

The significance Walker attached to the attack on Jefferson—creating a relationship between himself as a black author and Jefferson as both a historical figure and a white American—was directly connected to the stance he assumed in his pamphlet. At one level, Walker emphasized this connection by adopting a voice and a persona that many others had used. It was a voice using irony and a black authorial stance to undermine, as others had, Jeffersonian claims of white racial superiority. Thus, having reviewed not only Jefferson's remarks but, within a few pages, the comparative histories of Africa and Europe, he came to a tentative conclusion, "divested of prejudice either on the side of my colour or that of the whites." He felt compelled, he said, to "advance my suspicion of them, whether they are *as good by nature* as we are or not." With evidence at least as strong as Jefferson's, he combined refutation with parody in a way that reinforced the stance implicit throughout the pamphlet. With his stress on American hypocrisy, Walker placed himself as the superior observer on a topic into which history, no less than experience, gave him particular insight.[18]

For Walker, however, the superior position seems to have implied a need for an exclusiveness in black authorship that few of his predecessors ever suggested. To some extent, Walker drew on older motifs of literary exemplification when, talking about the need to refute Jefferson, he wrote, "Let no one suppose that the refutations which have been written by our white friends are enough," adding, "they are *whites*,—we are *blacks*." The act of refutation by blacks was in itself a part of the argument against Jefferson since it would show intelligence and reason.[19]

But Walker seems to have meant something more, something he captured toward the end of the pamphlet, in a tribute to Richard Allen, whom he had long idolized. "When the Lord shall raise up coloured historians in succeeding generations, to present the crimes of this nation, to the then gazing world, the Holy Ghost will make them do justice to the name of Bishop Allen, of Philadelphia," wrote Walker. The implications of the comment were profound, not only reinvoking the hand of providence in black history and destiny but emphasizing the extent to which the full story of that history, and of American history generally, would only be told when people of African descent began to write their own accounts. Whites, in Walker's view, could not, and would not, accurately represent black people to a broader world.[20]

In his assertion that only blacks could speak for blacks, Walker went beyond even *Freedom's Journal*. The *Journal*, after all, continued to find virtue in white representations. Moreover, Walker's views on authorship were not to have immediate impact on other black writers of the era. As will become apparent, they were to be mooted over the next several years by antislavery events that reinvigorated, rather than undermined, ideals of an interracial community of discourse. But Walker's contribution is not to be dismissed, for, if anything, it had much to do with that very reinvigoration, despite what Walker said.

Walker's *Appeal* was widely circulated in both the North and the South, and it was immediately controversial. The immediate controversy focused largely on what many saw as its incendiary character, its call for revolution. Walker tried to ensure that it would circulate in the South as well the North, and with some success. It was seized in Charleston; and the man charged with bringing it into the city was sentenced to a fine and a term in jail for encouraging "sedition" among the slaves. The grand jury's indictment stressed what appeared to be the *Appeal*'s incitements to violence, including Walker's hope for a new Hannibal to create a new Carthage. But reactions were sharp elsewhere as well. At least one southern state, North Carolina, instituted restrictions of black literacy in part as a response to Walker's work.[21]

The anxiety Walker inspired was reinforced by others. Walker's was not the only radical piece to appear during the period. Its messianism resembled, for example, that found in another 1829 pamphlet, Robert Young's *Ethiopian Manifesto*. Young also took a strongly prophetic stance in attempting "to call together the black people as a nation in themselves," while predicting the coming of a "leader" who would vindicate the rights of Africans in America. Young's was a vividly imagined projection, looking toward God's final vengeance on the American slaveholders.[22]

Nor was Walker's the only African American voice to produce a strong reaction. At least as important was that of the Virginia slave rebel Nat Turner, whose *Confessions*, rendered by the Virginia lawyer Thomas Gray, were published only about a year after the final edition of *Walker's Appeal*, shortly after Turner's execution, and were widely disseminated. This document has been deeply analyzed. Such scholars as William Andrews, Eric Sundquist, Mary Kemp Davis, and Kenneth Greenberg have done much to explore the complexities of its creation, the problems of distinguishing Gray's voice from Turner's, the problems inherent in trying to figure out who was controlling whom as Turner sought to force Gray to take his revelations of divine inspiration seriously and Gray sought to re-assure his readers that Turner was an aberration, an isolated fanatic whose actions had few implications for the health of slavery as a system. The problems are in many ways reminiscent of those facing white colo-nizationists who, in such documents as the 1826 Baltimore memorial of the free people of color, sought to create a convincingly black voice to serve their cause.[23]

In many ways Gray's effort reflected the diffusion of traditions in African American literature dating back to Jupiter Hammon and Phillis Wheatley. Perversely, it engaged in the same forms of authentication, a matter that, as Sundquist has noted, was of great importance to Gray himself. Gray declared he had committed Turner's statements to writing and published them "with little or no variation, from his own words," and he "annexed" the testimony of members of the Southampton County Court bearing witness to the document's authenticity based on Turner's approval of them when they were read in open court.[24]

Whether Turner or Gray was influenced by what could be read in the pages written by David Walker or Robert Young—and the matter was de-bated at the time, as it continues to be—the rendering of Turner's voice was credible enough to convince most observers of the *Confessions'* au-thenticity. The possibility of such a figure as Turner had been anticipated by Walker and Young. There was, in addition, much to place Turner's narrative within the larger traditions of African American spiritual auto-biography, especially as Turner was made to recount a near instanta-neous, miraculous literacy and a series of visions and revelations taken to be direct contact with God. Whether recording or creating the words of a black revolutionary, Gray's *Confessions* demonstrate, at the very least, how powerful certain conventions had become for framing a credible African American voice.

II

Such framing may help explain why the *Confessions* were taken as au-thentic by, most notably, one of the more seasoned white readers of African American writing, the emerging antislavery editor William Lloyd Garrison. In his first year as editor of the *Liberator*, when he was taking his place as a leading figure in the antislavery movement, Garrison did not find it difficult to accept the *Confessions* as genuine. He could even argue sarcastically that the pamphlet was so likely to create "among the blacks admiration for the character of Nat" that Gray and the pamphlet's printers ought to be subject to the same penalties as those that had been legislated against Walker—and himself—in many southern states. Although Garrison too was convinced that Turner was a fanatic, he saw nothing in the document itself to make him doubt its authenticity.[25]

Such voices as Turner's and Walker's played a major role in the formation of Garrison's own antislavery views. Garrison became aware of Walker's work soon after its publication and was highly impressed by it. He seems to have been the one who introduced it to Hezekiah Grice prior to the 1830 Philadelphia convention, remarking that "it was too early to have published such a book." At the time, the New Englander Garrison was working with Benjamin Lundy in Baltimore, assisting him with the *Genius of Universal Emancipation*. Reviewing the *Appeal* for Lundy's paper, he gave it a mixed notice. He described it as "a most injudicious publication," a view he shared with Lundy, who suggested that "acrimonious language should not be indulged, and even revengeful feeling should be repressed, as much as possible."[26]

At the same time, Walker's insurrectionist threats seemed quite credible to Garrison. As Robert Abzug has noted, Garrison believed that a race war was imminent in America if slavery was not abolished. Garrison saw in Walker's pamphlet a confirmation of his fears, and, as Abzug has also argued, he saw in those fears reason enough to adopt an immediatist position on the abolition of slavery. The pamphlet did much to encourage Garrison to focus his lifework on agitating against slavery through organization and, as a journalist, through the publication of a journal, the *Liberator*, devoted to the immediatist cause. He became still more determined when Turner's revolt occurred within months of the journal's inception.[27]

Such violent works as those of Walker and Turner were not, however, the only factors encouraging Garrison's move either to immediatism or to journalism. As Benjamin Quarles argued many years ago, Garrison's growing familiarity with people of color, beginning in the 1820s, had already led him to rethink many of his beliefs about slavery and about the place of people of color in American society. While working with Lundy he had developed ties with such leading men of color as Jacob Greener and William Watkins, the "Colored Baltimorean." By the time of the *Liberator*'s creation he had also become close to James Forten, who was to provide him substantial financial support, and to other prominent African American figures.[28]

What such ties meant in terms of the *Liberator* is revealed most clearly by the way Garrison and his black supporters talked about the paper and its purposes from the beginning. On the eve of the first issue, James Forten put the paper in the same framework that had helped define *Freedom's Journal* and other pioneering African American efforts. He expressed his hope for the *Liberator*'s success, congratulating both Garrison and Lundy for their efforts to "plead our cause," and his wish that Garrison's journal would be the means of "disposing these clouds of error, and of bringing many advocates to our cause." As the journal began its career, other black readers made the same point. A group of Philadelphians meeting in March 1831 urged support of Garrison's venture, describing the *Liberator* as "a noble and praiseworthy advocate in our behalf" (12 March 1831), one of many testimonials from black supporters Garrison reprinted in the paper.[29]

That he chose to print such testimonials is indicative of how important black support, and the black voice, was to Garrison. In responding appreciatively to one such testimonial, for example, he wrote that his correspondents' remarks had outweighed "in consolation all the abuse which has been heaped upon me." More importantly, he reprinted both the testimonial and his response in the pages of the *Liberator*, and made clear that his response was being made public at the request of its recipients.[30]

Such a series of exchanges suggests the uses Garrison and his supporters found for each other in the tumultuous conditions of the early 1830s. On the one hand, the testimonials indicate how much Forten and others felt they needed, and appreciated, a visible white champion. Thus, the very presence of the *Liberator* seems to have encouraged a dedication to the cause on the part of at least some pioneering black abolitionists, as Jehiel Beman and Sarah Douglass, for example, were later to testify. There was a feeling of being less than alone in an increasingly exclusionary America.[31]

On the other hand, these exchanges suggest that Garrison was eager to demonstrate that he had achieved black approval. This eagerness may have resulted, in part, from his need for black subscribers. Victor Ullman reports that blacks accounted for about 75 percent of the paper's subscription base during its earliest years. Still, these published testimonials also suggest that Garrison really did have an interest in what black people had to say, founded on the kinds of contacts he had already learned to value. In this, the testimonials clearly related to goals of interracial community that James Brewer Stewart has noted, more generally, at the founding of an immediatist abolition movement. This did not mean the rejection of color altogether. As Garrison's celebration of black support indicates, he continued to privilege the black voice primarily because it was black. But it did mean the creation of a common enterprise, bringing together individuals of like mind and attributes, across the color line, to reinforce one another in the battle against slavery and racial inequality.[32]

The testimonials Garrison received and his celebration of them suggest the extent to which he and his supporters saw the *Liberator* as an expression of such a common effort. They may also suggest that in publishing them Garrison was at least implicitly responding to David Walker's contention that only blacks should, or could, speak for blacks. Showing black approval for his efforts, Garrison also demonstrated the possibility for an interracial effort to achieve accurate representation. The testimonials, perhaps spurred by Walker's ideas, testified not only to the propriety of Garrison's journalistic efforts but also to his own place in the community he wanted to help create.

Reply to Walker or not, the *Liberator* developed policies that encouraged the kind of reciprocal relationships of influence and advocacy Forten, Garrison, and others had outlined and experienced since before the paper's founding. Such policies were evident, to some extent, in the *Liberator*'s treatment of David Walker. Donald Jacobs has suggested that, arriving in Boston, planning his journal, and realizing his need for black support, Garrison also discovered how much Boston's African Americans had admired Walker and appreciated his ideas. Whether simply to gain their support, as Jacobs suggests, or in keeping with ideals of interracial discussion, Garrison offered a decidedly evenhanded treatment of Walker's pamphlet in his paper. He included, over several issues in April and May 1831, a series of essays on the pamphlet by a white correspondent that, despite the writer's reservations about Walker's violent language, constituted a largely favorable commentary (which Garrison answered in footnotes) on the work.[33]

Previous to that series Garrison also published an exchange on Walker's *Appeal* by two black writers. Signing themselves "Leo" and "J.I.W.," the two differed sharply on the pamphlet. "Leo," in words Garrison too would use in reference to abolitionism, declared himself opposed to the pamphlet on the ground that "we are forbidden, by high authority, to do evil that good may come," and cited, as well, the crackdown on black expression that had occurred in North Carolina and elsewhere in the South (29 January 1831). His respondent urged him to read the pamphlet for himself, seeing in Leo precisely the kind of "colored man" Walker had condemned, one who let whites do his thinking for him (5 February 1831). Occurring early in the history of the *Liberator*, the exchange showed the kind of credibility the paper itself was to give to the black voice and the extent to which African Americans themselves saw it as a medium for debate both within and outside the community.

But a far more important clue to the *Liberator*'s purposes was the stance the paper took on colonization, and the way that stance was presented. The *Liberator*'s stance on colonization reflected the role African Americans had played in shaping Garrison's own views on the issue. Interest in colonization remained significant as the *Liberator* was getting under way. Canada remained a destination of some interest because, as one Brooklyn correspondent suggested, people of color were "received there by the Canadians as brethren and fellow subjects to his Majesty King William IV" (7 April 1832). Others began to think of Mexico, which offered a more hospitable climate and, a "free colored Floridian" suggested, was "entirely free from all prejudice against complexion."[34]

The *Liberator*'s approach to colonization was largely inspired, however, by the American Colonization Society's continuing efforts to publicize black support. The society had continued to solicit testimonials from satisfied colonists in Liberia for publication in the United States. In 1832, for example, the Maryland society published a little book called *News from Africa*, aimed at a readership among the free people of color in that state. The book contained a letter from George McGill, one of those involved in the 1826 memorial, celebrating the freedom he had found in Liberia, where, he declared, "the black face out-shines the white." The *African Repository* also printed a letter it had received from "a freeman of colour in Charleston" citing events in Ohio and elsewhere as proof of the depths of prejudice among Americans and suggesting Liberia as the only alternative for those who wished to be truly free.[35]

The purposes of the society were made especially clear in the case of Solomon Bayley, whose autobiography had appeared in the middle of the preceding decade. By 1827 he had decided to emigrate, and a white supporter, Willard Hall, had written to the society to ask for assistance. Hall pointed out that Bayley "can read and write" and that he was widely respected "among people of his colour," as well as "among the most respectable of our citizens." Hall felt that "should he go to Liberia and his life be spared"—Bayley was about sixty years old at the time—"he would be useful in making known that country to our coloured population and exciting a spirit of emigration among them."[36]

The society found a place for Bayley and about 1832 brought out his *Brief Account of the Colony of Liberia.* He acknowledged the problems emigration presented, especially the continuing high level of mortality among settlers and the "privations" facing those who encountered Liberia's frontier conditions. But he also noted that the "colored man in America, whether bond or free, is not likely, while living among the whites, to enjoy those civil rights and privileges, and opportunities of improvement" that should be his by right of birth. Liberia, "the land of his fathers," offered a more hopeful prospect for the future.[37]

The society also drew heavily on the services of John Russwurm, by this time settled in Liberia and editor of a paper there, the *Liberia Herald,* at least some copies of which circulated in the United States as well as in Africa. Russwurm too published testimonials to what was positive in the Liberian experience. Drawing on a tradition developed first in the *Repository,* Russwurm connected hopes for the Liberian venture with larger matters of history. He described the settlers as "pilgrims in search of Liberty," adding, "It is our duty to profit by the wisdom of those who have gone before us. I refer particularly to the pilgrim fathers of New England." Even more, he described a hope for Africa, and a credibility for the venture, in that greater history tying the present to the ancient past, to an Africa that could "claim the invention of letters" and whose primacy in literature, remnants of which remained visible in the demoralized tribes of the African coast, held hope for a civilization that could be realized again.[38]

By the time he founded the *Liberator* William Lloyd Garrison was deeply interested in the issue of colonization, having moved from moderate support for the society and its efforts to, by 1829, outright opposition to a venture he considered morally bankrupt. This new position was largely the result of Greener and Watkins's influence in Baltimore, especially that of Watkins, whose letters to Lundy's *Genius of Universal Emancipation* had done much to spread the anticolonizationist position. Garrison's change in position was also likely influenced by the stridently anticolonizationist language of Walker's *Appeal.*[39]

As Garrison worked to begin the *Liberator*, his African American supporters continued to instruct him in the ways of the colonization society. James Forten, for example, wrote to him in February 1831 complaining about a New Jersey woman who had made a sizable bequest to the society. Forten suggested that the money would have been better spent "to remove prejudice, improve the condition of the colored people by education and by having their children placed in a situation to learn a trade." He also noted that several of the founders of the society had promised to emancipate their slaves and send them to Africa; not one, said Forten, had kept the promise. It is not surprising that when Garrison began to speak out against colonization he revealed the influence of such figures as Greener, Watkins, and Forten and his familiarity, in general, with anticolonization arguments people of color had been developing since the colonization society's creation.[40]

The *Liberator* was to embody the kind of collaborative effort its supporters had seen as a part of its purposes, this time in opposition to colonization. The nature of that effort is exemplified by Garrison's adoption of the rhetoric of opposition long used by African Americans in response to the American Colonization Society. On a tour of the major eastern cities Garrison spoke before black audiences in an effort to build opposition to colonization and support for the *Liberator*. In these addresses he reminded his audiences that "you are no more natives of Africa" than the colonizationists should be considered "natives of Great Britain." As African Americans had done for the preceding decade and a half, and within the framework exploited by Walker only about a year before, Garrison denounced colonization as "a libel upon humanity and justice—a libel upon republicanism—a libel upon the Declaration of Independence—a libel upon christianity."[41]

African Americans continued to encourage Garrison's effort, and he continued to make clear how important that encouragement was to him. In the preface to a printing of what must have been the version of the address delivered in several places, he made clear that his remarks were being published at the request of his "colored brethren, in the various cities" where he had spoken. Whatever his motives, his effort to demonstrate black approval for his assuming the role of anticolonization spokesperson created the kind of discursive situation he and his supporters had hoped for, drawing on the resources of each to carry their message to a broader world.[42]

No less revealing of this project was the way the *Liberator* became a primary outlet for the publication of African American statements on the subject. In April 1831 the resolutions of a Baltimore anticolonization meeting appeared in the paper, declaring the society to be "founded more in a selfish policy, than in the true principles of benevolence." Garrison himself added editorially, "With such a knowledge of the feelings of the colored people—feelings which ought to be tenderly regarded—will really benevolent men continue to sustain this Society?" (2 April 1831). In October the address of a group in Rochester appeared, pointing out that "we do not consider Africa to be our home, any more than the present whites do England, Scotland, or Ireland" and declaring opposition to colonization and, significantly, declaring their intention "to do all in our power to support the Liberator, printed by Mr Garrison, and all other works in our behalf" (29 October 1831).

Letters from free men and women of color denouncing the society also appeared fairly often. In February and March "A Colored Philadelphian," probably James Forten, wrote to remind colonizationists that "we consider the United States our home, and not Africa as they wish to make us believe." Summarizing much that had been recently discussed, the writer noted, "If we do emigrate, it will be to a place or our own choice" (12 February 1831). The writer reiterated a suggestion that Forten had made to Garrison privately that free people would be better served if those devoting resources to the society were to help "establish good schools for our children as well as theirs, give them trades, and encourage them after they have become masters of their own businesses" (19 March 1831).

Such letters became a staple for the *Liberator,* as writers played upon conventions going back to 1817. "Hannibal," in a letter published on 12 March 1831, derided colonizationists as "boasters of freedom" and supported Forten's contention that "Afric's injured race" would be better aided by support in the United States. In the same issue Robert Roberts, a leading figure in the Boston anticolonization movement, heaped scorn on colonizationist "schemers" and society propaganda, suggesting that if Africa "flowed with milk and honey, you would not send a colored person to it." Subsequent letters from black writers remained firmly within the framework of convention. For example, John B. Vashon wrote: "Why establish a Society for the purpose of inducing the African to forsake this soil which he has enriched with his labor and watered with his tears; which the violence and rapacity of Europe and America have made his native land?" (31 March 1832).

The *Liberator* thus became a major forum for opposition to the American Colonization Society conveyed in ways consistent with the paper's aims and purposes. In 1832 Garrison supplemented this effort with the publication of a lengthy book devoted to making the case against the society, his *Thoughts on African Colonization.* The book was divided into three parts, two of which, following David Walker's lead, were intended to damn the society through its own words and those of its supporters, supplemented by Garrison's commentary. But particularly important was the second, middle part of the book, entitled "Sentiments of the People of Colour," in which Garrison documented black objections to the society and its schemes by quoting extensively from those objections. In keeping with his purposes and with his understanding of the peculiar circumstances of the black voice in American history, Garrison also sought to document the independence of that black opposition. Noting that he had been accused of actually creating a position for African Americans, he cited the lengthy, pre-Garrisonian history of black opposition, going back to 1817, and said that "their sentiments were familiar to me long before they knew my own."[43]

Garrison reprinted a wide range of documents in representing the sentiments of the people of color. He republished the earliest memorials from Philadelphia, Richmond, and elsewhere. He reprinted excerpts from letters addressed originally to the *Liberator* and to such other journals as the short-lived *African Sentinel*. Earlier anticolonization remarks from Hosea Easton and other prominent figures also appeared. Many of the expressions of sentiment came, however, from the kinds of public statements he had encouraged during his 1831 tour. These statements showed very clearly the essence of the anticolonization argument as it had diffused among free people of color. Virtually all stressed their authors' claims on citizenship as "natives of the United States" whose role in the country's creation entitled them to all the rights and privileges of citizenship. Virtually all concluded that Americans of African descent would be better served by encouragement, education, and support than by removal to a hostile and alien environment. Many suggested that should they remove, it should be to a place of their own choosing, "without asking the consent of a slaveholding party."[44]

Garrison's *Thoughts on African Colonization* was a more elaborate version of the framework for the development of a black voice created initially in the *Liberator*, for it drew at least some of its authority from the presentation of that voice, from investing it with a unique credibility that made such a voice crucial to a complete discussion of the colonization issue. And it is indicative of how African Americans understood their distinctive role that a black proponent of colonization had written to the *Liberator* in its early days, prior to the publication of Garrison's book, demanding a right to be heard in the colonization society's defense: "When you reflect that it is *my color* that is to be benefited by the Colonization system, you will acknowledge that I have a right to speak of those who would deteriorate its usefulness" (13 August 1831). It is a measure of the *Liberator*'s attempt to create a forum for African American voices that the letter appeared at all.

III

The issue of colonization and Garrison's understanding of the debate did much to define a more general relationship between the *Liberator* and an African American literary enterprise. Most significantly, black writers viewed the *Liberator* as an outlet for their efforts and contributed to it from the beginning. James Forten, who appeared often in the early issues encouraged his children to contribute as well, which they did. Forten told Garrison that the paper had quickly "roused up a Spirit in our Young People, that had been slumbering for years, and we shall produce writers able to vindicate our cause."[45]

At the same time, Garrison himself understood the importance of black literary effort. Whenever he printed a piece by a black writer, Garrison made sure to introduce it with the notation "By a colored person," or, often, "By a colored female." Black writers themselves joined in the effort. James Forten seems to have continued using "A Man of Color," and William Watkins remained "A Colored Baltimorean." Others used pseudonyms with fairly clear African associations, such as "Hannibal" or "Leo." Those who avoided such eponymous forms at least called attention to their color in their texts.

The relationship between black authorship and Garrison's enterprise was illustrated especially well by Garrison's introduction to a letter from "a colored resident of Georgia," who wrote, in a manner recalling the words of James Forten more than three decades earlier, "Although our senses are blunted and our spirits depressed by ignorance and slavery, yet the most abject and ignorant among us (thanks to the cupidity of the white man) are enabled by education, not only to express our feelings verbally, but to communicate them by writing to others." Providing his own assessment of the power of the word, the writer saw it as something that could prove black capability. Garrison seconded the assessment, saying that the letter displayed "talents highly creditable to its author," even as he printed the letter as testimony to black support for his own endeavors (11 February 1832).

The effort seems to have produced the desired effect. One white veteran of the abolition movement, looking back from 1865, recalled: "When I was young, there were no allusions to colored people in the newspapers, unless it was some grotesque caricature, pretending to be 'Cuffe's Speech at the Great Bobolition Meeting.'" The *Liberator*, "its columns full of speeches by intelligent colored men and women before audiences of educated white people," had created precisely the sort of alternative scenario for a black voice, and for the role that voice could play, that Forten, Garrison, and others had hoped for. Creating such a scenario was a big part of what the paper was about.[46]

The conventions, the themes, and, implicitly, the personae black writers assumed in the *Liberator* all accorded with the paper's purposes, giving credibility to both voice and journal alike. Because of the forum, as well as the possibilities for dialogue across the color line, that the *Liberator* provided, works by African American contributors presented images of people of color to a larger world that were consistent with hopes for the abolition of slavery and for a world of equality; at the same time, they helped cement the most significant conventions of African American thought and letters.

African American representations in the *Liberator* were many and varied, but they built on and helped consolidate earlier traditions. Most significantly, African Americans appeared in the paper's pages as exemplars of American virtues and African American achievement. Such an emphasis was in keeping with the paper's goals and with its supporters' ideals. Early on, as James Brewer Stewart has noted, notions of "respectability" were seen by many abolitionists, including such figures as Forten, Watkins, and Garrison, as a basis for that interracial community the *Liberator* attempted to foster. It also underlay such pioneering enterprises as the ultimately unsuccessful interracial effort in 1831 to create a college for young black men in New Haven. Writing to the *Liberator*, the college's black supporters cited the role of education in "cultivating the heart, restraining the passions, and improving the manners," whatever other skills its training might provide (24 September 1831). Although the effort's failure, as a result of white opposition, was to have implications of its own, the effort was an important indication of that community of respectability in which Forten, Garrison, and others put such faith.[47]

Perhaps the most important statement of such views within the framework of the *Liberator* was to be found in the speaking and writings of Maria Stewart, an admirer of David Walker, whose early career coincided with the paper's early years. Her works were reprinted and widely publicized in its pages, as well as in pamphlets issued by Garrison's press, and with his encouragement. Deeply religious, Stewart shared Walker's gift for strong language and his familiarity with biblical and secular history. She did much to consolidate traditions in African American literary culture as well.[48]

Stewart also shared many of Walker's and Garrison's views. Addressing black and white readers alike, in her first tract, "Religion and the Pure Principles of Morality, the Sure Foundation on which We Must Build," a piece that also appeared in the *Liberator* in October 1831, Stewart joined Walker and others in urging the importance of unity among the "sons and daughters of Africa" and reminded blacks and whites alike that a "sable hue" did not make one inferior in the sight of God. In keeping with the anticolonization sentiments all three held, she reminded readers that people of African descent had "enriched the soils of America with their tears and blood."[49]

Her indictments of American hypocrisy—like Walker, she distinguished "Americans" from Africa's descendants, despite her strong anticolonizationism—were as strong as Walker's, as strong as any in tradition, even as her prophecies of divine retribution echoed Walker's and Garrison's. "Oh, America, America, foul and indelible is thy stain!" Stewart declared. "The blood of her murdered ones cries to heaven for vengeance against thee" (39). Vengeance is God's, Stewart said, "and he will repay" (40). Like many, she assured her white readers that "our souls are fired with the same love of liberty and independence with which your souls are fired" (40), and the day could not be far off when, with God's direction, God's justice would triumph in America.

Still, much of Stewart's message focused on the need for "improvement" among the free people of color. "Oh, then, turn your attention to knowledge and improvement," Stewart concluded, "for knowledge is power. And God is able to fill you with wisdom and understanding, and to dispel your fears." Stewart's view that people of African descent had no hope for overcoming slavery and oppression without "improvement" led her to condemn failures she saw among the free people of color almost as vociferously as she did those among white Americans. She saw those failures as damaging to possibilities for concerted action, much as had the delegates at the early conventions; however, she could also write that "considering how little we have to excite or stimulate us, I am almost astonished that there are so many industrious and ambitious ones to be found" (46–47).

Stewart also believed that the improvements she advocated could help breach the color line. At some points, certainly, she appeared to echo Walker, as well as Hosea Easton, on the intractability of prejudice. In an 1832 address, for example, she lamented that no matter how accomplished young women of color might become, "it is impossible for them to rise above the condition of servants" given the power of white prejudice. Nevertheless she reached an optimistic conclusion: "Yet, after all, methinks were the American free people of color to turn their attention more assiduously to moral worth and intellectual improvement, this would be the result: prejudice would gradually diminish, and the whites would be compelled to say, unloose the fetters!" (46).

But Stewart's writings are particularly important for what they reveal about the role of gender in emerging abolitionist notions about respectability and improvement. So far as possibilities for African American development were concerned, Stewart was especially interested in the possibilities for free women of color. She argued that women of African descent had a special obligation to be virtuous and conform to the rules of right conduct in their roles as wives and mothers, to encourage their husbands to act boldly and live prudently and to raise children who were upright in their minds and manners. She saw women's improvement as a major part of the battle against prejudice. Not only might it help combat white illusions but it might also affect free men of color. "Did the daughters of our land possess a delicacy of manners, combined with gentleness and dignity, did their pure minds hold vice in abhorrence and contempt, did they frown when their ears were polluted with its vile accents, would not their influence become powerful?" (31). Stewart suggested that their influence would spur men to higher ambitions, and women would become examples of what black womanhood could be.

In offering such a vision of women's role in improvement Stewart was not, of course, departing very far from the gender ideals of her time. In the first decades of the nineteenth century an increasing value was placed in America on gentility, conceived as a matter of manners and refinement. There was also an increasingly firm association of respectability, gentility, and what were considered feminine virtues, including that "delicacy of manners" Stewart praised in her remarks. Certainly, such a vision did not offer only silence or subordination for women in the larger world; neither Stewart's words nor her career would support such an interpretation. But it does point toward a notion of respectability like that informing the creation of the *Liberator,* of a respectability based on education and a common culture, that many Americans would have understood.

On this, too, Stewart's views were not far from Garrison's, which may account for the encouragement he gave her. The kinds of gender ideals Stewart upheld also guided Garrison's efforts, at least in the *Liberator's* early years. Moreover, Garrison had offered a message of uplift himself as he traveled around the country in 1831 to up support for his journal and opposition to colonization, declaring to his black audiences that self-respect "is a lever which will lift you out of the depths of degradation, and establish your feet upon a rock, and put a song of victory into your mouths—victory over prejudice, pride and oppression." His was not simply a message of paternalism. Reflecting on friendships he had already made, he anticipated Stewart by praising the abilities already demonstrated by free people of color to achieve "respectability and affluence" in the face of the worst oppression, sarcastically noting his agreement "with the sentiment of Mr. Jefferson, that men must be prodigies who can retain their manners and morals under such circumstances."[50]

Because the ideals of moral improvement Stewart and Garrison held dear were so widely realized among free people of color, their expression, exemplification, and encouragement also played an important role in the kind of writing that appeared among those who sought to reach a sympathetic audience through the pages of the *Liberator*. The literary enterprise was itself seen as a force for both self-representation and uplift, a part of a more general effort at "mental cultivation" that, as one Philadelphia woman suggested, "not only beautifies and renders life a blessing, but it will irradiate the gloomy vale of death." Not simply knowledge but "mental cultivation," as this Philadelphian termed it, helped to instill the kind of purity and gentility Stewart and others felt should be prized (8 December 1832). Another correspondent, a "Man of Color," saw this possibility even in the contemplation of the literary achievements of people of African descent. "O Capitien, Sancho, Vassa, and Cugoano! send back your ambitious spirits into the bosom of your brethren, that they may sweetly repose under the shadow of your wisdom, and meditate upon your virtues with great delight," he implored, indicating the continuing life of some of the earliest works in an Anglo-African literary tradition among black readers, while redefining the purposes of those works under the rubric of uplift and exemplary virtues among the free people of color (19 February 1831).

This aspect of literary activity, as the historian Elizabeth McHenry has shown, figured no less significantly in the founding of a number of literary societies during this time. The first, in Philadelphia, predated Garrison's work, but some of the more significant were not only contemporary with the *Liberator* but also part of that interaction that made the paper so important. This was the case of a Philadelphia women's society founded in 1831. Its founders saw their purpose as trying to "break down the strong barrier of prejudice, and raise ourselves to an equality with those of our fellow beings who differ from us in complexion, but who are, with ourselves, children of one Eternal Parent."[51]

Garrison attended a meeting of the society, which he told one of the founders, Sarah Douglass, he saw as "a proof of the appreciation of knowledge by your sex," adding that it "puts a new weapon into my hands to use against southern oppressors." Thus, both Douglass and Garrison hoped that the Philadelphia group would inspire similar efforts in other cities, and Garrison hoped publication would spur further literary activity among African American women generally. Reminding Douglass of the *Liberator*'s "Ladies Department," he encouraged her and her colleagues to "occupy it as often as possible with your productions." He also encouraged such contributions when he visited the society.[52]

The power of the enterprise came to be both demonstrated and exemplified in the *Liberator* as the paper's contributors presented themselves and their works in ways that embodied the virtues literary activity helped develop. Among the most prominent was Sarah Forten, sixteen years old at the journal's inception, who published several pieces under the pseudonyms "Ada" and "Magawiska." A daughter of James and Charlotte Forten, who had done so much for Garrison, Sarah Forten as "Magawiska"—the name, as Todd Gernes has noted, taken from a heroic Native American character in a recent novel—demonstrated that she had learned well the language of her contemporaries. Her piece for the *Liberator* on "the abuse of liberty" condemned a society in which people of color could be "robbed of the rights by which they were endowed by an all-wise and merciful Creator." She also drew on the long tradition of confronting Jeffersonian ideas and language, describing the slaveholder as one "in constant dread lest they whom he unjustly condemns to bondage, will burst their fetters, and become oppressors in their turn," and reminding readers that God "is just and His anger will not always slumber" (26 March 1831).[53]

As "Ada" the teenage Forten took her poetry in several directions, most importantly that of condemning slavery. Her works reveal her familiarity with the basic conventions and images that had come before. Ada's very first poem appeared in one of the first issues of the *Liberator,* although Garrison professed ignorance of the author's identity. Entitled "The Grave of the Slave," it is reminiscent of George Moses Horton's "Slavery," which appeared in *Freedom's Journal* in 1828. No longer would the slave be subject to the demands and brutality of life, Forten wrote, concluding, "The Grave to the weary is welcomed and blest; / And death, to the captive, is freedom and rest" (22 January 1831). About two months later, her identity now known to Garrison, Forten recalled the tradition that even in the midst of bondage found freedom through faith:

> With thought of future joy and gain,
> The slave forgets his grief and pain,
> Forgets awhile his slavish fear;
> Forgets,—that fetters bind him here.

Published on 26 March 1831, the poem was destined to become a popular part of the antislavery literary tradition.[54]

Forten also moved outside of questions of slavery and color to write within the traditions of sentimentality becoming widely established in antebellum America. "A Mother's Grief," for example, captures images of the dying child and of motherhood so popular in genteel literature of the period. "There's nothing left for me to love, / This earth holds nothing dear," the mother laments, "Since *he,* my sweet—my gentle one, / Is now no longer here" (7 July 1832). In "The Farewell" Forten laments an unrequited love and the young man who "wilt soon forget / The stranger thou hast seen" (30 June 1832).

Writing the kind of verse often found in young women's commonplace books and scrapbooks at the time, Forten easily demonstrated her ability to live up to the ideals that Stewart, Garrison, and others considered so valuable in the battle against prejudice. Genteel in every way, young Sarah was the embodiment of what every young woman of color had the potential to be. In her writings she could join with Garrison to develop and help diffuse the kind of literary personality suited to the aims and ideas they and others believed the literary enterprise had the power to convey.

The same was true of several other correspondents to the paper. The unidentified "Zillah," whom Marie Lindhorst has suggested was Sarah Douglass, was a frequent contributor to the journal. The name Zillah drew on the same biblical verses, Genesis 4:19–23, in which the name "Adah" also appears. Both were wives of Lamech, and, while the allusion is far from clear, it at least suggests the kind of dialogue and exchange that was occurring among members of the Philadelphia society. Zillah offered a "leaf" from her scrap book as an example of pious reflection, recounting her return from a protracted meeting where she had heard the kind of "affectionate" preaching that moved her deeply and where she had encountered an array of characters who made her think about her own faith and its strengths (15 December 1832). Like Ada, however, Zillah most often combined sentimentality with her concerns about color and slavery, noting, for example, that her religion, "the religion of the meek and lowly Jesus," gave her hope for a world in which "black and white mingle together in social intercourse, without a shadow of disgust appearing on the countenance of either" (30 June 1832). In another effort, she described an evening contemplating the "beauties of moonlight." It made her reflect on many things—the death of a pious young friend, the virtues of her teacher, and her hope that "the time is not far distant, when the wronged and enslaved children of America shall cease to be a 'byword and a reproach' among their brethren" (7 April 1832).[55]

Ada's and Zillah's themes, motifs, and personae linked sentimentality in an appealing way with abolitionism, reform, and the construction of a literary community based on ideals of gentility and refinement. The two writers also drew on gender roles and conventions in ways that complemented the ideas of Maria Stewart and more general notions of "respectability" as these guided the *Liberator* and its purposes. Thus, these ideals showed up in a variety of contexts and apparently in the works of a number of writers. Another "young lady of color," for example, created such links in her "Sorrows of a Female Heart," evoking sympathy for "the polluted female who is driven away by man from society," the slave woman forced to "bid a final adieu to her friends and parents, to the husband of her bosom, and to her helpless offspring." Creating an image of one whose "tears flow, which no hand can wipe away," and whose "groans ascend, which no comforter can charm to peace," the writer worked within a sentimental world in which, she wondered, "Can no female heart reflect upon these things, and not be moved?" (31 March 1832).

The same may be said of those evocations of piety that both proved the character of their authors and exposed the nature of white American Christianity, bringing into the nineteenth century themes that may be traced back to the era of the Revolution. A Philadelphian who adopted the name of the tragic Carthaginian noblewoman Sophonisba—her name evoking ancient African nobility, while her words evoked a more contemporary gentility—picked up on an idea developed by Sarah Forten to write a brief sketch entitled "Ella." The writer evoked the thoughts of a young woman sitting in her cottage on a "happy Sabbath morning": "The sun shines with a peculiar brightness—the flowers send forth a sweet perfume—the birds sing melodiously in the trees—and my heart is filled with love to God." But Ella cannot engage in such a happy contemplation without being brought to a contemplation of a very different world, for "my heart is filled with sorrow for my enslaved sisters," who are denied the Bible and all access to "the matchless love of Jesus." She can take comfort only in thinking that even for the poor slave "Christ is near thee, even in thy heart!" and that the "time is approaching when Christ shall reign king of nations." Garrison published the piece accompanied by more than his usual annotation, saying, "[By a young lady of color.]—Beautiful!" (4 August 1832).

Living up to genteel ideals represented only one aspect, however, of the kind of literary personalities conveyed in the *Liberator.* The tradition on which Walker had built, that of a superior vision, a moral superiority, remained an important element in the African American voice cultivated in the *Liberator,* conveying, again, the paper's vision of a distinctive role for an African American voice in the community of discourse it was intended to create. African American writers found such a stance useful in reproaching, on the paper's pages, a professedly republican Christian America for its inconsistencies.

A contributor going by the initials "H.F.G.," identified as a "colored authoress" and presumably not the white antislavery poet Hannah F. Gould, combined a stance of moral superiority with ideals of gentility as she took on the discriminatory practices of religious institutions in a little poem entitled "The Black at Church" (21 May 1831). The poem explored, with a strong sense of irony, the real implications of white religious practices, reducing a segregated Sabbath to its most absurd dimensions. "God, is thy throne accessible to me— / Me of the Ethiop' skin?" she asked.

> Thou art our Maker—and I fain would know
> If thou hast different seats prepared above,
> To which the master and the servant go.

These lines recall, most likely unwittingly, the absurd remarks of the South Carolina mistress more than a century earlier who was concerned that her slaves, if converted, might actually join her in heaven. H.F.G. concluded with that motif that both Ada and Sophonisba had drawn on:

> Then will I meekly bear these lingering pains
> And suffer scorn, and be by man oppressed,
> If at the grave I may put off my chains,
> And thou will take me where the weary rest.

H.F.G. received at least one nice response to her poem, from a Philadelphian who signed herself "Ella." Noting how hurt she had often been when she was told at church, "This bench is for the black people," and saying that she made it a matter of principle "to sit with white Christians," Ella singled out H.F.G.'s poem "The Black at Church" for "expressing in such beautiful language, the sentiments of my heart." The combination of gentility with irony employed by H.F.G. was an important commentary on the nature of white Christianity, but it also served to create a stance that allowed Ella, like H.F.G., to assert her own superior understanding of the nature of a Christian community, her sadness not only about her treatment but also about a faith that recognized the evil of a bench "for the people of color" (4 June 1831).

If some writers worked within traditions of evangelical piety, still others spoke with the angry, prophetic voice that had also been a part of African American literary tradition. In a series of essays entitled "Prejudices of Society" a Massachusetts man of color provided a lengthy indictment of American hypocrisy "owing to prejudice" that detailed the failings of American religion, the white opposition to black ambitions and attainments, and the preservation of slavery and injustice. "Good

God!" he concluded, "are our statesmen, are our clergymen, are our churches given up to believe a lie that they may be damned? Is this country given over forever? God forbid!" (10 December 1831).

Black writers also continued to hold American society up to the professions of the Declaration of Independence, and to find that society lacking. In the most traditional of pieces, a Philadelphia correspondent, "Junius," quoted the Declaration's opening lines and wondered, "Can all this be true?" Not, he said, so long as slavery existed. How, he wondered, could a people "acknowledge such barefaced hypocrisy"? And in language reminiscent of James Forten's many years earlier, he drew on Shakespeare to ask, "'If ye prick us, do we not bleed?' If ye wrong us, are not our feelings the same as yours?" He quoted from Cowper, as writers had for years, to assert both human equality and slavery's evil (11 June 1831).

Even Ada, despite her usual tone of gentility, joined in the condemnation of American hypocrisy. Her poem "The Slave Girl's Address to Mother" begins with motifs of piety and patience but also asks, rhetorically, "Oh! ye who boast of Freedom's sacred claims, / Do ye not blush to see our galling chains. . . ?" (29 January 1831). And another piece, entitled "The Slave," condemns American professions of patriotism, saying, "The sweets of freedom now they know, / They care not for the captive's wo" (16 April 1831).

Another black writer took aim at the appropriation of republican rhetoric by the nullifiers of 1832, southern politicians who championed doctrines of state sovereignty and the need to resist what they saw as an oppressive federal government. Signing himself "A Colored Visiter," this Boston writer wondered, "What is the reason you all want to withdraw from the Union? You say, it is because you are oppressed." Evoking the regional origins of the movement, he asked, "Why, then, can you not let us have our liberty?" And looking back to Forten, he wrote, "Have we not the same feelings? Are we not of the same image and features? Our complexion is dark, but our blood is red." Reversing what were often familiar categories, he concluded, "Some of you ill-treat your own colored children—some make slaves of them. It makes me think that you are all still blind, like heathen. Perhaps you never read the bible" (25 August 1832).

Such a reference by the "Visiter" continued, of course, the denial of any special claims to civilization on the part the European world, including white America. Describing slaveholders as "heathen," moreover, evoked yet again that relativizing of savagery and civilization that writers had, for at least the last two decades, also reinforced with images of ancient history stressing African greatness. This, too, continued to be an important motif for correspondents to the *Liberator*. David Nickens, an Ohio leader and opponent of colonization, in an 1832 address printed in the paper suggested that "Africa was the garden and nursery where learning budded and education sprang. From Egypt the arts of civilization were carried into Greece, and from Greece to Europe" (11 August 1832). What Africans had achieved before, they could achieve again; and they could do it without being removed from the United States.

Such evocations of Africa could also be used to link an ancient heritage with an authorial voice and an implied superiority that supported the literary efforts of African American writers. "Euthymus," from Columbia, Pennsylvania, probably the Pennsylvania activist William Whipper, wrote a lengthy letter in 1831 identifying several of the most prophetic figures of the Old Testament, including "Solomon, whose head was an epitome of the world's wisdom," as men of color, while declaring that "The first white man, that we have an account of, became white for forging a falsehood" (27 August 1831). Though claiming merely to deny white claims to any divinely sanctioned superiority, Euthymus nonetheless joined Walker in referring to a comparative history in which one could see a firm basis for the superior stance of the descendants of a people of ancient greatness.

The same may be said of a brief poem from "A Colored Person" living in Newark, New Jersey, a poem signed only "C." and entitled "Afric's Lamentation." The poem begins:

> My harp is tuned to ages past,
> When bright my glory shown,
> My golden land was then the seat
> Of arts and science fair.

Continuing, the poem makes clear the contrast between African history and that of Europe:

My sons once noble, polished, brave,
Are led away in chains;
And doomed in distant lands to slave,
Where BOASTED FREEDOM reigns.

Predicting that ultimately "AFRIC once more shall RISE!" the poet drew on traditions of both African greatness and American irony to complement the moral stance other writers had taken in commenting on the failings and hypocrisy of American society (4 February 1832).

Garrison himself was obviously receptive to the position these writers took. Even in his 1831 address he had posed the possibility of an African American moral superiority, suggesting to his audiences that they could not be satisfied merely with equaling the whites in virtue: they must excel. He noted, "I do not think the task would be difficult to excel them," given the histories of the two peoples, even in the United States. Personalizing the sense such views could convey, Garrison had opened his address by stating that "I never rise to address a colored audience, without being ashamed of my own color," declaring his own hope of atonement even as he acknowledged the his audiences' peculiar moral authority to grant it to him. The moral relationship thus defined cohered closely with the status of the African American voice in the *Liberator*.[56]

But the strength of the framework the *Liberator* and its correspondents had created is illustrated especially well by its usefulness not only to black writers but also to those whites who continued to imagine an African American voice, including those who returned to the familiar form of the imagined dialogue, across the color line. These efforts often looked back to traditional forms and motifs, but they also complemented, built on, and helped to enhance the purposes defined for the paper by its creators.

Such pieces took many forms. In one reprinted piece initially dated 1826, for example, Garrison published a brief dramatization of a series of conversations among slaves, in stilted English, called "The Art of Preventing Slave Insurrections." In keeping with Garrison's own concerns, the piece suggests that a failure to grant freedom at the time could lead to violent revolution in the future, as the slaves likened their own desires for freedom with the patriotism that had motivated their masters at the moment of American independence (10 September 1831). No less striking is a dialogue exhibiting tendencies going back to Tryon and Meade but updated to address more contemporary concerns. It recounts a conversation between a slave and a minister in which the minister denies the validity of a religion based on dreams and visions—revelations the slave claimed for himself—and suggests that while God may have spoken through such devices in the past, the Bible is now the sole source of testimony to God's will. The slave replies that "poor negro, he got no Bible," noting, "Massa whip Cato if he read." Concluding, the slave says, "De white man keep de good book from poor negro, but God better than white man. He speak to 'um without de good book" (14 January 1832). Published only a few months after Nat Turner's rebellion and the widely publicized *Confessions*, the dialogue provided yet another warning from Garrison about the potential wages of slavery on a slaveholding society.

But particularly significant are several of the most fanciful imagined dialogues of the first half of the nineteenth century, apart, perhaps, from Robert Finley's evocation of the shades of Penn, Cuffe, and Jones. Somewhat in the tradition of Finley was an imagined dialogue set in heaven between Toussaint L'Ouverture and George Washington, written by one "G.X.," the product of reflections prompted by Washington's birthday. The dialogue builds on the kinds of analogies between insurrectionary slaves and Revolutionary patriots that informed other pieces, showing the influence of those assertions of the moral superiority in which Garrison himself had invested so much credibility.

Most importantly, though, it also reinforced the frame Garrison and his correspondents had built for an African American voice in the *Liberator*, since in the dialogue Washington is made to acknowledge that black superiority. Greeted by Toussaint as "the hero, the statesman, the patriot," Washington immediately grasps the irony and pleads, "Spare me, Toussaint. Spare me that reproachful look, that reproachful allusion to ill-deserved eulogies." Toussaint brings forth Washington's awareness of the hypocrisies of his countrymen, forcing Washington to admit that in contrast to the Americans', the Haitian's "motives were as pure, your cause at least as just, your people's wrongs far more imperiously calling for redress," and to condemn a nation whose "people boast of justice, and unjustly keep their fellow men in bondage, or drive them from the soil which is their own" (10 March 1832). The dialogue is an important dramatization of the ways in which the evolving character of an African

American voice had been understood and conventionalized by the time Garrison established his journal and of the importance those conventions could have in the debate over slavery.[57]

But perhaps most revealing are the antislavery fantasies signed them with the initials "T.T.," which have been analyzed by James Stewart. These two reported "dreams"—one of harmony, one of horror—encapsulate, as well, Garrison's own concerns about the consequences of an American failure to abolish slavery, and without delay. The more harmonious dream takes T.T. to a splendid social event at which blacks and whites are present in about equal number, "mingling with perfect ease in social intercourse." It reveals some interesting attitudes on T.T.'s part, as well as some hopes for a future in which "merit and virtue constituted the only distinctions among us." Finding himself in the presence of a young black woman, herself surrounded by gentlemen of every color, T.T. learns that in this new world "fair" no longer constitutes a compliment to a woman of beauty. He describes the young woman's soft and sweet voice as possessing a character "not unfrequently possessed by persons of African extraction." He joins in a conversation in which one "young white beau" suggests, only half facetiously, that slavery was put on the road to extinction when "the attractions of female loveliness first made the tyrants ashamed of their prejudices" (2 April 1831).[58]

In many ways, however, the conversations in which T.T. joins dramatize precisely the kind of discursive community the *Liberator* was attempting to create. Slavery ended, T.T. makes clear, because African Americans forced whites to realize that "black men have rights as well as whites, and are no more fond of having their rights trampled upon," and because they demonstrated the foolishness of any defense of slavery based on ideas of African inferiority—a demonstration implicit, clearly, in the "white beau's" evocation of a female loveliness transcending color. But some whites had played a role as well, seeking out talented people of African descent and introducing them "into society." The result was, by the time of the dream, the election of America's first black president, a man of such talent that no one could respectably vote against him. A joint effort of precisely the sort the *Liberator* represented had led to a society in which color no longer played a role (2 April 1831).

The alternative, for T.T. as for Garrison, involved exchanges very different from the polite banter that social integration made possible. Beginning with an evocation of Jefferson's expression of his fears of revolt in *Notes on the State of Virginia*, T.T. imagines the coming of a Liberian returnee who, as "a second Lafayette," had led a general revolt of the American slaves. The result was a complete role reversal, the whites driven from the South and the government in the hands of the newly free. The former slaves had also rejected a treaty with the United States, noting, "Our allies, the Cherokees, would laugh to scorn the idea of trusting to a treaty," and set upon an independent course (30 April 1831).

Here and elsewhere T.T. used a black voice to show the bankruptcy of much that white Americans were saying about themselves. He also used it to show the bankruptcy of what they were saying about slavery, especially as he staged a debate among the revolutionaries over what to do with the white people still living in the new republic. Many tend toward mercy so as not to repeat the sins of their former masters. But some express the view that "to think of their remaining among us on any footing of equality is as preposterous as to propose to allow a race of tigers to range our cities with the freedom of domestic animals," evoking an imagery reaching back to Grégoire. Hoping to find a solution "which unites at once a humane regard to this ill-deserving but much to be pitied race, with a due consideration for our own safety," the leaders of the new nation hit upon, not surprisingly, colonization, returning whites "to their native land, the land of their fathers, the region to which their constitutions are by nature adapted" (30 April 1831). The new government is urged to explore arrangements with the king of Portugal for the purchase of a suitable territory to which those of European descent may be returned. Reversing white colonizationist words as he put them into the mouths of African American speakers, T.T. sought not only to impress his readers with the foolishness of colonizationist arguments but also to evoke an imagery that questioned the integrity of the colonizationists themselves.

The fantasies that T.T. created were dramatizations in microcosm of the kind of discursive world the *Liberator* was meant to encourage. Without turning the dialogue into a roman à clef, it is not difficult to see a Sarah Forten in T.T.'s romantic fantasies and a James Forten in his political dreams. Nor is it difficult to see such angry ironists as David Walker in those who debate European colonization. To the extent that this is true, T.T. also showed, in microcosm, what the role of the black voice became in the context of abolitionism and in the context of the *Liberator*. It was a voice that both shaped and was shaped by the forces that defined the movement itself. The possibilities created by the *Liberator* were a major part of that process, pointing toward authorial stances and, even more, toward strengthening modes of mutual validation that would affect African American literary culture and representation for years to come.

6

Literary Expression in the Age of Abolitionism, 1833–1849

❧

THE DECADES of the 1830s and 1840s were among the most complex for free people of color in the United States since the era of the American Revolution, and in ways that had great impact on literary as well as other endeavors. The most important factor in helping to shape that impact was the continuing growth of the movement for immediate abolition, a movement that, if it remained small in size, was to gain in visibility throughout the era. Black men and women participated in the earliest and most influential of the abolitionist organizations. Important leaders who remained active through the history of the movement also emerged during this time, including such now familiar names as William Cooper Nell, Henry Highland Garnet, William Wells Brown, Martin R. Delany, and, best known of all, Frederick Douglass. They contributed financially to the movement and to its efforts to spread the antislavery message. They wrote for abolitionist publications—for the *Liberator*, the *Emancipator*, the *Pennsylvania Freeman*, the *Liberty Bell*, the *National Anti-Slavery Standard*. They also created important publications of their own. In 1837 the newspaper veteran Samuel Cornish, along with Philip Bell, founded the *Weekly Advocate*, renamed the *Colored American* a few weeks later. Subsequent efforts included the *National Reformer*, the *Mirror of Liberty*, the *Mystery*, the *Northern Star and Freeman's Advocate*, and the *Ram's Horn*. Toward the end of the decade the *North Star* was created by the man who had become the most visible black abolitionist, Frederick Douglass. Reaching broad audiences, these publications too were to play a major role in the abolitionist cause.

The Origins of African American Literature

I

An overview of the immediatist movement and of black participation in it indicates a number of things about the continued growth and development of an African American literary tradition. One is the continued collaboration of black and white abolitionists in the shaping of the African American voice. Certainly, toward the end of the 1840s powerful tensions developed around issues of independence and autonomy in that voice, with real anger expressed to some extent along lines of color. Still, it is important to note that such tensions developed late in the era and involved only a few abolitionists, black or white. For the most part, collaboration rather than division marked the work, especially the literary work, of black and white abolitionists. Tensions were understood and discussed in terms of a collaborative framework.

At the same time, the nature of the collaborative effort itself underwent significant change during those two decades. As James Brewer Stewart has argued, the *Liberator's* ideal of helping to end racial oppression through the cultivation of a community of respectability crossing lines of color was severely challenged by the mid-1830s. The literary and other evidence shows that this ideal was not entirely abandoned by either black or white abolitionists, and such outstanding figures as James McCune Smith, Charles Lenox Remond, and Charles Purvis did much to keep it alive. Nevertheless, it was to be supplemented by a number of strategies and motifs. The decade saw, for instance, a revival of interest in some of David Walker's ideas. This was demonstrated most famously in 1843, when Henry Highland Garnet delivered what he called an "Address to the Slaves" to an antislavery gathering. The address called for slave insurrection, deliberately rejecting earlier approaches to the abolition of slavery. These very shifts helped to create tensions within the movement, sometimes but not always involving issues of color as well.[1]

Finally, the multiplicity of African American voices was to be augmented by a new group of African American participants in the abolitionist cause. If black participation in the movement was significant from the beginning, most of those present at the founding were the sort of free men and women of color who had helped in the creation of the *Liberator*. Beginning in the mid-1830s, a new group began to assert itself and to find an important role in the abolitionist cause. These were fugitive slaves, bringing firsthand reports of the institution to eager abolitionist audiences. Although anticipated by an autobiographical tradition antedating the American republic, these fugitives could assume a role in the context of a focused abolition movement that had not been available before. They were to become the most visible symbols of the abolitionist cause. This group produced such stalwarts of the antislavery movement as William Wells Brown, Samuel Ringgold Ward, and Douglass.

No less important was the extent to which the immediatist movement continued, through the 1840s, to pursue the kinds of efforts the *Liberator* had initiated in 1831. Ideals of community, of a biracial effort to end slavery and achieve racial equality, and of a unique role for blacks continued to be important to many abolitionists through these decades. These were ideals that, as Paul Goodman has said, went well beyond tokenism. Certainly this was true in such places as Philadelphia and Boston, where the most important abolitionist organizations of the 1830s were the products of extensive African American participation, where conscious efforts were made to recruit black members, and where those members played an active role in the organizations' activities. Just as black activists had aided in the founding of the *Liberator*, they had aided in the creation of the American Anti-Slavery Society, serving in major offices and on important committees, and were among its most important mainstays in the early years. In such places as Philadelphia and Boston women's participation in interracial groups, especially the Boston Female Anti-Slavery Society and the Philadelphia Female Anti-Slavery Society—was particularly important, as was their role in determining the directions those societies would take. Although such participation was not universal, and some places, notably New York, tended toward racial exclusion, experiences such as those in Philadelphia and Boston were important indicators of at least some tendencies in the abolition movement more generally.[2]

In significant ways African American participation in the movement went beyond the purely organizational, intersecting both the public and private realms. Abolitionist meetings, rallies, and even festive occasions were marked by integrated crowds and integrated leadership. After 1838 this was to be particularly visible in the First of August celebrations abolitionists held in deliberate response to the American Fourth of July. These celebrations commemorated the culmination of British emancipation, an important event since, as Robert Forbes has said, it tended to confirm the possibility of peaceful, successful emancipation. They included picnics, singing, rallying, and speeches. Black and white abolitionists mingled on the grounds, provided the messages, and joined together to express a common cause against slavery.[3]

At a more personal level, for at least some within the movement the kinds of ties the *Liberator* represented actually grew. Melding public and private, perhaps, was the interracial abolitionist communitarian experiment at Northampton, Massachusetts, which has been documented by Christopher Clark, an experiment in which goals of racial equality were apparently sought and realized by the community's black and white members. Similarly institutionalizing ideals of mutuality was Beriah Green's experiment in interracial higher education, the Oneida Institute in New York. Becoming president in 1833, and heavily influenced by the *Liberator*, Green demanded an integrated admissions policy that embodied the ideal of an interracial community bound by ties of education and achievement. The school would produce such important African American abolitionists and leaders as Amos Beman, Thomas Sidney, Alexander Crummell, and William G. Allen.[4]

Equally important were less formal social ties that appeared early within the movement. Among women in Philadelphia and Boston, abolitionist activity led to more general interracial social networks. In Philadelphia, women in the Forten and Purvis families hosted a variety of interracial social functions; and similar events took place in Boston. The circle of friendships involving the Fortens, the Purvises, and Sarah Douglass included the Grimké sisters, Garrison, and Theodore Dwight Weld. The interracial wedding party for Weld and Angelina Grimké was only one of the more visible evidences of the friendships at least some black and white abolitionists felt for one another.[5]

Such social ties were not universal, as many people recognized. In 1837, in response to a letter from Angelina Grimké asking about "the effect of Prejudice" on her life, Sarah Forten wrote that "even our professed friends have not rid themselves of it—to some of them it clings like a dark mantle obscuring their many virtues and choking up the avenues to higher and nobler sentiments." It was an assessment with which Grimké strongly agreed.[6]

It should also be stressed that where they existed these social ties were often understood within the larger context of abolitionism and the character of black participation in it. For many white abolitionists, an identification with African Americans as an excluded, maligned people, similar to that found in turn-of-the-century evangelicalism, was not entirely absent from their approach to black social connections. As Lewis Tappan once wrote to Theodore Dwight Weld, "Christ went among the Publicans and samaritans (He *ate* with them. Oh horrible!)—they were the *colored people* of that day—and by so doing made himself of no reputation. Let us follow our Leader!"[7]

Such views even entered into personal ambitions, as white abolitionists sought to rid themselves of prejudice, using friendships with African American colleagues to cultivate the attitudes of sympathy and community on which the movement was to be based. Weld, during his days at Lane Seminary, seems to have deliberately sought out friendships "with the Colored people of Cincinnati" in what might be termed an exemplary manner, and he took what was, for him, great pride in doing so. The Grimkés, especially Weld's future wife, Angelina, did much the same thing and felt that their experiences were educational, whatever pleasures they derived from them. As Angelina wrote to Sarah Douglass, "The more I mingle with your people, the more I feel for their oppressions and desire to sympathize in their sorrows."[8]

One should not conclude from such words that interracial social ties were simply contrived. Nor does one find at this early date any overt expression on the part of black abolitionists of resentment over the patronizing attitudes white abolitionists' comments may seem to convey, although this did not always remain the case.

Still, it is not difficult to read into the remarks of Weld and others a reinscription of race within abolitionism, one that looked back to evocations of special validation found in the *Liberator* but also looked outward to the whole movement. As a number of historians have pointed out, abolitionists, and especially radical abolitionists, were well aware of the movement's separateness from the American mainstream. They acknowledged, even celebrated, the extent to which in their quest to overcome the American sin of slavery they were putting themselves at odds with most of their contemporaries and thus playing what they saw as a prophetic role in the shaping of American history.[9]

The kinds of relationships evoked in the words of a Weld or a Grimké were shaped by such perceptions, as were, in many ways, African Americans' roles in abolitionism. These relationships gave to black participation a still more pervasive role in validating the movement as a whole by further helping to define its distinctions from the corruption of the larger American world.

Such validation was enhanced, moreover, by a corresponding and not unrelated rise of antiblack sentiment accompanying the rise of radical abolitionism in the early 1830s. Historians' tendency to date the rise of a tradition of systematic racist thought in the United States to the early 1830s is well founded. Whether in the form of an increasingly vocal defense of slavery on racial grounds or in the form of a body of scientific thought emphasizing the innate, biologically based inferiority of nonwhite peoples, there was a new virulence in racial ideas designed to defend the oppression of African Americans, slave and free, in the 1830s. These efforts continued to gain in strength over the following two decades.[10]

So far as black Americans were concerned, thought continued to be translated into action, even against free people of color. One may note, for example, the move to disfranchise black voters on the part of the Pennsylvania convention charged with constitutional revision in 1837–38. Constitutional reform, undertaken in part to liberalize suffrage requirements for white males, had created the opportunity to remove blacks from the polls, a possibility strongly supported in many quarters. Debates on the issue made increasingly clear the extent to which many whites resented any black participation in Pennsylvania's political system; that they might actually exert political influence was seen as a real danger. A new constitution excluding black voters was ratified in October 1838.[11]

More subtle, perhaps, but no less challenging was the continuation of a tradition that had begun with the "bobalition" broadsides of the 1820s, given new force with the increasing popularity of blackface minstrelsy after about 1830. Using dialect and weird costuming to present ridiculous images of slaves and free people, and directed toward white urban audiences, these minstrel shows, whatever else they did, helped to fix representations of African Americans as a people both innately different from and innately inferior to the whites who created and enjoyed the spectacle.[12]

As Shane and Graham White have shown, the black middle class came in for special ridicule during this period, especially in such publications as Edward Clay's *Life in Philadelphia,* originally published in the late 1820s, and his still more vicious *Practical Amalgamation,* a work published in opposition to abolitionism in 1839. Caricaturing, pictorially and in words, the dress and manners of affluent people of color — and showing how they could never quite get their middle-class pretensions right — Clay and others portrayed what they saw as the unfitness of African Americans for true American respectability.[13]

Blacks involved in the abolition movement seemed to provoke special scorn, at least for some white observers. Even ostensibly straight reporting suggests the tenor of the times. A reporter for New York's *Commercial Advertiser* in 1833 ridiculed themes of ancient Africa, which were subjected to increasing publicity and attack during this period, by describing a discussion in which antislavery speakers went on "for hours — showing the extent and exactness of their learning, confounding Jurgatha and the Numidians, the Egyptians, Hannibal and the Carthagenians, with the race of Guinea." An Ohio paper in 1842 described a black-organized First of August observance as "The Darkies' Celebration" and concluded an apparently faithful account of one of the speeches with the words, "Well done Sambo."[14]

Still, antiabolitionist and antiblack sentiment merged most powerfully in the mob violence and riots of the period. In New York, Philadelphia, and elsewhere homes, churches, and community buildings were destroyed by white mobs. Abolitionists, white and black, were mobbed and beaten. Such violence continued through the 1830s and 1840s, reaching a peak in 1834 and 1835. Leading white abolitionists, including Garrison and Lewis Tappan, suffered at the hands of the mobs, as did such prominent black figures as Peter Williams Jr. As Emma Lapsansky has pointed out, the black middle class came in for special targeting as mobs enacted both a hatred for abolitionism and a resentment of black achievement.[15]

Both motives were most visible in the 1838 burning of Philadelphia's Pennsylvania Hall, a building erected to be a center for abolitionist activity. Its inaugural meetings, in which both black and white abolitionists participated, attracted hostile crowds, challenging delegates on their way to the hall. The crowds were enraged by the sight of black and white men and women walking together to the meetings. Identifying abolitionism with amalgamation—nothing new, but a theme that was to appear with increasing frequency in antiabolitionist rhetoric—the mob used both as a pretext for violence. Three nights after the building opened, the mob burned it down, then continued its violence, focusing on black institutions and homes, for two more nights.[16]

At one level, the meaning of all this for abolitionism, and for the role of blacks in the movement, was a strengthening of the solidarity of those abolitionists who had to face unruly mobs and episodes of discrimination. For some white abolitionists this involved maintaining a commitment to egalitarian precepts in the face of even the quotidian practices of American racism. Such was the case when Elizabeth Buffum Chace and some friends noisily protested the removal of a black couple from a segregated railway car or when Samuel J. May resisted the removal of African American parishioners from his church. At another level it involved the solidarity black abolitionists felt with white colleagues when given white support. Telling his own version of Chace's story, William Cooper Nell described an incident in 1840 when, traveling with Garrison, he was ordered out of a car. Leaving, he was joined by Garrison, who, as Nell put it, "permitted himself to be colonized (with his own consent)" into the car reserved for blacks. When Garrison joked that perhaps his skin had somehow darkened into the shade of a "col'd man," Nell replied "that he always knew how to feel as one."[17]

But above all, the solidarity such incidents implied helped to strengthen that peculiar validating role black and white collaboration could give to the separatist, prophetic stance abolitionists had chosen to give to the movement itself. One may see something of this in the 1836 response of the New Hampshire abolitionist newspaper *Herald of Freedom* to the remarks of one Colonel Barton calling it the "Nigger Herald." The paper responded, "A very good name, and we take this opportunity to inform the gallant colonel, that we will never complain, so long as he does not call it the Slaveholders' Herald." One may also note the pride Samuel May took in being able to reply forcefully to a Boston friend who questioned his actions in escorting one of the Forten sisters to an abolitionist meeting in Philadelphia. "I did," he said, "and should be happy to do it again." Since the charge of "amalgamationism" was so often flung at abolitionists, May's action and his defense of it were particularly striking evidence of how well he understood what the separateness of abolitionism entailed and how much that separateness rested on the cultivation of interracial connections deliberately flouting contemporary racial norms.[18]

Such words and actions indicate, finally, how interracial effort in a hostile world also gave a peculiarly public dimension to the validation black participation provided for the movement's distinctiveness. Susan Davis has suggested that by the 1830s and 1840s many white Americans sought to confine public spaces to use by whites alone. Abolitionists challenged this effort through their openly interracial meetings and, as May's remarks make plain, the friendships they displayed in those meetings. The *Herald of Freedom*'s response to Colonel Barton also supports David Henkin's argument that public space was broadly conceived at the time to include not only the publicness of physical space but also the publicness of space created through newspapers and other printed forms. By deliberately violating more exclusivist tendencies, abolitionists deliberately asserted not only their separateness from the American mainstream but, more than that, their critique of it and, again, the prophetic place the movement could occupy in American life. As James Forten Jr. wrote to James McCune Smith, the very persecution "the people of Color and our antislavery friends" received on the public stage had strengthened his belief that theirs was "the cause of God."[19]

Such a stance helps to reiterate the complexities of race relations both within abolitionism and looking outward. On the one hand, it reinforced that reinscription of race that allowed white abolitionists to validate themselves, not because they ignored the color line but because they treated it differently from their peers. It is not entirely cynical to see in this an abolitionist use of blacks that, in celebrating racial equality, nevertheless reinforced ideas of racial difference. There was more than a measure of this in the words of a May, a Weld, and even a Sarah Grimké as they celebrated their friendships across the color line, their standing up for black peers. It must also be acknowledged that such attitudes opened up a set of opportunities and possibilities that, building on past traditions, helped to enhance the role of a black voice within abolitionism and, ultimately, in the debates over slavery as such.

II

Through the 1830s and 1840s black speakers and writers played what everyone understood to be a special part in spreading abolitionist ideas. Much was in keeping with the special authority and special validation given to blacks as distinct but significant representatives of the cause. By the mid- to late 1830s a large group of African Americans, men and women representing a variety of backgrounds and a variety of interests, had achieved prominence. They would play an important role in addressing, sometimes consolidating, sometimes shaping, the various directions in which the abolition movement would go. They would participate fully in debates that broke out among abolitionists beginning in the late 1830s over such issues as gender equality, political activity, and, with Garnet's noted address, violence as a means for ending slavery. They took sides freely and did so efficaciously.

What made the black voice meaningful was not so much the positions black abolitionists sought to occupy on specific issues; rather, it was its distinctive authority in the context of racial complexities within the movement. This included the ways in which black and white abolitionists understood and characterized an African American authority, and what the nature of that authority meant for the roles a black speaker could assume.

To a great extent, the abolitionists' understanding of African American authority may be seen in the reassurances black and white abolitionists gave each other about the very efficacy of a black voice in the founding and shaping of abolitionism. The influence African Americans had exercised from the earliest days of the movement was widely acknowledged, especially the efficacy of an African American voice in, for example, turning such white figures as Garrison away from the chimera of colonization. In his 1834 address to the national convention of the free people of color William Hamilton urged his audience, "Cheer up, my friends! Already has your protest against the Colonization Society shown to the world that the people of color are not willing to be expatriated. Cheer up. Already a right feeling begins to prevail." Speaking to the American Anti-Slavery Society in 1837, the black abolitionist Charles Gardner made a similar point when he declared that "when William Lloyd Garrison was a schoolboy" free people of color had formed their own opposition to the scheme. It was a history widely acknowledged. Sarah Grimké, addressing "the free people of color" in 1837, suggested, "But for your virtuous and uncompromising hostility to the colonization society, a portion of our countrymen might never have been disabused of the idle and fallacious expectation, that this scheme would cure the moral evil of slavery." At about the same time Garrison himself wrote that "for more than thirteen years, before they ever saw or heard of me," free people of color had made their objections to colonization clear—an assertion matching the structure of his 1832 book on the subject.[20]

No less important, however, were those modes of presenting a black voice that confirmed its role in the abolition movement and, thus, abolitionism's role in relation to the larger society. These modes were visible in the ways black speakers asserted themselves in an array of contexts. They were also visible in the ways white abolitionists responded to those assertions.

Black abolitionists, continuing a long tradition, continued to use their position to remind white Americans of an American heritage to which African Americans were more faithful than those who would exclude them from America's blessings. Pennsylvania's 1830s move to disfranchise black voters produced an *Appeal of Forty Thousand Citizens, Threatened with Disfranchisement, to the People of Pennsylvania*, written by Charles Purvis and structured to make such a point. Describing the proposed disfranchisement as an "outrage upon the good old principles of Pennsylvania freedom," Purvis cast his own case in terms of a superior patriotism, pledging that "however others may forsake these principles, we promise to maintain them on Pennsylvania soil, to the last man." Such Revolutionary motifs became a staple of abolitionist rhetoric. William Lloyd Garrison, for example, once said that "Patrick Henry never spoke better." And he was likely making the same point a short time later when, following an early lecture by Frederick Douglass, he "rose, and declared that PATRICK HENRY, of revolutionary fame, never made a speech more eloquent in the cause of liberty."[21]

Such views slipped over fairly easily, moreover, into traditions of an African American moral superiority. Junius Morel put the matter in somewhat negative terms when, in a letter to the Philadelphia activist Frederick Hinton, he wrote of his unwillingness that "in the present day, the 'Colored American' shall be merged in all the guilty oppression and hypocrisy of his pale-faced brother. 'Tis meet the name should show the difference between the sinning and the sinned against."[22]

Others put the matter more positively, suggesting a special role for African Americans in preserving the destiny of the nation, and particularly in realizing American principles and Christian ideals. In its address to the American people in 1835 the national convention of free people of color declared that "if our presence in the country" could help produce moral and political reform, then, "although we have been reared under a most debasing system of tyranny, we shall have been born under the most favorable auspices to promote the redemption of the world." A few years later, Frederick Douglass made a still more trenchant observation when he said in New York, "I do not know but the United States would rot in its tyranny were not some negroes in this land—some to clink their chains in the ear of listening humanity, and from whose prostrate forms the lessons of liberty can be learned." James McCune Smith, making a similar point, connected the redemptive role of African Americans specifically with the role of the black voice in America when he assured an audience that "we are destined to produce the oratory of this Republic; for, since true oratory can only spring from honest efforts in behalf of the RIGHT, such will of necessity arise amid our struggles."[23]

As with evocations of the Revolutionary tradition, these assertions also fit within the framework for a black voice abolitionists had begun to evolve. Even Morel's rather pointed comments were intended for movement consumption, appearing as they did in the *Emancipator*, where they received a positive reception. Publishing Morel's letter, the editor of the *Emancipator* commented, "Greece and Rome have handed nothing down to us more noble." Thus, notions of black moral superiority became almost as common among white as among black abolitionists, building on the distinctiveness that all attached to black participation in the movement. One sees evidence of this, for example, in a letter Angelina Grimké wrote to Sarah Douglass to tell her approvingly of a remark the abolitionist Joshua Leavitt had made during a trip to Connecticut. Leavitt had suggested that "the Lord had a great work for the colord people to do" and, Grimké reported to Douglass, "that your long continued afflictions and humiliations was the furnace in which He was purifying you from the dross and the tin and the reprobate silver." Grimké herself agreed, and aware of the idea's implications, she added, "I fully believ you will after all get up abov us and be favored instruments [to] carry pure and undefiled Religion to the Heathen World."[24]

Such views even led to a sense within the movement that black abolitionists had a role to play in keeping its purposes, especially insofar as prejudice within the movement was concerned. Abolitionists, black and white, were troubled by that prejudice. Black abolitionists often decried the prejudice exhibited in abolitionist ranks. Sarah Forten's 1837 letter to Angelina Grimké is one example of this concern. Only a year or so later an angry B. F. Roberts, of Boston, wrote to Amos Phelps decrying the number of "hypocrites" in the movement, suggesting, "According to what I have seen of the conduct of some, a black man would be as unsafe in their hands as in those of southern slaveholders."[25]

But, again, such indictments fit well within the larger traditions of black authority. Significantly, Roberts was not reluctant to write his complaint to a white coworker, casting his indictment in a way that showed his hope to use his voice to raise white abolitionist consciousness. This was the same context in which Angelina Grimké used accounts such as Sarah Forten's to condemn segregationist tendencies of antislavery organizations in New York, writing that no proper abolition movement could exist there "while Prejudice banishes our colored sisters from an equal & full participation in its deliberations & labors." When Samuel Cornish, describing the goals of the *Colored American*, wrote that "our enemies generally, and our friends too frequently, indulge the erroneous idea that a dark complexion carries with it moral and mental inferiority," his remarks were publicized not only in his paper but also, with approval, in the white-edited *Pennsylvania Freeman*.[26]

Thus, from the beginning of the 1830s the view that black speakers and writers had a special part to play in shaping the abolitionist cause continued to be an element in the abolitionist discursive world. It was not only a moral role; it was an exemplary role as well. White leaders such as Garrison and Weld talked about the distinctiveness of that part, asserting, for one thing, the special power an eloquent black speaker could have in the fight against prejudice. Weld, optimistic in 1836, believed that "a specimen of free colored Elevation at the north" could even reach slaveholders: "The contrast between the free blacks of the North and the slaves of the south ought easily be such as to burn slavery out by the roots." A few years later, citing the accomplishments of such men as James McCune Smith, William Whipper, and Daniel Payne, among others, Weld wrote, "They would do more good in three months to kill prejudice (and our cause moves only as fast as that dies) than all our operations up to now." He also noted that "a colored man who is eloquent will in all parts of the North draw larger audiences than if white, in most places far larger."[27]

Weld was right, and some of the very men he cited achieved celebrity status in the United States and abroad in the 1830s and 1840s. Audiences clamored for them at antislavery rallies. A few even inspired celebratory poems. In the early 1840s one abolitionist paid poetic tribute to some of the more prominent when he wrote,

> SMITH, WRIGHT, REMOND and CORNISH rise,
> With other kindred souls, erect,
> Faint sending o'er benighted skies,
> The gleam of negro intellect.

The poet had been inspired, he said, "on hearing Mr. C. L. Remond, a young colored man of talent, but slight education, lecture on Prejudice against Color in the United States." The poem was testimony to the possibilities Weld had suggested and to the ideals that held the abolitionist discursive community together.[28]

Still, if men like Remond and Smith could draw antislavery audiences, the arrival of the fugitive slaves was to greatly reinforce and further shape the character of black participation in abolitionism. These fugitives, still legally slaves, could use their experiences to add both personal poignancy and authenticity to the antislavery cause. As Robert Hall has pointed out, abolitionists were often charged with having no firsthand knowledge of the institution they attacked. Clearly, no such charge could be leveled against the fugitives, who had been slaves and who by law remained slaves still. Abolitionists understood the importance of this. Weld, for example, early in his career noted his own reluctance to highlight the institution's cruelties in speeches against slavery. This was partly a matter of principle, for he hoped not to detract from the moral focus of the case, but it was also because no matter how well he presented instances of brutality, he tended to be greeted with cries of "deceptions" and "exceptions." As he was to appreciate, such cries were less likely when the stories came "burning" from the lips of one who had experienced them firsthand.[29]

Fugitives joined free people of color in spreading the abolitionist word. Many achieved a celebrity status of their own. During the 1830s and even more in the 1840s such fugitives as Samuel Ringgold Ward, Henry Bibb, Lewis Clarke, William Wells Brown, and especially Frederick Douglass traveled widely on the abolitionist circuit, in the United States and abroad. They recounted their experiences and helped fulfill Weld's goal of giving credibility to abolitionist images of slavery. So great was their popularity generally that by 1842, as the historian Robert Hall has noted, the abolitionist John A. Collins could write to Garrison about the clamoring of antislavery audiences to hear a black speaker, "particularly a *slave*." By that same year such a fugitive as Douglass, still at the beginning of his career, could already receive one of the first of many poetic tributes. This was in the form of a piece entitled "The Fugitive Song," composed and "respectfully dedicated" to him by the noted Hutchinson Family, a popular group of abolitionist singers.[30]

The fugitives thus entered quickly into the world of abolitionism, and they were conscious of their importance to it. As Weld wrote, they could give credibility to the movement it otherwise had difficulty claiming. Frederick Douglass made this clear in one of his earliest speeches, in 1841. He said, "My friends, I have come to tell you something about slavery—what I *know* of it, as I have *felt* it." Praising the abolitionists for their knowledge of the institution, he said, nevertheless, that "though they can give you its history—though they can depict its horrors, they cannot speak as I can from *experience*; they cannot refer you to a back covered with scars, as I can."[31]

Fugitives also added to the credibility of the cause when, on the stump, they submitted to questions from their audiences, probing still further into the details of their experiences in bondage. "Are families often separated?" one might be asked, as Lewis Clarke was, or, "What do slaves know about the Bible?" Creating such a dialogue on the stump was an important way of reinforcing the significance of the fugitives' role to the antislavery cause.[32]

But lending credibility to accounts of slavery was only one role fugitives played within the abolition movement. In addition, and like talented free people of color, they also played an exemplary role. Several of the fugitives were recognized for their eloquence, and the contrast between their obvious virtues and their putative status could easily comment on racial stereotypes. As John Blassingame has emphasized, Frederick Douglass was commonly introduced to audiences, especially by Garrison, as "a thing from the South," as a piece of "property," an inhuman category that Douglass belied by his very presence. His eloquence before a crowd more than implied, at the same time, the extent to which he and other abolitionists were above such a view. Even though Douglass would later claim to have resented the language, he understood its significance and its utility early on and often made use of it himself. In one speech, quoted by Blassingame, he told an English audience, "I have come to England, and behold the change! The chattel becomes a man." In another English address he used very Garrisonian language, as well as the language of southern law, to ridicule the notion that in America he would be considered "'a chattel personal to all intents, purposes, and constructions whatsoever'; 'a thing' to be bought and sold." It was a language, as Blassingame notes, that Douglass himself used in introducing his fugitive colleagues.[33]

It is not difficult to document fugitives' importance to the movement. One may note, again, the popularity of fugitives in abolitionist meetings. One may also note the special attention they began to draw from the proslavery South. In a noted attack on abolitionism in 1845 James Henry Hammond condemned the extent to which "the research and ingenuity, aided by the invention of runaway slaves—in which faculty, so far as improvizing falsehood goes, the African race is without rival—have succeeded in shocking the world with a small number of pretended instances of our barbarity." So saying, he paid at least tacit tribute to the power the fugitives had attained in furthering the abolitionist cause.[34]

In many ways, then, a black voice had a distinctive and important role to play in furthering the abolitionist cause. Through the 1830s and 1840s its character and modes of representation were crucial to the movement's impact, its message, and its representation of itself. This is not to say that no tensions or conflicts were involved. The divisions in the movement as a whole often spilled over into tensions over the proper role and nature of the black voice itself. More crucially, as many historians have shown, issues of independence and autonomy were to arise within the movement, and among some of the most prominent black abolitionists, by at least the end of the 1840s. To see these tensions more clearly, however, it is useful to turn from issues of the black voice as such—whose efficacy and significance no one doubted—to the more substantive issues of how that voice was constituted.

III

Much that guided black literary effort in the 1830s and 1840s grew out of the unique role of African Americans within abolitionism. In writing, as on public occasions, acknowledging the authority in the black voice was an important way in which these black and white abolitionists could work together to enhance the moral standing of the movement as a whole. Recognizing the eloquence and authority of black writers, no less than encouraging black participation in the movement, was an assertion of freedom from the failings of the American mainstream, as black and white abolitionists alike asserted the moral superiority that many saw in the black perspective on American life.

This joint effort was clearly apparent in the literary realm, as abolitionist journals continued to publish pieces by African American writers with the familiar identifications "by a colored man," "by a colored young lady," "by a colored youth." They also made much of the exemplary character of such figures. The *Emancipator*, in typical fashion, in its brief introduction to James Forten Jr.'s widely printed address to Philadelphia's integrated Ladies' Anti-Slavery Society in 1836 identified him as one "who belongs to that proscribed class, which can 'scarcely be reached, in their debasement, by the heavenly light,' 'out of which no individual can be elevated, and below which, none can be depressed!!'" The paper's sarcasm underlined the exemplary role a man like Forten could play, through his eloquence, in the abolition movement while making clear, in terms coherent with the distinctive stance abolitionists took toward American society, the editor's own appreciation for that role.[35]

The history of that achievement also continued to provide a moral grounding for the movement against prejudice and slavery, and in ways that also supported that movement's stance toward the larger society. The great writers of the Anglo-American past figured significantly in abolitionist rhetoric. The accomplishments of writers of African descent, from Equiano and Wheatley through Banneker, Lemuel Haynes, and David Walker, formed a worthy backdrop to the accomplishments of the present even as they gave African American writers a history that should confound prejudice. To these early writers could be added distinguished literary stars from elsewhere—Aleksandr Pushkin, Alexandre Dumas, and the Cuban poet Diego Gabriel de Concepción Valdez, known as Plácido. All became widely known in abolitionist and African American literary circles. James W. C. Pennington, the prominent clergyman and abolitionist, showed something of both the extent and the significance of the tradition itself when he praised young Ann Plato, in 1841, by saying that she had "followed the example of Phillis Wheatly, and of Terence, and Capitain, and Francis Williams, her compatriots."[36]

Thus, as Pennington's remarks make clear, grounds of authority rooted in history had great importance in the 1830s and 1840s. The enterprise of tracing those achievements also remained important. This period saw one of the first critical treatments of African American literature by an African American scholar in William G. Allen's 1849 *Wheatley, Banneker, and Horton*, offering a selection of their works. Allen had been a student at the Oneida Institute, an editor, and "Professor of the Greek and German languages and of Rhetoric and Belles Lettres" at the abolitionist Central College in New York—his own early career pointing up some possibility for inclusiveness within the movement. Examining the three authors he had chosen and discussing such others as Pushkin and Plácido, Allen drew the clear implications that black voices had their place in the world mainstream, that what "the African" could become, "the past clearly evinces."[37]

Allen joined a legion of writers on the African and African American literary pasts and helped others in the continuing creation of an African American canon. In 1836 Lydia Maria Child published her highly influential *Appeal in Favor of Americans Called Africans*. The book put Child herself at the center of an abolitionist literary life, a position she would maintain through her contributions as editor and writer for such important periodicals as the *Liberty Bell* and the *National Anti-Slavery Standard*, where she did much to encourage black writers. The *Appeal*, described by James Forten Jr. as "one of the best productions of the subject that I have ever read," was directed above all at disproving notions of black intellectual inferiority. It relied heavily on literary history to make its case, including such figures as Wheatley, Equiano, and Sancho, with much of the discussion derived from Grégoire.[38]

Allen and Child also joined an increasing number of writers who continued to forge links between such figures as Wheatley and Plácido and a larger history of African achievement. In 1836 Robert Lewis produced his *Light and Truth*, a historical compendium of past and contemporary achievements that put African Americans in the historical mainstream. More influential were Hosea Easton's 1838 book *A Treatise on the Intellectual Character and Civil and Political Condition of the Colored People of the U. States; and of the Prejudice Exercised Toward Them*, James Pennington's 1841 *Text Book of the Origin and History, &c. &c. of the Colored People*, and, in 1848, Henry Highland Garnet's published address *The Past and Present Condition, and the Destiny of the Colored Race*. All used the ground of historical achievement as a way of denying inferiority while, like Lewis, Child, and Allen, inserting people of African descent into the history of the modern world.

Here, too, one sees the force of canon formation. All these works carried forward traditions of celebrating ancient Africa as a way of asserting the claims of modern African Americans to a place in the American social order. Child, for example, cited Herodotus, the German naturalist Johann Friedrich Blumenbach, and Volney, among others, to claim for Africa—and the ancestors of contemporary African Americans—the creation of the bases for modern science. "Egypt was the great school for knowledge in the ancient world," she wrote, making a point that would be developed by other writers as well. Garnet noted that the black people of ancient Egypt had "astonished the world with their arts and sciences, in which they reveled with unbounded prodigality."[39]

It was easy to take pride in such a heritage, and many did. It was also easy to continue to see in such a past hopes for a better future. One reader of Garnet's address felt that its presentation of history was "enough to arouse and animate every one — man and woman, to great exertions and action, to reach that pinnacle of human excellence waiting in store for us." Pennington made the connection between ancient greatness and contemporary literary achievement in his introduction to a collection of Ann Plato's works. Like many, he described Egypt's influence on the other great ancient civilizations and suggested, "As Greece had a Plato why may we not have a Platoess?" Similar connections were made by Julius Ames in an 1843 book, *Legion of Liberty!* The book included a long chapter, "The African Character," citing Volney, Herodotus, Wheatley, Remond, Cornish, Jacob Oson, as well as Toussaint L'Ouverture and James Forten.[40]

It was perhaps this sense of the importance of history that led to a greater self-consciousness in both the use and the evocation of tradition by abolitionist thinkers and writers themselves. An obvious case was the decision of the 1849 Ohio state convention of free people of color to re-publish Henry Highland Garnet's 1843 address advocating slave insur-rection in an edition with David Walker's *Appeal*, deliberately evoking a tradition of militant rhetoric. But this identification of tradition was done in a variety of ways that both maintained the tradition and educated people in it. Thus, the critics Kenny Jackson Williams and Frances Fos-ter have noted how such writers as Ann Plato and the spiritual autobiog-rapher Jarena Lee looked back to and drew from Phillis Wheatley's writings in their own work. Foster has also shown how Lee positioned herself within the larger tradition of black spiritual autobiography.[41]

In a more strictly political realm one may note Theodore Dwight Weld's lengthy quotation of George Moses Horton in an 1835 address, as well as a reprinting in that year's *Anti-Slavery Record* of the speech by a slave rebel comparing his quest to that of George Washington, from Robert Sutcliff's 1812 *Travels in North America*. One may also note that in an 1849 speech Frederick Douglass paid tribute to James Forten and quoted from his words in opposition to colonization.[42]

Other writers similarly positioned themselves and showed the force of a continuing tradition, some going back to the eighteenth century. A fugitive "Mr. Johnson," appearing before the Massachusetts Anti-Slavery Society, told of his kidnapping from Africa while engaged in innocent play. Calling his Gambia home "a fine country," he added, "But here we are called heathen in dis Christian—no—I don't know what to call it—in dis—enlightened heathen country." In an 1847 speech Douglass also demonstrated his familiarity with the oldest sentimental conventions as he took his audience imaginatively to a "little village on the West Coast of Africa," a place where "the profound stillness is only relieved by the melodious hum of tropical insects. How still the scene." Then, as writers had done more than a half-century earlier, Douglass brought a slave ship onto the scene. "A few moments, and the village is in flames," its people led off to slavery. "Grim death and desolation reigns, where before was life, peace, and joy." Both Douglass's subsequent description of the slavery awaiting the captives and Johnson's characterization of his experiences owed too much to tradition to be divorced from it. Both strengthened its continuing role in the realm of antislavery ideas.[43]

The history of African American literary culture remained important. So did the continuing cultivation of an African American literary voice, by blacks and whites alike. Sarah Forten, writing as "Ada," continued her prolific career, even if, unlike Ann Plato, for instance, her verse was never collected for publication in a volume. Although the *Liberator* remained her primary outlet—which is not surprising, given Garrison's closeness to the Forten family—her verse appeared in other places as well, including *The Abolitionist* and the *Emancipator*.

As a poet Forten continued to write on a range of subjects, although the movement remained at the center of her attention. A tribute to Garrison, on his way to Britain in 1833, was widely reprinted in the abolitionist press. Much of her poetry reveals that she perceived the movement as a kind of community, one in which membership brought fulfillment. In 1833, shortly after the adjournment of the founding convention of the American Anti-Slavery Society in Philadelphia, which she had attended, Forten wrote a brief poem called "The Separation" in which, remembering the convention, she wrote, "We feel the void which absence makes, / With joy, and sorrow too," joy in what had been accomplished, sorrow in the departure of "friends—the firm and true!"[44]

Forten was certainly justified in her feelings. Through her poetry, as well as her gentility, she made herself a visible member of the antislavery world, keeping alive that community of respectability, however challenged it might become, created with the *Liberator*'s founding. Her efforts did not go unacknowledged. Both her literary and personal gentility are celebrated in the poet John Greenleaf Whittier's tribute to her and the other Forten sisters in his poem "To the Daughters of James Forten, Philadelphia," published initially in the *Liberator*. It was in part an effort—similar to those of other abolitionists—to declare a transcendence of his own prejudices, and those of the larger society, through his appreciation for those young women, who, through "excellence of mind, / The chaste demeanor and the taste refined" compelled him to proclaim them "sisters" to himself. It was also a confirmation of the ideals Forten herself exemplified by her works.[45]

Neither Forten nor Whittier mentioned it, but, taken together, their efforts would have had additional significance, given the growing tendencies toward caricature, particularly caricature of the black middle class. Certainly, everyone was aware of those tendencies. Joseph Willson, who wrote one of the first treatments of a black middle-class world, his 1841 *Sketches of the Higher Classes of Colored Society in Philadelphia*, noted that even the title could "excite the mirth of the prejudiced community on its annunciation." He suggested that such readers would "expect burlesque representations, and other laughter exciting sketches, and probably be led to procure this little volume for the purpose of gratifying their *penchant* for the ludicrous." Willson, a black writer but not a member of the Philadelphia elite, thus knew the contrast he was making when he portrayed a gentility wholly unlike the caricatured renditions created by Edward Clay and others. It was a contrast the abolitionist press reinforced, reprinting his work and citing it as further support for the abolitionist cause. Forten and Whittier both proved the possibilities for transcending those renditions, while asserting in the literary realm a stance toward the larger society marked by its moral distinction.[46]

Perhaps just as revealing was an effort growing out of the 1836 publication of Angelina Grimké's "Appeal to the Christian Women of the South." As Todd Gernes has shown, Grimké's "Appeal" led to what appears to have been a three-way conversation involving Grimké, Forten, and a white abolitionist poet named Eliza Earle. Earle also began to use the name Ada for poems appearing in the *Liberator*, the *Massachusetts Spy*, and elsewhere. According to Gernes, Earle, writing as "Ada," responded to the "Appeal" with a poetic tribute to Grimké, written for the *Liberator* and reprinted in the *Emancipator*, describing Grimké as her "gifted sister" and defining a distinctive role for women in the fight against slavery: "There's much in woman's influence, ay much, / To swell the rolling tide of sympathy," wrote Earle.[47]

In her words to Grimké, Earle was to a great extent echoing sentiments Forten had expressed in a poem published in the *Liberator* in 1834 on the duties of women in the abolition movement, "An Appeal to Women." Addressed to white abolitionists, Forten's poem had been introduced by Garrison with the comment that the writer's family was one that had "forced the respect even of those who would wish to crush the people of color to the earth." The poem urged women to recognize a unity in character transcending color. It produced at least two poetic responses. One, by James Scott, writing from Rhode Island, endorsed Ada's sentiments and urged her to continue to "use thy tongue and pen and mental power" to aid the cause. Another, signed only "Augusta," similarly recognized the power of Forten's words and, as if to demonstrate the poem's impact, declared, "Daughter of Eve!—my sister and my friend, / To thee the hand of friendship I extend." Earle, joining in with poetic tribute a short time later, also joined the kind of conversation these writers, especially Forten and Grimké, had created.[48]

It is not impossible to see the conversation itself as helping to form the core of one of Angelina Grimké's most important works, her *Appeal to the Women of the Nominally Free States*, issued under the auspices of the 1837 Anti-Slavery Convention of American Women. Grimké indicated her debt to Forten by using a stanza from the 1834 "Appeal to Women" as the epigraph for her appeal, including the lines, "Our skins may differ, but from thee we claim / A sister's privilege, and a sister's name." The body of Grimké's *Appeal* built on the concerns Forten had expressed in her poem and in her 1837 letter decrying prejudice. Grimké herself urged northern white women to put aside prejudice and work with their black counterparts to overcome slavery and discrimination. In the very cooperative venture Grimké demanded, both writers helped to define what each saw as a set of standards within abolitionism and an authoritative stance for the movement toward society as a whole.[49]

As this extended example also indicates, gender ideals informing the cultivation of an inclusive genteel community in the early 1830s remained important. And as Whittier's poem indicates, the compelling combination of genteel and feminine virtues represented by young women like Sarah Forten did much to augment ideals of abolitionist community, even as Eliza Earle and Angelina Grimké saw in these ideals a stimulus for reaching across lines of color to create a distinctive abolitionist sisterhood.

Still, one should not be too quick to stress gender alone in seeking to explain the continuation of genteel traditions in African American writing. Women, after all, were never alone in creating genteel, sentimental literature, and this was to be the case in the abolitionist world too. By the time Forten and Earle began their conversation, and despite any eclipse of "respectability" as the primary strategy for abolitionism, many writers, male and female, had begun to try their hands at producing the kind of genteel work Forten and others had helped develop in the movement's early years.

The young Ann Plato, of Hartford, whose works had received Pennington's imprimatur, was one whose work rested heavily on genteel ideals. Several of the Forten sisters, as well as their brother Robert B. Forten, made their contributions within the conventions of popular sentimental verse of the period. Other Philadelphians, including Sarah Douglass and her brother Robert, also contributed fairly frequently, and to a variety of publications. The effort was, however, hardly confined to Philadelphia. The Pittsburgh native and activist George Vashon in the 1840s wrote a widely published tribute called "The Seasons," in which he used sentimental imagery of nature and its beauties. The abolitionist and activist Charles L. Reason wrote on topics ranging from abolitionism to the beauties of spring. Even figures not noted for a poetic bent contributed an occasional verse to one publication or another, reinforcing both antislavery and genteel traditions. In 1848, for example, the *North Star* published a poem entitled "The Things I Love," by Henry Highland Garnet:

> I love to hear the summer sigh,
> When I am wandering in the dale,
> I love to see the clear blue sky
> When breathes the gale.[50]

Such examples as Garnet's poem, together with the wide variety of works from the period, emphasize the extent to which literary activity as such had become an aspect of the African American "public man" of the 1830s and 1840s, whatever the gender implications of the phrase. The historian Edward Maceo Coleman once argued that in French-speaking New Orleans such creoles of color as Armand Lanusse, Camille Thierry, and Victor Séjour, whose works were collected in the 1845 volume *Les Cenelles,* wore their taste for largely sentimental verse as a badge of refinement and taste. Though they had little influence in the English-speaking, abolitionist world, their efforts represented an impulse similar to that found in more northern regions. Literary achievement and public persona, exemplified by Garnet's poetic endeavors, for instance, were significantly linked.[51]

Perhaps this understanding of literary effort also helps to explain why, in a more public realm, poetry and other literary efforts usually marked important events, whatever else occurred. Thus, for example, the First of August celebration at Troy, New York, in 1839 included not only an address by Henry Highland Garnet, then a student at the Oneida Institute, but also an original ode composed by Daniel A. Payne, then a young minister, later to become one of the most influential bishops of the African Methodist Episcopal Church. Drawing on traditional themes of providence, Payne declared, "SHOUT! ye islands of the ocean, / Jehovah hath made you free," as he and others celebrated the emancipation of Britain's West Indian slaves.[52]

Payne himself was to be a fairly prolific poet during the period, on top of all his work for his church. He seems to have begun writing fairly early in his life. Born in Charleston, where he began his work as a teacher in 1834—prior to beginning his ministerial career—he wrote one of his first poems in response to South Carolina legislation, passed that same year, prohibiting any free person of color from teaching other people of color, free or slave, to read and write. Perhaps testifying to the importance of literacy—and poetry—during the era, Payne was so devastated by the legislation that he almost immediately turned to verse to express his sorrow, producing a poem entitled "The Mournful Lute, or the Preceptor's Farewell." The poem conveys Payne's own love for education, pleading, "Come, wisdom, clothe me in they sacred flame," while lamenting the imminent closing of his school:

> When Carolina's laws shall shut the doors
> Of this fine room, where science holds his reign,
> The humble tutor, hated Daniel Payne.[53]

Payne continued to write throughout the period. His short poem "The Hour of Prayer," represented as "an early production," appeared initially in the *Colored American* and was reprinted in the *Emancipator* in 1837. Like many other poets, and continuing a tradition common in American letters as well as in the works of such figures as Phillis Wheatley and Ann Plato, Payne also wrote obituary poetry. And he produced pieces for a variety of commemorative occasions associated with abolitionism and with African American community affairs. To be "literary" was as much a part of Payne's endeavors as were his more clearly ministerial labors.[54]

Probably no arena did more to encourage such a view, and to provide a foundation for it, than that provided by the literary societies. Several important ones were founded during the 1830s and 1840s, including the Philadelphia Library Company of Colored Persons and the Phoenix Society in New York, both founded in 1833. These organizations developed independent libraries and met regularly for lectures, readings, recitations, and discussions. They cemented social ties and activism among their members. Regular contributors to the *Colored American*, for example, along with its editors, shared a common membership in the New York Philomathean Society, whose activities were regularly reported in the paper's pages.[55]

Members continued to have high hopes for their societies, tying them in with more general efforts at "improvement" among free people of color, attaching educational as well as social purposes to them. Such societies would, moreover, provide further evidence of what people of African descent could achieve. "They will tend," one participant suggested, "to clear us from the charge of indolence, or indifference, to our own welfare, which has been heaped upon us; and also, from that foul aspersion, as to the inferiority of our intellectual capacities, with which many has been pleased to brand us." They also continued to provide an important setting for creative efforts, as meetings were structured around brief essays and original poems written by the members themselves.[56]

The literary societies took an approach to literary production that helped to keep traditions alive. By emphasizing improvement and literary attainments the societies ensured an interest in genteel themes on the part of even such men as Garnet. And by emphasizing a distinct and meaningful place for blacks in the sphere of public discourse they also encouraged a continuation of that tradition of commentary that had always been a part of African American tradition. Within the framework the literary societies adopted, literary activity remained part of, and helped maintain, the kind of abolitionist discursive world that had emerged with the founding of the *Liberator*.

It is perhaps not surprising, therefore, that abolitionist publications and even African American papers continued to make the imagined black voice a part of the case against the institution, and within this same frame. Garrison's *Liberator*, the *Emancipator*, the *Colored American*, and, later, Douglass's *North Star* all continued to offer poems in the language of the suffering slave, imagined dialogues on the merits and demerits of colonization, and imagined retorts of slaves to the pretensions of the slaveholders. These too showed a connection to older traditions, as in the imagined "Negro's Soliloquy on the Ten Commandments," which appeared in the British press and was reprinted in *The Abolitionist* in 1833. Contemplating God's biblical command that "Thou shalt have none other gods, but me," the poor slave wonders, "What can it mean? my massa make me too much 'fraid; he tell me negro must 'bey him first:—den he same like first God to me. But God tell me, I must 'bey him first. What sal I do?"[57]

A few older pieces even saw new life, indicating the existence of an abolitionist canon not wholly composed of African American works. Lydia Maria Child published portions of John Stedman's 1796 *Narrative of a Five Years' Expedition Against the Revolted Negroes of Surinam* in an 1834 antislavery book called *The Oasis*. She focused on the story of Stedman's affair with the slave Joanna, not, she assured her readers, because it portrayed a widespread abolitionist wish "to marry a mulatto," a charge much bandied by the movement's opponents, but because of the nobility it showed in Stedman and Joanna alike. Documenting its appeal, Garrison's associate Isaac Knapp reproduced this version of Stedman's work as a separate volume in 1838. At about the same time, the *Amistad* incident, which so mobilized antislavery sentiment, brought new life to William Cullen Bryant's poem "The African Chief," Bryant's poetic creation being readily identified with Cinque, the leader of the Amistad captives. The fugitive Lewis Clarke, speaking to antislavery audiences, gave new life to the old story, from oral tradition and turn-of-the-century jest books, of the slave who refused to be buried next to his master since "When the debbil come take you body, he make mistake and get mine."[58]

But perhaps the most striking appearance of the imagined voice was in antislavery songsters, such as the 1848 *Anti-Slavery Harp*, compiled by and with the imprimatur of the black abolitionist William Wells Brown, "A Fugitive Slave." Drawing on a variety of sources and containing a few of Brown's own works, the songster included such pieces as "The Slave's Lamentation," to be sung to a familiar tune, in which presumably black and white congregations would sing of how "All hope of freedom hath fled from me now, / Long, long ago — long, long ago." They might also join in singing the imagined words of "Zaza — the Female Slave," remembering "Where the sween Joliba kisses the shore, / Say, shall I wander by thee nevermore." Or, if they were using John A. Collins's *Anti-Slavery Picknick*, they could join in a rhetorical tradition looking back to 1817 and collectively reiterate the "Colored Man's Opinion of Colonization: "Home, sweet home, / Till force drives us from it, this, this is our home."[59]

Such imagined voices garnered black as well as white attention. African American publications, including the *Colored American* and the *North Star*, readily republished pieces from white writers and white papers as part of their own efforts to speak out against slavery. Douglass's paper, for example, gave a place to Henry Wadsworth Longfellow's poem "The Slave's Dream," a piece filled with exotic imagery of Africa that recounts the death of a slave resulting from an existence marked by pain and fatigue. One may also note the African American writer Susan Paul's 1835 *Memoir of James Jackson*, which drew on evangelical traditions of youthful and black piety. Paul's story helps to illustrate not only the versatility but also the continuing appeal of traditional representations. The appearance of these pieces and their republication emphasizes, yet again, the collaborative character of literary activity and African American authority within the context of the abolition movement.[60]

IV

For all, however, the distinctive claim of African Americans to an authoritative voice and the nature of that authority are most clearly conveyed in the narratives of fugitive slaves. These narratives were destined to become the most important form of African American literary expression in the nineteenth century.

Slave biographies and autobiographies, though they had a history going back to the eighteenth century and had never been absent from the antislavery literary tradition, took on special significance in the abolition movement, beginning in about the mid-1830s, as a stream of articulate, dedicated fugitives began to enter the antislavery ranks. The clamoring by audiences to hear fugitives John Collins had described to Garrison in 1842 represented an enthusiasm that carried over into the literary realm. The abolitionist press was soon filled with their narratives. As those narratives began to appear as books and pamphlets, they achieved a popularity matching that of the performances on the platform. Frederick Douglass's 1845 narrative had sales of about thirty thousand copies in about five years. Many went into multiple editions, usually, as in the case of Lewis Clarke's work, due to popular demand. Several of those who produced such narratives hoped to support themselves through sales of the books and were able to do so.[61]

A variety of issues confronted the fugitives and their stories, whether in printed form or on the stump. Credibility was always a matter for discussion, both inside and outside abolitionism. It dogged those fugitive slaves who took to the stump, especially those who were noted for their eloquence, such as Frederick Douglass. A rumor was rife, even in New England, that Douglass "was an educated free negro"; thus, at least one of his reasons for putting his narrative into print was to give evidence of his former condition. As he told an audience in Scotland, the rumors had so plagued him that in order to dispel them, "he sat down and wrote out his experience of slavery, telling the name of the state in which he had been a slave, the name of the county, the name of the town, and the name of the man who dared to call him his property." Henry Bibb's 1849 narrative, written after Bibb had been active in the abolition movement for half a decade, was intended to serve much the same purpose.[62]

Even after publication, questions of credibility plagued the written narratives. One of the earliest of the fugitive narratives, Charles Ball's *Slavery in the United States*, "compiled" by the abolitionist Isaac Fisher, came under immediate attack despite Fisher's assurance that he had taken the narrative "from the mouth of the adventurer himself" and that the "sense and import" of Ball's words had been "faithfully preserved." One reviewer of Ball's work, Elizur Wright, contended that whether or not the narrative was exactly true, no one could doubt "the perfect accuracy of its picture of slavery." Nevertheless, given the role of the narratives in abolitionism, it was impossible to be so sanguine about the credibility of their origins. There were many who disagreed with a view such as Wright's. And even Wright expressed a wish that in Ball's case "there had been an appendix of some sort, containing documentary evidence" to back up at least some of what Ball had to say.[63]

Similar issues of credibility persisted throughout the period. They were encouraged, in part, by the publication of a variety of narratives besides Ball's about which questions of authenticity could be raised, including the infamous James Williams narrative of 1838. Williams, perhaps a free man of color from the North, dictated his memoirs to the abolitionist poet John Greenleaf Whittier, who edited them and arranged for their publication. The resulting work, published with the imprimatur of the American Anti-Slavery Society, was advertised as the "Authentic Narrative of an American Slave." Shortly thereafter, serious questions began to be raised about the accuracy of Williams's account, including the existence of the plantation where, according to Williams, many of the events he recounted had taken place. The abolitionist press was filled with discussion of the truth of the narrative, and a committee was formed to evaluate the veracity of the work, with somewhat inconclusive results. As the critic William Andrews has emphasized, the Williams narrative was never actually proven false. But the questions raised were considered serious enough that after some investigation the work was temporarily withdrawn from sale; it was ultimately reoffered because of the quality of its descriptions of the institution. As Lydia Maria Child said, echoing Elizur Wright, to those "who look on the *foundations* upon which slavery rests, it is not of the slightest consequence whether James Williams told the truth or not." Even she acknowledged, however, that credibility problems were causing "mischief" in many quarters.[64]

Most other memoirs preempted the objections raised to those by Williams and Ball by including documentary evidence to support the fugitives' claims, as Elizur Wright had suggested. Amanuenses offered "indubitable vouchers" of the credibility of their sources, as George Thompson did in putting forth Moses Grandy's narrative in 1844. Many, like William Hayden in 1846, published documentary evidence that supported the facts of their stories. Henry Bibb, like James Williams, went through a committee investigation, though with happier results.[65]

Still, charges against the narratives remained common and serious, as Bibb's scrutiny by a committee makes clear. Even Frederick Douglass faced such questioning once his narrative appeared. His former "owner," Thomas Auld, called into question both Douglass's authorship and the facts of the narrative. Another writer, A. C. C. Thompson, submitted a lengthy commentary to prove that Douglass's narrative was "a budget of falsehoods, from beginning to end." Douglass had little trouble responding, and he felt confident enough to publish much of the exchange in his own newspaper, but the importance of the issue never really lessened during the period, nor would it so long as narratives remained a part of the abolition movement.[66]

The authentication of narratives and, in cases like those of Douglass and William Wells Brown, of their actual authorship had an important role within the context of abolitionism, for black and white abolitionists alike. Here was where authenticating testimonials, usually but not always by whites, such as the well-known introductions by Garrison and Wendell Phillips to Douglass's *Narrative*, came in. These testimonials have often been interpreted as creating a white control over the black author and his voice. Certainly, for men like Douglass and Brown, and others who claimed authorship of their own accounts, measures of authority and independence were involved, measures that were to become increasingly important to their own understanding of their antislavery endeavors.

But such issues should not obscure what was, within abolitionism, the more important concern. Again, almost as soon as fugitives began to play an active role in the movement, the narratives were used, by white and black abolitionists alike, to authenticate the movement itself. Credibility was not only a matter of asserting or questioning the accuracy of a particular account. It was demanded by the authenticating role such narratives had to play in the movement, a role that involved giving credence to abolitionist perspectives on slavery and on African Americans themselves.

This is why the reactions of Elizur Wright and Lydia Child were so ambivalent when they were faced with the possibly spurious narratives of

Ball and James Williams. They, like other abolitionists, may have appreciated the value of an imagined fugitive's portraying what they saw as the true character of slavery. Richard Hildreth's 1836 novel about a fugitive, *Archy Moore*, was widely appreciated on precisely such grounds, and it was not the only effort of its kind. But there was still a need for the credible, apparently authenticating narrative of one who had actually experienced all slavery had to offer if abolitionism were to be truly sustained. This need could only be filled by actual fugitives themselves.

Such a need helped to frame both the role of the narratives and their character. Above all, they served to corroborate much of the more general abolitionist argument against slavery and for abolitionism. At times this process could be pretty simple. Both Henry Watson and William Wells Brown, for example, published selections from Theodore Dwight Weld's influential 1839 book *American Slavery as It Is*, a compendium of materials, mainly from southern sources, using the South's own words to document slavery's most brutal features. Brown even made a point of noting how he had seen, with his own eyes, specific events Weld had described in the book. The effect was not simply to use correlative material from Weld to corroborate their own accounts but, by embedding it in their experiences, to give further veracity to what Weld had compiled.[67]

In addition, autobiographers could give experiential testimony to abolitionist claims in the larger debates over slavery. James W. C. Pennington, in his 1849 narrative, wrote about his desire, after escaping, to make his mark against the institution but said that he felt he had nowhere to return. As he recalled, in 1828 and 1829, his first years of freedom, there was no antislavery society, and the alternatives that presented themselves were less than attractive. "At one time," he wrote, "I had resolved to go to Africa and to react from there; but without bias or advice from any mortal, I soon gave up that, as looking too much like feeding a hungry man with a spoon." Putting a mark of validity on organized abolitionism while exposing the weakness of colonization—and verifying the assertion, made by many, that blacks needed no Garrison to turn them from the American Colonization Society—Pennington used his experiences to support the claims of black and white abolitionists to speak for a real African American constituency.[68]

Given such purposes, it is not surprising that the content of narratives that evolved beginning in the 1830s quickly became highly conventionalized, as the critic James Olney has noted. Olney's "Master Plan for Slave Narratives," as he has called it, accounts for virtually all the major elements, from the authenticating testimonials, through the description of early life, of the events of plantation slavery, particularly its brutality, the family separations, and the auctions, and on to the fugitive's escape and emergence into a life of freedom. The form grew out of many sources, including the give and take on the stump, and traditional motifs, including motifs long associated with African American and antislavery sources, merged with evolving abolitionist focuses. That it was so deeply rooted probably explains why such readers as Wright and Child could find a "truth" in the narratives of Ball and Williams despite those works' uncertain provenance.[69]

At the same time, perhaps because it was so deeply rooted, the form took on enough power to be quickly adaptable to a variety of specific stories. It was, for example, sufficiently well established that the evangelist Zilpha Elaw could draw on it for her 1846 spiritual autobiography. Describing one foray into the South, she told of the vulnerability of anyone of her "complexion and features" to enslavement in a way that would have had meaning for anyone familiar with the fugitive tradition. In a more perverse testimony to the clarity of the narrative form, as early as 1835 the white scholar and novelist Jerome B. Holgate, writing as "Oliver Bolokitten," could burlesque it fairly successfully in his bogus "Memoirs of Boge Bogun," which, the "title page" claimed, were "Written by Himself." The burlesque was part of a larger work, A Sojourn in the City of Amalgamation, written in opposition to abolitionism.[70]

However formulaic, the narratives brought the apparent power of firsthand experience to the indictment of slavery, and they sought to employ that power not only to authenticate the indictment but also to reveal its physical and emotional core. When, for example, the fugitives described the auctions and the separations of families, they could give an undeniably authentic account of the pain such actions caused. When Henry Watson, in his 1848 narrative, related how, subjected to the insults of potential "buyers" while standing on the block, he "burst into tears, and wept so" that he became insensible to the proceedings surrounding him, he gave his readers a sense of exactly what the block could mean to one who had to undergo its torments. The same may be said of the inescapable evocations of violence in the narratives. The fugitives recounted episodes of brutality, which they portrayed graphically. Moses Roper, for example, described in excruciating detail the floggings he underwent, the ways he was tied, the lashes he received. He provided pictures with captions that made his point especially clear. Most other narratives were similarly graphic, if not always illustrated.[71]

Certainly, in an era of heightened concern about the body, as Lindon Barrett and Elizabeth Clark have shown, such evocations of physical pain were powerful. Physical punishment was being increasingly questioned in a variety of realms; its evocation in the narratives would have heightened their power. No less important in the context of abolitionism were the sources of such gruesome stories, whether in print or on the platform. These were, after all, coworkers, and in some cases friends, of the abolitionists.[72]

The relationships the narratives sought to cultivate between fugitives and their antislavery audiences paralleled those that used the bridging of the color line to reinforce the moral stance of the abolition movement. One way of cultivating these relationships was to evoke a moral identity between black and white Americans. J. W. C. Pennington, in his 1849 narrative, asked his white readers quite specifically to make the imaginative leap of putting themselves in his place. Describing the beating of his father, he wrote, "Let me ask any one of Anglo-Saxon blood and spirit, how would you expect a *son* to feel at such a sight?" Similarly, Lewis Clarke, after describing the depredations to which slave women were exposed, asked his audience, "Now who among you would like to have *your* wives, and daughters, and sisters, in *such* a situation?"[73]

In evoking such a moral identity the fugitives and their readers continued, at one level, a process that went back to the roots of antislavery thought in the eighteenth-century ethic of sympathy, an ethic that nineteenth-century abolitionists had stressed since the early days of the fugitive accounts. In 1836, for example, Angelina Grimké wrote in her "Appeal to the Christian Women of the South": "Let every slaveholder apply these queries to his own heart; Am *I* willing to be a slave— Am *I* willing to see *my* wife the slave of another—Am *I* willing to see my mother a slave, or my father, my sister or my brother?" The empathy, as well as Christian morality, that Grimké's words demanded became an important measure of the abolitionist response to the fugitive narratives. Strong feelings figured prominently, with abolitionists urging one another to "let the tear of sympathy roll freely from your eyes," as Charles

Stearns put it in his preface to Henry "Box" Brown's narrative, when contemplating the fugitives' tales. Wilson Armistead made a similar point in an 1848 appreciation of Douglass's narrative, suggesting that no person of human feeling could read it "without a tearful eye, a heaving breast, an afflicted spirit," leading to an "abhorrence" of slavery.[74]

But the key way in which evoking strong feelings and empathetically bridging lines of color marked an abolitionist moral community was by the contrasts the narratives created involving themselves, their abolitionist allies, and the slaveholders' world whence they had come. It was a world in which, unlike in the world of the fugitives, the very empathy cultivated by the narratives was absent. As the fugitive William Hayden put it, "All the feelings of humanity are lost upon the slave-holder, when he contrasts his worldly importance—his increasing wealth and standing in society, with the poor slave—he, whose toils and privations are the very means of acquiring that wealth and standing." The slaveholders' failure to achieve empathy was part of a larger moral failing in slave society, one the fugitives had little trouble documenting.[75]

From the earliest times, attacks on slavery had focused on the religious hypocrisy of those who held slaves, and this continued to be the case in the abolition movement. Indictments of slaveowner hypocrisy filled the fugitive narratives. The brutal slaveholding Christian became a stock figure in the narrative tradition. A slaveowning Mr. Gooch, for instance, who tormented the fugitive Moses Roper during his years in captivity, was described as "a member of a Baptist church," which Roper could not attend because of the congregation's policy of strict segregation. William Wells Brown recalled an owner who made a regular practice of seasoning family worship with rounds of mint juleps. Brown's own clumsiness in serving the juleps once led to his punishment "as soon as prayer was over." James W. C. Pennington described a brutal beating received by a man whose daughter was subsequently sold away. According to Pennington, "This poor slave and his wife were both Methodists, so was the wife of the young master who flogged him."[76]

Indictments of slaveholder' religious hypocrisy were matched by those of their licentiousness, grounded, again, in the fugitives' very lives. Whatever other problems there may have been, no one would have found incredible the opening of James Williams's narrative, in which he suggested that his mother was the daughter of her owner and thus he was the grandson. Nor would anyone have had difficulty with Moses Roper's far more common assertion that he was the child of his owner. The device was well enough established that "Bolokitten" could satirize it in his antiabolitionist piece. Nor would many readers have been likely to doubt the story so crucial to Frederick Douglass's account of his dawning awareness of the meaning of slavery, that of the brutal beating of his Aunt Hester for her refusal to submit to the sexual demands of her master. Such reports, particularly when set within the larger abolitionist framework of gentility, represented another way in which fugitives were able to use their experiences to link issues of color, morality, and slavery. That there was a more than tacit challenge to proslavery condemnations of abolitionist "amalgamationism" is also clear, perhaps inspiring the "Bolokitten"'s anxious response to the form.[77]

It is also not difficult to see how such stories of hypocrisy and licentiousness might underline the moral standing of the fugitive as one who could see through the pretensions of a slaveholding Christian society and easily claim a moral superiority to those who would hold him inferior. For several of the fugitives this positioning was reemphasized by what was to become a standard device within the narratives, as William Andrews has shown: the dramatization of a dialogue between slave and slaveholder in which the slave gets the moral better of the master. Recapturing the antislavery dialogue tradition that went back to the end of the eighteenth century in works such as Warner Mifflin's *Defense* or Caleb Bingham's *Columbian Orator*, these dialogues confronted the slaveholder with the immorality of his position, simultaneously putting the writer in a position of moral superiority.[78]

The dialogue form reached a kind of apogee in what became a significant literary device within abolitionism, the open letter from an escaped slave to his former master. These letters were widely published. The most famous, that of Frederick Douglass to Thomas Auld, appeared initially in the *North Star* and later as an appendix to a second version of his autobiography, *My Bondage and My Freedom*. Even before Douglass, however, both Henry Bibb and J. W. C. Pennington produced open letters to their former owners, Bibb in response to a letter from the master himself; shortly thereafter, William Wells Brown published one as well.[79]

In these letters the writers celebrated their own freedom and recounted the cruelties they and others had suffered at the hands of the recipient. Bibb confronted his former master William Gatewood with the anguish created by being "compelled to stand by and see you whip and slash my wife without mercy, when I could afford her no protection"; he recalled how his "infant child was also frequently flogged by Mrs. Gatewood, for crying, until its skin was bruised literally purple." Brown urged his former master, "When you look upon your own parents, sisters and brothers, and feel thankful that you are kept in safety together, think of him who now addresses you, and remember how you, with others tore from him a beloved mother, an affectionate sister, and three dear brothers, and sold them to a slave trader, to be carried to the far South."[80]

Such public confrontations of former masters based in experience not only lent further validity to the fugitives' narratives as such but also created a relationship, outside that of bondage, with the masters themselves, and that relationship was clearly one between moral superiors and inferiors. Pennington made this clear in religious terms when he wrote, "I could wish to address you (being bred, born, and raised in your family) as a father in Israel, or as an elder brother in Christ, but I cannot; mockery is a sin." Brown made a similar point, and drew on a long tradition, when he said to his former master, "You profess to be a Christian, and yet you are one of those who have done more to bring contempt upon Christianity in the United States, by connecting that religion with slavery, than all other causes combined." Instructing their former owners in the real truths of Christianity, or, as Brown also did, in the nature of republican duty, these former slaves asserted a moral stance that represented the role they had taken in abolitionism and in the larger society as well.[81]

That they asserted that position successfully is clear. Again, one may note the anxiety this black voice created. Douglass, for instance, could with pleasure report stories of legal prosecutions in Virginia aimed at individuals "feloniously and knowingly circulating the Narrative of the Life of Frederick Douglass." Such stories were testimony both to the book's circulation and to its power to frighten slaveholders. It is similar testimony to the narratives' reach and influence that criticism of the credibility of Ball and Williams came from the South, evidence, at the simplest level, of the breadth of the audience the works had reached and the anxiety they had created.[82]

It became increasingly apparent that such attacks evoked concern not only about the impact of fugitive testimony but also about the stories that were appearing in the narratives. Thus, when he sought to defend slavery in more positive terms, and not simply to dismiss fugitive testimony altogether, James Henry Hammond, for example, singled out family separations, so stressed in the narratives, as an issue to be addressed. He did so in ways that directly emphasized a main theme, the pain such separations caused. "Negroes," he wrote, "are themselves both perverse and comparatively indifferent in the matter." He also emphasized the availability of religious instruction and suggested that "our slaves are the happiest three millions of human beings on whom the sun shines."[83]

If anything, Hammond's words, emerging by no later than the mid-1840s, may indicate the early stages of precisely the kind of exchanges fugitives and their supporters incorporated into narrative conventions and into letters to former masters. Even as they stung such men as Hammond into addressing matters of family separations and religious impoverishment, the kinds of defenses Hammond proposed encouraged a still greater focus on experience in the narratives to deny what Hammond said. The exchange may go back even farther. In 1835 and 1836 the *Anti-Slavery Record* published two stories about fugitive mothers who were willing to kill themselves and their children rather than face a return to slavery. One, anticipating Hammond, was entitled "Contented and Happy."[84]

Hence, too, one may account for the historian Walter Johnson's finding based on a survey of the narratives that they tended to focus, even more than earlier abolitionist writing, on the meaning of the auction block in the lives of slaves. Stressing, as Johnson says, the impossibility that a slave system in which men and women were subject to sale could be benevolent, the evocation of such imagery in the narratives went to the heart of Hammond's contention that no one could be happier than southern slaves.[85]

V

In important ways, then, an African American voice was crucial to the larger abolition movement of the 1830s and 1840s, as black and white abolitionists appreciated. It was required to authenticate abolitionist arguments; it was required, no less, to authenticate the movement itself in its stance toward American society. Still, significant tensions developed in regard to the role of the black voice in abolitionism. These tensions did not undermine the role of that voice; if anything, they strengthened it. But they pointed to a self-consciousness on the part of black and white abolitionists alike about the nature of the black voice and its significance.

Given the combination of abolitionist desires and abolitionist needs, it is perhaps not surprising that issues of control and independence arose for black speakers and writers. Again, these have often been noted with regard to the fugitive narratives, particularly given the role of white abolitionists in their presentation. But these issues were to become increasingly important among African American activists during this period, underlying a series of debates and divisions that took place among them.

Although one can see some precedent for these debates in such events as Walker's call for a generation of black historians, the signs of division began to appear more clearly later in the 1830s, initially in what appeared to be a series of exchanges over terminology — over what, among other things, African Americans should call themselves. The debate was not without precedent; it had assumed a public shape even in such early outlets as *Freedom's Journal*, and it had never really gone away. In 1834, for example, the *Liberator* had run a brief anticolonization piece by "a colored Bostonian" that asserted an American identity but nonetheless concluded, "We are American Africans!"[86]

In the late 1830s, however, a number of events made the issue seem more pressing. Most important was the founding by William Whipper and other elite Philadelphians of the American Moral Reform Society at a meeting in 1836. At the meeting, Whipper led a caucus that, in response to a resolution supporting improved educational opportunities for free people of color, rejected references to the term *color*. According to Whipper and his allies, the society should consider the needs of all Americans; moreover, they asserted, any focus only on people of color simply accepted the bases for discrimination and exclusion prevalent in America.[87]

Whipper was firm in his position, and the debate he provoked was strong. His position had extensive support. There was always a substantial group opposed to anything that might appear to compromise the interracial character of any movement devoted to racial equality. James McCune Smith even opposed a convention of African American leaders set for 1841 on the ground that it represented "a 'caste convention' in order to abolish caste."[88]

Still, many who had initially worked with Whipper in creating the society, notably Junius Morel and Frederick Hinton, broke with him. Others began to express their opposition in the pages of Samuel Cornish's *Colored American*, which had faced a "names" controversy of its own only a few months before. Cornish himself ridiculed the Whipper position, suggesting of "some of our brethren in Philadelphia" that "nothing can be more ridiculous nor ludicrous, than their contentions about NAMES—if they quarrel it should be about THINGS." In a series of letters, the Pittsburgh activist Lewis Woodson, writing as "Augustine," made a somewhat stronger point. Arguing that "national prejudice must not only have been originally allowed, but intended by the Creator," he wrote about the positive role national pride and feeling could play in achieving precisely the goals Whipper and his colleagues championed. It was want of national pride, he said, that led too many African Americans to "the neglect of public works," especially education and "public accommodation." Although Woodson rejected what he described as "prejudice of caste," he believed that "national prejudice" and independent development could play an important role in strengthening the African American community.[89]

Woodson's views were far from eccentric, echoing, for example, the letter Junius Morel had written to Fredrick Hinton asserting his unwillingness that "the 'Colored American' should be merged in all the guilty oppression and hypocrisy of his pale-faced brother." Beyond that, Morel had said, it was important that the history of people of African descent be clearly understood. "Let our exertions to be free, our struggling after knowledge, our patience in adversity, our almost superhuman efforts to ascend the hill of science, unaided and alone, our throes of sorrow and our shrieks of bitter anguish, and our staid and unimpaired confidence in the providence of God—let them! yes, I say let them be written and read as the chronicles of the Colored Man." "The eyes of the civilized world are turned toward us," Morel wrote, concluding, "Let us stand, then, unmasked on the eminence of our own erection, and be seen of the whole world as we are."[90]

In his letter, then, Morel asserted more than the distinctive moral authority of African Americans. Echoing Walker, he also asserted the importance of autonomy of action and self-representation that encompassed more than the processes of mutual authentication found in abolitionism.

Such ideas had been put in the background by the dominating aims and purposes embodied in the founding of the *Liberator*. But their reappearance revealed much about issues relating to a black voice that had been taking shape in abolitionism in the years up to his writing.[91]

It is important to reemphasize that Morel's position did fit within the framework of abolitionism. His letter was, after all, published with glowing commentary in the white-edited *Emancipator*. Taken together, however, the letter and the commentary indicate the areas in which tensions had to develop regarding a black abolitionist voice. On the one hand, they show, again, the significance many abolitionists, black and white, invested in an independent, autonomous black voice. That voice served as a manifestation of the capability of African American people unsullied by the oppressiveness and hypocrisy of a slaveowning America. On the other hand, and like those indictments of white abolitionist prejudice appearing throughout this period, the dynamic surrounding Morel's letter shows how the very celebration of the black voice pointed up the extent to which the abolition movement, for all its professions of racial equality, continued to reinscribe notions of difference. This tension had increasing significance for African American writers and activists from the late 1830s through the 1840s, in proportion, not at all paradoxically, with the increasingly visible role African Americans played in antislavery and related movements against discrimination and exclusion.

The tendencies Morel represented were particularly apparent in discussions on the importance of an African American press during the period. Again, the 1830s and 1840s saw the founding of a spate of black-owned, black-edited papers, most of them short-lived, some continuing for several years. In 1837 the newspaper veteran Samuel Cornish, along with Philip Bell, founded the *Weekly Advocate*, renamed the *Colored American* a few weeks later. In the following year William Whipper created the *National Reformer*. David Ruggles also began publishing his *Mirror of Liberty*. The 1840s saw the creation of the *Mystery* by Martin Delany in Pittsburgh, the *Northern Star and Freemen's Advocate* by Stephen Myers in Albany, and the *Ram's Horn*, edited by Thomas Van Rensselaer and Frederick Douglass in New York. Most important was Douglass's creation of the *North Star* in Rochester in 1847.[92]

All these ventures, even Whipper's, asserted the importance of an independent voice. The *Weekly Advocate* made its purposes clear in its first issue, in words that looked back to those of Cornish's *Freedom's Journal*. "O how often have we been insulted and degraded, and how frequently do we feel the want of an ADVOCATE among us!" the editors wrote, and recalling the problems of *Freedom's Journal* and the *Rights of All*, they urged their friends to support the paper.[93]

In March 1837 the paper discarded the title *Weekly Advocate* in favor of *Colored American*, emphasizing still further the editors' understanding of their purposes. At the same time, Samuel Cornish, writing for the paper, declared purposes well in line with the kinds of ideas Junius Morel would put forward later in the year. In an editorial entitled "Why We Should Have a Paper," he declared that "without such an organ we can never enlist the sympathy of the nation in our behalf and in behalf of the slave." He continued, "Before the wise and good awake and consecrate themselves to our cause, we ourselves must have proclaimed our oppression and wrongs from the HOUSE-TOP," and he cited the precedents of Greece and Poland in support of his view.[94]

In addition, Cornish wrote, there were other factors to consider. A key reason for establishing the paper, he said, was "because no class of men, however pious and benevolent can take our place in the great work of redeeming our character and removing our disabilities. They may identify themselves with us, and enter into our sympathies," he wrote. "Still it is ours to will and to do." The very name of the paper was related to its purposes, an assertion of an identity that was American as well as one of "color." Anticipating the fight with Whipper, Cornish wrote that "the peculiarity of our circumstances require special instrumentalities and action." Both autonomy and authority were at the base of the *Colored American*'s understanding of its significance and role.[95]

This quest for autonomy and authority did not mean that the paper sought to speak to a wholly black audience. To the contrary, it intended to take its place within the complex of abolitionist journalism. It actively sought, and received, the endorsement of leading whites in the movement. In its second issue, for example, the *Colored American* published a letter of endorsement from the leading white abolitionists Arthur and Lewis Tappan, Joshua Leavitt, Simeon Jocelyn, and Elizur Wright commending it "to the patronage of Abolitionists throughout the land, and especially to their colored fellow-citizens." Needing, as always, to raise support, a few months later it published a long letter from a white Maine abolitionist, Mary Bright, endorsing the editors' opinion that only blacks could truly press the claim of humanity at the core of the abolitionist cause. The processes of mutual authentication remained as important for the development of an independent press as they had been within the movement generally.[96]

Such purposes continued to guide the *Colored American* while also guiding more general thinking about the importance of the press during the era. In 1841, for example, the Pennsylvania state convention of the free people of color urged the utility of a black-edited paper in words quite similar to those Cornish had used a few years before, resolving that "it is just as absurd to imagine, that we can become intelligent and enterprising, by others speaking and writing for us, as that we can become fat by their eating and drinking for us." "It is true," they added, "that kind friends may persuade the master to unrivet the fetters of the slave and the Legislature to repeal all unjust and unwholesome laws; but here their kind offices measurably end; the balance of the work is chiefly ours." Asserting, as well, the extent to which a paper could help unite the community, the convention nonetheless understood that both autonomy and authority, as well as the presentation of an African American voice to the outside world, were a crucial part of what an African American newspaper could accomplish.[97]

Many of these issues came to a head in 1847, when Frederick Douglass struck out with Martin Delany to establish the *North Star*. The complexities and difficulties involved in the founding of the paper, an act that has been seen as Douglass's declaration of independence from his longtime Garrisonian connections, themselves appear to have been related to tensions involving issues of autonomy and authority in the abolition movement.[98]

Writing about his purposes, perhaps mindful of the conflict lying behind the creation of his paper, Douglass too asserted the importance and the distinct authority of an autonomous African American voice. "It is neither a reflection on the fidelity, nor a disparagement of the ability of our friends and fellow-laborers, to assert what 'common sense affirms and only folly denies,'—that the man STRUCK is the man to CRY OUT." He added, in words that maintained the same purposes as Cornish's had a decade earlier. "It is evident," he wrote, "we must be our own representatives and advocates, not exclusively, but peculiarly"; they should speak with a distinct voice that brought its own message, and its own credibility, to the larger cause. Printing endorsements from black and white abolitionists alike, and relying on a subscriber base made up of about five times as many whites as blacks, Douglass saw in his paper the possibilities for mutual, reciprocal authentication that had shaped his career as an antislavery lecturer for the preceding seven years.[99]

Still, the emphasis on mutuality found in these papers should not obscure a deeper tension underlying their founding, a deeper drive for autonomy that seems to have pushed many, if not all, African American writers during this period. Frederick Douglass's career, which commenced especially with the founding of the *North Star,* provides something of a paradigm for this shift. The well-documented Garrisonian opposition to Douglass's venture was strong and in a few cases insulting. There were some who thought Douglass was acting with an unforgivable impudence. Edmund Quincy, who substituted for Garrison as editor of the *Liberator* through much of the controversy, was especially offensive, writing as though Douglass should claim no independence at all, saying that his efforts were simply the product of an excess of ego.[100]

To be sure, it is possible to exaggerate the opposition Douglass received, particularly its racial dimensions. Again, he was able to print endorsements from white as well as black abolitionist sources for his venture, and his paper had a strong white subscriber base. The *Pennsylvania Freeman,* going to the heart of his concerns, editorialized at the outset that whether or not his choice to create the paper was wise, "we cheerfully concede to him the right to be his own judge in the case, and cordially welcome him to the editorial fraternity." Even Garrison's Massachusetts Anti-Slavery Society, lamenting the potential loss of Douglass from the lecture circuit, resolved in January 1848 that he would continue to have influence, "let it be put forth in whatever direction he may think best."[101]

Nevertheless, the opposition had appeared, and it clearly had a significance for Douglass that went beyond a simple question of suspicion or, on his part, overexaggeration. In November 1849 Douglass wrote to the abolitionist Elizabeth Pease lamenting what he saw as a lack of support from many of his "best friends." He also noted a hesitancy on the part of black writers "about speaking through the columns of papers conducted by white persons." The accuracy of Douglass's perceptions is less important than the perceptions themselves.[102]

The issue of whether Douglass should found a paper was also part of a larger set of concerns he had about his career during the late 1840s, and perhaps before. Historians have often quoted Douglass's famous recollection in the 1850s of efforts by such figures as Garrison, Parker Pillsbury, and others to control his speaking, to add "a *little* of the plantation manner" to his speech, to stick to the facts, leaving to white abolitionists "the philosophy." Even if, as several historians have noted, neither the nature of the praise he received from his white colleagues nor Douglass's speeches indicate that the efforts were quite as constraining as he remembered, the recollection captures the concern about autonomy, the sense of its necessity, and a drive for independence that would ultimately come to fruition with the founding of the paper.[103]

By the late 1840s Douglass had removed himself from the kind of setting his recollections described, and in many ways. He had begun to move toward "political" abolitionism, largely under the influence of other black abolitionists. He had begun to see his role in the abolition movement circumscribed by Garrisonian demands. He had begun to seek an identity more clearly of his own making. Using the *North Star* as his outlet, he had revealed the existence of an abolitionist framework that, however confirming, could also be seen as confining. James McCune Smith's well-known comment about Douglass, in a letter to Gerrit Smith, that "only since his Editorial career has he begun to become a *colored man!*" is undoubtedly an important reflection of what Douglass's new independence really meant, both to him and to others.[104]

Douglass was certainly not the first to feel such constraints. In his 1838 letter to Amos Phelps decrying the hypocrisy of white abolitionists, Benjamin Roberts had also written about his perception of the need for an independent black press, suggesting not only that a paper would fill important needs but that otherwise independence would be impossible even in the context of abolitionism. Another writer, looking in a slightly different direction, argued that given the nature of American society, anything promulgated in even a mixed setting would "go forth as the sentiments and opinions of white men." Problems of control and autonomy remained crucial even as such eloquent figures as Douglass, Delany,

Bibb, and Cornish made their mark in the fight against prejudice and slavery.[105]

Given such a background of concern about autonomy, it is not surprising that an assertion of independence, as well as a sense that such assertions were needed, became part of African American rhetoric during the 1840s. In 1843, for example, when Henry Highland Garnet made his powerful call for insurrection, though he received some white support and met with some black opposition, he interpreted the opposition generally in terms similar to those Douglass and Roberts had expressed. In reply to an article written by Maria Chapman for the *Liberator*, Garnet defended not only his position but also his equally controversial turn to political abolitionism through his involvement in the new Liberty Party. He reminded Chapman, "Were I a slave of the Hon. George McDuffie, or John C. Calhoun, I would not be required to do anything more than to think and act as I might be commanded." He especially took Chapman to task for suggesting that his views were the product of "bad counsel," presumably, he suggested, "the '*counsel*' of some anglo-saxon." Reminding her that as an abolitionist she ought to appreciate his ability to think "without counsel," he cited precisely the kinds of constraints, and the deeper implications of those constraints, that Douglass would begin to feel by the end of the decade.[106]

Douglass's actions and Garnet's words reveal important tensions. In the final analysis, those tensions represented nothing like a permanent breach within the movement along lines of color. More crucial is what the words and actions of Garnet and Douglass say about the nature of the movement itself and the implications of the simple fact that black and white abolitionists all understood the black voice to be essential to its progress. That people disagreed on how it should be used is testimony, above all, to an African American authoritative role in defining the movement as a whole: it mattered where leading African Americans stood. That such figures as Douglass and Garnet sought to seize the voice for themselves remains an important reminder of how distinct that voice remained. Its very authoritativeness produced a conflict of confirmation and constraint that would mark African American literary efforts for some time to come.

7

African American Voices in the American Crisis, 1850–1861

Beginning in 1850 the developing political crisis in the United States over slavery had profound effects on African American writers and on the role of the African American voice in American life. Important continuities from the preceding decades still framed much that characterized African American literary forms. Thematic constants based on the experiences of slavery and oppression remained key elements in African American writing. Issues of authority and independence that had been taking shape within abolitionism for the preceding twenty years were further elaborated and debated as the movement matured and black participation increased.

Nevertheless, the 1850s brought concerns of their own, from the passage of the Fugitive Slave Law in 1850, to a revival of colonization activity among whites, to an increasing factionalism in the movement's final years. All helped to shape, and in some ways to reshape, tendencies in literature and thought. Most significantly, the debate over slavery itself grew increasingly strong and increasingly vitriolic during the decade as American expansion, American party politics, and the very success of abolitionism produced a more assertive proslavery position, in the North as well as the South. This aggressive proslavery position also helped to define a war of words in which the African American voice played a prominent role, for both sides.

The Origins of African American Literature

I

At the center of this war and also at the center of continuity and change in regard to African American letters was the experiential evidence blacks could provide against slavery and prejudice. The evoked black voice, especially the evoked voice of the slave, continued to be a critical part of the antislavery effort. The unique authority that fugitives brought to the argument against slavery remained particularly crucial. Figures whose careers had begun during the preceding decades, including Frederick Douglass and William Wells Brown, were joined by more recent escapees to lend the weight of their experiences to images of slavery as a brutal, dehumanizing institution.

The ongoing power of the fugitives' testimonies was exerted in several arenas. They continued to take to the stump, supplementing argument with narrative to bring home the brutality of the slave system. Their efforts continued to receive special recognition. The fugitive Samuel Ringgold Ward, touring with Henry Bibb in 1850, reported a good turnout for a meeting in Lowell, Massachusetts. He also heard, however, "that more persons would have attended, had they known that the S. R. Ward, advertised to speak, was a black man. Supposing me to be *nothing but a white man*, they did not take pains to attend. Well."[1]

Fugitives' published narratives also continued to play a major role in the literary efforts of the abolition movement, both in the United States and abroad, especially in Britain. An American critic quoted approvingly by a British writer suggested in 1850 that the "fugitive slave literature is destined to be a powerful lever," adding that "argument provokes argument, reason is met by sophistry; but narratives of slaves go right to the hearts of men." The opinion was widely echoed. An editorialist for the Canada-based *Voice of the Fugitive*, perhaps its editor Henry Bibb, noted that "all the literary productions of the colored population of this country are purely original with themselves, which renders them more interesting to the unprejudiced reader; not so with the white population —their writings are mostly made up of speculations." The narratives of life in slavery, this writer added, "have called the attention of the civilized world to its enormity" in ways nothing else could.[2]

Thus, the appeal of the narratives continued to be great, and as Bibb's words indicate, the fugitives' stories were seen by abolitionists to give people of African descent a special place in the world of American letters. Wendell Phillips made this point in 1853, when he approvingly cited Fredrika Bremer's opinion that "the fate of the negro is the romance of our history." A few years later, the abolitionist Thomas Wentworth Higginson, recounting the escape of William and Ellen Craft, wrote, "The romance of American history will, of course, be found by posterity in the lives of fugitive slaves."[3]

Moreover, the narratives continued to sell well. Frederick Douglass's *My Bondage and My Freedom*, an 1855 revision of his earlier *Narrative*, reportedly sold five thousand copies within two days of its publication. Solomon Northup was a northern free man of color kidnapped into more than a decade of slavery. Upon his rescue he became front-page news, and he was offered three thousand dollars for the rights to his story.[4]

Thus, the appeal of fugitives remained great, so great that by the mid-1850s the abolitionist press often ran stories warning sympathetic antislavery audiences of black speakers falsely representing themselves as fugitives, asking for assistance and support. It was not unusual for such people to do a "good business at begging" as they played on the sympathy of their audiences, as one Ohio case illustrated.[5]

Still, fugitives were not the only African Americans to contribute to abolitionism. Free people of color also continued to occupy a significant place in the movement. Those whose careers had begun earlier—James McCune Smith, William Cooper Nell, Charles Lenox Remond—were joined by new figures, including Frances Ellen Watkins and Charlotte Forten, whose work came to be incorporated into antislavery agitation during the 1850s. Their literary efforts continued to be understood within the framework of exemplary accomplishment. Thus, one may understand the thrust of William Lloyd Garrison's well-known introduction to Frances Ellen Watkins's first book of poems, which appeared in 1854. "The critic will remember," Garrison wrote, "that they are written by one young in years, and identified in complexion and destiny with a depressed and outcast race, and who has had to contend with a thousand disadvantages from earliest life." And he added that the pieces could only "deepen the interest already so extensively felt in the liberation and enfranchisement of the entire colored race."[6]

Thus, certain patterns of authority, both exemplary and legitimating, continued into the 1850s and beyond. As Garrison's words indicate, the

very fact that Watkins had suffered for her color gave a certain significance to her work. Both he and William Cooper Nell assured readers
that she had been close enough to slavery, given her Baltimore background, to make up for the fact that she had not been a slave herself.
Watkins herself emphasized her identity with her "poor blighted and
crushed people" in stressing her commitment to the antislavery cause,
providing a foundation for her career in the experiences created by her
color.[7]

The importance of such identity was not lost on African American
writers. Charlotte Forten—Robert B. Forten's daughter and Sarah Forten's
niece—began to write poetry and other pieces during her teenage years.
She seems to have understood the value of both her connections and her
color for her access to the abolitionist press and to have appreciated that
the two were intertwined. Receiving a pair of packages from Charles
Sumner, the antislavery Massachusetts senator, she remarked excitedly
about the signed extract of one of his speeches, along with the autographs of a host of important British and American personages. Grateful
for Sumner's kindness, she added, "I suppose I have to thank my color
for it."[8]

As Forten's words indicate, a measure of curiosity continued to underlie the recognition blacks could attain within the abolition movement
and elsewhere. It was the sort of curiosity that brought spectators to John
Mercer Langston's theology classes at Oberlin in 1853, as William and
Aimee Cheek have noted. Moreover, as Frances Foster has stressed in an
analysis of Garrison's introduction to Watkins's poems, the white celebration of abolitionism's racial inclusiveness could become patronizing,
even demeaning. This bothered Robert Purvis, for example, despite his
closeness to Garrison and others. It came through in the resentment he
expressed in 1860 after a white colleague boasted of how "he had eaten
with black men; he had *slept* with a black man; and this perhaps was as
severe a test as a man's antislavery character could be put to." Purvis responded, "A white man may eat and otherwise associate with colored
men, without conferring thereby any favor. It is quite possible that the
favor may be on the other side!" The notion that egalitarianism was a test
for whites was never far below the surface in abolitionist thinking; such
a white-centered approach to abolition remained an underlying current
up to the Civil War.[9]

Still, one should not conclude that collaborationist activities and purposes were severely undermined. They remained as strong, and as mutually encouraging, as they had since the early 1830s. In the literary realm, these purposes were particularly visible in Charlotte Forten's early career. Living in Salem with the family of the prominent abolitionist Charles Lenox Remond and socializing with the leading figures in the movement, Forten began to publish in the abolitionist press as early as 1855, when she was sixteen years old. Among her first pieces was the poem "To W. L. G.," which appeared in Garrison's *Liberator*. It was a response to "My Chosen Queen," a little poem written by Garrison. Describing his own commitment to liberty, "the passion of my soul," Garrison's lines led to Forten's praise. "Than thee," she wrote, "thy chosen Queen shall never find / A truer subject nor a firmer friend."[10]

Forten continued to write, and with some visibility. That same year, she produced a parting hymn for her class at the State Normal School in Salem, a piece William Cooper Nell inserted into Garrison's paper as evidence of what Boston's young black men and women were achieving. In 1858 her lengthy essay "Glimpses of New England" appeared unsigned in the *National Anti-Slavery Standard*, inaugurating a series of pieces Forten wrote for the magazine. A few months later the *Standard* printed, and the *Liberator* reprinted, her love poem "The Wind Among the Poplars," a ballad of a loved one lost at sea. In 1860 she wrote "The Slave Girl's Prayer" for insertion in the *Standard* and had it reprinted in the *Liberator*. Drawing on one of the oldest antislavery literary traditions, Forten portrayed a slave girl, facing "the doom of shame and sorrow," who prayed for death as "the refuge which the broken-hearted / Find only in the quiet of the grave."[11]

Frances Ellen Watkins joined Forten in receiving a fair amount of celebrity in the 1850s. She too published widely, aided, perhaps, by her being a niece of William Watkins, the "Colored Baltimorean" of earlier times. Like Forten, she wrote pieces for, and her work appeared in, the *Standard* and the *Liberator*. She also wrote for *Frederick Douglass' Paper*, which succeeded the *North Star* in 1851, the *Anti-Slavery Bugle* of Ohio, and, later, the *New York Anglo-African*. Unlike Forten, Watkins became prominent as an antislavery lecturer, her obvious gentility and eloquence contributing to the popularity of her work and to her celebrity. Accounts of her lectures, no less than her literary efforts, appeared often in the antislavery press. By 1857 her reputation was great enough that John Dixon Long, the moderately antislavery Maryland Methodist, could take notice of her abilities in his *Pictures of Slavery in Church and State*. In a passage defending southern literary achievement he acknowledged that the South had "given birth to but few poets" but added that there were some, including "Nathan C. Brooks, Amelia Welby, Edgar A. Poe, and Frances E. Watkins," all of whom, he noted, were Marylanders.[12]

Like Forten, Watkins derived much of her fame from her ability to work within the most clearly established traditions of abolitionist African American letters. Much of her work was religious, moralistic, and genteel, and much was devoted to the antislavery cause. Watkins brought the streams of genteel abolitionism together, drawing on antislavery traditions, as in her 1854 poem "The Slave Auction," in which she described a sale at which "young girls were there / Defenseless in their wretchedness." She described their "stifled sobs" and the tears of mothers whose children were being sold away.[13]

Watkins also wrote topical works. In 1856 the rector of Philadelphia's Church of the Epiphany, D. A. Tyng, was forced to resign following a moderately antislavery sermon. Watkins responded with a poem that was initially published in the *New York Tribune* and later reprinted in the abolitionist press in which she commented sarcastically on Tyng's dismissal:

> What holy horror filled our hearts —
> It shook our church from dome to nave —
> Our cheeks grew pale with pious dread,
> To hear him breathe the name of slave![14]

Because of their family connections, their ties to abolitionism, and their recognized ability, Forten and Watkins occupied a prominent place in the abolition movement as African American writers. Certainly, they were not alone. A fair number of African Americans continued to find a place in the major abolitionist publications, including the *Liberator*, the *Standard*, and *Frederick Douglass' Paper*. Smaller journals, including the *Bugle*, the *Pennsylvania Freeman*, the *Voice of the Fugitive*, and the *Provincial Freeman*, all provided important outlets for black writers. Most of their work, like that of Forten and Watkins, was devoted to the antislavery cause or to the evocation of those ideals of piety and gentility that had long informed African American writing.

A few of these writers did achieve a certain celebrity during the 1850s, including the poets Joseph Holly, James M. Whitfield, James Madison Bell, and Elymas Payson Rogers, a graduate of Beriah Green's Oneida Institute. Although none had the national audience Watkins and Forten were able to achieve, Holly and Whitfield had pieces published in the volumes of Julia Griffiths's important *Autographs for Freedom* in 1853 and 1854, joining such luminaries as Douglass and Harriet Beecher Stowe, James McCune Smith and Ralph Waldo Emerson.

The opportunities abolitionism could present for an African American writer were demonstrated particularly well, however, by the career of William Wells Brown, after Douglass the most prominent African American literary figure of the decade and certainly the most prolific. Not only had the fugitive Brown published a popular narrative of his life in the late 1840s, he had, even then, ventured outside the form with the *Anti-Slavery Harp*, his popular compilation of abolitionist songs and poems. During the 1850s he continued to produce autobiographical work in one form or another but also branched out to write one of the first novels by an African American, *Clotel*, several dramas, and the first travel account written by an African American, recounting his experiences in Europe. In all, he used his fugitive status to ground his authority as a writer and observer and as a marketing tool as well.

Both the importance and the nature of Brown's status are evident in his accounts of his European travels. Having begun to build a reputation in the United States, Brown left the country for Europe in the summer of 1849. He did so, he said, to follow in the footsteps of such illustrious predecessors on the English abolitionist stage as Douglass and Remond and also because he had been chosen by the Garrisonian-dominated American Peace League to serve as an American delegate to an international peace congress in Paris. He remained out of the country until 1854, supporting himself largely by writing and speaking, and arranging for the education of his daughters in an environment unmarked by the prejudice they would have had to face in an American school.[15]

Throughout his time abroad Brown maintained his celebrity status. He wrote for newspapers and periodicals in Britain during his time there and spoke widely, beginning with a highly praised address to the Paris Peace Conference. By 1856, according to his daughter, biographies of Brown had appeared not only in the United States and Great Britain but in Germany and in Paris, "in the French language," as well. Brown also wrote letters, mainly for *Frederick Douglass' Paper*, recounting his European experiences for an American audience. These were to serve as the basis for his travel book, *Three Years in Europe*, published in England in 1852 and appearing in an expanded American edition as *The American Fugitive in Europe* in 1855.[16]

In introducing this book, Brown made much of the significance of his status. Writing for his British readers, Brown conceded that "most of the contents of these Letters will be interesting chiefly to American readers," but he expressed "the hope, that the fact of their being the first production of a Fugitive Slave, as a history of travels, may carry with them novelty enough to secure for them, to some extent, that attention of the reading public of Great Britain." The book did find an English audience, and it was generally well reviewed in the English press, especially as evidence of what could be done by "one who has had to surmount so many difficulties in his literary career." The *Pennsylvania Freeman*, which praised the book as a first, stated that "if nothing else were attained by its publication, it is well to have another striking proof of the capability of negro intelligence."[17]

In the book itself Brown encouraged such readings. Validating his own background, he spoke of how, over the preceding decade, "a great impetus has been given to the anti-slavery movement in America by coloured men who have escaped from slavery. Coming as they did from the very house of bondage, and being able to speak from sad experience, they could speak as none others could." What Brown made clear in his book, however, was an ability to "speak as none others could" on an array of issues, based on the distinctive experience of being a man of color in the nineteenth-century world.[18]

Above all, Brown could use his distinctive status to comment on the nature of prejudice in America, contrasting his experiences there with his experiences abroad, where prejudice "vanished as soon as I set foot on the soil of Britain." He particularly seemed to relish recounting events at the Paris Peace Conference, at which his address had enhanced his European celebrity. He emphasized, above all, being put in a position to snub one of several American delegates who had subjected him to an icy hostility during their voyage across the Atlantic. According to Brown, all had been nasty, but he had particularly resented one who had suggested, in Brown's hearing, that "that nigger had better be on his master's farm." In the wake of his conference address, Brown had been approached by some of the most eminent Europeans, including Richard Cobden and the great Victor Hugo. As Brown was chatting with them, that same American approached, introduced himself, and requested an introduction to Cobden and Hugo. Brown wrote, "I need not inform you that I declined introducing this pro-slavery American to these distinguished men." Exposing the falsity of American pride in a situation where few could act as he had, Brown stressed the unique authority he brought to revealing the true nature of American prejudice.[19]

Still, no African American writer, not even Brown, was able to match the authority and stature of Frederick Douglass, whose influence ranged still farther, and in so many different ways. No one was more widely known than Douglass; accounts of his speeches and exploits were staples of the antislavery press. Even his political influence was remarkable. When, in 1855, New York's state assembly passed a resolution to end suffrage restrictions on blacks—a resolution ultimately tabled by the Senate—Douglass was widely given credit for its initial success, proving at least some real influence. What the abolitionist Robert Raymond said of Douglass in 1856 was widely echoed in the antislavery community, namely, that "his present character, attainments, and position constitute a phenomenon hitherto perhaps unprecedented in the history of intellectual and moral achievement," given his or igins and what he had been able to attain.[20]

Thus, the career he had begun in the 1840s continued to develop through the 1850s and beyond. His newspaper, renamed *Frederick Douglass' Paper*, gave him great visibility within the abolition movement. With its largely white readership and financial support, both of which Douglass cultivated, it put him, as an editor, on a plane with Garrison and such other influential abolitionist journalists as Oliver Johnson, William Goodell, and Sidney Howard Gay. White abolitionists, no less than black, sought a place in its pages, and Douglass's literary authority was enhanced by his editorial work. A revealing story that appeared well after emancipation gives some hint of this. In the early 1850s a teenage white New Yorker whose family home had been used by escaping fugitives decided to write a short story. It was, he recalled, "one containing all the horrors of slave life which the imagination of a boy filled with abolitionism could invent." Having it read by friends, he was thrilled by his ability to move his audience to laughter and tears, and he took the story to Douglass for possible publication. Douglass told him to improve it, saying that in time the young man would "feel ashamed of this effort and thank me for rejecting it." The fledgling writer was crushed. Later, however, he described the episode with praise for Douglass, for he realized that "Douglass was right after all, and couldn't buy that story to-day for lots of money."[21]

This did not mean, however, that Douglass had escaped the problem of color, even within the movement. Even the would-be writer whose work Douglass had criticized recalled his anger at being rejected by a "nigger," however much he later regretted the feeling. Douglass's own awareness of such tendencies informed his continuing quest for autonomy as the strivings for independence he and others began to demonstrate at the close of the 1840s became, if anything, somewhat stronger during the 1850s. Douglass is an important exemplar of such tendencies, for he openly rejected his initial Garrisonianism to become a political abolitionist, and an open hostility developed between him and some of the Garrisonians. In addition to using *My Bondage and My Freedom* to condemn, retrospectively, Garrisonian efforts to constrain him intellectually, he also took on prejudice within the movement, noting that, despite their calls for racial equality, "even abolitionists do not reduce their theory to practice" by treating blacks as equals in everyday life.[22]

During the 1850s Douglass's desire for independence led him to reassess both the history and the leadership of the abolition movement. In 1851, for example, he sought to undermine any impression of Garrison's intellectual leadership of the movement by calling attention to the roles of such black pioneers as James Forten, Richard Allen, and Hosea Easton in the development of the antislavery argument. By 1855 he was denying Garrison credit for anything but immediatism, and even this, he said, was a doctrine with precedents established "before Mr. Garrison was born." Perhaps in line with such purposes, Douglass encouraged others to learn the true pedigree of abolitionism in the works of earlier eras.[23]

Others in the movement felt some of the same impulses that influenced Douglass's career. Robert Purvis, perhaps reflecting his resentment of white patronization, in an exchange with the movement veteran Bayard Taylor denied that Taylor could truly comprehend American prejudice. Purvis said, "It takes a man of African blood to understand the contempt which is cherished by a certain class against people of African blood." New and influential figures as Samuel Ringgold Ward, Jermain W. Loguen, and especially Martin R. Delany similarly argued that black men needed to speak for themselves, that others could not speak for them. Each saw danger in excessive white influence; each saw potential constraints in paying too close attention to white opinion. Loguen described the core of the impulse in a letter to Douglass concerning white abolitionists who demanded unconditional loyalty. They seemed to believe, he said, that "the colored man is 'all right;' he is a 'good *nigger*' so long as he will worship at their shrine, and pour money into their coffers; but let him only presume to think and act for himself, like an independent and accountable being, and above all, to put his own penny into his own pocket, and he is no longer a 'good *nigger!*'"[24]

Delany's outspokenness on the issue of independence fit within this same framework. His influential 1852 book *The Condition, Elevation, Emigration, and Destiny of the Colored People of the United States*, an early statement of emigrationist views that would become stronger as the decade progressed, was no less a call for independent thought and action. In it Delany decried what he saw as a submissiveness among African Americans to white authority and an unwillingness to recognize brilliance among African Americans themselves. "Indeed," he wrote, "the most ordinary white person is almost revered, while the most qualified colored person is totally neglected." Along with Douglass, Delany condemned the prejudice he found among abolitionists. He too saw the problem as one of control. "Politicians, religionists, colonizationists, and abolitionists, have each and all, at different times, presumed to *think* for, dictate to, and *know* better what suited colored people, than they knew for themselves," he wrote. The result, he said, was a prevailing white ignorance of black people, as well as a continuing attempt to deny black men and women their proper place in abolitionism and elsewhere.[25]

Sentiments such as Delany's brought an ambivalent response from white abolitionists. For one thing, it was difficult to deny the truth of much of what Delany had said. Garrison, for example, in giving Delany's book favorable notice in the *Liberator*, endorsed Delany's strictures against abolitionist prejudice. He raised questions mainly about Delany's treatment of Garrison's own early colonizationist past and about "a tone of despondency, and an exhibition of the spirit of caste" in what he saw as the work's separatist and, especially, emigrationist thrust. Delany replied respectfully to Garrison, apologizing for errors of fact and promising to correct them in subsequent editions. But he added that although he was "not in favor of caste," he could see no future for black people in America except a life in which they were "subservient" to whites, "existing by mere *sufference*, as we, the colored people, do, in this country."[26]

Other exchanges were not so respectful. At least one abolitionist editor, Oliver Johnson, of the *Pennsylvania Freeman*, found Delany's book wholly offensive, suggesting that it might have been better "for his own credit, and that of the colored people," if Delany had not published the book. He suggested that much in the book was "bunglingly and egotistically presented." Delany responded harshly to Johnson's comments. Accusing Johnson of "negro-hate," he wrote that the charge of egotism "is but a prejudicial sneer at a black man, for daring to do anything upon his own responsibility."[27]

As Delany's words make clear, both knowledge and power were at issue, something Douglass, Loguen, and others recognized as well. This recognition influenced the thought and actions of men like Douglass and Delany, whose independent courses of action during the 1850s are well known. Even committed Garrisonians such as James McCune Smith and William Cooper Nell and such longtime integrationists as William Whipper saw some need for independence as the 1850s progressed.

At the same time, independence, as even Delany's remarks to Garrison indicate, did not mean entire separation, despite Garrison's interpretation. Even in his call for independence Delany sought and appreciated Garrison's support, classing him among those "*few* excellent exceptions" to the generality of white Americans who refused to recognize black equality. It was a measure of his respect for Garrison that he promised in his letter to correct the errors concerning Garrison in his book. It may have been even more a measure of that respect that, shortly thereafter, according to historian Vernon Loggins, Delany responded to abolitionist objections by ordering a halt to the book's circulation. Delany wanted independence, but like Douglass, he conceived of it in the context of an interracial antislavery movement that recognized the unique authority he could bring to it.[28]

The tendencies Delany displayed were particularly evident in the African American press, which continued to play an important part in abolitionism during the 1850s. A spate of papers appeared in the decade, including the weekly *Anglo-African*, edited by Thomas Hamilton in New York, the Cleveland *Aliened American*, and the Canadian-based *Voice of the Fugitive* and *Provincial Freeman*. Virtually all sought white as well as black support, white as well as black readers, even if the potential they represented for presenting an independent black voice was an express part of the purposes all professed. An editorial in the black-edited *Provincial Freeman* caught the sense of a need for an independent voice, its writer urging the need for a black-edited paper in Ohio to advocate black rights. "The papers of their country, conducted by *white men*, have *not* done it *properly*," the writer said, "and we doubt very much whether they will, at least for some time to come." Only a black-edited paper could be truly devoted to the cause of racial justice. At the same time, as the historian Jane Rhodes has noted, the *Provincial Freeman*, like most papers, sought to deliver its message to a readership that was white as well as black and depended heavily on white subscribers for support. The existence of such a readership was part of most editors' sense of the realm in which an authoritative, independent voice needed to make its distinctive influence felt.[29]

Such ideals and ambitions continued to inspire editorial efforts through the decade, culminating in the founding in 1859 of what was to be the first intellectually oriented periodical edited by African Americans, Thomas Hamilton's New York–based *Anglo-African Magazine*. The magazine offered articles on topics from chess and astronomy to black history and calls for education and uplift. Its writers included men and women of stature whose careers spanned the entire period of abolitionism. Sarah Douglass contributed to the journal, as did such longtime celebrities as Nell, Pennington, James McCune Smith, and Daniel Payne. So did more recent prominent writers, including Delany, Frances Ellen Watkins, and William J. Wilson. The plan was, as Hamilton stated in the first issue, that all articles, "not otherwise designated, will be the products of the pens of colored men and women," a plan the magazine adhered to throughout its brief existence.[30]

The magazine was well received, if not sufficiently supported financially to survive beyond its first year. Douglass, in his own relatively new

Douglass' Monthly, successor to his newspaper, described the magazine as "a bright new fact, and we trust the beginning of an era in the mental moral and religious history of the colored people in this republic." No less important, however, Hamilton was able to cite significant testimony from such white-edited antislavery papers as the *New York Independent* and the *Washington National Era* praising the magazine's quality and its value in the cause of racial equality.[31]

Thus, the 1850s saw a number of continuing trends, including conflict and cooperation, in the shaping of African American writing, especially within abolitionism. These were to be reinforced and modified by the specific events of the 1850s. Certainly foremost among these events was the Compromise of 1850, which many abolitionists viewed as a capitulation by northern politicians to the slave South both in its approach to slavery's expansion and in its specific provision for a strongly enforced Fugitive Slave Law. The new law made it easier for southern slaveholders to claim black men and women as runaways; it also obliged all U.S. citizens to assist in the capture of runaways.

The law brought terror to African American communities in the North, increasing the vulnerability of all people of color, free and fugitive alike. Even prominent men and women, including William Wells Brown, Jermain Loguen, and William and Ellen Craft, had to face the dangers the law created for them. The more famous found safety serving the abolitionist cause abroad, but in the wake of the law thousands were forced to flee the United States, going mainly to Canada.[32]

The law had major effects on abolitionist thought and on African American thought as well, as many historians have documented. In some ways it served to unite black and white abolitionists in the common purpose of saving fugitives from reenslavement through both legal resistance and direct action, as in such highly publicized cases as those of the Crafts, Anthony Burns, Shadrach Minkins, and Thomas Sims. Reaction to the law on the part of many northerners, especially in Boston but elsewhere too, built new support for the abolitionist cause out of resentment against a perceived southern aggressiveness, if nothing else.[33]

Among African Americans the law also provoked the interest in emigration that Delany sought to encourage in his controversial 1852 book. This interest grew during the 1850s, with a focus initially on Canada that broadened at various points to include Haiti and West Africa as possible destinations. At various times emigration interested such prominent black abolitionists as William J. Watkins (son of the "Colored Baltimorean" of earlier days), William Wells Brown, and the poet James Whitfield, as well as Delany, who, more than anyone, looked to Africa as a possible home for disfranchised African Americans. Growing emigrationist sentiment led to the formation of the African Civilization Society near the end of the decade, a group strongly supported and publicized by Thomas Hamilton's *Weekly Anglo-African*. Though the society was a source of great controversy among black abolitionists, it was nevertheless an important effort to formulate emigrationist ideas. Its stated ambition was to use African colonization to "establish a grand centre of negro nationality, from which shall flow the streams of commercial, intellectual, and political power which shall make colored people respected everywhere." Harking back in obvious ways to the emigrationist movements of the late eighteenth century and especially to the aims of Paul Cuffe in the early nineteenth, the society, despite strong opposition from such leaders as Douglass, Remond, and Nell, attracted the support of others, including Garnet, Pennington, and the poets James Madison Bell and Elymas Payson Rogers, as well as Delany.[34]

From the point of view of an African American literary voice, the main impact of this movement was to augment the force of the authoritative criticism of American society that the distinctive stance color created. In particular, the Fugitive Slave Law served to enhance the moral authority of the fugitives themselves and, by implication, of all persons who, because of color, were rendered vulnerable to its workings. A new language of moral defiance focused on the need to resist the law became a common part of African American rhetoric from the time of its passage. For example, within a month the outspoken fugitive Jermain W. Loguen, in an address to an audience in Syracuse, proclaimed his refusal to obey the law. "I was a slave; I knew the dangers I was exposed to," he told his audience, but he had determined to escape slavery, and he had succeeded. "I will not, nor will I consent, that anybody else shall countenance the claims of a vulgar despot to my soul and body." His freedom, he said, had come from God, and only God could take it away.[35]

Philadelphia's black leaders offered a response to the law that did still more to underscore its moral bankruptcy and, by implication, their own claims to a moral superiority. Meeting in 1854, they resolved that men and women "without crime" had been "condemned and treated as out-laws" by the American government, and they therefore declared them-selves "absolved from all obligations to obey its slaveholding behests, and fall back upon our natural rights." Henceforward, they said, all should adopt the motto "Liberty or death." Paraphrasing a revolutionary motto hallowed by time, they concluded, "Resistance to the slave-hunters is obedience to God," and they pledged themselves "to resist all such laws by such means as we shall deem right and expedient." Others, too, cited the "example of the Revolutionary Fathers" as a guide for their own course in the face of oppressive national legislation.[36]

Whatever the determination for resistance these words evoked, their claim to a true inheritance from the Founding Fathers found a full ex-pression. As they had earlier in American history, African American writ-ers used their own position to claim a truer faith in America's heritage than that of their oppressors. This point was reinforced by a renewed con-centration on the role of African Americans in the Revolution itself. As had been the case in responses to colonization, black contributions to American independence highlighted the injustice of 1850s policies. As William J. Watkins said, addressing proslavery whites, given that role, "why should you, in point of privileges, like Capernium of old, be ele-vated to heaven, and we be cast down to Hell?" But no one did more to establish the Revolutionary role of blacks than William Cooper Nell, whose compendium *Colored Patriots of the American Revolution* ap-peared in 1855. Intended, as he told Wendell Phillips, to "show the world Colored American valor and antecedents," Nell's book was also intended to reiterate for African Americans their claim to America's Revolution-ary past. The book was well received in the abolitionist press and else-where. The *New Bedford Standard* recommended, "Read this book, and learn that patriotism, courage, and talents are not confined to particular races, or complexion." The book continued to be cited through the decade for the way it emphasized black claims to citizenship and, even more, highlighted the hypocrisy of those who would deny those claims.[37]

Within such a context it was not difficult to create a literary response to the Fugitive Slave Law that worked within older traditions to offer a condemnation of slavery and discrimination in the United States. The freeborn Ohio poet Joshua McCarter Simpson described Canada in a poem from the 1850s entitled "The Bondman's Home," in which he played on American hypocrisy—and Revolutionary traditions—by writing, "There men protected are / By the Lion's paw," and declaring, "John Bull is the man for me." At least two poets took their inspiration from Stephen Foster's popular song "O, Susannah" to indict American failings. One, in a poem entitled "Away to Canada," published in Henry Bibb's *Voice of the Fugitive*, deliberately evoked folk tradition to indict both the political and the religious hypocrisy of slavery's defenders:

> I heard old master pray last night—
> heard him pray for me
> That God would come and in his might,
> From Satan set me free.
> So I from Satan would escape,
> And flee the wrath to come—
> If there's a fiend in human shape,
> Old Master must be one.
> O! Old Master,
> While you pray for me,
> I'm doing all I can to reach the land of Liberty.

The other poem, purportedly sung by a group of arriving fugitives, concluded simply, "I'm going up to Canada, / Where colored men are free."[38]

II

As these poems indicate, even emigration could be viewed as an abolitionist act in the 1850s. As such, it was also an act occurring within the context of political and ideological debates over slavery as an institution. The decade of the 1850s saw a steady heightening of sectional tensions in the United States, focused especially on the potential expansion of slavery into newly acquired western territories and, as the debates came to be defined, over the continuing existence of slavery itself. As the sections became increasingly polarized, the rhetorics of slavery and antislavery themselves became increasingly violent, especially as growing antislavery sentiment in the North and elsewhere put the white South increasingly on the defensive.

In this debate the credibility and authoritative character of the African American voice occupied a central place. Abolitionists had long drawn on that voice as a measure of their own authenticity and legitimacy. The voice itself had played a key role in the development and elaboration of abolitionist arguments. Because of the experiential authority African Americans had annexed, the African American voice was something slavery's defenders had to confront. The resulting confrontation helped to shape the meaning of African American writing, which, in the 1850s came to take on increasing significance in light of the main lines of debate involving pro- and antislavery forces.

Although direct encounters between black spokespeople and proslavery figures were rare—William Wells Brown's opportunity to snub a racist American was unusual—they did occur. In 1855 the fugitive Lewis Hayden was able to confront the Alabama slaveholder John Githell at a hearing before the Massachusetts legislature regarding a bill to limit the reach of the Fugitive Slave Law. Githell had come to Massachusetts to testify against the legislation. Hayden, noting that both were "from the South," used his own experiences to dismiss the slaveholder's efforts to defend the institution. Another celebrated confrontation took place in London in 1860 when Martin Delany was introduced in glowing terms to delegates of the International Statistics Congress. Proslavery and southern delegates from the United States, including former vice president George Mifflin Dallas and the Georgian Augustus Baldwin Longstreet, declared themselves offended by Delany's reception. They were even more offended by Delany's declaration, in response to the introduction, that he had "only to say *that I am a man*," words that received hearty applause from the rest of the audience.[39]

Even if direct confrontations were rare, however, implicit confrontations much like those that occurred during the 1840s became increasingly visible as the debate over slavery heated up in the 1850s. The power of the black voice also remained very much at issue as slavery's defenders sought to make their case. This was made clear, at one level, by their efforts to use that voice for their own purposes, harking back to Edmund Botsford's efforts early in the century. One may note, among the more imaginative efforts, an 1850 dialogue in the *Southern Literary Messenger*. As described by the historian Thomas Virgil Peterson, the dialogue featured articulate representatives of the races of "Ham" and "Japheth," the descendant of "Ham" declaring his acceptance of an eternal role as servant and dependent to the white sons of Japheth and his appreciation for that longstanding proslavery reading of Scripture. Less fancifully, this effort also underlay by proslavery portrayals of slave contentment in fiction, reportage, and such proslavery travelogues as Nehemiah Adams's *South-Side View of Slavery*, with its many purported interviews with happy slaves. No less pointed was the recruitment of at least one proslavery slave to make the proslavery argument. In 1861, as sectional tensions reached a peak, a group of white Georgians sponsored an attack on abolitionism by a slave named Harrison Berry, including testimony from a slaveholding sponsor authenticating Berry's authorship of the work. The slaveholder wrote, "The sentiments are his, for I have heard him express them time and again, long before I ever dreamed of his writing a book." Berry argued, in essence, that slavery was an institution hallowed by both history and holy writ.[40]

Still, the main line of attack by proslavery writers continued the effort, seen in the work of James Henry Hammond and others, to question the role of fugitive slaves and blacks in abolitionism and to challenge the narratives that were so important in shaping the abolitionist cause. In 1853, for example, the South Carolinian David McCord wrote for the *Southern Quarterly Review* a lengthy review of a new edition of Charles Ball's 1836 narrative, reiterating questions, on factual grounds, of Ball's account of the treatment of slaves. In 1852 Mary Howard Schoolcraft echoed Hammond by condemning fugitive slaves generally as "fugitives from labor" and specifically taking on the role they had played "under the revolutionizing patronage of the abolitionists." A few years later she even more pointedly described "all the *lies* told to Abolitionists by *runaway* negroes" as "pure inventions of their own wicked deceits."[41]

It is difficult not to see in such words a recognition by proslavery writers of the power the fugitives were exerting, especially as these writers played on the issue in so many ways. Elaborating, perhaps, on School-craft's comments, the northern proslavery writer Nehemiah Adams criticized a northern tendency to view the fugitive as "the incarnation of injured innocence," the perception that "liberty, priceless liberty, is personated in him." Similarly, an English critic of the role of fugitives in the British antislavery movement, referring to Ellen Craft, was reported by the *National Anti-Slavery Standard* to have said, "Show them (meaning the people of England) a Congo wench, with a face like a bull dog, and they will bow in homage to her charms." The Georgia theorist Thomas

R. R. Cobb, having echoed Thomas Jefferson's strictures on Phillis Wheatley, made the same point when he identified the attainments of some of the more celebrated fugitives as consisting chiefly of "moving in the first circles of society in Great Britain."[42]

In still other ways proslavery forces sought to undermine the credibility of African Americans and the role of the African American voice in the debate over slavery. Sometimes the challenges were quite direct, as when, in 1852, proslavery southerners in England sought to discredit Ellen Craft, by then a visible member of the fugitive opposition to slavery in Britain, by circulating a rumor that she had "grown so tired of liberty" that she sought to return to southern slavery.[43]

Finally, friends of slavery—and opponents of abolitionism—turned to more familiar literary devices. Harking back to the "bobalition" parodies of the 1820s and 1830s, they continued, for example, to find ways to use dialect to ridicule the black voice and its role in abolitionism. Louisa McCord, David McCord's wife and a celebrated advocate of slavery in her own right—she once wrote that Charles Lenox Remond was hoping to create in America "the highest perfection of African Cannibal civilization"—did so in an essay condemning abolitionism and feminism at the same time. Portraying a scene with "the lovely Miss Caroline, the fascinating Miss Martha, elbowing Sambo for the stump," she had the victorious Sambo declare, "Ebery man must help hisself. I git de stump anyhow, and so, fellow-citizens, Sambo will show how Miss Marta desarve what she git."[44]

Something similar may be seen in many of the lecture parodies that became a staple of the minstrel stage in the 1840s and especially the 1850s. Directly descending from the "bobalition" tradition, and even from the slave "scientist" burlesqued by Henry Hugh Brackenridge in *Modern Chivalry*, these joke lectures, in dialect, ridiculed what were presented as both intellectual and political pretensions among African Americans, covering everything from abolitionism to astronomy, from literary topics to literature itself. Some could be quite direct in their references to contemporary African American writing, as in a series of mock letters from Europe ascribed by their author, William Levison, to one "Professor Julius Caesar Hannibal." At the heart of Levison's parody, dramatizing T. R. R. Cobb's comment, was an effort to challenge the celebrity of fugitives in Britain and, by implication, their authority in abolitionism generally. Thus, Levison had his protagonist recount "Hannibal"'s first meeting with a well-to-do Englishwoman, who, especially pleased to have a black guest, wanted to know if he was a fugitive. Excitedly, she asked, "In de name ob heaven, 'ow *did* you git away from them — 'ave you bin beaten much, or branded wid 'ot hirons, do let's look at you."[45]

Levison then went on to make "Hannibal" a celebrity. As "Hannibal" was made to recount, "It got noised round de naborhood dat I wus riv, and de letters ob inwatations and de nabors flocked in from all quarters." He "had inwite, de fust ting, to lecture at de *Eggbeaters' Hall* in de Strand, de greatest temple ub Abolishunism and Deism in all 'Urope." He even got to meet with "Mrs. Victoria Coburg, de Queen, to wisit her at de Buck ob Dukeinham's Palace in St. Jeemes's Park." The references to the kinds of accounts fugitives in Europe were sending back to the abolitionist press in America, and especially the references to so widely noticed a work as Brown's *Three Years in Europe*, were clear. So, too, was the effort to address, through ridicule, the problem of fugitive authority in the debate over slavery.[46]

Given the anxiety such efforts reveal, it is not difficult to suggest a mutually reinforcing relationship between the abolitionist evocation of a black testimony against slavery and at least some of the directions proslavery rhetoric took during the 1850s. This relationship focused, in part, on the credibility of that voice as such. So far as African American writing was concerned, the debate also helped reinforce earlier emphases, while giving greater relevance to the role of that voice in abolitionism.

One can see some evidence of this focus in regard to dialect and to burlesque as such. Abolitionist papers often ran some of the uglier versions of proslavery caricature in their pages, demonstrating their own recognition of the form and their rejection of it. In 1850, for example, the *Liberator* published an account of an abolition meeting from the *New York Era* in which the speakers were referred to as "Garrison's band of nigger minstrels." In 1855 leading New York abolitionists, black and white, organized a celebration of West Indian emancipation. Sidney Howard Gay spoke, as did William Lloyd Garrison. A sizable contingent of black and white New Yorkers attended. The *New York Evening Mirror* also sent a correspondent, who characterized the "sable gentry" of the city by exclaiming, "Lor de Massy, how they yah, yah'd at their own display, Miss Phillisy proudly cachinating at sight of the tall plumes of Massa Pompey." The writer also presented a version of the hymn to free-dom composed for the occasion:

> De Lord he lubs good nigga well,
> He know de nigga by de smell;
> And while de pitch holds out to burn,
> De brackest nigga may return.

Both the *Liberator* and the *National Anti-Slavery Standard* ran the *Mir-ror*'s version of the day's events, along with their own more straightfor-ward accounts, in an effort, analogous to the *Mirror's*, to turn ridicule back on the burlesque tradition, while commenting on the issues of credibility that tradition raised. Doing so was consistent with the earliest abolitionist purposes, for it allowed both papers and their supporters to re-assert their moral superiority to an American society in which prejudice ruled as they conveyed, through apparent ridicule, their freedom from such views. At the same time, through the contrast they created, they em-phasized the significance to the cause of the more valid representation they had to offer, again putting them in the context of the increasingly vitriolic debates over slavery and race.[47]

This dualistic stance toward minstrelsy-derived proslavery representa-tions may also help to explain the continuing presence of antislavery di-alect pieces within the antislavery movement. Abolitionist papers of the decade continued to print poems and dialogues putting antislavery mes-sages in dialect form. Antislavery orators, including Douglass and Brown, found the evocation of antislavery dialect a useful way to enliven their lectures while, at least implicitly, giving dialect a dimension its minstrel forms tended to deny.

More important, however, is the extent to which black abolitionist voices and those of slavery's advocates entered more fully into the kind of dialogue that had begun in the mid-1840s. The dialogue itself would be-come increasingly clear in the critical atmosphere of the 1850s. The themes and images on which each chose to focus reflected a need to re-spond to the other. This was the case, for example, in regard to the con-troversy created by the duchess of Sutherland, in England, who in 1853 sponsored an "Affectionate and Christian Address of Many Thousands of the Women of England to Their Sisters, the Women of the United States of America." This antislavery appeal, inspired in part by the publication of Harriet Beecher Stowe's *Uncle Tom's Cabin*, condemned the institution as contrary to Christianity, especially because it brought about the separation of families and because it denied the enslaved an education in "the truths of the Gospel."[48]

The address produced a storm of proslavery criticism, including replies from such prominent, offended American women as Louisa McCord and Julia Gardner Tyler, the wife of the former president. Tyler's response was publicized especially widely, appearing in pamphlet form, in the *Southern Literary Messenger,* and even in the *New York Times.* Echoing the earlier words of Hammond, she described programs of religious instruction for the slaves on southern plantations, "often by colored pastors," and asserted that the separation of families was "of rare occurrence among us, and then attended by peculiar circumstances." The duchess's picture of slavery, Tyler suggested, "could only have been derived from some dealer in, and retailer of fiction," probably Stowe herself.[49]

Tyler's response was itself ripe for rebuttal and helped to spark one of the first public statements from a fugitive slave who would later become quite prominent. Harriet Jacobs drew on her own experiences to deny Tyler's contentions. Jacobs, whose remarks originally appeared in the *New York Tribune* and were reprinted in the abolitionist press, focused in an open letter on Tyler's assertion that families were separated only under "peculiar circumstances." Signing herself "A Fugitive Slave," she drew on her experience to demonstrate that those "peculiar circumstances" could hardly redound to the credit of a slaveholding South, since her mother and sisters had been torn from her to satisfy "her mistress's jealousy and her master's brutal passion." Mrs. Tyler, Jacobs could testify, was telling nothing like the truth about the nature of slavery in the South.[50]

Tyler also called forth a rebuttal from the Georgia fugitive John Brown, or it at least helped shape the narrative given the imprimatur of Brown's experiences. Speaking through his amanuensis, the British abolitionist L. A. Chamerovzow, Brown spoke of the family separations he had witnessed, noting, "It is all very well for Mrs. Tyler to say that families are not often separated. I know better than that, and so does she." As these responses to Tyler help to emphasize, neither the proslavery case

nor the black testimony serving the cause of abolition occurred in ignorance of the other. Throughout the 1850s there were ways in which they
helped to shape each other, each defining key themes, emphases, and
rhetorical strategies in the other.[51]

One certainly sees this in the issues Tyler raised, and her opponents
addressed, especially that of family separations. For both fugitives and
proslavery writers this continued to be a matter of central concern, something fugitives always stressed when recounting the horrors of the system.
Many of those who defended slavery treated stories of family separation
as Mrs. Schoolcraft did, as one of the "monstrous falsehoods" abolitionists had used to build sympathy for their cause. Others, including the
northern proslavery writer Nehemiah Adams, echoed Tyler in describing
such separations as rare occurrences. William Harper, among others,
simply asserted that such separations could not be too painful for the
slaves since blacks were deficient in family feeling.[52]

The very denials, coupled with attacks on fugitive testimony, testify
both to a proslavery awareness that fugitives were helping to shape perceptions of slavery and to a sensitivity to what was being said. The same
may be said of the related charges of brutality and licentiousness that
played such an important role in fugitive narratives, entering, from there,
into abolitionist rhetoric. Again, proslavery writers were at pains to deny
both the character and the origins of the charges made against them.
The South Carolina writer William Grayson, introducing his proslavery
poem "The Hireling and the Slave," said of abolitionists that they "regard
slavery as a system of chains, whips, and tortures. They consider its
abuses as its necessary condition, and a cruel master its fair representative." He at least acknowledged the importance of fugitive accounts
when he added, "With these people the cruelty of slavery is an affair of
tropes and figures. But they have dealt so long in metaphorical fetters
and prisons, that they have brought themselves to believe that the Negroes work in chains and live in dungeons." In asserting, as he would,
that slavery could be something very different, he showed the impact of
those metaphors on his own thinking as well.[53]

Grayson revealed his sense of their impact even more when he suggested that any cruelty that did exist in the system had to be considered
"abuse," adding that such "abuses of slavery are as open to all reforming
influences as those of any other civil, social, or political condition." As

Eugene D. Genovese has shown, such reformist tendencies were widespread among slavery's more thoughtful defenders during the 1850s, and the very abuses Tyler felt compelled to deny were those reformers sought to correct, including family separations and ignorance of the Gospel, along with problems of violence and sexual abuse. Although, as Genovese has noted, the reformers' focus was determined largely by their own ideals of a Christian slaveholding society, it is not difficult to see how abolitionist narratives of brutality led to at least some of the reforming focus in the proslavery South.[54]

But, again, one can also see the specific responses of proslavery writers adding to the urgency of an African American testimony against the institution. When Frances Ellen Watkins evoked the "shriek" of a slave mother about to lose her son in the lines "She is a mother, and her heart / Is breaking in despair," that familiar motif became all the more important to stress, given the charge by William Harper and others that blacks lacked family feeling. Thus, if the great number of narratives describing the breakup of plantations out of economic necessity continued to make family separations an endemic characteristic of slavery, the constant evocation of images of slaveholders wholly indifferent to the sufferings caused by family separations directly responded to such proslavery charges. Descriptions such as Solomon Northup's of slaveholders as "entirely deaf" to the kinds of shrieks Watkins evoked were a staple of the narrative tradition by the time he offered it in 1853.[55]

The same was true of so much else to be found in African American writings. For every assertion, such as that of William Harper, that female slaves were lacking in chastity, one could find more than one fugitive account of slaveholder lasciviousness, much like that with which Harriet Jacobs answered Julia Tyler. For every assertion, such as that of E. N. Elliott, that "we are instructing them in the principles of our common Christianity," one could find continuing narrative accounts of slaves denied access to religion or even punished for their beliefs.[56]

Still, the differences ultimately had to do with more than specifics. At one level, they had to do with the nature of the system itself. For slavery's defenders, the system could be described in terms of that paternalism and organic stability that many historians have seen at the center of proslavery thought. Recognizing the humanity of their slaves —they saw them as more than "things," despite what abolitionists charged—slaveowners were, they said, on the road to creating a peaceful, balanced social system that would benefit both groups. So much in the fugitive narratives was aimed at giving the lie to such views. So much supported the contention of the Georgia fugitive John Brown, through his amanuensis, that "cruelty is inseparable from slavery as a system of forced labor; for it is only by it, or through fear of it, that enough work is got out of the slaves to make it profitable to keep them."[57]

And above all it was a system whose victims were far from content with their status, whose lives were filled with a hope for freedom. Fugitive narratives continued to follow the precedent set by Douglass in documenting an awareness of that hope from an early age and a dedication to seeing it fulfilled. Proslavery writers showed their awareness of this aspect of the narratives' case when they confronted it in their works, trying, for example, to dismiss the hope as misguided. Albert Taylor Bledsoe suggested that "a wrong desire in one relation of life is not a reason for a wrong act in another relation thereof," a complex way of saying simply that no one should abolish slavery simply because some slaves claimed to want it. Louisa McCord, more colorfully, simply said of "Quashee" that "if we teach him to bray out for liberty, i.e., for idleness, verily it is as easy for him to bray to that tune as to any other."[58]

Black testimony thus occupied an important place in the debate over slavery, and it was enhanced by that debate. Its authenticating power for abolitionism helped to define the issues for both sides. Its credibility and authority also became crucial. Even Abraham Lincoln, a friend to neither slavery nor blacks, recognized its import, disputing a proslavery theologian who had asserted that "it is better for *some* people to be slaves," meaning blacks in particular. Suggesting, hypothetically, that the theologian might have a slave named Sambo, Lincoln noted, in debating this particular issue, that "no one thinks of asking Sambo's opinion on it." Not entirely right in his assessment of Sambo's silence—just ask Louisa McCord—he was nevertheless absolutely correct in citing the relevance that many people felt should be attached to the slave's voice.[59]

III

If the importance of African American testimony was enhanced by the debate over slavery, the impact of that voice on the debate itself was even further augmented by the appearance in 1851 and 1852 of Harriet Beecher Stowe's *Uncle Tom's Cabin*. As its inspiration of the duchess of Sutherland's "Address" emphasizes, the novel's influence was felt widely—in the North and the South, in England and Europe, among black and white readers alike. Its influence was such as to focus many of the issues relating to an African American voice over the preceding two decades. Among abolitionists and defenders of slavery it raised issues of strategy and authenticity in the debate over the institution. More than any earlier work, it raised issues about how African Americans were to be represented in antislavery writing. Also more than any earlier work, it helped produce important transformations in African American writing.

Stowe's purposes in writing *Uncle Tom's Cabin* were compatible with much that inspired other abolitionist writers. She hoped to expose not only the character of slavery but the extent to which it was "a system so necessarily cruel and unjust" as to be impossible to justify. More importantly, she wanted hers to be an accurate portrayal of the institution, a goal she felt she had achieved. There were many, especially in the South, who would know the "fidelity" to slave society of the scenes she recounted. In keeping with abolitionist traditions, she felt she could use the experiences of slaves, as related in fugitive narratives, to provide the most damning and accurate testimony against the institution.[60]

The book's immediate impact has been well documented. It sold rapidly—some 100,000 copies within two months of its initial publication. Stowe became a celebrity within the antislavery movement in both the United States and Britain. William Wells Brown observed that by September 1852 some seven different publishers in England alone had produced editions of what he described as a "wonderful book." As so many have noted, nothing did as much to increase both the visibility and the popularity of abolitionism as did *Uncle Tom's Cabin*, as a novel, as a play, and in a variety of other forms as well.[61]

Proslavery as well as antislavery forces perceived the power of *Uncle Tom's Cabin*. Stowe was considered foremost among those makers of "tropes" said to have been taken in by lying fugitives, and almost as soon as her book appeared proslavery writers began to attack its credibility and its potential influence. Louisa McCord wrote of Stowe that "her black angels are as hard to find as her white devils, both being creations whose existence belongs to the *terra incognita* of her own brain." A writer for Boston's *Christian Observer* agreed that Stowe had engaged in caricature and also worried that the work cast too much opprobrium on the "conscientious, devoted, and true" Christians of the South. The novel brought forth a raft of replies, including some answering southern fiction.[62]

The virtually symbiotic relationship between Stowe's novel and the narrative tradition has also been well documented. Richard Blackett's comment that the narrative tradition helped pave the way for Stowe's success is well justified. So is Richard Yarborough's view that the novel helped shape the narrative tradition as such after 1852. It certainly helped to enhance an interest in the fugitives themselves, especially in England. Samuel Ringgold Ward, for example, was induced to leave Canadian labors for England in 1853 in large part to take advantage of feelings awakened there "by the unprecedented influence of Mrs. Stowe's masterpiece." So notable were these quickened feelings that William Levison used his "Julius Caesar Hannibal" to ridicule them from the minstrel stage. Looking for London lodgings, "Hannibal" was asked by a landlady, "Are you one ob thim poor hoppressed people Mrs. Butcher Store has so beautifully wrote on, from that barberous savage country, North America?" Hannibal, "wid an eye to de lodgins," agreed that he was, gaining a place for himself in a comfortable home.[63]

To the extent that the credibility of Stowe's book derived from the authority invested in the fugitives, Stowe appreciated the background those narratives provided. Not only did she contact Douglass for assistance but she read widely in the narrative tradition. She spoke directly with fugitives, whom she contacted through a network of servants she knew and employed. She acknowledged these debts in her "concluding remarks" to the novel and in a book she published two years later, *Key to Uncle Tom's Cabin.* There she provided clear, full references for the accounts upon which she had drawn, accompanied by supporting extracts, giving to the narratives the authority for her contentions that they had long received within abolitionism.[64]

Abolitionists appreciated both Stowe's debt and the credibility it gave her work. Martin Delany, for example, identified the specific narratives that had informed *Uncle Tom's Cabin* even before her *Key* appeared. That she had "draughted largely on all of the best fugitive slave narratives," he asserted, citing Douglass's, Brown's, and Bibb's, "only makes her work the more valuable, as it is the more *truthful.*" *Uncle Tom's Cabin* also provided a framework within which the reputation of fugitive narratives and other works was still more enhanced. Not uncommon was a review of Solomon Northup's *Twelve Years a Slave* that not only compared the work to Stowe's but gave Northup's a higher recommendation, suggesting that hers was "only an ingenious and powerfully wrought novel, intended to illustrate what Solomon saw and experienced." Even William Wells Brown's account of his European travels benefited from a comparison with *Uncle Tom's Cabin* that cited his account as an example of "what a real fugitive slave has to say for himself."[65]

Much of the earliest criticism of Stowe's novel from within abolitionism can also be understood within the framework of authenticity fugitive narratives had helped create. Much focused on the ending of the novel and Stowe's decision to have her most militant character, George Harris, depart for Liberia. Many critics expressed concern that this would be taken as representative of African American desires. Robert Purvis wrote to the *Pennsylvania Freeman* that "the imposture in the chapter referred to should cause its condemnation as pernicious to the well-being of the colored people in this country." Delany too took Stowe to task for her colonizationism, asserting in a letter to Douglass that such sentiments proved "she knows nothing about us," meaning "the *Free* Colored People of the United States." Two years later a writer in the *Provincial Freeman*, probably Samuel Ringgold Ward, characterized that conclusion as "a piece of needless and hurtful encouragement of the vile spirit of Yankee Colonizationism."[66]

Stowe's emphasis on authenticity also underlay some of the criticism of the character of Tom and the extent to which he appeared to represent an unhealthy submissiveness to tyranny, actually reinforcing, for some readers, proslavery ideas. According to such critics as Wendell Phillips and William Watkins, Stowe's Tom could easily fit into widespread proslavery images of slave contentment, undermining contrary representations of the slaves' hope for freedom. As Richard Yarborough notes, such proslavery writers as William Gilmore Simms and Nehemiah Adams did seek to appropriate Tom as an example of the success of slavery in transforming a savage into a Christian.[67]

Still, the dominant reaction among abolitionists to Stowe's novel was positive. Frederick Douglass was only one early champion of the work, which was described in his *Paper* as a "truly great work." According to an early review, perhaps written, as Robert Levine has suggested, by Douglass's English collaborator Julia Griffiths, Stowe "evinced great keenness of insight into the workings of slavery, and a depth of knowledge of all its various parts, such as few writers have equalled, and none, we are sure, have exceeded." Whoever wrote the review, the sentiments were certainly Douglass's, since, as Levine has said, Douglass endorsed Stowe and her work in a variety of publications and speeches.[68]

Other endorsements were as strong. William Craft, in England, defended the novel against proslavery attacks in the London newspapers, focusing particularly on Stowe's development of slave characters. While suggesting that one slaveowning character, the kindly Mrs. Shelby, might be a rare type, he vouched wholly for the characters of Tom, Aunt Chloe, and George Harris. Craft, like many, cited his own experiences in slavery to support his contentions. Douglass's view of the novel's potential to affect the debates over slavery were still further endorsed by the 1853 Colored National Convention, whose delegates included the most significant black abolitionists. Recognizing the influence Stowe's novel had achieved, the delegates described it as "a work plainly marked by the finger of God, lifting the veil of separation which has too long divided the sympathies of one class from another." Despite the critics, most black and white abolitionists approved of Stowe's novel and generally endorsed the picture of slavery it presented.[69]

Perhaps nothing was a better testimony to the importance many African American writers saw in Stowe's work than the extent to which it both inspired further work and even became a part of the common vocabulary of debate. No one acknowledged this importance more than Solomon Northup, whose experiences Stowe recounted in her *Key*. Dedicating his own narrative to her, Northup presented it as "another Key to Uncle Tom's Cabin," authenticating her work and his at the same time and placing both within the tradition of black testimony against slavery. Frances Ellen Watkins was especially drawn to Stowe's novel. In early 1854 she published a poetic tribute to Stowe in *Frederick Douglass' Paper*, thanking Stowe "for thy pleading / For the helpless of our race." She also wrote widely published poetic renditions of Eliza Harris's escape across the ice and, for Douglass's paper, of the death of Eva.[70]

References based on *Uncle Tom's Cabin* entered the vocabulary of debate in other ways. Only a short time after the novel was published, various characters in the novel began to provide reference points for expressing important views. Among black abolitionists at least, these references often contained a good deal of implicit criticism, as when William J. Wilson informed readers of *Frederick Douglass' Paper* of "a large and increasing number of George and Eliza Harris's" prepared to use "sterner methods" than prayer to resist their own enslavement. Even Frederick Douglass, despite his admiration for the novel, warned a New York audience in 1857 that the slaves were not simply "a nation of Uncle Toms, who could shout 'glory' and sing hymns." Proslavery writers were not immune to the appeal of such figures. Albert Taylor Bledsoe criticized abolitionist claims that slavery turned men into brutes, while implying that slaveholders also held "a George Harris—or an Eliza—or an Uncle Tom—in bondage."[71]

But perhaps the most important result of *Uncle Tom's Cabin*'s success was the confirmation of the significance of literature to the success of the antislavery movement. Such a belief had informed Stowe from the beginning. As she put it in her preface, one of her purposes was, "under the allurements of fiction," to "breathe a humanizing and subduing influence, favorable to the development of the great principles of Christian brotherhood." At least a few newspapers reported very concrete results of the novel's publication. The *Pennsylvania Freeman* described how several Kentucky slaves had been inspired by Stowe's stirring tale of the escape of George and Eliza Harris to run away themselves. The same paper also told of a Missouri slaveholder who was inspired by the novel "to execute a bill of emancipation for his slave man," a far from typical outcome but significant nonetheless.[72]

There was nothing entirely new in the faith Stowe's novel inspired in the efficacy of literature. The celebration of black authors, antedating the abolition movement, was at least in part an expression of faith in the power of literature to change minds. This faith remained a part of abolitionist thinking through the period. By 1858 John Mercer Langston, celebrating the body of antislavery literature as an "important and splendid achievement" in its own right, could assert that "one good book is more powerful than a thousand soldiers clad in arms." Still, the enormous popularity and impact of Stowe's mixture of fact and fiction was unprecedented, and an important inspiration to the further development of an African American testimony against slavery.[73]

The years following publication of *Uncle Tom's Cabin* saw an explosion in efforts to use fiction to dramatize the inherent evils of slavery. Stowe's novel loomed large in most of these efforts, as did the demands posed by the rhetoric of national debates over slavery. The decade also saw the writing of the first novels by African Americans, including William Wells Brown's *Clotel* (1853), Frank Webb's *The Garies and Their Friends* (1857), and Harriet Wilson's *Our Nig* (1859). And the art of autobiography began to move in directions fiction had helped define. For instance, recent scholars, including William Andrews and Carla Peterson, have documented an increasing quest for authorial control in the narratives of the 1850s, one drawing on the kind of assertion of an authorial voice that lay at the bottom of the novelist's enterprise.[74]

These developments did not mean an end to a concern for authenticity. Not only did autobiographers continue to assert the truth of their stories; so, too, did authors of fiction. William Wells Brown relied heavily on documentation and true stories for *Clotel*, and this was not unusual. Other works, including Mattie Griffith's *Autobiography of a Female Slave*, of 1856, sought to blur the line between fact and fiction as novels in traditional narrative form did. In some ways Griffith's *Autobiography* was the archetypical work of the era, given the author's background as a slaveholder in Kentucky who had herself been converted to the abolitionist cause. Documenting in the novel itself the potential impact of abolitionist literature, Griffith also authenticated herself as an abolitionist by sympathetically evoking a black voice even as she authenticated the significance of that voice as the most effective argument against the institution. The work was widely admired for its significance as well as its skill. Both Lydia Maria Child and Charlotte Forten praised Griffith for her "genius," as well as for what the novel said about the nobility of Griffith's life.[75]

As Griffith's novel also helps bring home, the fictional works of black and white antislavery writers hardly existed independently of each other. More striking, in fact, is the way in which authors borrowed from each other, as in William Wells Brown's well-documented use of an 1842 story by Lydia Maria Child, "The Quadroons," for elements of *Clotel*. Nor, given the body of writing, is it easy to find thematic elements distinctive to one group of writers or the other. More important for understanding the development of African American literature is the way in which abolitionist fiction helped to refine still further the creation of a black voice within a framework defined by the role of that voice in the ongoing debate over slavery.[76]

Fiction, both drawing on and going beyond narrative, allowed for a dramatizing of arguments in striking ways. Though Frank Webb's book *The Garies and Their Friends* is set in Philadelphia, Webb imagined a dialogue between an antislavery white southerner, "Winston," and a black waiter, "Ben," that both looked back to and gave the lie to the proslavery assertions of a Nehemiah Adams, for instance, by ridiculing images of slave contentment, while challenging the apparent testimony on which those images were based. Asked by Winston if he was a runaway, Ben replies, "I was sot free," adding, "in a whining tone," his wish that "I was back agin on the old place—hain't got no kind marster to look after me here, and I has to work drefful hard sometimes." When Winston turns on Ben, saying that "any man that prefers slavery to freedom deserves to be a slave," Ben bolts from the room, rushing to relate his experiences to the other waiters, "talking as correct English, and with as pure Northern accent as one could boast." While challenging the credibility of proslavery observers, Webb also took advantage of the possibilities fiction offered to dramatize a scene that was credible within antislavery traditions, and in a peculiarly vivid way.[77]

With such roots in older traditions of black testimony, antislavery fiction developed its conventions fairly quickly. Scenes of family separation and the auction block were staples. So were evocations of terrible brutality, both its physical and its psychological dimensions often being graphically described. Like Webb, most writers of abolitionist fiction also found dialect appealing, sometimes following the minstrel tradition of using it for comic relief, as did Brown in *Clotel*. More often, they redeemed it by showing a strength and dignity below the surface or by demonstrating that not all people of African descent used it.

The power of such conventions, and of the models they implied, was great, reinforcing much that the narratives had already done to create images of slavery. But the possibilities of antislavery fiction were to be especially important in regard to two key themes that, while they did not originate with Stowe nor even in the 1850s, would take on increasing importance in that decade, in part as a result of her work. One of these was given special impetus by Stowe's Uncle Tom and by the piety and submissiveness with which she endowed him. The romantic racialism embodied in Tom's character was not original with Stowe, having its roots in the evangelical representations of the late eighteenth and early nineteenth centuries. Still, her novel did much to put it at the center of abolitionist thinking even as it helped shape responses to the novel among black and white readers alike.

For most of Stowe's contemporaries, as for Stowe herself, the main tenets of romantic racialism were primarily in keeping, as they had been for more than half a century, with the kinds of ideas that invested a moral equality, if not superiority, in people of African descent. In 1850 a writer for the *Pennsylvania Freeman* identified at least one aspect of the "mission of the People of Color" in America as being "to soften the rough features and sharp energy of the Anglo-Saxon character by the natural gentleness, cheerfulness, and untaught delicacy of the African." The black emigrationist Joseph Holly echoed the view two years later, when he suggested that "the races on this Continent will finally merge or fuse into each other," each bringing its own virtues. For the African, he said, the contribution would be "its sociality, its spirituality."[78]

For many, this spirituality was tangibly embodied in the piety of the Christian slave. It was also embodied in peculiar gifts, especially those of feeling and expression. When an observer of the 1853 National Convention of Colored Citizens noted, in reference to the fine speeches he had heard, that "eloquence, like song, is a peculiar forte of our people," he was drawing on the kinds of ideas that had influenced Stowe. So, too, was Martin Delany when he said, though with some ambivalence, that "the colored races" were "civil, peaceable, and religious to a fault." He conceded to whites a superiority in mathematics, commerce, and science, while claiming that in "languages, oratory, poetry, music, and painting," along with "ethics, metaphysics, theology, and legal jurisprudence," blacks would "yet instruct the world."[79]

The moral authority to be found in romantic racialism played an important role in the kind of characterization antislavery writers developed, in the kinds of voices they evoked. Much of the strength and dignity of dialect-speaking folk characters was based in ideas of romantic racialism;

writers evoked men and women who, Tom-like, endured their sufferings while providing living testimony to the beauties of Christian faith. Still, probably the most striking way in which the ideals and images of romantic racialism found significant life in the antislavery writing of the 1850s was in the great emphasis, in various contexts, on the characters, especially the young women, of mixed race.

The portrayal of such young women was not new in the 1850s; one can find a number of precedents in the antislavery fiction and autobiography of the 1830s and 1840s and even before. But their prevalence in the fiction of the 1850s is striking. They were absent from few works, and from almost no novels. It would be an oversimplification to suggest that they can be interpreted wholly in the light of romantic racialism since, as a number of scholars have pointed out, they could serve a variety of functions in antislavery fiction. As presented in most novels, such characters tended to be have a very light complexion, often light enough that they could pass for white, which helped to create an identity between a largely white audience and a slave character. By their very color and condition, moreover, they helped to call into question the very racial categories upon which slavery was usually defended, as Werner Sollors has stressed. At the same time, they stood as a rebuke to proslavery white southerners, as evidence of the sexual licentiousness that had long existed at the heart of slavery, as both its product and its potential victims.[80]

Within the context created by ideals of romantic racialism, however, mixed-race figures, particularly young women, also came to be treated in terms of the kind of merger, or fusion, discussed by Joseph Holly in his 1852 letter to Douglass. As Holly's comments make plain, the kinds of virtues he and others associated with the "African" character were those usually associated with ideals of gentility and femininity, and such ideas were not unique to him. As George Frederickson has noted, such abolitionists as Moncure Conway and Gilbert Haven wrote of a fusion very like that Holly described and went on to champion intermarriage as a result. Such ideas tended to be embodied in fiction as well. Elizabeth Livermore, in her 1855 novel *Zoë; or, The Quadroon's Triumph*, described her heroine as one who combined "Anglo-Saxon" virtues of "courage, energy, self-reliance and practical power" with the "fiery temperament, imagination, strong affections and religious aspirations" of that other "division of the human family" that was part of her makeup. Again, it would be difficult to cite romantic racialism as the dominant motive in the use of mixed-race characters in abolitionist fiction. Too many other issues were involved. Nevertheless, there seems little reason to doubt that ideals of romantic racialism, perhaps evoking images going back to T.T.'s fantasies of 1831, reinforced and enriched the connotations such characters created.[81]

The classic such character, after Eliza Harris, was William Wells Brown's Clotel, "her features as finely defined as any of her sex of pure Anglo-Saxon," but a slave nevertheless. Overtly mixing fact with fiction, Brown did much to set the model for the way such a character was presented. Describing Clotel's relationship to her first lover—with whom she lives as a wife though she is legally his slave—and her ultimate betrayal by him, even as he drew on earlier works, he anticipated an approach to the mixed-race character that many were to follow during the decade. In an auction-block scene, in which Clotel is exposed to the coarsest of buyers, the auctioneer stressing her chastity and purity, Brown set up that confrontation between natural virtue and a calculating hardness that had structured romantic racialist ideas from the beginning. Brown took themes long pursued in auction-block scenes and gave them the still greater impact that the combined languages of gentility, gender, and sex could provide.[82]

The dialectic Brown dramatized did much to evoke the contrasts between virtue and viciousness on which the antislavery argument was built. In this, as Werner Sollors says, the story of the mixed-race character went back to a tradition established in the eighteenth century, in the legend of Inkle and Yarico, with its own emphases on virtue, vulnerability, and betrayal. At the same time, in the context of the 1850s the contrasts had further meaning, helping to define the debate over slavery as well.[83]

The sexual vulnerability of the female slave, especially the female slave of mixed race, evoked in Brown's auction scene, was to be a central motif in abolition literature from the 1850s; certainly, it had been present earlier, but it came into its own in this decade's heated debates. Henry Wadsworth Longfellow's poem "The Quadroon Girl," printed in *Frederick Douglass' Paper,* among other places, provided a succinct example of the theme, and in its strongest form, in its portrayal of a planter's sale of his own daughter to a slaver. The planter knew "whose blood ran in her veins," but at the sight of the "Slaver's gold" sent her off, nonetheless, to be a buyer's "slave and paramour / In a strange and distant land!" Describing a quadroon who was both childlike and virtuous, her eyes betraying "the features of a saint," Longfellow built on a dialectic of virtue and greed in ways that epitomized the romantic, racialized images such characters could embody and reinforced those images of slaveholder evil others had helped to create.[84]

Such a work as Longfellow's, along with those of Stowe, Brown, and others, also helped prepare the way for that merging of novelistic and narrative forms that is generally recognized as the most candid treatment of the female slave's sexual vulnerability, Harriet Jacobs's 1861 *Incidents in the Life of a Slave Girl*. It was the first and only full-length account by a fugitive women, as Joanne Braxton has stressed. Jacobs, herself the daughter of parents of "mixed" ancestry, had begun thinking about writing her story since at least the early 1850s. In her letter replying to Julia Tyler, she had also taken note of *Uncle Tom's Cabin*. Suggesting that the novel had not "told the half" concerning slavery's evils, she said that she wished only for the "genius" to tell the rest. By the end of the decade, working with Lydia Maria Child, she felt able to do so.[85]

Even in her own account Jacobs asserted, she had had to show restraint. While telling the truth, she wrote, her descriptions, no less than Stowe's, had fallen "short of the facts." Nevertheless, as she described her master's constant harassment of her, his efforts to fill her mind "with unclean images, such as only a vile monster could think of," she presented a full account of unending southern degradation and licentiousness. She presented, as well, an account that, perhaps reflecting her long involvement with the abolitionist cause, was a point-by-point refutation of the proslavery position. She did that at one level by creating, as her predecessors had, dialogues in which, with great vigor, she challenged the power represented by her master. At another, however, her entire story was focused, perhaps more than any other, on refutation. Documenting family separations, sexual terrorism, and slaveholder coarseness, not to mention her own becoming "prematurely knowing, concerning the evil ways of the world," she directly contradicted proslavery representations of the system as paternalistic and benevolent. With sex as her keystone, she used her experiences to deny the claim of Mississippi Senator Albert Gallatin Brown that slavery was, in his words, "a great moral, social, and political blessing; a blessing to the master, and a blessing to the slave."[86]

Drawing on ideals of romantic racialism, such representations of sex did much to dramatize the conflict between virtue and vice at the heart of the debate over slavery. This conflict was further dramatized by the extent to which characters of mixed race were informed by another theme in the debate, that having to do with "amalgamation." From the 1830s through the 1850s abolitionists were often charged by their opponents with desiring amalgamation, including intermarriage between blacks and whites. Levison, in one of his minstrel-show sketches, suggested that the root of abolitionism was an unhealthy sexual desire: "De abolish'nists won't let our gals alone," one of his characters said. During the suffrage debates in New York, debates in which Douglass and others figured so strongly, the charge was frequently leveled by the proponents of continuing restriction. Some abolitionists responded by denying its truth, as Child did in her introduction to Stedman's *Joanna*. Others met it head on by suggesting that eventually the challenge would be meaningless as marriages across the color line inevitably became commonplace. As Gilbert Haven declared, drawing on themes of romantic racialism, "The loveliest maidens of the South are often of mixed blood. A pure and noble man will seek a pure and noble mate, and he is more apt to find her in that class than any other, for the pride and bitterness of the white and slaveholding women do not defile her soul."[87]

Within the body of antislavery literature the acceptance of "amalgamation" in the form of legitimate relationships across the color line, including marriage, was actually fairly common. Certainly it is true, as has often been noted, that many of the stories end unhappily. The figure of the "tragic mulatta," a beautiful young woman whose unrequited love across the color line leads to her doom, was a powerful presence in antislavery fiction. Brown's Clotel is a case in point, her betrayal ultimately leading her to suicide. The presence of such characters might suggest an evasion or even a tacit rejection of "amalgamation" as a possibility for those separated by lines of color. Such a reading is not, however, supported by the general range of antislavery fiction. Werner Sollors has rightly noted that the scholarly stereotype of the "tragic mulatta" was developed in more recent times. The actual case was far more complex, with marriage and a happy ending as common as the tragic death associated with the type, if not more so. The happy ending audiences demanded of Dion Boucicault for his initially tragic 1859 play *The Octoroon* is only one example of this. In such novels as Mary Pike's 1859 *Caste*, a work endorsed by Douglass, or Hezekiah Hosmer's 1860 *Adela, the Octoroon* mixed-race characters are rescued from slavery by white men who take them as brides. Even Frank Webb's *The Garies and Their Friends*, while generally tragic in the stories it tells, begins with the legitimation of a relationship between the white Garie and the beautiful Emily, whom he originally bought as a slave before ultimately making her his wife and taking her out of the South. The later death of both Garies in an outburst of northern mob violence heightens rather than diminishes the sense of how proper their relationship was in contrast to the ugliness of the mob that took their lives.[88]

Such fictionalized accounts dovetailed with more factual or ostensibly factual ones. When William G. Allen was forced to flee New York for England following his marriage to a white woman, few abolitionists condemned the marriage. Many condemned those who had forced him to flee. More in keeping with literary versions was a story, presented as fact in an 1854 piece for the *Boston Telegraph*, by a man, apparently white, who claimed to have married a fugitive slave of light complexion. Describing her beauty in words much like those of Gilbert Haven, the writer cited her character to ridicule southern fears of "the horrors of amalgamation." But above all he offered a sympathetic account of his love for a bride who had to hide her past for fear of capture and reenslavement in the South.[89]

In any event, whether tragic or happy, all these stories share common characteristics. All deny the relevance of color to refinement. All present heroes and heroines of color whose virtue and character put many whites to shame. And all, reflecting more general abolitionist views, highlight both the acceptability and the propriety of love and even marriage across lines of color, however happy or tragic the ending might be.

In all these ways the stories reinforced frameworks of African American authority that had defined antislavery thinking for many years. By illuminating possibilities for interracial relationships that could—and these stories said should—exist, they again put people of African descent at the center of thinking about American virtue as that thinking was informed by the romantic ideals of the era. At one level they allowed for still sharper distinctions between slavery's opponents and its advocates by dramatically counterposing the romantic love they portrayed with southern realities of sexual brutality.

But at another level these stories held out, still more dramatically, those possibilities of conversion that had been exemplified by white Americans from Warner Mifflin and the Grimkés to Mattie Griffith and Moncure Conway. Building on the imagery of T.T.'s earlier dream, these stories of testing and love wrought by color used romantic ideals to describe the power of African Americans to bring enlightenment and virtue to previously obtuse white men and women. There was a sense in which the virtuous young women portrayed by Mary Pike and Hezekiah Hosmer did as much to rescue their young men from sin as those young men did in efforts to rescue their wives from slavery.

By the same token, because of the virtues these mixed-race figures portrayed, and because of the ways antislavery writers used them, they reasserted, in a new and vivid manner, the special role of a distinctly African American testimony for measuring the gaps between American professions and American realities. By the very tests such characters represented in their relations across the color line, they posed a contrast between virtue and reality that raised questions about the white American commitment to ideals of gentility, to romantic ideals of family and love. Here, on a new front, that calculated marginality at the heart of a prophetic African American voice was presented in a way that raised deeper concerns about American virtue. Whatever other purposes such characters had—and they had many—they provided an important way to bring modes of African American social criticism into the context of mid-nineteenth-century America.

Still, as the response to *Uncle Tom's Cabin* by readers from Wendell Phillips to William J. Watkins made plain, not everyone was entirely happy with the imagery romantic racialism entailed. As many historians have emphasized, its ideals of passivity and endurance, rather than resistance, were troubling to many. Despite traditions of nonresistance, a number of abolitionists during the 1850s began to contemplate violence in more positive terms. They were galvanized, in part, by the Fugitive Slave Law and by those episodes of violent resistance to the law that had occurred in Boston, Ohio, Syracuse, and elsewhere during the decade.

They were galvanized by the war in Kansas, the first open battle over slavery. They were moved, finally, as John Stauffer has suggested, by popular ideals of "primitive masculinity," complementing more feminine notions of gentility, that held an attraction for such men as Gerrit Smith and James McCune Smith no less that for others in the mid-nineteenth century.[90]

Throughout the decade, in contradistinction to such figures of suffering as Clotel and Harriet Jacobs, a number of writers, including Stowe, focused attention on the heroic rebel rather than on the tragic or even redeemed victim. To some extent, they may have been responding directly to the celebration of Uncle Tom. This has often been suggested of Martin Delany and Frederick Douglass in their works of fiction from the 1850s. Douglass, whose novella "The Heroic Slave" appeared in 1853, created a fictional version of Madison Washington, a slave rebel from 1841 who had interested Douglass for several years. Washington, in life and in Douglass's story, both spoke and took action against slavery, leading a violent revolt aboard a slave ship in an effort to free himself and his comrades. Delany's *Blake*, appearing late in the decade, focused on a more fictional rebel, tracing the title character's exploits from the United States to Canada and Cuba.[91]

Such works were to point in important directions for antislavery fiction. Neither actually broke from the main purposes or the main traditions of the abolition movement. Nor did either author place his efforts wholly outside the movement. But both helped to mobilize those traditions in ways that looked toward a more active response to slavery and oppression.

Douglass's novella appeared in his friend Julia Griffiths's *Autographs for Freedom*, surrounded by the works of other prominent writers. It drew, like most antislavery fiction, on the facts of slavery in its retelling of Madison Washington's story, a part of slavery's history Douglass had begun to recount for audiences by 1849. As early as 1849 Douglass had begun to use Washington's story to counter proslavery assertions of slave timidity, assertions "that there is no fight in us," as Douglass told a New York audience.[92]

In the novella, even as he emphasized his own move away from Garrisonian nonresistance—celebrating Gerrit Smith rather than Garrison—Douglass also helped elaborate more connections among heroism and moral authority, black testimony and antislavery ideals. Contributing to the tradition also exploited by Nell, he linked the slave revolutionary, a Virginian, to a larger Revolutionary context, describing Madison Washington as "a man who loved liberty as well as did Patrick Henry,—and who deserved it as much as Thomas Jefferson."[93]

At the same time, Douglass used fiction to imagine Washington as a rebel who still dramatized abolitionist, even Garrisonian possibilities. Creating an encounter between a northern traveler, Listwell, and the still enslaved Washington, Douglass put words of a hope of freedom and an evocation of despair into Washington's mouth that impressed Listwell powerfully. "Here is a man," Listwell was made to think, "of rare endowments—a child of God,—guilty of no crime but the color of his skin." Replicating in microcosm what had long been a key aspect of the impact of black testimony within abolitionism, Listwell proclaims, "From this hour I am an abolitionist," proving it by his continuing support of Washington for the rest of the story.[94]

No less important, however, is the way Douglass dramatized the impact of Washington's shipboard rebellion. Rather than reporting the events directly, Douglass had them recounted by two white veterans of the affray. Here there were no overt conversions, but the inability of one reporter to suppress his admiration for Washington is striking. At one point, the sailor says that he forgot Washington's "blackness in the dignity of his manner, and the eloquence of his speech." Even this man, so dominated by prejudice, reinforces Douglass's synthesis of celebration and irony by confessing, "It was not that his principles were wrong in the abstract; for they were the principles of 1776. But I could not bring myself to recognize their application to one whom I deemed my inferior." His failure was one in which many Americans shared. His words recalled motifs found in American rhetoric since the era of the early republic.[95]

"The Heroic Slave" was important as a measure of emerging moods in abolitionism and of Douglass's shifting career, as many scholars have said. It was no less important, however, for taking those emerging moods and reminding readers of their compatibility with revolutionary tendencies long latent in abolitionist ideals. Revolutionary ideas had long played their role, even in Garrison's thinking. By returning to the movement's revolutionary potential Douglass not only proclaimed his appreciation for that tradition but also helped emphasize the consistency of violent action with the moral authority the movement had long claimed. He used the African American hero and the African American voice to claim a place for new strategies within the traditions of the antislavery movement.

Delany, in *Blake*, similarly moved between offering something relatively new and placing his work within the context of abolitionist tradition. He asked Garrison for help in getting the novel published, a measure of his wish for it to play a role within the movement. That he did so with the confidence that Garrison, along with Wendell Phillips and Edmund Quincy—whose help he also sought—had "always taken so great an interest in anything eminating from Col'd People" showed his understanding of the kind of possibilities that existed for black writers.[96]

With its multiple settings, *Blake* is a complicated work. Some of its American action takes place in the South, where Delany's hero is a slave. Escaping from his home plantation, he goes, not to the North, but further south, seeking, unsuccessfully, to foment insurrection. Leaving the South, the hero ultimately makes his way to Cuba, where, working with the legendary Cuban poet Plácido, he again does the work of rebellion. This time the consequences are tragic, reminiscent of those facing blacks in Charleston in the wake of Denmark Vesey's aborted plot. The plans of Blake and his compatriots also foiled, Cubans of African descent are confronted with a reign of oppression of cruel proportions. Delany concludes the novel, however, with a vow on the part of those Cubans to resist and a threat of greater insurrection to come. Delany uses the failed attempt to assert that courage and virtue lay in unity and resistance.

Despite its complications, any reader familiar with abolitionist traditions would have found much that was familiar in *Blake*. Delany drew on the traditions of the fugitive narratives for much of the book. He also drew on larger traditions of abolitionist literature. He used excerpts from Harriet Beecher Stowe's poetry as epigraphs for each of the novel's two parts. He used a poem by James Whitfield, "How Long," which had appeared in *Autographs for Freedom*. He inserted poems of his own in the text, poems that also conformed to abolitionist conventions. Much of the dialogue involved set pieces that similarly lived up to form. His use of a Cuban setting was new. Still, the invocation of the life of Plácido, long celebrated by abolitionists, tied Delany's novel to familiar reference points, as did other overt mixtures of fact and fiction. However complex,

Blake nonetheless followed the track of Delany's career by placing its distinctive properties in the context of larger abolitionist frames.

There can be no doubt, however, that Delany did much to expand those frames. His peripatetic rebel was hardly in the usual fugitive mold. Nor was his tale of Cuban revolution, although it drew on Haitian motifs and offered a picture of African nobility and dignity no abolitionist would have found incredible. But that in itself is what Delany's novel was about. Like Douglass, he used conventions that had for so many reasons come to characterize the African American literary enterprise to ground a case for violence within a moral framework that, as his approach to Garrison and others indicates, he believed his readers could understand.

Again, Douglass and Delany were far from unusual in contemplating and celebrating black revolutionaries during the decade, and doing so in ways that used those figures to provide testimony on behalf of important tendencies in abolitionist thought. In an 1854 lecture on Santo Domingo, William Wells Brown recounted the heroism of Haiti's rebels, warning, "Who knows but that a Toussaint, a Christophe, a Rigaud, a Clervaux, and a Dessalines, may some day appear in the Southern States of this Union? That they are there, no one will doubt." If there were Toms, there were also Nat Turners and Toussaint L'Ouvertures in the world, a point made by writers as diverse as Samuel Ringgold Ward, Harriet Beecher Stowe, and Wendell Phillips, as well as Delany, Douglass, and Brown.[97]

As the decade drew to a close, such figures became more prominent in abolitionist writings. Stimulated by what appeared to be increasing southern aggressiveness, by the Dred Scott Decision, and by the possibilities offered by an increasingly militant antislavery politics, the interest in insurrection and black heroism grew in abolitionism. The testimony of that heroism also became more compelling. It would begin to peak in important ways in 1859, spurred by events that made it apparent to many that slavery's end would be brought about, and fairly soon, by conflict.

8

The War for Emancipation
and Beyond

IF THERE WAS MUCH in the 1850s to encourage thinking about conflict
and violence among abolitionists, the end of the decade saw a series of
events that made such thought seem more pressing still. To some extent
such thought was born of a pessimism brought on by such events as the
Supreme Court's 1857 Dred Scott Decision, which in effect institutionalized racial prejudice as the basis for all of American law and practice.
That same pessimism underlay, for example, the widespread interest
in emigration by about 1859 and 1860. For many abolitionists, there was
an increasing sense that Garrisonian moral suasion was not going to
be enough to bring slavery to an end, a sense that something more was
needed.

That something more had been anticipated, during the 1850s, by
violent confrontations over slavery. The war in Kansas was one such
episode, as pro- and antislavery settlers came to violence over whether
the territory should ultimately be slave or free. Still more important was
John Brown's 1859 raid on the Harper's Ferry federal arsenal in Virginia
and his later martyrdom. A veteran of the Kansas war, Brown led a raid-
ing party of twenty-one men, including five African Americans, in an attack that he hoped would incite slave insurrections and inspire an all-out
armed assault on slavery itself. Ten of his men, including two of the black
recruits, were killed in the action, and seven, including Brown himself,
along with the black volunteers John A. Copeland and Shields Green, a
fugitive, were captured. Brown was executed on 2 December 1859, and
Copeland and Green, two weeks thereafter.[1]

The Brown raid, and black participation in it, was part of the discussion that had been framed by ideas of romantic racialism, notably in the controversy over Stowe's Uncle Tom, and by such works as Martin Delany's *Blake* and Douglass's "Heroic Slave," among others. As Jeffrey Rossbach has noted, a few white abolitionists even questioned whether slaves would fight for their own freedom. Black participation in Brown's raid was crucial, and Copeland's martyrdom was widely noted in the abolitionist press. Letters that Copeland wrote from his cell shortly before his execution were widely reprinted in the *Liberator* and elsewhere. In those letters Copeland spoke as a martyr, and in the tradition that equated black revolutionaries with the heroes of America's own Revolutionary past, commenting, as they did, on America's own dedication to that past. "Could I die in a more noble cause?" Copeland asked. His courage was exemplary, and those who celebrated his martyrdom knew that it was representative as well.[2]

In the context of the sectional crisis such a black voice with revolutionary potential became an increasingly important element in abolitionist literature and in the evocation of an African American presence. The heightened tensions between North and South during the 1860 presidential campaign and following Lincoln's election were reflected, in part, by a growing interest in black insurrectionist heroism. In early 1860 *Frederick Douglass' Paper* published a story written for the paper about a group of "Liberators" conspiring to create an insurrection in Virginia. Such fictional accounts were supplemented by those based on fact, especially with the outbreak of war in 1861. Antebellum heroes whose very actions testified to the slaves' willingness to fight and die for freedom enjoyed new visibility. The abolitionist Thomas Wentworth Higginson, who had been involved with Brown, paid tribute to Nat Turner in the June 1861 issue of the *Atlantic Monthly* and wrote a sketch of Denmark Vesey the following month, both of which were reprinted in *Douglass' Monthly*; the following year, he celebrated Gabriel's 1800 plot in Richmond. William Wells Brown drew on Higginson's work for his own tribute to Turner, which appeared as a column in James Redpath's *Pine and Palm*; Brown provided a brief sketch of Madison Washington for the paper as well.[3]

Such accounts provided a framework for more contemporary representations of black heroism. Osborne Anderson, who had been with

Brown at Harper's Ferry, the only black raider to escape, published a first-hand account of his experiences and about Brown using the framework of history to give meaning to his own aims and motivations. He wrote, "There is an unbroken chain of sentiment and purpose from Moses of the Jews to John Brown of America; from Kossuth, and the liberators of France and Italy, to the untutored Gabriel, and the Denmark Veseys, Nat Turners and Madison Washingtons of the Southern American States." All had been martyrs for freedom. Their lives and careers supported Anderson's own claim to a heroism comparable to that of any revolutionary and legitimized the contention that a revolutionary spirit could be found in the hearts of men of African descent.[4]

The power of such imagery was great. In 1861 and 1862, as African Americans agitated for the right to join the Union cause and the Union armies, they could refer to such heroes and martyrs as a basis for their own claim to recognition. Early in the war, a fugitive who distinguished himself by spying on the Confederates near Washington was celebrated in even the mainstream white press as a "rival of Toussaint L'Ouverture." His exploits were noted in the abolitionist papers as well, although Phillip Bell, of San Francisco's *Pacific Appeal*, suggested that the analogy was not quite apt, L'Ouverture having been a diplomat and statesman as well as a military hero.[5]

These same kinds of references, similarly integrated into the wartime context, appeared as well in James Gilmore's 1862 novel, *Among the Pines*, continuing important conventions from abolitionist letters. The novel was a strange one, and as the literary historian Blyden Jackson has noted, was Unionist in sentiment without being entirely hostile to the South. Represented as an account of a northern visitor's travels through the South, the novel put its protagonist, Edmund Kirke, in the company of a black driver who, speaking a thick dialect, professed his own dignity and devotion to freedom, his support for the northern cause, and even his hope for insurrection. When "Kirke" suggests that the insurrectionists might have little hope for success, the driver replies, "I knows most ob de great men, like Washington and John and James and Paul, and dem ole fellers war white, but dar war Two Sand (Toussaint L'Ouverture), de Brack Douglass, and de Nigga Demus (Nicodemus), dey war brack." Far from ridiculing the driver, Gilmore indicated that his Kirke, following the model of the white convert, was strongly persuaded of a potential for rebellion that he had thought the slaves did not possess.[6]

Still, nothing brought such connections home more clearly than a theme that emerged even as blacks were agitating for the right to fight, the theme of black patriotism. Following William Cooper Nell's well-known *Colored Patriots of the American Revolution*, other writers traced the role of African Americans in the war that had created the nation. The editor of the A.M.E. Church's *Christian Recorder*, for example, wrote a series of articles on the topic designed to demonstrate the contribution of black people to the founding of the republic. Nell's book enjoyed a revival during the Civil War. Amos Beman urged it on the young people of his New Haven church in 1863; and Nell himself felt he could justify a new edition of the book in 1864.[7]

Celebrations of black patriotism and heroism gained momentum as African Americans began to take their place in the Union armies after 1863. Abolitionist newspapers printed accounts of black bravery in the field. Letters and other documents from black soldiers became common. Songs sung by black troops headed for battle were also common and helped demonstrate both the bravery and the loyalty of the soldiers. In 1863, for example, the *Liberator* printed "A Negro Volunteer Song," in which the troops proclaimed their faith that "God is for the right" and concluded, "The Union must be saved by the colored volunteer."[8]

That such accounts were deemed effective was at least partially shown by Amos Beman's review of one of the most elaborate evocations of black bravery and patriotism, Epes Sargent's novel *Peculiar*, which appeared in 1864. Drawing on traditions of antislavery fiction, it told of a fugitive slave named "Peculiar Institution," of his heroism in slavery and in helping to bring the institution to an end. It concluded with his courageous death as a soldier. Reviewing the book favorably for an antislavery publication, Beman wrote that it was the kind of story that would "strengthen the purpose of all friends of freedom and of the country to toil on for the utter destruction of the old Bastille of American oppression."[9]

What made such accounts especially significant within the framework of black patriotism was what they said about African Americans themselves. At one level they continued a tradition whereby African Americans could make a stronger claim to a place in America than could many of those who received the privileges of citizenship to a greater degree. As one writer said in a letter to the *Pacific Appeal* at a time when blacks were still excluded from the army, "We were considered aliens, while the Irish, Germans, French and Italians were all welcomed to the call." The writer asserted, "We were not discouraged. No; why should we be? The only true loyalists of the South were the blacks," and added that "the only true heroism that has yet been manifested by the South showed itself in Robert Small," the black seaman who had served the Union forces in South Carolina.[10]

At another level this idea of black patriotism reinforced the abolitionist standard that made commitment to racial equality a crucial test of commitment to American political and cultural ideals. From the beginning of the war, even as abolitionists worked to define the conflict as a war to end slavery, both sides, in one way or another, put blacks themselves at the center. If abolitionists wanted to define the conflict as one devoted to black freedom, others saw it as the product of an abolitionist obsession with black people. A popular parody of "Yankee Doodle" entitled "Nigger Doodle" appeared in the northern Democratic press. The chorus summarized African American and abolitionist goals:

> Nigger Doodle's all the go,
> Ebon shins and bandy,
> "*Loyal*" people all must bow
> To Nigger Doodle dandy.

Even President Lincoln suggested that the presence of blacks had been responsible for the death and destruction the country had suffered.[11]

Such charges undoubtedly helped to maintain the vigor during wartime of earlier charges and countercharges regarding "amalgamation." Leveled against abolitionists, the charges were advanced musically in "Nigger Doodle," a new national hero who, according to the song, "favors 'malgamation." The charges were advanced more formally in such pamphlets as David Croly and George Wakeman's well-known *Miscegenation*, of 1864, initially presented as an abolitionist argument in favor of intermarriage. In their parody Croly and Wakeman quoted directly from such abolitionists as Wendell Phillips and Theodore Tilton, who were initially believed by some to be its authors, and in general drew heavily on abolitionist rhetoric. When, for example, they wrote, "Let us then embrace our black brother; let us give him the intellect, the energy, the nervous endurance of the cold North, which he needs, and let us take from him his emotional power, his love of the spiritual, his delight in the wonders which we understand only through faith," their words were not too different from those of Haven and others during the 1850s. As Sidney Kaplan showed, such abolitionists as James McCune Smith, Angelina Grimké Weld, and Parker Pillsbury responded positively to the pamphlet. And it received warm reviews in the *Anglo-African* and the *National Anti-Slavery Standard*.[12]

Such language and ideas could seem credible during the war because abolitionists, black and white, continued to contrast their own attitudes with those of southern slaveholders through stories of interracial marriage, as opposed to the interracial sexual abuse of slavery. Epes Sargent's *Peculiar* tells the harrowing story of the marriage of a young white man to the slave Estelle. Seeking to escape to the North, the two are captured and beaten, Estelle's sufferings leading to her death at the hands of a jealous slaveholder. The contrast between slavery's opponents and advocates, as Sargent dramatized it, was well in keeping with prewar motifs, and Sargent was not alone in drawing it. A year earlier Louisa May Alcott, in her short story "M. L.," wrote about a young white woman who learned that her prospective husband had African ancestry but married him anyway. The story captured the essence of abolitionism, as the young bride's rejection of her own prejudice and growing alienation from those who could not overcome theirs became the vehicle by which she came to recognize "the emptyness of her old life."[13]

Toward the end of the war the same motif was used by Mrs. Julia Collins, wife of a prominent African Methodist Episcopal leader, in a novel serialized for the A.M.E. *Christian Recorder* from February to September 1865. Mrs. Collins wrote about a young man, Richard Tracy, who, although from a slaveholding family, married a beautiful quadroon named Lina, going with her to New England to escape the opposition of his parents and the strictures of his society. Forced to return to New Orleans, Richard remains true to Lina despite his father's efforts to separate them. But in what turns out to be a prolonged absence a distraught Lina dies. The couple's daughter, Claire Neville, born in New England, later finds herself in New Orleans employed as a governess in the home of the Tracy family. Unaware of her mother's ancestry, she plans marriage with a young white man, only to have the secret of her ancestry exposed.

Claire's fate was never to be revealed, since Mrs. Collins died before she could finish the novel. But as she told the story up to the time of her death she, like others, clearly saw the propriety of love across the color line, creating through her "black" characters dramatic proofs of possibilities for American virtue, as well as dramatic demonstrations of American failings.[14]

Still, both the testing role of African American figures and their authoritative voice in asserting that role found more direct expression in wartime, as the works of two poets in 1862 indicate. The minister and fugitive slave J. Sella Martin told of a black man joining a Boston crowd that included a decorated, wounded Union hero. Suddenly one of the crowd says contemptuously,

> "There's a 'nigger' everywhere—
> In the church, and state, and barracks,
> Still his woolly head pops in."

As the poem continues, the speaker's contempt turns to shame, showing that Massachusetts had always been at the forefront of any battle for freedom and that under the circumstances the ugly words supported tyranny rather than liberty. He embellished the story with an account of how, in the battle in which the soldier earned his stars, the black man, then a slave, had saved the hero's life. An appreciation for the former slave's own heroism, Martin wrote, was itself a test of Massachusetts's continuing dedication to liberty.[15]

Another poem from the same year, appearing in the *Pacific Appeal*, made a similar point. The poet introduced the piece by saying that it had been inspired by a remark from a white man who, speaking of the causes of "the present rebellion," said, "The Negroes have done it." Surveying the history of black patriotism, the poet replied,

> Yes! few people on earth
> Would still love the land,
> (Tho' it gave them their birth,)
> Where oppressed and enslaved
> As we have been.

Celebrating such true patriotism, the poet turned the white man's charge into a vehicle for conveying an understanding of American history that was superior to that of the white man who had made the charge, a vehicle that made an understanding a what black people had done a test of loyalty.[16]

Given such views, it is not surprising that African Americans, including fugitives, continued to exercise the authority they had assumed in the context of abolitionism since the 1830s. Douglass, Brown, Loguen, Pennington, and other prominent fugitives lent the weight of their authority to the Union cause, and to the effort to make black soldiers an integral part of the Union effort. Less prominent fugitives also provided testimony in support of the Union. Miss Oneda De Bois, a former Alabama slave who had emigrated to Haiti, returned to the United States for a lecture tour in the North. Distinguished by "her able vindication" of people of African descent, along with "her proud disdain of the contumely so heaped upon them, her defence of their soldierly qualities," and her ability to place American events in the context established by the revolution in Haiti, her lectures were well received. One journalist described her words as "exceedingly touching, even eloquent."[17]

The authority of fugitives and others extended beyond that of testimony on behalf of the Union cause. One of the most celebrated instances of the assertion of a distinctly African American authority occurred in Britain, in a much-publicized exchange between the fugitive William Craft and the British social scientist James Hunt. The exchange took place at a meeting of the British Association for the Advancement of Science, following the reading of a paper by Hunt in which he attempted to demonstrate black inferiority. During the time devoted to discussion Craft, having recourse to abolitionist tradition, cited Roman prejudices against the "stupid people" they had enslaved in Britain and cited black progress, against enormous odds, in Haiti and America as evidence of African equality. According to at least one account, he spoke "with great fluency, and at the same time with great modesty," and was "loudly applauded" for his efforts.[18]

No less celebrated was the series of pieces Charlotte Forten wrote detailing her experiences as a black teacher in Union-held territory in South Carolina. She began her efforts in late 1862, with letters addressed to Garrison that she hoped he would publish in his *Liberator* "if he thinks it worth printing, which I do not," a comment typical of those she tended to make about her own work. Not surprisingly, Garrison did publish them, noting that they were "from a young colored lady," a "granddaughter of the late venerable James Forten," whose name, Garrison said, "is not unfamiliarly associated with those of Benjamin Franklin and Rush, of the old Revolutionary days." No less prominently, in 1864 Forten had two lengthy accounts of her South Carolina experiences published in the *Atlantic Monthly*. Sponsored by the abolitionist poet and longtime family friend John Greenleaf Whittier, Forten was identified by Whittier as one "herself akin to the long-suffering race whose Exodus she so pleasantly describes." In Forten's accounts, no less than in the works of other men and women of color, race, authority, and the moral status of abolitionism were as strongly linked in wartime as they had been throughout the course of the abolition movement.[19]

Forten's pieces also helped to convey the multiplicity of messages informing African American writing during the war. In working to convey both her sympathy for and distance from the freedmen and freedwomen of the islands, Forten helped emphasize the genteel possibilities that had informed her career and those of other black writers since at least the early 1830s. Presenting herself to be as much an outsider as the white northern teachers she joined in South Carolina, she helped challenge the racial determinism at the core of any case for black inferiority.

At the same time, in her articles Forten was one of several writers who began to look more closely at the world of the slaves, now freed, themselves. Despite her well-documented ambivalence about the people she encountered, she was one of a number of people who began to record folk forms, especially folk hymns, for publication to a wider audience. If, in her diary, she described one of those songs—a funeral hymn with the chorus "Sing, O graveyard"—as "a strange wild thing," when she wrote her *Atlantic* articles she was ready to acknowledge "the deep pathos" of that refrain. Suggesting that the words had "but little meaning," she nevertheless said of the "tones" that "a whole lifetime of despairing sadness is concentrated in them." In conveying such a sensibility, Forten joined a number of abolitionists who saw in the voices of the slaves, and the freedmen and freedwomen, a testimony to their humanity and, both within and outside the conventions of romantic racialism, their fitness for freedom.[20]

The recording of folk traditions began almost as soon as Union troops and observers began to take control of parts of the South in 1861 and continued throughout the war. In September 1861 the *Weekly Anglo-African* published an account of "Contraband Singing" in which the author described one song's "simple melody of nature, fresh and warm from the heart." By the end of 1861 one of the most prominent songs, "Let My People Go," was becoming very well known, and for more than simplicity and warmth. In introducing it a correspondent for the *National Anti-Slavery Standard* wrote that it had had to be sung stealthily during slavery and could be performed openly only by those out of slavery's reach. "The verses surely were not born from a love of bondage," he wrote, "and show in a portion, if not in all of the South, the slaves are familiar with the history of the past, and are looking hopefully toward the future."[21]

It is not surprising that the prophetic role African American voices had asserted since at least the days of Phillis Wheatley continued to be assumed in the era of the Civil War. The poet James Madison Bell, who spent the war years in San Francisco, published a lengthy poem written for the city's 1862 First of August celebration detailing the "challenge of Slavery to Liberty" as the chief cause of the War. And he declared:

> America! America!
> Thine own undoing thou has wrought,
> For all they wrongs to Africa,
> This cup has fallen to thy lot.

Others adopted a similarly prophetic voice in calling attention to the sin against Africans that had brought America's fratricidal war upon the nation.[22]

Still, if the Civil War enhanced African American writers' assertion of the moral authority underlying African American testimony, it also exacerbated other issues for which African American history and African American self-assertion were equally critical. These, too, helped define important directions for African American writing. The most significant issues emerged with force as even the most ardent Unionists realized that the war had come to be defined as a war for emancipation. This realization led to renewed debate, however rooted in the antebellum period, over the fitness of African Americans for freedom. As the historian James McPherson has shown, the debate brought out all of the evidence that had previously been adduced, including the history of black achievement, not to mention more recent annals of heroism and patriotism, the evocation of ancient African greatness, and the exemplary character of prominent men and women.[23]

The debate also gave rise to a variety of works intended to prove the fitness of black people for freedom. Even as the era saw an explosion of interest in black revolutionaries, there was a renewed interest in intellectual and literary figures, all of whom helped make the case for racial equality. Such publications as the *Liberator* and the *Standard* reprinted works by Phillis Wheatley and Ignatius Sancho. Hollis Read, in his book *The Negro Problem Solved*, of 1864, linked figures from the past with such modern talents as Frances Ellen Watkins and Charlotte Forten to show that "the gifts of nature are of no rank or color." The Virginia slaveholder turned abolitionist Moncure Conway wrote a sketch of Benjamin Banneker for the 1863 *Atlantic Monthly* in which he cited the famous correspondence with Jefferson and asserted that "the most original scientific intellect which the South has yet produced was that of the pure African, Benjamin Banneker."[24]

Still, the most noticed wartime book to celebrate black accomplishments was William Wells Brown's 1863 book *The Black Man, His Genius and His Achievements*. Aimed at the "calumniators and traducers of the Negro," Brown's lengthy book also reviewed African and African American history, including stories of ancient Africa, to prove racial equality. But it was composed mainly of brief biographies of men and women of achievement—from Banneker and Wheatley to Douglass, Nell, and Remond—all of whom exemplified what men and women of African descent were capable of accomplishing.[25]

The book was not without controversy. Brown's biographer William Edward Farrison reported that Charlotte Forten found it "a silly book" despite the favorable attention she received in its pages. A reviewer for the *Pacific Appeal* thought Brown had left too much out, that he had neglected too many important people and put in too much about himself. Another of the paper's correspondents defended Brown, noting that any author had to be selective and suggesting that the book would "do much good." The reviewer for *Douglass' Monthly* similarly praised the book, emphasizing not only the book's usefulness but also its imprimatur owing to Brown's being "a man of colour" and a former slave. Hollis Read borrowed from it heavily for his own 1864 study of the prospects of emancipation, *The Negro Problem Solved*. Read not only identified Brown as "a colored writer and ex-slave" but also singled him out as an exemplar of what black people were contributing "to the science, the literature, and the intellectual advancement of the country." Despite the controversy, then, the book did well. Samuel May, who was critical of much that had been written on African American prospects as either too "eulogistic" or "hostile," singled out *The Black Man* as "a quite sensible & useful book, for ordinary purposes & popular reading."[26]

Emancipation did not mean an end to the needs Brown's volume sought to address. If anything, those needs were heightened. How freedmen and freedwomen would assume their new status, as well as the role they, and all African Americans, would play in an America without slavery, was itself a matter for discussion. A number of abolitionists, following the lead of Charlotte Forten and her colleagues in South Carolina, began to devote themselves to training freedmen and freedwomen for freedom. Harriet Jacobs, for example, helped to open schools for the freed in northern Virginia even before the war ended. In 1865 Lydia Maria Child produced a primer that sought to inculcate racial pride by providing "accounts of what colored people *have* done," including "the best specimens of colored authors." In the tradition of abolitionism, it also sought "to diminish prejudice against color at the North" by, again, presenting the testimony black achievement and, especially, literature provided against negative ideas.[27]

As Child's effort indicates, at least in the immediate aftermath of emancipation there was a general tendency to view events, and to define purposes, within the framework created in the abolition movement. The prophetic role of African American voices retained its vigor with the coming of emancipation. With the advent of freedom, however, that role could be enhanced, celebrating the practical accomplishments of black soldiers in quelling the southern rebellion and the larger role of African Americans, whose emancipation meant a realization of the larger purposes of American liberty. It could also mean the recognition of equal rights on the part of freedmen and freedwomen as yet another test the country must pass to prove, still further, its dedication to stated principles. As a California state convention resolved in October 1865, African Americans would prove their own loyalty to the reunited nation "if the

American government will become sufficiently just to accord to us the full rights of citizenship."[28]

Further development of an African American voice took place within the framework such words implied, all informed by a mood of anxious optimism. The voice remained strongly assertive, and there was good evidence for its efficacy in the visibility of some of its strongest figures. Antebellum celebrities, including Douglass, Frances Ellen Watkins Harper, and William Wells Brown, continued to occupy a place within the old abolitionist world, speaking widely to receptive audiences of black and white Americans. For at least a few years after the war the interracial ideals that had brought them fame and authority continued to play a role in their careers. New celebrities also appeared, including those whose autobiographies were intended to capture the imaginations of black and white readers alike and those who hoped to use the stories of their lives to provide financial support for themselves and their families.

Still, things did not stay exactly the same. For one thing, what many believed to be the end of the antislavery cause changed the possible settings for an African American voice significantly. Garrison's *Liberator* was discontinued in 1865, and the *National Anti-Slavery Standard* ceased publication about five years later. These, along with the black-edited papers, all of them having subscriber lists that transcended color, had been the major outlets for black writers hoping to reach an interracial audience. Nothing arose to take the place of the major abolitionist papers, and the African American press changed markedly after emancipation, increasingly serving an exclusively black readership. This had not necessarily been their intent. When the *Elevator* was founded in 1865, the veteran editor Phillip Bell announced, "We wish to obtain as large a circulation among our white fellow-citizens as among colored," following a precedent he and his colleagues had laid down before the Civil War. William McFeely has shown that the *New National Era*, founded at the end of the decade, similarly sought an interracial audience but failed to gain white subscribers despite Frederick Douglass's prominence as editor. The creation of an African American press to serve the African American community was the trend in post-emancipation America, as newspapers multiplied rapidly throughout the country, reaching local audiences and attuned to local affairs.[29]

Thus, through the years of Reconstruction, African American writers continued to produce. One can trace the continuing careers of writers begun during the antebellum period, including those of Brown, Harper, Bell, and Whitfield. One can see the emergence of new figures whose careers began in the aftermath of emancipation and continue beyond the end of Reconstruction, notably Elijah Smith and John Willis Menard. Since their works appeared in black-edited publications with mainly black readers, however, they failed to receive the national stature their predecessors had achieved. When, in the 1890s, such writers as Charles Chesnutt and Paul Laurence Dunbar became so widely recognized as "firsts," theirs was a celebrity based on historical amnesia growing out of a nearly thirty-year absence of black writers from the national stage.

Still, what might be considered a national hiatus brought on by the post-Reconstruction "nadir" in American race relations could not entirely diminish the special authority that had been defined for an African American voice during the debate over slavery. Writers themselves continued to stress certain key themes, including the ironies inherent in American professions of liberty in a land of oppression and the special perspective African Americans, as a people at the margins, brought to understanding the nature of American history and society. A dominating gentility, little different from that of the antebellum era, expressed the overwhelming aspirations of African Americans for a place in the mainstream of American life.

The dynamic created by abolitionism was not present in the closing years of the nineteenth century. It would never quite return to American literary life until it was re-created, in a sense, by the Civil Rights movement of the 1950s and 1960s, when, again, the African American voice, along with that of other American minorities, was invested with a distinctive moral authority that it continues to hold for many readers. Still, the themes and images, and the stances created in the context of the abolition movement, building on frameworks going back to the seventeenth century, were kept alive by African American writers for a long time. Revitalized by events, made relevant by circumstances, they have continued to shape American ideals, and American anxieties, down to our own time. Until the color line is truly abolished, if it ever is, they are likely to continue to shape American culture, and American consciousness, for some time to come.

Notes

1. Background to an African American Literature

1. Africanus, *History and Description of Africa*, 1:185; Hawkins, "Third troublesome voyage," 10:65; Jordan, *White over Black*, ch. 1.

2. Jordan, *White over Black*, 67, 78, 82; Vaughan, *Roots of American Racism*, 131–34.

3. Berlin, "From Creole to African."

4. Ibid., 276–78; Twombley and Moore, "Black Puritan," 235–36; Hodges, *Root and Branch*, 13–14.

5. Twombley and Moore, "Black Puritan," 227; Breen and Innes, *Myne Own Ground*, 104; Aptheker, *Anti-Racism in U.S. History*, 28; Foote, "Black Life in Colonial Manhattan"; Berlin, *Many Thousands Gone*, 59–60.

6. Jordan, *White over Black*, 105.

7. Ibid., 125–27; Berlin, *Slaves without Masters*, 127.

8. Berlin, "Time, Space," 46, 54; Greene, *Negro in Colonial New England*, 114–15; Gilroy, *Black Atlantic*, 12; Bolster, *Black Jacks*, 4.

9. Wood, *Women's Work, Men's Work*, 29; Morgan, "Black Life in Eighteenth-Century Charleston," 193–97; Olwell, *Masters, Slaves, and Subjects*, 172.

10. Wood, *Black Majority*, 175, 182; Kay and Cary, *Slavery in North Carolina*, 142–44; Frey, *Water from the Rock*, 14.

11. Berlin, "Time, Space," 53–54.

12. Piersen, *Black Yankees*, 137–39; Reidy, "Negro Election Day," 102–9.

13. Seeman, "Justise Must Take Plase," 400–401.

14. Wood, *Black Majority*, 135–36; Vibert, "Society for the Propagation of the Gospel in Foreign Parts," 171–74.

15. Greene, *Negro in Colonial New England*, 266, 276–77.

16. Raboteau, *Slave Religion*, 128–30.

17. Ibid., 120; Kay and Cary, *Slavery in North Carolina*, 201; Greene, *Negro in Colonial New England*, 285; Wood, *Women's Work, Men's Work*, 29; Frey and Wood, *Come Shouting to Zion*, 64; Frey, *Water from the Rock*, 36–37; Piersen, *Black Yankees*, 77.

18. Billings, "Cases of Fernando and Elizabeth Key"; Berlin, "Time, Space," 50.

19. Billings, "Cases of Fernando and Elizabeth Key," 470.

20. Godwyn, *Negro's and Indians Advocate*, 140; Van Horne, *Religious Philanthropy*, 186; Davis, *Problem of Slavery in Western Culture*, 203.

21. Butler, *Awash in a Sea of Faith*, 140; [Bacon], *Two Sermons*, 14.

22. Godwyn, *Negro's and Indians Advocate*, 34, 36, 41, 55, 58; Mather, *Negro Christianized*, 23.

23. Fawcett, *Compassionate Address*, 3–4; Jordan, *White over Black*, 201, 214; Stein, "George Whitefield on Slavery," 246, 252, 253; Wood, *Black Majority*, 137–38; Kay and Cary, *Slavery in North Carolina*, 207.

24. Moore, "First Printed Protest," 266; Bruns, *Am I Not a Man*, 71; Davis, *Problem of Slavery in Western Culture*, 309.

25. Le Jau, *Carolina Chronicle*, 102; Godwyn, *Negro's and Indians Advocate*, 61.

26. Creel, *A Peculiar People*, 92–94; Frey, *Water from the Rock*, 24.

27. Davies, *Duty of Christians*, 44.

28. Greene, *Negro in Colonial New England*, 236–37, 277; Piersen, *Black Yankees*, 37.

29. Raboteau, *Slave Religion*, 116.

30. Brown, *Strength of a People*, ch. 1, quotation on 27.

31. Van Horne, *Religious Philanthropy*, 124, 226.

32. Vibert, "Society for the Propagation of the Gospel in Foreign Parts," 176, 199; Van Horne, *Religious Philanthropy*, 255; Raboteau, *Slave Religion*, 117.

33. Ingersoll, "Releese us out of this Cruel Bondegg," 779; Le Jau, *Carolina Chronicle*, 70.

34. Lambert, "I Saw the Book Talk," 190; Jordan, *White over Black*, 212–13.

35. Lambert, "I Saw the Book Talk," 190; Juster, *Disorderly Women*, 33.

36. Cadbury, "An Early Quaker Anti-Slavery Statement," 492; Fox, *Gospel of Family Order*, 14; Sewall, *Selling of Joseph*, unpaginated.

37. Greene, *Negro in Colonial New England*, 248.

38. Sheldon, "Negro Slavery," 54; A Lady of Boston, *Memoir of Mrs. Chloe Spear*, 9, 12.

39. Chace, *Anti-Slavery Reminiscences*, 10.

40. Bruns, *Am I Not a Man*, 91; Piersen, *Black Yankees*, 106; Huston, "Experiential Basis," 621.

41. Piersen, *Black Legacy*, 43–44; Gomez, *Our Country Marks*, 199.

42. Anstey, *Atlantic Slave Trade*, 151.

43. [Appleton], *Considerations*, 5.

44. Dathorne, *Black Mind*, 1974. See also Capitein, *Agony of Asar*.

45. Walvin, *Black and White*, 9; Jonson, "Masques of Blackness and Beauty."

46. Davis, *Problem of Slavery in Western Culture*, 371–73.

47. Tryon, *Friendly Advice*, 155, 160, 175.

48. Ibid., 208, 209; Davis, *Problem of Slavery in Western Culture*, 372.

49. Cox, *Renaissance Dialogue*, 5–7; Eliot, *John Eliot's Indian Dialogues*, 61.

50. Behn, *Oroonoko*, 5, 6.

51. Mullin, *Africa in America*, 40; Josselyn, *John Josselyn*, 24; Piersen, *Black Legacy*, 76, 78.

52. Price, *Inkle and Yarico Album*, 6, 14; Sollors, *Neither Black nor White*, 193.

53. Curtin, *Africa Remembered*, 17; Donnan, *Documents*, 4:424.

54. Donnan, *Documents*, 4:426–27.

55. Sypher, *Guinea's Captive Kings*; Grainger, *Sugar-Cane*, 136.

56. Krise, "True Novel," 153; "Speech of Moses Ben Sàam."

57. "Speech of Moses Ben Sàam," 21.

58. Ibid.; Krise, "True Novel," 153.

59. Haskell, "Capitalism," 147, 151; Sollors, *Neither Black nor White*, 195; *Royal African*, 40.

60. Shields, *Civil Tongues*, xvii, xxvii.

61. Sheldon, *History of Deerfield*, 2:899; Foster, *Written by Herself*, 27.

62. Jackson, *History of Afro-American Literature*, 29–31; Sheldon, *History of Deerfield*, 2:899.

63. Foster, *Written by Herself*, 26–27.

64. Sheldon, "Negro Slavery," 55.

65. Jackson, *History of Afro-American Literature*, 32–33; Kaplan and Kaplan, *Black Presence*, 239–41.

66. Sekora, "Is the Slave Narrative a Species of Autobiography?" 102.

67. Porter, *Early Negro Writing*, 525.

68. Ibid., 523; Andrews, *To Tell a Free Story*, 32, 42–43.

69. Sekora, "Is the Slave Narrative a Species of Autobiography?" 106; Costanzo, *Surprizing Narrative*, 92.

70. Porter, *Early Negro Writing*, 528; Costanzo, *Surprizing Narrative*, 94; Hartman, *Providence Tales*, 9–10.

71. Richards, "Nationalist Themes," 123; Jackson, *History of Afro-American Literature*, 33–34.

72. Porter, *Early Negro Writing*, 529.

2. The Age of Revolution

1. Nash and Soderlund, *Freedom by Degrees*, 76; Wood, "The Dream Deferred," 176.

2. Frey, *Water from the Rock*, 54; Quarles, *Negro in the American Revolution*, 24; Berlin, *Slaves without Masters*, 16.

3. Olwell, *Masters, Slaves, and Subjects*, 232; Long, *History of Jamaica*, 1:25.

4. Bailyn, *Ideological Origins*, 235–39; Bruns, *Am I Not a Man*, 104.

5. Wheatley, *Poems*, 115. Unless otherwise noted, all references to Wheatley's poems are to this edition.

6. Shields, *Civil Tongues*, 219.

7. Wheatley, *Poems*, 133, 134.

8. Loggins, *Negro Author*, 16–18.

9. Wheatley, *Poems*, 185n; Grimsted, "Anglo-American Racism," 371; Welch, *Spiritual Pilgrim*, 144.

10. Gates, "James Gronniosaw," 58; Carretta, *Unchained Voices*, 54.

11. Wheatley, *Poems*, 185, 195.

12. See Silverman, *Cultural History*, 215.

13. Nash, *Race and Revolution*, 8–9.

14. Wheatley, *Poems*, 125.

15. Ibid., 123, 52.

16. Adams, *Works*, 2:322; Ferguson, *American Enlightenment*, 10–13; Zafar, *We Wear the Mask*, 18.

17. Wheatley, *Poems*, 83, 171; Waldstreicher, *In the Midst of Perpetual Fetes*, 317.

18. Wheatley, *Poems*, 204; Akers, "Our Modern Egyptians," 405–7.

19. Wheatley, *Poems*, 128–30; Richmond, *Bid the Vassal Soar*, 4–5; Odell, *Memoir*, 11.

20. Wheatley, *Poems*, 7; Smith, "To Maecenas," 581.

21. Wheatley, *Poems*, 204; Akers, "Our Modern Egyptians," 75; Nott, "From 'Uncultivated Barbarian' to 'Poetical Genius,'" 26, 28. See also Winans, "Slaves and Citizens," 28.

22. Melish, *Disowning Slavery*, 135; Grimsted, "Anglo-American Racism," 340.

23. Bruns, *Am I Not a Man*, 286, 289.

24. Ibid., 104; [Hopkins], *Dialogue Concerning the Slavery of Africans*, 42; Quarles, *Negro in the American Revolution*, 34.

25. Day and Bicknell, *Dying Negro*, 28; [Allen], *Watchman's Alarm*, 26–27.

26. Carretta, *Unchained Voices*, 76; Silverman, *Cultural History*, 292.

27. Nisbet, *Slavery Not Forbidden by Scripture*, 25n; Romans, *Concise Natural History*, 105; Gates, *Figures in Black*, 68–71.

28. Isani, "British Reception," 145–47; Isani, "Contemporaneous British Poem," 565–66; Wheatley, *Poems*, 29.

29. See O'Neale, *Jupiter Hammon*, 69, 77.

30. Hammon, *America's First Negro Poet*, 24, 87, 94.

31. O'Neale, *Jupiter Hammon*, 209.

32. Bruns, *Am I Not a Man*, 340; Roberts, "Patriotism and Political Criticism," 574; Bogin, "Battle of Lexington," 501.

33. Bogin, "Liberty Further Extended"; Brown, "Not Only Extreme Poverty," 508; *Sermon on the Present Situation*, 10.

34. Greene, *Negro in Colonial New England*, 241; *An Appendix*, 7; Bruns, *Am I Not a Man*, 200; Kaplan and Kaplan, *Black Presence*, 203; Davis, *Problem of Slavery in the Age of Revolution*, 277; Winans, "Slaves and Citizens," 36–37, 50.

35. *An Appendix*, 9–10.

36. Davis, "Emancipation Rhetoric," 254–55; Porter, *Early Negro Writing*, 254–55.

37. In Kaplan and Kaplan, *Black Presence*, 12.

38. Davis, "Emancipation Rhetoric," 258; Aptheker, *Documentary History*, 8–10; Bruns, *Am I Not a Man*, 428, 452–53.

39. Wood, *Radicalism*, 243–44.

40. Bailyn, *Ideological Origins*, 130–31.

41. Day and Bicknell, *Dying Negro*, 16–17; [Appleton], *Considerations*, 19.

42. Wheatley, *Poems*, 83, 163; Richards, "Phillis Wheatley," 169; Isani, "Gambia on My Soul," 66; Ferguson, *American Enlightenment*, 172.

43. *Views of American Slavery*, 35.

44. [Appleton], *Considerations*, 5.

45. Bruns, *Am I Not a Man*, 286, 287.

46. Bailyn, *Ideological Origins*, 138.

47. Bruns, *Am I Not a Man*, 452.

48. Shields, "Phillis Wheatley's Subversive Pastoral," 640; Stiles and Hopkins, *To The Public*, 5; Wheatley, *Poems*, 211; Erkkila, "Phillis Wheatley"; Zafar, *We Wear the Mask*, 22–23.

49. Jefferson, *Notes*, 138, 139, 163.

50. Dwight, *Oration*, 13.

51. Grimsted, "Anglo-American Racism," 437.

52. *Boston Magazine* 1 (1784): 488, 619–20; Wheatley, *Poems*, 178n; Nott, "From 'Uncultivated Barbarian' to 'Poetical Genius,'" 28.

53. Kaplan and Kaplan, *Black Presence*, 132; Jefferson, *Notes*, 140.

54. Imlay, *Topographical Description*, 229.

55. Huddleston, "Matilda's 'On Reading the Poems of Phillis Wheatley,'" 61–62; *New-York Magazine*, n.s., 1 (1796): 550.

56. *Tyrannical Libertymen*, 14.

57. Kaplan and Kaplan, *Black Presence*, 244.

58. *American Museum* 1 (1787): 539.

59. Ibid., 541.

60. Ibid., 539; Foster, *Written by Herself*, 44; Pitcher, "A 'Complaint'"; Carretta, "An 'Animadversion.'"

61. *Massachusetts Magazine* 3 (1791): 573–74.

62. Kaplan and Kaplan, *Black Presence*, 139, 140.

63. Jordan, *White over Black*, 451n; McHenry, "Account of a Negro Astronomer," 558; Kaplan and Kaplan, *Black Presence*, 145; Gordon-Reed, *Thomas Jefferson and Sally Hemings*, 239. See also Bay, *White Image*, 17.

64. Newman, Rael, and Lapsansky, *Pamphlets of Protest*, 4–5; Edwards and Walvin, *Black Personalities*, 62–63; Mifflin, *Defense*, 4–5. See also McColley, *Slavery and Jeffersonian Virginia*, 155ff.

65. Hammon, *America's First Negro Poet*, 64; *American Museum* 9 (1791): 153, 204.

66. Bingham, *Columbian Orator*, prefatory note, 240–42; Douglass, *Autobiographies*, 41.

67. Jefferson, *Notes*, 140; [Smith and Wolcott], *Pretension of Thomas Jefferson*, 8.

68. White, *Somewhat More Independent*, 188.

69. Brackenridge, *Modern Chivalry*, 130–31. See also Dain, "Hideous Monster of the Mind," 151–52.

70. *Merry Fellow's Companion*, 26. See also Levine, *Black Culture*, 35; and Porter, *Early Negro Writing*, 75.

71. "What the Negro Was Thinking," 68; Williams, *Slavery and Freedom in Delaware*, 160.

72. Creel, *A Peculiar People*, 138; Spangler, "Salvation Was Not Liberty," 222–23.

73. Mathews, *Religion in the Old South*, 66–67; Little, "George Liele," 188–89.

74. Hatch, *Democratization*, 112.

75. Raboteau, *Slave Religion*, 135; Asbury, *Journal and Letters*, 1:298; Rippon, *Baptist Annual Register*, 333.

76. Brooks, "Evolution," 12; Little, "George Liele," 190; Daniel, "Southern Presbyterians," 309–10; Richards, "Nationalist Themes," 127–28; Allen, *Life Experience*, 21; George, *Segregated Sabbaths*, 30.

77. Raboteau, *Slave Religion*, 138; Brooks, "Evolution," 11; Nash, *Forging Freedom*, 113.

78. Allen, *Life Experience*, 17–18.

79. Potkay and Burr, *Black Atlantic Writers*, 4, 10; Eslinger, *Citizens of Zion*, 175; Rippon, *Baptist Annual Register*, 332.

80. *American Museum* 6 (1789): 78; Parrish, *Remarks*, 51; Hodges, *Root and Branch*, 166.

81. Mackenzie, *Slavery*, 4.

82. Parrish, *Remarks*, 49; Nash, *Forging Freedom*, 188; Newman, "Transformation of American Abolitionism," 131–32.

83. Loggins, *Negro Author*, 36; Jordan, *White over Black*, 547.

84. "What the Negro Was Thinking," 49, 51, 52; *American Museum* 4 (1788): 414.

85. *American Museum* 6 (1789): 80.

86. Ibid., 76.

87. Porter, *Early Negro Writing*, 74; Douglass, *Annals*, 31.

88. Wheatley, *Poems*, 190; Parrish, *Remarks*, 49.

89. In Raboteau, *Slave Religion*, 117.

90. Breen, "Ideology and Nationalism," 27; Onuf, "To Declare Them a Free and Independent People," 22–23.

91. Wheatley, *Poems*, 203; Porter, *Early Negro Writing*, 67, 74.

92. Hammon, *America's First Negro Poet*, 69; Porter, *Early Negro Writing*, 322.

93. Porter, *Early Negro Writing*, 313, 315, 322.

94. Buxbaum, "Cyrus Bustill"; [Sansom], *Poetical Epistle*, 21; Jordan, *White over Black*, 496n.

95. Cowper, *Poetical Works*, 372; Monaghan, "Anti-Slavery Papers of John Jay," 492.

96. Equiano, *Life and Adventures of Olaudah Equiano*, 36; Loggins, *Negro Author*, 30.

97. Wesley, *Prince Hall*, 201.

98. Kaplan and Kaplan, *Black Presence*, 203–10; Wesley, *Prince Hall*, 71–72.

99. Porter, *Early Negro Writing*, 65, 66; Marrant, *Sermon*, 20.

100. Porter, *Early Negro Writing*, 73, 68.

101. Allen, *Life Experience*, 17–18; Carretta, *Unchained Voices*, 39; Cugoano, *Thoughts and Sentiments*, 70n.

102. Rippon, *Baptist Annual Register*, 340.

103. Potkay and Burr, *Black Atlantic Writers*, 91; Zafar, *We Wear the Mask*, 61.

104. Nash, *Forging Freedom*, 123–25.

105. Jones and Allen, *Narrative*, 22.

106. Ibid., 23, 20.

107. Ibid., 20.

108. *American Jest Book*, 73.

109. Stedman, *Narrative of a Five Years' Expedition*, 369.

110. Ibid., 54, 59, 267n; Pratt, *Imperial Eyes*, 92, 96; Sollors, *Neither Black nor White*, 198–99.

111. Stedman, *Narrative of a Five Years' Expedition*, 61–62.

112. Norris, *Memoirs of the Reign of Bossa Ah'adee*, vi, viii.

113. Ito, "Olaudah Equiano," 93.

114. Equiano, *Interesting Narrative*, 36, 40; Carretta, "Olaudah Equiano or Gustavus Vassa?" 96.

115. Porter, *Early Negro Writing*, 539; Desrochers, "Not Fade Away," 50.

116. Porter, *Early Negro Writing*, 539, 534; Desrochers, "Not Fade Away," 53–55.

117. Murphy, "Olaudah Equiano," 558n; Bingham, *Columbian Orator*, 292; Colman, *The Negro Boy*.

118. Newton, *Journals*, 105; Equiano, *Narrative*, 56; "What the Negro Was Thinking," 51.

119. Egerton, *Gabriel's Rebellion*, 47. See also Dain, "Haiti and Egypt," 139–40; Gellman, "Race, the Public Sphere, and Abolition," 632–34.

120. Equiano, *Narrative*, 45; Marrant, *Sermon*, 20.

121. Porter, *Early Negro Writing*, 557.

3. Literary Identity in the New Nation

1. Curry, *Free Black in Urban America*, 199; Perlman, "Organizations of the Free Negro."

2. Porter, *Early Negro Writing*, 379.

3. Berlin, *Slaves without Masters*, 92–97, 101; Kulikoff, "Uprooted Peoples," 150.

4. Pease and Pease, *They Who Would Be Free*, 18–19; Jordan, *White over Black*, 412; Heyrman, *Southern Cross*, 223–24.

5. Waldstreicher, *In the Midst of Perpetual Fetes*, 333.

6. Ibid., 209–10. See also Melish, *Disowning Slavery*, 168–69.

7. Nash, *Forging Freedom*, 182–83.

8. Forten, *Letters*, 5, 8.

9. Ibid., 3, 9.

10. Ibid., 10.

11. Winch, *Philadelphia's Black Elite*, 20.

12. *Virginia Religious Magazine* 2 (1806): 126–28; Prentiss, *Blind African Slave*, 112–15.

13. Branagan, *Preliminary Essay*, 17–19; Nash, *Forging Freedom*, 178; Gravely, "Rise of African Churches," 72; Branagan, *Penitential Tyrant*, 87.

14. Prentiss, *Blind African Slave*, 203.

15. Swan, "John Teasman," 347–48; Teasman, *Address*, 5.

16. Haynes, *Nature and Importance of True Republicanism*, 11–12.

17. Haynes, *Black Preacher to White America*, xii–xiii; Brown, "Not Only Extreme Poverty," 511.

18. "Some Letters of Allen and Jones," 442–43.

19. Prentiss, *Blind African Slave*, 72.

20. Heyrman, *Southern Cross*, 224.

21. For White's narrative, see Hodges, *Black Itinerants*, 52.

22. Ibid. 70. See also Andrews, *To Tell a Free Story*, 53–55.

23. See Gravely, "Rise of African Churches," 63.

24. See Nash, *Forging Freedom*, 118–19; and Gravely, "Rise of African Churches," 60.

25. Hodges, *Black Itinerants*, 89, 94; Saillant, "Traveling in Old and New Worlds," 481–82.

26. Hodges, *Black Itinerants*, 115; Gates, *Signifying Monkey*, 163; Saillant, "Traveling in Old and New Worlds," 478.

27. Hodges, *Black Itinerants*, 168, 169.

28. "Some Letters of Allen and Jones," 436; Heyrman, *Southern Cross*, 306n; Prentiss, *Blind African Slave*, 148–49; Teasman, *Address*, 10.

29. Parrish, *Remarks*, 51.

30. Hodges, introduction, ix, xv; Grégoire, *Enquiry*, 15.

31. Grégoire, *Enquiry*, 103–6.

32. [LaVallée], *Negro Equalled by Few Europeans*.

33. Waldstreicher, *In the Midst of Perpetual Fetes*, 321–22; "Philanthropos," *African Miscellanist*, 32, 33, 37.

34. Waldstreicher, *In the Midst of Perpetual Fetes*, 328–31; Gravely, "Dialectic of Double-Consciousness," 303; Quarles, *Black Abolitionists*, 119.

35. Davis, *Parades and Power*, 16; Waldstreicher, *In the Midst of Perpetual Fetes*, 328–29; Hodges, *Root and Branch*, 188–89.

36. Porter, *Early Negro Writing*, 348–49; Swan, "John Teasman," 344.

37. Porter, *Early Negro Writing*, 372, 565; Swan, "John Teasman," 344.

38. Parrott, *Oration*, 4–5; Winch, *Philadelphia's Black Elite*, 189n.

39. Morse, *Discourse*, 11, 12; Moss, *Life of Jedidiah Morse*, 94–95.

40. Waldstreicher, *In the Midst of Perpetual Fetes*, 343.

41. Porter, *Early Negro Writing*, 36–37; Waldstreicher, *In the Midst of Perpetual Fetes*, 343.

42. Cmiel, *Democratic Eloquence*, 46, 58.

43. Porter, *Early Negro Writing*, 36.

44. Ibid., 353.

45. Ibid., 37; Nash, *Forging Freedom*, 115.

46. *Massachusetts Missionary Magazine* 1 (1803): 165. See also Heyrman, *Southern Cross*, 224.

47. [Botsford], *Sambo and Toney*, 5. On Botsford, see Raboteau, *Slave Religion*, 135; and Frey and Wood, *Come Shouting to Zion*, 103–4.

48. Meade, *Sermons*, 143.

49. Aron, *How the West Was Lost*, 189.

50. Meade, *Sermons*, 141.

51. [Botsford], *Sambo and Toney*, 43, 15, 8; Meade, *Sermons*, 153.

52. See Bruce, "Significance of African American History," 13–14; and Heyrman, *Southern Cross*, 222–23.

53. *Lay-Man's Magazine* 1 (1816): 131.

54. Coker, *Dialogue*, 5.

55. Ibid., 16–17, 38; Berlin, *Many Thousands Gone*, 279.

56. Coker, *Dialogue*, 39. See also Smith, "Slavery and Theology," 500; and Aptheker, "Afro-American Superiority."

57. Prentiss, *Blind African Slave*, 148.

58. Glaude, *Exodus!* 45.

59. [Saunders], *Sons of Africans*, 8; Glaude, *Exodus!* 54, 83.

60. Parrott, *Oration*, 4; Grégoire, *Enquiry*, 113.

61. Porter, *Early Negro Writing*, 346, 368; Teasman, *Address*, 5.

62. Porter, *Early Negro Writing*, 368. This point is explored for a later period in Price and Stewart, *To Heal the Scourge of Prejudice*, 27–28.

63. Egerton, "The Scenes Which Are Acted in St. Domingo."

64. Egerton, *Gabriel's Rebellion*, 102; Ferguson, *American Enlightenment*, 170.

65. Grégoire, *Enquiry*, 57; "Humanitas," *Hints*, 14n.

66. Equiano, *Interesting Narrative*, 43–44; Prentiss, *Blind African Slave*, 62; Hirschberg, "Problem of the Judaized Berbers," 314–15, 319. I am grateful to Daniel Schroeter for pointing out this reference.

67. Miller, *Sermon*, 4.

68. Volney, *Ruins*, 17; Dain, "Hideous Monster of the Mind," 144; Bruce, "Ancient Africa," 689–90.

69. Grégoire, *Enquiry*, 4.

70. Dain, "Hideous Monster of the Mind," 208–10; Porter, *Early Negro Writing*, 393, 396; *Columbian Magazine* 2 (1788): 152.

71. Grégoire, *Enquiry*, 10; Porter, *Early Negro Writing*, 393, 396.

72. Porter, *Early Negro Writing*, 393–94.

73. Oson, *Search for Truth*, 5, 6, 11. On Oson, see *African Repository* 4 (1828): 283–84.

74. Oson, *Search for Truth*, 7.

75. Wheatley, *Poems*, 50; Jefferson, *Notes*, 142; Grégoire, *Enquiry*, 16; *An Address Delivered Before the New York African Society*, 13, 14.

76. Coker's address, quoted in Aptheker, *Documentary History*, 68; *Doctrines and Discipline of the African Methodist Episcopal Church*, 5.

77. Brooks, "Providence African Society's Sierra Leone Emigration Scheme," 187; Jordan, *White over Black*, 546–47; Sherwood, "Early Negro Deportation Projects," 487, 490–91, 503; Hunt, "William Thornton," 43; Porter, *Early Negro Writing*, 255. The discussion that follows draws on Bruce, "National Identity and African-American Colonization," used by permission of *The Historian*.

78. Miller, *Search*, 10–11; Kaplan and Kaplan, *Black Presence*, 208; Douglass, *Annals*, 26, 183–202.

79. Kaplan and Kaplan, *Black Presence*, 208; McCoy, *Elusive Republic*, 86–90, quotation on 90.

80. Brooks, "Providence African Society's Sierra Leone Emigration Scheme," 192; Douglass, *Annals*, 28.

81. Kaplan and Kaplan, *Black Presence*, 151–52.

82. The most thorough treatments of Cuffe's career are in Miller, *Search*; Thomas, *Rise to Be a People*; and Cuffe, *Captain Paul Cuffe's Logs and Letters*.

83. Carter and Ripley, *Black Abolitionist Papers*, 16:991.

84. Porter, *Early Negro Writing*, 260; Jefferson quotation in Kohn, *Idea of Nationalism*, 276.

85. Thomas, *Rise to Be a People*, 62; Miller, *Search*, 29, 44; Williams, *Discourse*, 11, 12; Porter, *Early Negro Writing*, 260; Sundquist, *To Wake the Nations*, 543.

86. Carter and Ripley, *Black Abolitionist Papers*, 17:165.

87. Ibid., 16:1069, 17:256.

88. Thomas, *Rise to Be a People*, 32, 81; Sherwood, "Paul Cuffe," 198.

89. Loomis, "Evolution of Paul Cuffe's Black Nationalism," 197; Sherwood, "Early Negro Deportation Projects," 195–97; Cuffe, *Captain Paul Cuffe's Letters and Logs*, 252–53.

90. Carter and Ripley, *Black Abolitionist Papers*, 16:1025; Thomas, *Rise to Be a People*, 77.

91. Porter, *Early Negro Writing*, 259, 260.

4. The Era of Colonization

1. Staudenraus, *African Colonization Movement*, 17; Castiglia, "Pedagogical Discipline."

2. Finley, *Thoughts*, 7.

3. Ibid., 5.

4. Egerton, "Its Origin Is Not a Little Curious," 469; Foster, "Colonization of Free Negroes," 52–53; Streifford, "American Colonization Society," 207, 211.

5. Staudenraus, *African Colonization Movement*, 29–32.

6. *National Intelligencer*, 30 December 1816.

7. Ibid.

8. Ibid.

9. Ibid.

10. Staudenraus, *African Colonization Movement*, 31–32; Nash, *Forging Freedom*, 236–38.

11. Nash, *Forging Freedom*, 238.

12. See Garrison, *Thoughts on African Colonization*, pt. 2, pp. 9–10.

13. Ibid., 2, 63.

14. Staudenraus, *African Colonization Movement*, 33; Porter, *Early Negro Writing*, 265–66.

15. Finley, "Dialogues," 316; see also Waldstreicher, *In the Midst of Perpetual Fetes*, 307. I am grateful to Professor Waldstreicher for calling this document to my attention.

16. Finley, "Dialogues," 325–26, 327.

17. Ibid. 317, 330, 333.

18. Ibid., 329, 336.

19. See Waldstreicher, *In the Midst of Perpetual Fetes*, 307.

20. *Poulson's American Daily Advertiser*, 18 November 1819.

21. American Colonization Society, *Third Annual Report*, 122.

22. Ibid., 118.

23. Lynch, "Pan-Negro Nationalism," 47; Markwei, "Rev. Daniel Coker," 205; Phillips, *Freedom's Port*, 138; Smith, *Biography*, 36.

24. Markwei, "Rev. Daniel Coker," 207–8.

25. Bracy, Meier, and Rudwick, *Black Nationalism*, 47.

26. Coker, *Journal*, 14.

27. Ibid., 22.

28. Ibid., 44.

29. Ibid., 17–19; American Colonization Society, *Fourth Annual Report*, 19.

30. Rankin, *Letters on American Slavery*, 57; Kirk, *Randolph of Roanoke*, 125; Huston, "Experiential Basis," 640.

31. *Genius of Universal Emancipation* 1 (1821), 15.

32. Grimes, *Life of William Grimes*, iii, iv.

33. Ibid., 68. See also Andrews, *To Tell a Free Story*, 90.

34. Saillant, "Remarkably Emancipated," 122–40.

35. Porter, *Early Negro Writing*, 101.

36. Harris, *Discourse*, 12.

37. Andrews, *To Tell a Free Story*, 67; Porter, *Early Negro Writing*, 587, 590, 599.

38. Ladd, *Some Account of Lucy Cardwell*, 4; *Washington Theological Repertory* 3 (1821): 63. See also Teute, "In 'the gloom of the evening,'" 45.

39. Alford, *Prince among Slaves*, 81–82, 105–6, 114, 137–38 (brackets in Alford); Austin, *African Muslims*, 460–61.

40. *Abolition Intelligencer* 1 (1822): 56.

41. *Short History of the African Union Meeting*, 20–21.

42. Ibid.; *Genius of Universal Emancipation* 1 (1822): 138, 116.

43. Hodges, *Root and Branch*, 196–97; Stewart, "Emergence of Racial Modernity," 192–93.

44. Egerton, *He Shall Go Free*, 214–15; Evarts, "On the Condition of Blacks," 244–45.

45. Nash, *Forging Freedom*, 254–59; White, "It Was a Proud Day," 33, 36–37; Gates, *Signifying Monkey*, 90–92.

46. *African Repository* 1 (1825): 79, 172; 2 (1826): 152.

47. Ibid. 1 (1825): 236; Mathew Carey to John H. B. Latrobe, 8 November 1818, John H. B. Latrobe Papers, Library of Congress.

48. *African Repository* 1 (1825–26): 96, 253, 373, and 4 (1828): 77–81; Staudenraus, *African Colonization Movement*, 101.

49. *African Repository* 1 (1825): 212–13, 12. See also Melish, *Disowning Slavery*, 197.

50. Saunders, *Haytian Papers*, iii; Winch, *Philadelphia's Black Elite*, 50–51.

51. Lewis, *W. E. B. Du Bois*, 43–44; Staudenraus, *African Colonization Movement*, 83–84.

52. George, *Segregated Sabbaths*, 148; McGraw, "Richmond Free Blacks," 209–10.

53. Much of the subsequent discussion is adapted from Bruce, "Black and White Voices."

54. *African Repository* 2 (1826): 294, 298; Charles C. Harper to Ralph R. Gurley, 13 December 1826, American Colonization Society Records, Library of Congress; George, *Segregated Sabbaths*, 148; Phillips, *Freedom's Port*, 214.

55. Campbell, *Maryland in Africa*, 52, 64, 100.

56. Harper to Gurley, 13 December 1826.

57. *Genius of Universal Emancipation* 2 (1826–27): 94, 141, 150.

58. Harper to Gurley, 28 December 1826, American Colonization Society Records.

59. *African Repository* 2 (1826): 297, 298.

60. Ibid., 294.

61. Ibid. 3 (1827): 301, 302, 307; Saillant, "Circular," 492n.

62. Fisher, "Lott Cary," 382–83, 389–90.

63. Saillant, "Circular," 482; Abasiattai, "Search for Independence," 112.

64. *Latter Day Luminary* 6 (1825): 356; *African Repository* 1 (1825): 155, 3 (1827), 249.

65. Saillant, "Circular," 503.

66. Ibid., 495, 496, 500; McGraw, "Hues and Uses of Liberia," 198.

67. Saillant, "Circular," 494.

68. See Swift, *Black Prophets of Justice*, 21–23, 37–40; William B. Davidson to Gurley, 6 February 1827, American Colonization Society Records; and *Genius of Universal Emancipation* 2 (1826): 92.

69. Foner, "John Brown Russwurm," 393, 397.

70. Gross, "Freedom's Journal," 442–43; Brewer, "John B. Russwurm," 414; *Freedom's Journal*, 16 March 1827. Subsequent references to *Freedom's Journal* in this chapter appear in parentheses in the text.

71. *Genius of Universal Emancipation* 2 (1827): 152.

72. Dillon, *Slavery Attacked*, 140.

73. Cooper, "Elevating the Race," 605–7.

74. Dain, " Hideous Monster of the Mind," 239–40; Bay, *White Image*, 26–30.

75. Jackson, *History of Afro-American Literature*, 83; Sherman, introduction, 1–8; Richmond, *Bid the Vassal Soar*, 91, 97.

76. Horton, *Black Bard*, 75, 89.

77. Sherman, introduction, 14.

78. Richmond, *Bid the Vassal Soar*, 107–9; Horton and Horton, *In Hope of Liberty*, x; Horton, *The Hope of Liberty*, 3.

79. On the poem's authorship see *Liberator*, 10 March 1832.

80. *African Repository* 4 (1829): 376; Gross, "Freedom's Journal," 280–81.

81. Easton, *An Address*, 6, 10; Price and Stewart, *To Heal the Scourge of Prejudice*, 3–10, 54, 58.

5. The *Liberator* and the Shaping of African American Tradition

1. *Rights of All,* 29 May 1829; Swift, *Black Prophets of Justice,* 41, 45.

2. *Genius of Universal Emancipation* 11 (1831): 179, 197.

3. Baily, "From Cincinnati, Ohio, to Wilberforce," 427–28.

4. Ibid.," 430–31; Wade, "Negro in Cincinnati," 51–52, 55.

5. Baily, "From Cincinnati, Ohio, to Wilberforce," 432; Wade, "Negro in Cincinnati," 56; Swift, *Black Prophets of Justice,* 43–44; *Rights of All,* 14 August 1829.

6. Porter, *Early Negro Writing,* 295, 297; Steward, *Twenty-Two Years a Slave,* 177.

7. George, *Segregated Sabbaths,* 156; "The First Colored Convention" (1859), in Bell, *Minutes of the National Negro Conventions,* unpaginated; Glaude, *Exodus!* 12–15.

8. Porter, *Early Negro Writing,* 178–80.

9. Ibid., 180.

10. "First Colored Convention"; Peter Hinks, in Walker, *David Walker's Appeal,* xlv.

11. Hinks, *To Awaken My Afflicted Brethren,* 92–93; *Freedom's Journal,* 19 December 1828.

12. Hinks, *To Awaken My Afflicted Brethren,* 105.

13. Ibid., 181; Walker, *David Walker's Appeal,* 12, 19, 21.

14. Walker, *David Walker's Appeal,* 67.

15. Ibid., 22; Hinks, *To Awaken My Afflicted Brethren,* 180.

16. Walker, *David Walker's Appeal,* 19. See also Aptheker, "Afro-American Superiority," 340.

17. Walker, *David Walker's Appeal,* 14, 28–29; Jefferson, *Notes,* 143.

18. Walker, *David Walker's Appeal,* 19–20. See also Bay, *White Image,* 35.

19. Walker, *David Walker's Appeal,* 17.

20. Hinks, *To Awaken My Afflicted Brethren,* 66; Walker, *David Walker's Appeal,* 77.

21. Pease and Pease, "Walker's *Appeal* Comes to Charleston," 291–92; Richmond, *Bid the Vassal Soar,* 117–18.

22. Young, *Ethiopian Manifesto,* 8–9; Stuckey, *Ideological Origins,* 7–8.

23. Andrews, *To Tell a Free Story,* 75–76; Sundquist, *To Wake the Nations,* 50–52; Greenberg, *Confessions of Nat Turner,* 10–11; Davis, *Nat Turner before the Bar of Judgement,* 63–64.

24. Sundquist, *To Wake the Nations,* 44–45; Greenberg, *Confessions of Nat Turner,* 40, 42.

25. *Liberator,* 17 December 1831. Subsequent references to the *Liberator* in this chapter appear in parentheses in the text.

26. "First Colored Convention"; Abzug, "Influence of Garrisonian Abolitionists' Fears," 18; *Genius of Universal Emancipation* 11 (1830): 16.

27. Abzug, "Influence of Garrisonian Abolitionists' Fears," 18.

28. Quarles, *Black Abolitionists,* 19.

29. Porter, "Early Manuscript Letters," 200.

30. Garrison, *Letters,* 1:126–27.

31. See, e.g., Lindhorst, "Politics in a Box," 265–66.

32. Ullman, *Martin R. Delany,* 16; Stewart, "Emergence of Racial Modernity," 197.

33. Jacobs, "David Walker and William Lloyd Garrison," 15; Thomas, *The Liberator,* 145–46.

34. *Genius of Universal Emancipation* 12 (1831): 87.

35. Staudenraus, *African Colonization Movement*, 190–91; *News from Africa*, 3; Porter, *Early Negro Writing*, 303.

36. Willard Hall to Secretary of the American Colonization Society, 27 September 1827, American Colonization Society Records.

37. Bayley, *Brief Account*, 8.

38. *Liberia Herald*, 6 March 1830.

39. Phillips, *Freedom's Port*, 221; Thomas, *The Liberator*, 101–3, 145–46; Goodman, *Of One Blood*, 41.

40. Sterling, *Speak Out in Thunder Tones*, 59.

41. Streifford, "American Colonization Society," 213; Staudenraus, *African Colonization Movement*, 194–95; Garrison, *Address*, 18–19.

42. Garrison, *Address*, 2–3.

43. Garrison, *Thoughts on African Colonization*, pt. 2, p. 8.

44. Ibid., 20.

45. James Forten to William Lloyd Garrison, 2 March 1831, Antislavery Collection, Boston Public Library/Rare Books Department. This and subsequent citations courtesy of the Trustees.

46. *Independent*, 25 December 1865.

47. Stewart, "Emergence of Racial Modernity," 197; Goodman, *Of One Blood*, 47–48.

48. Richardson, introduction, 7, 10–11, 23.

49. Stewart, *Maria W. Stewart*, 29, 34, 35. Subsequent references to this book appear in parentheses in the text.

50. Garrison, *Address*, 6.

51. McHenry, "Dreaded Eloquence," 48–49.

52. Garrison, *Letters*, 1:143–44; McHenry, "Dreaded Eloquence," 48; Sarah Douglass to Garrison, 29 February 1832, Antislavery Collection.

53. Gates and McKay, *Norton Anthology*, 277; Gernes, "Poetic Justice," 234.

54. Gernes, "Poetic Justice," 235–36.

55. Ibid., 230n; Lindhorst, "Politics in a Box," 271.

56. Garrison, *Address*, 3, 6–7.

57. Dain, "Hideous Monster of the Mind," 325–26.

58. Stewart, "Emergence of Racial Modernity," 186–87.

6. Literary Expression in the Age of Abolitionism

1. Stewart, "Emergence of Racial Modernity," 208.

2. Quarles, *Black Abolitionists*, 23–25; Winch, "You Have Talents," 116–17; Soderlund, "Priorities and Power," 69; Yee, *Black Women Abolitionists*, 90–92; Goodman, *Of One Blood*, 254.

3. Forbes, "Slavery and the Meaning of America," 2:599; Kachun, "Faith That the Dark Past Has Taught Us," 118.

4. Clark, *Communitarian Moment*; Sernett, *Abolition's Axe*, 20–21, 52.

5. Yee, *Black Women Abolitionists*, 13–14; Hansen, *Strained Sisterhood*, 101.

6. Barnes and Dumond, *Weld-Grimké Letters*, 1:276–77; Jeffrey, *Great Silent Army*, 126–28.

7. Barnes and Dumond, *Weld-Grimké Letters*, 1:276.

8. Kraditor, *Means and Ends*, 242–43; Friedman, *Gregarious Saints*, 174–75; Barnes and Dumond, *Weld-Grimké Letters*, 1:273, 364.

9. Friedman, *Gregarious Saints*, 44; Clark, *Communitarian Moment*, 7–8.

10. Frederickson, *Black Image in the White Mind*, 73–75.

11. Winch, *Philadelphia's Black Elite*, 141–42.

12. Roediger, *Wages of Whiteness*, 124.

13. White and White, *Stylin'*, 114–16.

14. *Liberator*, 28 December 1833; Carter and Ripley, *Black Abolitionist Papers*, 4:411.

15. Richards, *Gentlemen of Property and Standing*, 16–19; Lapsansky, "Since They Got Those Separate Churches," 55, 64, 75; Grimsted, *American Mobbing*, 36–37.

16. Winch, *Philadelphia's Black Elite*, 146–48.

17. Chace, *Anti-Slavery Reminiscences*, 16; May, *Some Recollections*, 270–71; William Cooper Nell to Wendell Phillips, 31 August 1840, Crawford Blagden Collection of the Papers of Wendell Phillips, bMS Am 1953 (924), Houghton Library, Harvard University. This and subsequent citations by permission of the Houghton Library, Harvard University.

18. *Herald of Freedom*, 30 April 1836; May, *Some Recollections*, 288.

19. Davis, *Parades and Power*, 45; Henkin, *City Reading*, 122–23; James Forten Jr. to James McCune Smith, 8 September 1835, Antislavery Collection. See also Lehuu, *Carnival on the Page*, 26.

20. Hamilton, *Address*, 6; *Emancipator*, 18 May 1837; [Grimké], *Address*, 21; Garrison, *Letters*, 2:319.

21. *Colored American*, 2 June 1836, 30 May 1840; Garrison, *Letters*, 2:608; Douglass, *Autobiographies*, 4.

22. *Emancipator*, 16 November 1837; Bay, *White Image*, 41.

23. "Minutes of the Fifth Annual Convention for the Improvement of the Free People of Colour in the United States" (1835), in Bell, *Minutes of the National Negro Conventions*, 22; Douglass, *Papers*, 2:125; Smith, *Destiny of the People of Color*, 15.

24. *Emancipator*, 16 November 1837; Barnes and Dumond, *Weld-Grimké Letters*, 1:365.

25. Barnes and Dumond, *Weld-Grimké Letters*, 1:380; Carter and Ripley, *Black Abolitionist Papers*, 2:498.

26. Ceplair, *Public Years*, 126; *Pennsylvania Freeman*, 11 April 1839.

27. Barnes and Dumond, *Weld-Grimké Letters*, 1:263, 2:811.

28. *Liberator*, 28 January 1842.

29. Barnes and Dumond, *Weld-Grimké Letters*, 1:297, 523; Hall, "Massachusetts Abolitionists," 83.

30. Hall, "Massachusetts Abolitionists," 83; song in Frederick Douglass Papers, Library of Congress.

31. Douglass, *Papers*, 1:3.

32. Clarke, *Narrative*, 70; *National Anti-Slavery Standard*, 20 October 1842. See also Fabian, *Unvarnished Truth*, 106–7.

33. [Blassingame], "Introduction to Series One," li; Douglass, *Papers*, 2:28.

34. Hammond, "Hammond's Letters on Slavery," 127.

35. *Emancipator*, 26 May 1836.

36. Pennington, "To the Reader," xviii.

37. Allen, *Wheatley, Banneker, and Horton*, 7.

38. Forten to Smith, 8 September 1835.

39. Child, *Appeal*, 149; Garnet, *Past and the Present Condition*, 7.

40. *North Star*, 7 April 1848; Pennington, "To the Reader," xviii; [Ames], *Legion of Liberty!* unpaginated.

41. Bell, "Expressions of Negro Militancy," 12–13; Williams, introduction, xlviii; Foster, *Written by Herself*, 57, 69.

42. *Anti-Slavery Record* 1 (1835): 111, 143; Douglass, *Papers*, 2:165–66.

43. Massachusetts Anti-Slavery Society, *Fifth Annual Report*, xxvi; Douglass, *Papers*, 2:75–76.

44. *Liberator*, 21 December 1833.

45. Ibid., 3 September 1836.

46. [Willson], *Sketches*, 5–6.

47. *Liberator*, 29 October 1836; *Emancipator*, 10 November 1836.

48. *Liberator*, 1, 22 February, 1 March 1834. See also Gernes, "Poetic Justice," 265.

49. [Grimké], *Appeal*, title page; Foster, *Written by Herself*, 81.

50. *North Star*, 28 April 1848.

51. Coleman, *Creole Voices*, xix.

52. *Colored American*, 28 September 1839.

53. Payne, *Recollections*, 26–27, 30, 31.

54. *Colored American*, 9 September 1837; *Emancipator*, 26 October 1837.

55. McHenry, "Dreaded Eloquence," 44, 45; Perlman, "Organizations of the Free Negro," 194.

56. *Colored American*, 11 March 1837.

57. *The Abolitionist* 1 (1833): 14.

58. Child, *Oasis*, 65; [Stedman], *Narrative of Joanna*; *Liberator*, 11 October 1839; *Emancipator*, 19 September 1839; Clarke, *Narrative*, 83.

59. Brown, *Anti-Slavery Harp*, 14, 30; Farrison, *William Wells Brown*, 138–39; Collins, *Anti-Slavery Picknick*, 107.

60. *North Star*, 17 March 1848; Paul, *Memoirs of James Jackson*.

61. Hall, "Massachusetts Abolitionists," 83; Andrews, *To Tell a Free Story*, 97; Clarke and Clarke, *Narratives*, preface; Gates, *Figures in Black*, 103; Fabian, *Unvarnished Truth*, 105.

62. Douglass, *Papers*, 1:89, 133; Andrews, *To Tell a Free Story*, 106; McFeely, *Frederick Douglass*, 113.

63. Ball, *Slavery in the United States*, preface; [Wright], "Life and Adventures," 375, 393; Fabian, *Unvarnished Truth*, 96–98.

64. Nichols, *Many Thousand Gone*, xiii; *Liberator*, 13 June, 28 September, 2 November 1838; Andrews, *To Tell a Free Story*, 88; Barnes and Dumond, *Weld-Grimké Letters*, 2:735–36.

65. Katz, *Flight from the Devil*, 107–8; 221; Hayden, *Narrative*, 149–56; Bibb, *Narrative*, ii–iii.

66. *Liberator*, 20 February 1846; *North Star*, 13 October 1848.

67. Watson, *Narrative*, 42; Katz, *Flight from the Devil*, 133.

68. Pennington, *Fugitive Blacksmith*, 54.

69. Olney, "I Was Born," 152–53. See also Browder, *Slippery Characters*, 20–21.

70. Andrews, *Sisters of the Spirit*, 91; Bolokitten, *Sojourn*, 70–71; Fabian, *Unvarnished Truth*, 108.

71. Roper, *Narrative*, 45; Bibb, *Narrative*, 112–13.

72. Barrett, "African American Slave Narratives," 421; Clark, "Sacred Rights of the Weak," 465, 470.

73. Pennington, *Fugitive Blacksmith*, 7; Ripley, *Black Abolitionist Papers*, 3:395.

74. Ceplair, *Public Years*, 50; Brown, *Narrative of Henry Box Brown*, iv; Armistead, *Tribute*, 454.

75. Hayden, *Narrative*, 66.

76. Roper, *Narrative*, 17; Katz, *Flight from the Devil*, 123; Pennington, *Fugitive Blacksmith*, 11.

77. *Narrative of James Williams*, 3; Roper, *Narrative*, 1.

78. Andrews, "Dialogue," 92–93.

79. McFeely, *Frederick Douglass*, 158.

80. Bibb, *Narrative*, 177; Woodson, *Mind of the Negro*, 216.

81. Pennington, *Fugitive Blacksmith*, 83; Woodson, *Mind of the Negro*, 215.

82. *North Star*, 29 June 1849.

83. Hammond, "Hammond's Letters on Slavery," 133.

84. *Anti-Slavery Record* 2 (1836): 170.

85. Johnson, *Soul by Soul*, 217–18.

86. *Liberator*, 22 February 1834.

87. McCormick, "William Whipper," 33.

88. Birney, *Letters*, 2:624.

89. *Colored American*, 15 March, 2 June 1838; Miller, "Father of Black Nationalism," 312–13.

90. *Emancipator*, 16 November 1837.

91. Ibid.

92. Hutton, *Early Black Press*, 165–66.

93. *Weekly Advocate*, 7 January 1837.

94. *Colored American*, 4 March 1837.

95. Ibid.

96. Ibid., 11 March 1837; Swift, *Black Prophets of Justice*, 106; Quarles, *Black Abolitionists*, 89.

97. Foner and Walker, *Proceedings of the Black State Conventions*, 1:114.

98. Levine, *Martin Delany*, 20; Bell, "National Negro Conventions," 258–59; McFeely, *Frederick Douglass*, 146–47.

99. *North Star*, 3 December 1847; Ullman, *Martin R. Delany*, 81.

100. McFeely, *Frederick Douglass*, 147.

101. *Pennsylvania Freeman*, 7 October 1847; Massachusetts Anti-Slavery Society, *Sixteenth Annual Report*, 42.

102. Frederick Douglass to Elizabeth Pease, 8 November 1849, Antislavery Collection.

103. Douglass, *Autobiographies*, 367; [Blassingame], "Introduction to Series One," xlviii–xlix, lii; McFeely, *Frederick Douglass*, 91, 95.

104. Martin, *Mind of Frederick Douglass*, 57; Carter and Ripley, *Black Abolitionist Papers*, 5:715.

105. Pease and Pease, "Organized Negro Communities," 24.

106. Woodson, *Mind of the Negro*, 194–95.

7. African American Voices in the American Crisis

1. Carter and Ripley, *Black Abolitionist Papers*, 6:453.
2. *Fugitive Slaves*, 12; *Voice of the Fugitive*, 20 May 1852.
3. Phillips, *Speeches, Lectures, and Letters*, 132; Higginson, "Romance of History," 47.
4. Chesebrough, *Frederick Douglass*, 47; *Anti-Slavery Bugle*, 9 April 1853.
5. *Anti-Slavery Bugle*, 13 February 1858.
6. William Lloyd Garrison, preface to Watkins, *Poems on Miscellaneous Subjects*.
7. *Liberator*, 8 September 1854; *National Anti-Slavery Standard*, 18 February 1860.
8. Grimké, *Journals of Charlotte Forten*, 289. See also Jeffrey, *Great Silent Army*, 195, 196.
9. Cheek and Cheek, *John Mercer Langston*, 178; Foster, *Brighter Coming Day*, 26–27; Bacon, "Double Curse of Sex and Color," 69.
10. *Liberator*, 23 February, 16 March 1855.
11. Ibid., 24 August 1855; *National Anti-Slavery Standard*, 2 April 1859, 14 January 1860.
12. Long, *Pictures of Slavery*, 175.
13. *Frederick Douglass' Paper*, 22 September 1854.
14. *Liberator*, 19 December 1856.
15. Jefferson, introduction, 3.
16. See Farrison, *William Wells Brown*, 148–49, 200; and Brown, *Biography of an American Bondman*, 1.
17. Brown, *Three Years in Europe*, xxxi; Farrison, *William Wells Brown*, 207; *Pennsylvania Freeman*, 30 October 1852.
18. Brown, *Three Years in Europe*, 259.
19. Ibid., 7, 34–35.
20. Wesley, "Participation of Negroes," 64, 69; Field, *Politics of Race*, 93; Raymond, "Outline of a Man," 1:155.
21. *New National Era*, 17 April 1873.
22. See Sweet, *Black Images of America*, 145; and Douglass, *Papers*, 2:443.
23. Douglass, *Papers*, 3:23–24.
24. *National Anti-Slavery Standard*, 8 December 1860; *Frederick Douglass' Paper*, 6 April 1855.
25. Delany, *Condition*, 190, 10.
26. *Liberator*, 7, 21 May 1852.
27. *Pennsylvania Freeman*, 29 April 1852; *Liberator*, 28 May, 21 July 1852.
28. *Liberator*, 21 May 1852; Loggins, *Negro Author*, 184.
29. *Provincial Freeman*, 3 November 1855; Rhodes, *Mary Ann Shadd Cary*, 107.
30. *Anglo-African Magazine* 1 (1859): 4.
31. *Douglass' Monthly*, February 1859, 20; *Weekly Anglo-African*, 5 November 1859.
32. See Quarles, *Black Abolitionists*, 198–99.
33. Ibid., 205–11; Melish, *Disowning Slavery*, 262; Bell, "Expressions of Negro Militancy," 14; Browne, "To Defend Mr. Garrison," 432; Collison, *Shadrach Minkins*, 83; Wellman, "This Side of the Border," 384.
34. Stuckey, *Ideological Origins*, 183; Bell, *Search for a Place*, 30–31; *Frederick Douglass' Paper*, 8 July 1859; Ripley, *Black Abolitionist Papers*, 4:155n. See also Dixon, "Ambivalent Black Nationalism."

35. Foner and Branham, *Lift Every Voice*, 225.
36. *National Anti-Slavery Standard*, 24 June 1854; *Liberator*, 11 October 1850.
37. Watkins, *Our Rights as Men*, 11; Nell to Phillips, 8 July 1855, Crawford Blagden Collection of the Papers of Wendell Phillips; *Radical Abolitionist*, November 1856, supplement, unpaginated.
38. The poems are quoted in Simpson, *Emancipation Car*, 38; *Voice of the Fugitive*, 15 January 1851; and *Liberator*, 20 May 1853.
39. Ripley, *Black Abolitionist Papers*, 4:266; Rollin, *Martin R. Delany*, 104–5.
40. Peterson, *Ham and Japheth*, 93–94; Berry, *Slavery and Abolitionism*, viii. See also Faust, *Creation of Confederate Nationalism*, 63.
41. McCord, "Life of a Negro Slave," 206–7; [Schoolcraft], *Letters*, 25; Schoolcraft, *Black Gauntlet*, 72.
42. Adams, *South-Side View of Slavery*, 132; *National Anti-Slavery Standard*, 8 May 1851; Cobb, *Enquiry*, 45. See also Accomondo, "The Laws Were Laid Down," 235.
43. Woodson, *Mind of the Negro*, 265.
44. McCord, *Political and Social Essays*, 331, 115.
45. [Levison], *Black Diamonds*, 347. See also Mahar, *Behind the Burnt Cork Mask*, 72.
46. [Levison], *Black Diamonds*, 347, 348.
47. *National Anti-Slavery Standard*, 11 August 1855; *Liberator*, 31 August 1855; Fabian, *Unvarnished Truth*, 108–10.
48. The address appears in McCord, *Political and Social Essays*, 477–78.
49. *New York Times*, 5 February 1853.
50. *Pennsylvania Freeman*, 30 June 1853.
51. [Chamerovzow], *Slave Life in Georgia*, 165–66.
52. [Schoolcraft], *Letters*, 17; Adams, *South-Side View of Slavery*, 68–69; Harper, "Slavery in the Light of Social Ethics," 580.
53. Grayson, *Hireling and the Slave*, v.
54. Ibid., vii; Genovese, *Consuming Fire*, 17; Forbes, "Slavery and the Meaning of America," 2:606.
55. Watkins, *Poems on Miscellaneous Subjects*, 6, 8; Northup, *Twelve Years a Slave*, 58.
56. Harper, "Slavery in the Light of Social Ethics," 580; Elliott, *Cotton Is King*, ix.
57. [Chamerovzow], *Slave Life in Georgia*, 165–66.
58. Bledsoe, "Liberty and Slavery," 302; McCord, *Political and Social Essays*, 228.
59. Lincoln, *Collected Works*, 3:204.
60. Stowe, *Uncle Tom's Cabin*, xiii–xiv.
61. Herzog, *Women, Ethnics, and Exotics*, 103; William Wells Brown to Phillips, 1 September 1852, Crawford Blagden Collection of the Papers of Wendell Phillips.
62. McCord, *Political and Social Essays*, 310; *Voice of the Fugitive*, 6 May 1852; Van Deburg, *Slavery and Race*, 36.
63. Blackett, *Building an Antislavery Wall*, 26; Yarborough, "Strategies of Black Characterization," 73; Ward, *Autobiography*, 227; [Levison], *Black Diamonds*, 347.
64. Hedrick, *Harriet Beecher Stowe*, 218–19.
65. *Frederick Douglass' Paper*, 29 April 1853; *New York Tribune*, 19 August 1853; Brown, *American Fugitive in Europe*, 317.

66. *Pennsylvania Freeman*, 29 April 1853; *Frederick Douglass' Paper*, 6 May 1853; *Provincial Freeman*, 22 July 1854; Levine, *Martin Delany*, 59–60. For a useful overview, see Banks, "*Uncle Tom's Cabin*."

67. Stewart, *Wendell Phillips*, 105; Watkins, *Our Rights as Men*, 8; Yarborough, "Strategies of Black Characterization," 60.

68. *Frederick Douglass' Paper*, 8 April 1852; Levine, "*Uncle Tom's Cabin*," 72–74.

69. *Pennsylvania Freeman*, 9 December 1852; "Proceedings of the Colored National Convention Held in Rochester, July 6th, 7th, and 8th, 1853," in Bell, *Minutes of the National Negro Conventions*, 40.

70. Northup, *Twelve Years a Slave*, dedication; *Frederick Douglass' Paper*, 3 February 1854.

71. *Frederick Douglass' Paper*, 2 February 1855; Douglass, *Papers*, 3:148; Bledsoe, "Liberty and Slavery," 416.

72. Stowe, *Uncle Tom's Cabin*, xiii; *Pennsylvania Freeman*, 28 April 1853.

73. Langston, *World's Anti-Slavery Movement*, 19.

74. Peterson, "*Doers of the Word*," 147–49; Andrews, "Novelization of Voice," 23–34.

75. Lockard, afterword, 407; Grimké, *Journals of Charlotte Forten*, 189; Lydia Maria Child to Louis Gilman Loring, 8 February 1857, in Child, *Collected Correspondence*. See also Browder, *Slippery Characters*, 33.

76. Farrison, *William Wells Brown*, 224.

77. Webb, *Garies and Their Friends*, 39, 40.

78. Moses, *Black Messiahs and Uncle Toms*, 60–61; *Pennsylvania Freeman*, 1 August 1850; *Frederick Douglass' Paper*, 15 April 1852.

79. *Anti-Slavery Bugle*, 23 July 1853; Stuckey, *Ideological Origins*, 203.

80. See Sollors, *Neither Black nor White*, 232–35. See also Castronovo, *Fathering the Nation*, 227; Bruce, "Toward a Borderland Identity," 6–7; and Browder, *Slippery Characters*, 24–25.

81. Frederickson, *Black Image in the White Mind*, 121–22; Livermore, *Zoë*, 98–99.

82. Brown, *Clotel*, 8.

83. Sollors, *Neither Black nor White*, 194–95.

84. *Frederick Douglass' Paper*, 16 February 1855.

85. Braxton, *Black Women Writing Autobiography*, 23; *Pennsylvania Freeman*, 30 June 1853.

86. Andrews, "Dialogue," 93–95; Jacobs, *Incidents*, xiii, 26, 125; Painter, "Of *Lily*, Linda Brent, and Freud," 249.

87. [Levison], *Black Diamonds*, 29; Haven, *National Sermons*, 148.

88. Sollors, *Neither Black nor White*, 228, 353.

89. *Anti-Slavery Bugle*, 28 October 1854.

90. Stauffer, "Advent among the Indians," 258.

91. Levine, *Martin Delany*, 177; Sundquist, *To Wake the Nations*, 117–19.

92. Douglass, *Papers*, 2:154.

93. Douglass, "Heroic Slave," 1:175.

94. Ibid., 181–82. See also Reid-Pharr, *Conjugal Union*, 50.

95. Douglass, "Heroic Slave," 235, 238.

96. Martin R. Delany to Garrison, 2 February 1859, Antislavery Collection. See also Delany, *Blake*.

97. Brown, *St. Domingo*, 32.

8. The War for Emancipation and Beyond

1. Oates, *To Purge This Land with Blood*, 327–28.

2. Rossbach, *Ambivalent Conspirators*, 8–9; Aptheker, *Documentary History*, 443.

3. *Fredrick Douglass' Paper*, 17 February 1860; *Douglass' Monthly*, July 1861, 488; Farrison, *William Wells Brown*, 369.

4. Anderson, *Voice from Harper's Ferry*, 1.

5. *Pacific Appeal*, 10 May 1862.

6. Jackson, *History of Afro-American Literature*, 379; Gilmore, *Among the Pines*, 21 ("translations" in original).

7. Swift, *Black Prophets of Justice*, 325; *New Orleans Tribune*, 17 November 1864.

8. *Liberator*, 19 June 1863.

9. Clipping in Amos Gerry Beman Scrapbooks, vol. 2, James Weldon Johnson Collection, Beinecke Rare Book and Manuscript Library, Yale University.

10. *Pacific Appeal*, 6 December 1862.

11. Chorus in Olsen, *Negro Question*, 41; Blight, *Frederick Douglass' Civil War*, 139.

12. Hodes, *White Women, Black Men*, 132–33; Olsen, *Negro Question*, 40; Frederickson, *Black Image in the White Mind*, 171–72; [Croly and Wakeman], *Miscegenation*, 24; Kaplan, "Miscegenation Issue," 286–89, 292–93, 306.

13. Alcott, "M. L.," 153.

14. *Christian Recorder*, 16 December 1865.

15. Martin, *Hero and the Slave*, 4.

16. *Pacific Appeal*, 5 July 1862.

17. Blight, *Frederick Douglass' Civil War*, 158; *Liberator*, 8 April 1864.

18. *London Times*, 31 August 1863.

19. Grimké, *Journals of Charlotte Forten*, 407; *Liberator*, 12 December 1862; Forten, "Life on the Sea Islands," 587.

20. Grimké, *Journals of Charlotte Forten*, 409; Forten, "Life on the Sea Islands," 666–67.

21. *Weekly Anglo-African*, 14 September 1861; *National Anti-Slavery Standard*, 21 December 1861.

22. Bell, *A Poem*, 2, 8.

23. McPherson, "The Negro," 79–82.

24. Read, *Negro Problem Solved*, 190; Conway, "Benjamin Banneker," 80, 84.

25. Brown, *Black Man*, 1.

26. Farrison, *William Wells Brown*, 372–73; *Pacific Appeal*, 30 May 1863; *Douglass' Monthly*, January 1863, 771; Read, *Negro Problem Solved*, 180, 183; Samuel J. May to Richard D. Webb, 19 September 1865, Antislavery Collection.

27. Karcher, *First Woman of the Republic*, 496, 504; Child to James Thomas Fields, 23 August 1865, in Child, *Collected Correspondence*; *National Anti-Slavery Standard*, 25 November 1865.

28. Foner and Walker, *Proceedings of the Black State Conventions*, 2:175.

29. *San Francisco Elevator*, 14 April 1865; McFeely, *Frederick Douglass*, 286.

Works Cited

Manuscript Collections

Beinecke Rare Book and Manuscript Library, Yale University
    Amos Gerry Beman Scrapbooks, James Weldon Johnson Collection
Boston Public Library/Rare Books Department
    Antislavery Collection
Houghton Library, Harvard University
    Crawford Blagden Collection of the Papers of Wendell Phillips
Library of Congress
    American Colonization Society Records
    Frederick Douglass Papers
    John H. B. Latrobe Papers

Newspapers and Periodicals, 1680–1870

Abolition Intelligencer
The Abolitionist
African Repository
Aliened American
American Museum
Anglo-African Magazine
Anti-Slavery Bugle
Anti-Slavery Record
Boston Magazine
Christian Recorder
Colored American
Columbian Magazine
Douglass' Monthly
Emancipator (New York)
Frederick Douglass' Paper
Freedom's Journal
Genius of Universal Emancipation
Gentleman's Magazine
Herald of Freedom

Latter Day Luminary
Lay-Man's Magazine
Liberator
Liberia Herald
Liberty Bell
Massachusetts Magazine
Massachusetts Missionary Magazine
National Anti-Slavery Standard
National Intelligencer
New National Era
New Orleans Tribune
New-York Magazine
New York Times
New York Tribune
North Star
Pacific Appeal
Pennsylvania Freeman
Poulson's American Daily Advertiser
Provincial Freeman

Works Cited

Radical Abolitionist
Rights of All
San Francisco Elevator
Virginia Religious Magazine

Voice of the Fugitive
Washington Theological Repertory
Weekly Advocate
Weekly Anglo-African

Published Sources

Abasiattai, Monday B. "The Search for Independence: New World Blacks in Sierra Leone and Liberia, 1787–1847." *Journal of Black Studies* 23 (1992): 107–16.

Abzug, Robert. "The Influence of Garrisonian Abolitionists' Fears of Slave Violence on the Antislavery Argument, 1829–40." *Journal of Negro History* 55 (1970): 15–28.

Accomondo, Christina. "'The Laws Were Laid Down to Me Anew': Harriet Jacobs and the Reframing of Legal Fictions." *African-American Review* 32 (1998): 229–45.

Adams, John. *The Works of John Adams, Second President of the United States.* 10 vols. 1850–56. Rpt. New York, 1971.

Adams, Nehemiah. *A South-Side View of Slavery; or, Three Months at the South in 1854.* 2d ed. Boston, 1855.

An Address Delivered Before the New York African Society for Mutual Relief, of the African Zion Church, 23rd March, 1815, Being the Fifth Anniversary of Their Incorporation, By a Member. New York, 1815.

Africanus, Leo. *The History and Description of Africa and of the Notable Things Contained Therein.* Trans. John Pory, ed. Robert Brown. 3 vols. 1896. Rpt. New York, n.d.

Akers, Charles W. "'Our Modern Egyptians': Phillis Wheatley and the Whig Campaign against Slavery in Revolutionary Boston." *Journal of Negro History* 60 (1975): 397–410.

Alcott, Louisa May. "M. L." In *Louisa May Alcott: Selected Fiction*, ed. David Shealy, Madeline B. Stern, and Joel Myerson, 131–55. Boston, 1990.

Alford, Terry. *Prince among Slaves.* New York, 1977.

[Allen, John]. *The Watchman's Alarm to Lord N———h; or, The British Parliamentary Port-Bill Unwraped.* Salem, Mass., 1774.

Allen, Richard. *The Life Experience and Gospel Labors of the Rt. Rev. Richard Allen.* Nashville, 1960.

Allen, William G. *Wheatley, Banneker, and Horton; With Selections from the Poetical Works of Wheatley and Horton, and the Letter of Washington to Wheatley, and of Jefferson to Banneker.* Boston, 1849.

American Colonization Society. *Third Annual Report of the American Society for Colonizing the Free People of Colour of the United States.* Washington, D.C., 1820.

———. *The Fourth Annual Report of the American Society for Colonizing the Free People of Colour of the United States.* Washington, D.C., 1821.

The American Jest Book: Containing a Curious Variety of Jests, Anecdotes, Bon Mots, Stories, &c. Pt. 1. Philadelphia, 1789.

[Ames, Julius R.]. *The Legion of Liberty! And Force of Truth, Containing the Thoughts, Words, and Deeds, of Some Prominent Apostles, Champions and Martyrs.* 2d ed. New York, 1843.

Anderson, Osborne P. *A Voice from Harper's Ferry.* Boston, 1861.

Works Cited

Andrews, William L. "Dialogue in Afro-American Autobiography." In *Studies in Auto-biography*, ed. James Olney, 89–98. New York, 1988.

———. "The Novelization of Voice in Early African American Narrative." *PMLA* 105 (1990): 23–34.

———. *To Tell a Free Story: The First Century of Afro-American Autobiography, 1760–1865.* Urbana, Ill., 1986.

———, ed. *Sisters of the Spirit: Three Black Women's Autobiographies of the Nineteenth Century.* Bloomington, Ind., 1986.

Anstey, Roger. *The Atlantic Slave Trade and British Abolition, 1760–1810.* London, 1975.

An Appendix; or, Some Observations on the Expediency of the Petition of the Africans, living in Boston, &c. lately presented to the General Assembly of this Province. Boston, [1773].

[Appleton, Nathaniel]. *Considerations on Slavery. In a Letter to a Friend.* Boston, 1767.

Aptheker, Herbert. "Afro-American Superiority: A Neglected Theme in the Literature." *Phylon* 31 (1970): 336–43.

———. *Anti-Racism in U.S. History: The First Two Hundred Years.* Westport, Conn., 1993.

———, ed. *A Documentary History of the Negro People in the United States.* New York, 1951.

Armistead, Wilson. *A Tribute for the Negro.* 1848. Rpt. Miami, 1969.

Aron, Stephen. *How the West Was Lost: The Transformation of Kentucky from Daniel Boone to Henry Clay.* Baltimore, 1996.

Asbury, Francis. *The Journal and Letters of Francis Asbury.* Ed. Elmer T. Clark. 3 vols. Nashville, 1958.

Austin, Allan D. *African Muslims in Antebellum America: A Sourcebook.* New York, 1984.

Bacon, Margaret Hope. "'The Double Curse of Sex and Color': Robert Purvis and Human Rights." *Pennsylvania Magazine of History and Biography* 121 (1997): 53–76.

[Bacon, Thomas]. *Two Sermons Preached to a Congregation of Black Slaves, and the Church of S. P. in the Province of Maryland. By an American Pastor.* London, 1749.

Baily, Marilyn. "From Cincinnati, Ohio, to Wilberforce, Canada: A Note on Antebellum Colonization." *Journal of Negro History* 58 (1973): 427–40.

Bailyn, Bernard. *The Ideological Origins of the American Revolution.* Cambridge, Mass., 1967.

Ball, Charles. *Slavery in the United States: A Narrative of the Life and Adventures of Charles Ball, a Black Man.* 1836. Rpt. Detroit, 1970.

Banks, Marva. "*Uncle Tom's Cabin* and Antebellum Black Response." In *Readers in History: Nineteenth-Century American Literature and the Contexts of Response*, ed. James L. Machor, 209–27. Baltimore, 1993.

Barnes, Gilbert H., and Dwight L. Dumond, eds. *Letters of Theodore Dwight Weld, Angelina Grimké Weld, and Sarah Grimké, 1822–1844.* 2 vols. 1934. Rpt. New York, 1970.

Barrett, Lindon. "African American Slave Narratives: Literacy, the Body, Authority." *American Literary History* 7 (1995): 415–42.

Bay, Mia. *The White Image in the Black Mind: African-American Images of White People, 1830–1925.* New York, 2000.

Bayley, Solomon. *A Brief Account of the Colony of Liberia*. Wilmington, Del., n.d.

Behn, Aphra. *Oroonoko and Other Writings*. Ed. Paul Salzman. New York, 1994.

Bell, Howard Holman. "Expressions of Negro Militancy in the North, 1840–1860." *Journal of Negro History* 45 (1960): 11–20.

———. "National Negro Conventions of the Middle 1840's: Moral Suasion vs. Political Action." *Journal of Negro History* 42 (1957): 247–60.

———, ed. *Minutes of the National Negro Conventions*. New York, 1969.

———. *Search for a Place: Black Separatism and Africa, 1860*. Ann Arbor, 1969.

Bell, James Madison. *A Poem: Delivered August 1st, 1862, by J. Madison Bell, at the Grand Festival to Commemorate the Emancipation of the Slaves in the District of Columbia, and the Emancipation of the Slaves in the British West Indian Isles*. San Francisco, 1862.

Berlin, Ira. "From Creole to African: Atlantic Creoles and the Origins of African-American Society in Mainland North America." *William and Mary Quarterly* 53 (1996): 251–88.

———. *Many Thousands Gone: The First Two Centuries of Slavery in North America*. Cambridge, Mass., 1998.

———. *Slaves without Masters: The Free Negro in the Antebellum South*. New York, 1974.

———. "Time, Space, and the Evolution of Afro-American Society in British Mainland North America." *American Historical Review* 85 (1980): 44–78.

Berry, Harrison. *Slavery and Abolitionism, as Viewed by a Georgia Slave*. Atlanta, 1861.

Bibb, Henry. *Narrative of the Life and Adventures of Henry Bibb, An American Slave. Written by Himself*. 3d ed. 1850. Rpt. Miami, 1969.

Billings, Warren M. "The Cases of Fernando and Elizabeth Key: A Note on the Status of Blacks in Seventeenth-Century Virginia." *William and Mary Quarterly* 30 (1973): 467–74.

Bingham, Caleb, ed. *The Columbian Orator; Containing a Variety of Original and Selected Pieces; Together with Rules; Calculated to Improve Youth and Others in the Ornamental and Useful Art of Eloquence*. 3d ed. Boston, 1800.

Birney, James Gillespie. *Letters of James Gillespie Birney, 1831–1857*. Ed. Dwight L. Dumond. 2 vols. New York, 1938.

Blackett, R. J. M. *Building an Antislavery Wall: Black Americans in the Atlantic Abolitionist Movement, 1830–1860*. Baton Rouge, 1983.

Blassingame, John. "Introduction to Series One." In *The Frederick Douglas Papers*, ed. John Blassingame, 1:xxi–lxix. 5 vols. New Haven, 1979–92.

Bledsoe, Albert Taylor. "Liberty and Slavery: or, Slavery in the Light of Moral and Political Philosophy." In *Cotton Is King, and Pro-Slavery Arguments*, ed. E. N. Elliott, 269–458. 1860. Rpt. New York, 1969.

Blight, David W. *Frederick Douglass' Civil War: Keeping Faith in Jubilee*. Baton Rouge, 1989.

Bogin, Ruth. "'The Battle of Lexington': A Patriotic Ballad by Lemuel Haynes." *William and Mary Quarterly* 42 (1985): 499–506.

———. "'Liberty Further Extended': A 1776 Antislavery Manuscript by Lemuel Haynes." *William and Mary Quarterly* 40 (1983): 85–105.

Works Cited

Bolokitten, Oliver [Jerome B. Holgate]. *A Sojourn in the City of Amalgamation, in the Year of Our Lord 19——*. New York, 1835.

Bolster, W. Jeffrey. *Black Jacks: African American Seaman in the Age of Sail*. Cambridge, Mass., 1997.

[Botsford, Edmund]. *Sambo and Toney: A Dialogue in Three Parts*. Georgetown, S.C., 1808.

Brackenridge, Hugh Henry. *Modern Chivalry*. Ed. Lewis Leary. New Haven, 1965.

Bracy, John H., August Meier, and Elliot Rudwick, eds. *Black Nationalism in America*. Indianapolis, 1970.

Branagan, Thomas. *The Penitential Tyrant; or, Slave Trader Reformed: A Pathetic Poem in Four Cantos*. 2d ed. New York, 1807.

———. *A Preliminary Essay on the Oppression of the Exiled Sons of Africa*. Philadelphia, 1804.

Braxton, Joanne M. *Black Women Writing Autobiography: A Tradition within a Tradition*. Philadelphia, 1989.

Breen, T. H. "Ideology and Nationalism on the Eve of the American Revolution: Revisions *Once More* in Need of Revising." *Journal of American History* 84 (1997): 13–39.

Breen, T. H., and Stephen Innes. *Myne Own Ground: Race and Freedom on Virginia's Eastern Shore, 1640–1676*. New York, 1980.

Brewer, William M. "John B. Russwurm." *Journal of Negro History* 13 (1928): 413–22.

Brooks, George E. "The Providence African Society's Sierra Leone Emigration Scheme, 1794–1795: Prologue to the African Colonization Movement." *International Journal of African Historical Studies* 7 (1974): 183–202.

Brooks, Walter H. "The Evolution of the Negro Baptist Church." *Journal of Negro History* 7 (1922): 11–22.

Browder, Laura. *Slippery Characters: Ethnic Impersonators and American Identities*. Chapel Hill, 2000.

Brown, Henry Box. *Narrative of Henry Box Brown, Who Escaped from Slavery, Enclosed in a Box Three Feet Long, Two Wide, and Two and a Half High, Written from a Statement of Facts Made by Himself*. Boston, 1849.

Brown, Josephine. *Biography of an American Bondman, by His Daughter*. Boston, 1856.

Brown, Richard D. "'Not Only Extreme Poverty, but the Worst Kind of Orphanage': Lemuel Haynes and the Boundaries of Racial Tolerance on the Yankee Frontier, 1770–1820." *New England Quarterly* 61 (1988): 502–18.

———. *The Strength of a People: The Idea of an Informed Citizenry in America, 1650–1870*. Chapel Hill, 1996.

Brown, William Wells. *The American Fugitive in Europe: Sketches of Places and People Abroad*. 1855. Rpt. New York, 1969.

———. *The Black Man: His Antecedents, His Genius, and His Achievements*. 2d ed. 1863. Rpt. New York, 1969.

———. *Clotel; or, The President's Daughter*. Ed. Joan Cashin. Armonk, N.Y., 1996.

———. *St. Domingo: Its Revolutions and Patriots*. Boston, 1855.

———. *Three Years in Europe; or, Places I Have Seen and People I Have Met*. London, 1852.

Works Cited

————, comp. *The Anti-Slavery Harp: A Collection of Songs for Anti-Slavery Meetings.* Boston, 1848.

Browne, Patrick T. J. "'To Defend Mr. Garrison': William Cooper Nell and the Personal Politics of Antislavery." *New England Quarterly* 70 (1997): 415–42.

Bruce, Dickson D., Jr. "Ancient Africa and the Early Black American Historians." *American Quarterly* 36 (1984): 684–99.

————. "Black and White Voices in an Early African-American Colonization Narrative: Problems of Genre and Emergence." In *Criticism and the Color Line: Desegregating American Literary Studies,* ed. Henry B. Wonham, 112–25. New Brunswick, N.J., 1996.

————. "National Identity and African-American Colonization, 1773–1817." *The Historian* 58 (1995): 15–28.

————. "The Significance of African American History for American Studies." In *HUSSE Papers: A Selection from the Papers Read at the Second Conference of the Hungarian Society for the Study of English, Szeged, 26–28 January, 1995,* ed. György Novák, 11–16. Szeged, Hungary, 1995.

Bruce, Emily Sarah. "Toward a Borderland Identity: The Mulatta Myth in Anti-Slavery Fiction from Cuba and the United States." A.B. thesis, Princeton University, 1996.

Bruns, Roger, ed. *Am I Not a Man and a Brother: The Antislavery Crusade of Revolutionary America, 1688–1788.* New York, 1977.

Butler, Jon. *Awash in a Sea of Faith: Christianizing the American People.* Cambridge, Mass., 1990.

Buxbaum, Melvin. "Cyrus Bustill Addresses the Blacks of Philadelphia." *William and Mary Quarterly* 29 (1972): 99–108.

Cadbury, Henry J., ed. "An Early Quaker Anti-Slavery Statement." *Journal of Negro History* 22 (1937): 488–93.

Campbell, Penelope. *Maryland in Africa: The Maryland State Colonization Society, 1831–1857.* Urbana, Ill., 1971.

Capitein, Jacobus Elisa Johannes. *The Agony of Asar: A Thesis on Slavery by the Former Slave, Jacobus Elisa Johannes Capitein, 1717–1747.* Trans. with commentary by Grant Parker. Princeton, 2001.

Carretta, Vincent. "An 'Animadversion' upon a 'Complaint' against 'the Petition' of Belinda, An African Slave." *Early American Literature* 32 (1997): 187–88.

————. "Olaudah Equiano or Gustavus Vassa? New Light on an Eighteenth-Century Question of Identity." *Slavery and Abolition* 20 (1999): 96–105.

————, ed. *Unchained Voices: An Anthology of Black Authors in the English-Speaking World of the Eighteenth Century.* Lexington, Ky., 1996.

Carter, George E., and Peter Ripley, eds. *Black Abolitionist Papers, 1830–1865.* New York, 1981. Note references are to the microfilm edition, by reel and frame.

Castiglia, Christopher. "Pedagogical Discipline and the Creation of White Citizenship: John Witherspoon, Robert Finley, and the Colonization Society." *Early American Literature* 33 (1998): 192–214.

Castronovo, Russ. *Fathering the Nation: American Genealogies of Slavery and Freedom.* Berkeley and Los Angeles, 1995.

Ceplair, Larry, ed. *The Public Years of Sarah and Angelina Grimké: Selected Writings, 1835–1839.* New York, 1989.

Works Cited

Chace, Elizabeth Buffum. *Anti-Slavery Reminiscences*. Central Falls, R.I., 1891.

[Chamerovzow, L. A.]. *Slave Life in Georgia: A Narrative of the Life, Sufferings, and Escape of John Brown, a Fugitive Slave*. Ed. F. N. Boney. Savannah, Ga., 1972.

Cheek, William, and Aimee Lee Cheek. *John Mercer Langston and the Fight for Black Freedom, 1829–1865*. Urbana, Ill., 1989.

Chesebrough, David B. *Frederick Douglass: Oratory from Slavery*. Westport, Conn., 1998.

Child, Lydia Maria. *An Appeal in Favor of Americans Called Africans*. 1836. Rpt. New York, 1968.

———. *The Collected Correspondence of Lydia Maria Child, 1817–1880*. Ed. Patricia G. Holland and Milton Meltzer. Millwood, N.Y., 1980. Microfiche.

———, ed. *The Oasis*. Boston, 1834.

Clark, Christopher. *The Communitarian Moment: The Radical Challenge of the Northampton Association*. Ithaca, N.Y., 1995.

Clark, Elizabeth B. "'The Sacred Rights of the Weak': Pain, Sympathy, and the Culture of Individual Rights in Antebellum America." *Journal of American History* 82 (1995): 463–93.

Clarke, Lewis. *Narrative of the Sufferings of Lewis Clarke, During a Captivity of More than Twenty-five Years, Among the Algerines of Kentucky, One of the So-Called Christian States of America*. Boston, 1845.

Clarke, Lewis, and Milton Clarke. *Narratives of the Sufferings of Lewis and Milton Clarke, Sons of a Soldier of the Revolution, During a Captivity of More than Twenty Years Among the Slaveholders of Kentucky, One of the So-Called Christian States of North America*. 1846. Rpt. New York, 1969.

Cmiel, Kenneth. *Democratic Eloquence: The Fight over Popular Speech in Nineteenth-Century America*. Berkeley and Los Angeles, 1990.

Cobb, Thomas R. R. *An Enquiry into the Law of Negro Slavery in the United States of America. To Which Is Prefixed, An Historical Sketch of Slavery*. 1858. Rpt. New York, 1968.

Coker, Daniel. *A Dialogue Between a Virginian and an African Minister*. Baltimore, 1810.

———. *Journal of Daniel Coker, a Descendant of Africa, from the time of Leaving New York, in the Ship Elizabeth, Capt. Sebor, on a Voyage for Sherbro, in Africa, in Company with Three Agents, and about Ninety Persons of Colour*. Baltimore, 1820.

Coleman, Edward Maceo. *Creole Voices: Poems in French by Free Men of Color First Published in 1845*. Washington, D.C., 1945.

Collins, John A. *The Anti-Slavery Picknick: A Collection of Speeches, Poems, Dialogues, and Songs; Intended for Use in Schools and Anti-Slavery Meetings*. Boston, 1842.

Collison, Gary. *Shadrach Minkins: From Fugitive Slave to Citizen*. Cambridge, Mass., 1997.

Colman, George. *The Negro Boy, Sung by Mr. Tyler*. N.p., [1796].

Conway, Moncure. "Benjamin Banneker, the Negro Astronomer." *Atlantic Monthly* 11 (1863): 79–84.

Cooper, Frederick. "Elevating the Race: The Social Thought of Black Leaders, 1827–50." *American Quarterly* 24 (1977): 604–25.

Costanzo, Angelo. *Surprizing Narrative: Olaudah Equiano and the Beginnings of Black Autobiography*. New York, 1987.

Works Cited

Cowper, William. *The Poetical Works of William Cowper.* Ed. H. S. Milford. 4th ed. London, 1934.

Cox, Virginia. *The Renaissance Dialogue: Literary Dialogue in Its Social and Political Context, Castiglione to Galileo.* Cambridge, Eng., 1992.

Creel, Margaret Washington. *"A Peculiar People": Slave Religion and Community-Culture among the Gullahs.* New York, 1988.

[Croly, David G., and George Wakeman]. *Miscegenation: The Theory of the Blending of the Races, Applied to the American White Man and Negro.* New York, 1864.

Cuffe, Paul. *Captain Paul Cuffe's Logs and Letters, 1808–1817: A Black Quaker's "Voice from within the Veil."* Ed. Rosalind Cobb Wiggins. Washington. D.C., 1996.

Cugoano, Ottobah. *Thoughts and Sentiments on the Evil and Wicked Traffic of the Slavery and Commerce of the Human Species, Humbly Submitted to the Inhabitants of Great-Britain.* 1787. Rpt. London, 1969.

Curry, Leonard P. *The Free Black in Urban America, 1800–1850: The Shadow of the Dream.* Chicago, 1981.

Curtin, Philip D., ed. *Africa Remembered: Narratives by West Africans from the Era of the Slave Trade.* Madison, Wis., 1968.

Dain, Bruce R. "Haiti and Egypt in Early Black Racial Discourse in the United States." *Slavery and Abolition* 14 (1993): 139–61.

———. "A Hideous Monster of the Mind: American Race Theory, 1787–1859." Ph.D. diss., Princeton University, 1996.

Daniel, W. Harrison. "Southern Presbyterians and the Negro in the Early National Period." *Journal of Negro History* 58 (1973): 291–312.

Dathorne, O. R. *The Black Mind: A History of African Literature.* Minneapolis, 1974.

Davies, Samuel. *The Duty of Christians to Propagate Their Religion among Heathens: Earnestly Recommended to the Masters of Negro Slaves in Virginia. A Sermon Preached in Hanover, January 8, 1758.* London, 1758.

Davis, David Brion. *The Problem of Slavery in the Age of Revolution, 1770–1823.* Ithaca, N.Y., 1975.

———. *The Problem of Slavery in Western Culture.* Ithaca, N.Y., 1966.

Davis, Mary Kemp. *Nat Turner before the Bar of Judgment: Fictional Treatments of the Southampton Slave Insurrection.* Baton Rouge, 1999.

Davis, Susan G. *Parades and Power: Street Theatre in Nineteenth-Century Philadelphia.* Philadelphia, 1986.

Davis, Thomas J. "Emancipation Rhetoric, Natural Rights, and Revolutionary New England: A Note on Four Black Petitions in Massachusetts." *New England Quarterly* 62 (1989): 248–63.

Day, Thomas, and John Bicknell. *The Dying Negro, a Poem.* 1773. Rpt. London, 1793.

Delany, Martin R. *Blake; or the Huts of America.* Boston, 1970.

———. *The Condition, Elevation, Emigration, and Destiny of the Colored People of the United States.* 1852. Rpt. New York, 1969.

Desrochers, Robert E., Jr. "'Not Fade Away': The Narrative of Venture Smith, an African American in the Early Republic." *Journal of American History* 84 (1997): 40–66.

Dillon, Merton L. *Slavery Attacked: Southern Slaves and Their Allies, 1619–1865.* Baton Rouge, 1990.

Works Cited

Dixon, Chris. "An Ambivalent Black Nationalism: Haiti, Africa, and Antebellum African-American Emigrationism." *Australasian Journal of American Studies* 10 (1991): 10–25.

The Doctrines and Discipline of the African Methodist Episcopal Church. Philadelphia, 1817.

Donnan, Elizabeth. *Documents Illustrative of the Slave Trade to America*. 4 vols. 1930–35. Rpt. New York, 1965.

Douglass, Frederick. *Autobiographies*. Ed. Henry Louis Gates Jr. New York, 1994.

———. *The Fredrick Douglass Papers*. 5 vols. New Haven, 1979–92.

———. "The Heroic Slave." In *Autographs for Freedom*, ed. Julia Griffiths, 1:174–239. 2 vols. 1853–54. Rpt. Miami, 1969.

Douglass, William. *Annals of the First African Church, in the United States of America, Now Styled the African Episcopal Church of St. Thomas, Philadelphia*. Philadelphia, 1862.

Dwight, Theodore. *An Oration, Spoken Before the Connecticut Society, for the Promotion of Freedom and the Relief of Persons Unlawfully Holden in Bondage*. Hartford, Conn., 1794.

Easton, Hosea. *An Address: Delivered Before the Coloured Population of Providence, Rhode Island, on Thanksgiving Day, November 27, 1828*. Boston, 1828.

Edwards, Paul, and James Walvin. *Black Personalities in the Era of the Slave Trade*. London, 1983.

Egerton, Douglas R. *Gabriel's Rebellion: The Virginia Slave Conspiracies of 1800 and 1802*. Chapel Hill, 1993.

———. *He Shall Go Free: The Lives of Denmark Vesey*. Madison, Wis., 1999.

———. "'Its Origin Is Not a Little Curious': A New Look at the American Colonization Society." *Journal of the Early Republic* 5 (1985): 463–80.

———. "The Scenes Which Are Acted in St. Domingo: The Legacy of Revolutionary Violence in Early National Virginia." In *Antislavery Violence: Sectional, Racial, and Cultural Conflict in Antebellum America*, ed. John R. McKivigan and Stanley Harrold, 41–64. Knoxville, 1999.

Eliot, John. *John Eliot's Indian Dialogues: A Study in Cultural Interaction*. Ed. Henry W. Bowden and James P. Ronda. Westport, Conn., 1980.

Elliott, E. H., ed. *Cotton Is King, and Pro-Slavery Arguments*. 1860. Rpt. New York, 1969.

Equiano, Olaudah. *The Interesting Narrative and Other Writings*. Ed. Vincent Carretta. New York, 1995.

———. *The Life and Adventures of Olaudah Equiano; or Gustavus Vassa, the African, from an Account Written by Himself*. Abridged by A. Mott. New York, 1829.

Erkkila, Betsy. "Phillis Wheatley and the Black American Revolution." In *A Mixed Race: Ethnicity in Early America*, ed. Frank Shuffleton, 225–40. New York, 1993.

Eslinger, Ellen. *Citizens of Zion: The Social Origins of Camp Meeting Revivalism*. Knoxville, 1999.

Evarts, Jeremiah. "On the Condition of Blacks in this Country." *Panoplist* 16 (1820): 241–45.

Fabian, Ann. *The Unvarnished Truth: Personal Narratives in Nineteenth-Century America*. Berkeley and Los Angeles, 2000.

Works Cited

Farrison, William Edward. *William Wells Brown: Author and Reformer.* Chicago, 1969.

Faust, Drew Gilpin. *The Creation of Confederate Nationalism: Ideology and Identity in the Civil War South.* Baton Rouge, 1988.

Fawcett, Benjamin. *A Compassionate Address to the Christian Negroes in Virginia.* 1756. Rpt. New York, 1975.

Ferguson, Robert A. *The American Enlightenment, 1750–1820.* Cambridge, Mass., 1997.

Field, Phyllis. *The Politics of Race in New York: The Struggle for Black Suffrage in the Civil War Era.* Ithaca, N.Y., 1982.

Finley, Robert. "Dialogues on the African Colony." In *Memoirs of the Rev. Robert Finley, D.D.,* ed. Isaac V. Brown, 313–45. New Brunswick, N.J., 1819.

———. *Thoughts on the Colonization of Free Blacks.* Washington, D.C., 1816.

Fisher, Miles Mark. "Lott Cary, the Colonizing Missionary." *Journal of Negro History* 7 (1922): 380–418.

Foner, Philip S., ed. "John Brown Russwurm, a Document." *Journal of Negro History* 54 (1967): 393–97.

Foner, Philip S., and Robert James Branham, eds. *Lift Every Voice: African-American Oratory, 1787–1900.* Tuscaloosa, Ala., 1998.

Foner, Philip S., and George E. Walker, eds. *Proceedings of the Black State Conventions, 1840–1865.* 2 vols. Philadelphia, 1979.

Foote, Thelma Wills. "Black Life in Colonial Manhattan, 1664–1786." Ph.D. diss., Harvard University, 1991.

Forbes, Robert Pierce. "Slavery and the Meaning of America, 1819–1837." 2 vols. Ph.D. diss., Yale University, 1994.

Forten, Charlotte. "Life on the Sea Islands." *Atlantic Monthly* 13 (1864): 587–96, 666–76.

Forten, James. *Letters from a Man of Colour, on a Late Bill Before the Senate of Pennsylvania.* N.p., [1813].

Foster, Charles I. "The Colonization of Free Negroes." *Journal of Negro History* 38 (1953): 41–66.

Foster, Frances Smith, ed. *A Brighter Coming Day: A Frances Ellen Watkins Harper Reader.* New York, 1990.

———. *Written by Herself: Literary Production by African American Women, 1746–1892.* Bloomington, Ind., 1993.

Fox, George. *Gospel of Family Order, Being a Short Discourse Concerning the Ordering of Families, Both of Whites, Blacks and Indians.* N.p., 1676.

Frederickson, George M. *The Black Image in the White Mind: The Debate over Afro-American Character and Destiny, 1817–1914.* New York, 1972.

Frey, Sylvia. *Water from the Rock: Black Resistance in a Revolutionary Age.* Princeton, 1991.

Frey, Sylvia, and Betty Wood. *Come Shouting to Zion: African American Protestantism in the American South and British Caribbean to 1830.* Chapel Hill, 1998.

Friedman, Lawrence J. *Gregarious Saints: Self and Community in American Abolitionism, 1830–1870.* Cambridge, Eng., 1982.

Fugitive Slaves: Douglass, Pennington, Wells Brown, Garnett, Bibb, and Others. Leeds, n.d.

Garnet, Henry Highland. *The Past and the Present Condition, and the Destiny of the Colored Race: A Discourse Delivered and the Fifteenth Anniversary of the Female Benevolent Society of Troy, N.Y., Feb. 14, 1848.* 1848. Rpt. Miami, 1969.

Garrison, William Lloyd. *An Address Delivered Before the Free People of Color, in Philadelphia, New-York, and Other Cities During the Month of June, 1831.* Boston, 1831.

———. *The Letters of William Lloyd Garrison.* Ed. Walter M. Merrill and Louis Ruchames. 6 vols. Cambridge, Mass., 1971–81.

———. *Thoughts on African Colonization.* 1832. Rpt. New York, 1968.

Gates, Henry Louis, Jr. *Figures in Black: Words, Signs, and the "Racial" Self.* New York, 1987.

———. "James Gronniosaw and the Trope of the Talking Book." In *Studies in Autobiography,* ed. James Olney, 51–72. New York, 1988.

———. *The Signifying Monkey: A Theory of African-American Literary Criticism.* New York, 1988.

Gates, Henry Louis, Jr., and Nellie Y. McKay, eds. *The Norton Anthology of African American Literature.* New York, 1997.

Gellman, David N. "Race, the Public Sphere, and Abolition in Late Eighteenth-Century New York." *Journal of the Early Republic* 20 (2000), 607–36.

Genovese, Eugene D. *Consuming Fire: The Fall of the Confederacy and the Mind of the White Christian South.* Athens, Ga., 1998.

George, Carol V. R. *Segregated Sabbaths: Richard Allen and the Emergence of Independent Black Churches, 1760–1840.* New York, 1970.

Gernes, Todd S. "Poetic Justice: Sarah Forten, Eliza Earle, and the Paradox of Intellectual Property." *New England Quarterly* 71 (1998): 229–65.

Gilmore, J. R. *Among the Pines; or, South in Secession Time, by Edmund Kirke.* New York, 1862.

Gilroy, Paul. *The Black Atlantic: Modernity and Double-Consciousness.* Cambridge, Mass., 1993.

Glaude, Eddie S., Jr. *Exodus! Religion, Race, and Nation in Early Nineteenth-Century Black America.* Chicago, 2000.

Godwyn, Morgan. *The Negro's and Indians Advocate, Suing for their Admission into the Church: Or, Persuasive to the Instructing and Baptizing of the Negro's and Indians in Our Plantations.* London, 1680.

Gomez, Michael A. *Our Country Marks: The Transformation of African Identities in the Colonial and Antebellum South.* Chapel Hill, 1998.

Goodman, Paul. *Of One Blood: Abolitionism and the Origins of Racial Equality.* Berkeley and Los Angeles, 1998.

Gordon-Reed, Annette. *Thomas Jefferson and Sally Hemings: An American Controversy.* Charlottesville, 1997.

Grainger, James. *The Sugar-Cane: A Poem in Four Books, With Notes.* London, 1764.

Gravely, William B. "The Dialectic of Double-Consciousness in Black American Freedom Celebrations, 1808–1863." *Journal of Negro History* 67 (1982): 302–17.

———. "The Rise of African Churches in America (1786–1822): Re-examining the Contexts." *Journal of Religious Thought* 41 (1984): 58–73.

Grayson, William. *The Hireling and the Slave, Chicora, and Other Poems.* Charleston, S.C., 1856.

Works Cited

Greenberg, Kenneth S., ed. *The Confessions of Nat Turner and Related Documents.* Boston, 1996.

Greene, Lorenzo Johnston. *The Negro in Colonial New England, 1620–1776.* New York, 1942.

Grégoire, Henri. *An Enquiry Concerning the Intellectual and Moral Faculties, and Literature of Negroes.* Trans. David Bailie Warden, ed. Graham Russell Hodges. 1810. Armonk, N.Y., 1997.

Grimes, William. *The Life of William Grimes, the Runaway Slave, Written by Himself.* New York, 1825.

[Grimké, Angelina]. *An Appeal to the Women of the Nominally Free States, Issued by an Anti-Slavery Convention of American Women.* 2d ed. Boston, 1838.

Grimké, Charlotte Forten. *The Journals of Charlotte Forten Grimké.* Ed. Brenda Stevenson. New York, 1988.

[Grimké, Sarah]. *An Address to Free Colored Americans.* New York, 1837.

Grimsted, David. *American Mobbing, 1828–1861: Toward Civil War.* New York, 1998.

———. "Anglo-American Racism and Phillis Wheatley's 'Sable Veil,' 'Lengthen'd Chain,' and 'Knitted Heart.'" In *Women in the Age of the American Revolution,* ed. Ronald Hoffman and Peter J. Albert, 338–444. Charlottesville, 1989.

Gross, Bella. "Freedom's Journal and the Rights of All." *Journal of Negro History* 17 (1932): 435–43.

Hall, Robert L. "Massachusetts Abolitionists Document the Slave Experience." In *Courage and Conscience: Black and White Abolitionists in Boston,* ed. Donald M. Jacobs, 75–99. Bloomington, Ind., 1993.

Hamilton, William. *Address to the Fourth Annual Convention of the Free People of Color of the United States.* New York, 1834.

Hammon, Jupiter. *America's First Negro Poet: The Complete Works of Jupiter Hammon of Long Island.* Ed. Stanley Austin Ransom Jr. Port Washington, N.Y., 1970.

Hammond, J. H. "Hammond's Letters on Slavery" (1845). In *The Pro-Slavery Argument; as Maintained by the Most Distinguished Writers of the Southern States.* 1852. Rpt. New York, 1968.

Hansen, Debra Gold. *Strained Sisterhood: Gender and Class in the Boston Female Anti-Slavery Society.* Amherst, Mass., 1993.

Harper, William. "Slavery in the Light of Social Ethics." In *Cotton Is King, and Pro-Slavery Arguments,* ed. E. N. Elliott, 547–626. 1860. Rpt. New York, 1969.

Harris, Thaddeus Mason. *A Discourse Delivered Before the African Society in Boston, 15th of July, 1822, on the Anniversary Celebration of the Abolition of the Slave Trade.* Boston, 1822.

Hartman, James D. *Providence Tales and the Birth of American Literature.* Baltimore, 1999.

Haskell, Thomas. "Capitalism and the Origins of the Humanitarian Sensibility, Part 2." In *The Antislavery Debate: Capitalism and Abolitionism as a Problem in Historical Interpretation,* ed. Thomas Bender, 136–60. Berkeley and Los Angeles, 1992.

Hatch, Nathan O. *The Democratization of American Christianity.* New Haven, 1989.

Haven, Gilbert. *National Sermons: Speeches and Letters on Slavery and Its War: From the Passage of the Fugitive Slave Bill to the Election of President Grant.* 1869. Rpt. New York, 1969.

Hawkins, John. "The third troublesome voyage made with the Jesus of Lubeck, the Minion, and foure other ships, to the parts of Guinea, and the West Indies, in the yeeres 1567 and 1568 by M. John Hawkins." In *The Principal Navigations Voyages Traffiques and Discoveries of the English Nation*, ed. Richard Hakluyt, 10:64–74. 12 vols. Glasgow, 1903–5.

Hayden, William. *Narrative of William Hayden, Containing a Faithful Account of His Travels for a Number of Years, Whilst a Slave, in the South. Written by Himself.* 1846. Rpt. Philadelphia, 1969.

Haynes, Lemuel. *Black Preacher to White America: The Collected Writings of Lemuel Haynes, 1774–1833.* Ed. Richard Newman. Brooklyn, 1990.

———. *The Nature and Importance of True Republicanism; With a Few Suggestions Favorable to Independence. A Discourse Delivered at Rutland, (Vermont), the Fourth of July, 1801.* N.p., 1801.

Hedrick, Joan D. *Harriet Beecher Stowe: A Life.* New York, 1994.

Henkin, David. *City Reading: Written Words and Public Spaces in Antebellum New York.* New York, 1999.

Herzog, Kristin. *Women, Ethnics, and Exotics: Images of Power in Mid-Nineteenth-Century American Fiction.* Knoxville, 1983.

Heyrman, Christine Leigh. *Southern Cross: The Beginnings of the Bible Belt.* New York, 1997.

Higginson, Thomas Wentworth. "The Romance of History in 1850." *Liberty Bell* 16 (1858): 47–53.

Hinks, Peter P. *To Awaken My Afflicted Brethren: David Walker and the Problem of Antebellum Slave Resistance.* University Park, Pa., 1997.

Hirschberg, H. Z. (J. W.). "The Problem of the Judaized Berbers." *Journal of African History* 4 (1963): 313–39.

Hodes, Martha. *White Women, Black Men: Illicit Sex in the Nineteenth-Century South.* New Haven, 1997.

Hodges, Graham Russell. Introduction to *An Enquiry Concerning the Intellectual and Moral Faculties, and Literature of Negroes*, by Henri Grégoire. Trans. David Bailie Warden, ed. Graham Russell Hodges. 1810. Armonk, N.Y., 1997.

———. *Root and Branch: African Americans in New York and East Jersey, 1613–1863.* Chapel Hill, 1999.

———, ed. *Black Itinerants of the Gospel: The Narratives of John Jea and George White.* Madison, Wis., 1993.

[Hopkins, Samuel]. *A Dialogue Concerning the Slavery of the Africans; Shewing It to Be the Duty and Interest of the American Colonies to Emancipate All Their African Slaves: With an Address to the Owners of Such Slaves.* Norwich, Conn., 1776.

Horton, George Moses. *The Black Bard of North Carolina: George Moses Horton and His Poetry.* Chapel Hill, 1997.

———. *The Hope of Liberty. Containing a Number of Poetical Pieces.* Raleigh, N.C., 1829.

Horton, James Oliver, and Lois E. Horton. *In Hope of Liberty: Culture, Community, and Protest among Northern Free Blacks, 1700–1860.* New York, 1997.

Huddleston, Eugene L. "Matilda's 'On Reading the Poems of Phillis Wheatley, the African Poetess.'" *Early American Literature* 5 (1971): 57–67.

Works Cited

"Humanitas." *Hints for the Consideration of the Friends of Slavery, and the Friends of Emancipation.* Lexington, Ky., 1805.

Hunt, Gaillard. "William Thornton and Negro Colonization." *Proceedings of the American Antiquarian Society,* n.s., 30 (1920): 32–61.

Huston, James L. "The Experiential Basis of the Northern Antislavery Impulse." *Journal of Southern History* 56 (1990): 609–40.

Hutton, Frankie. *The Early Black Press in America, 1827–1860.* Westport, Conn., 1992.

Imlay, Gilbert. *A Topographical Description of the Western Territory of North America: Containing a Succinct Account of Its Soil, Climate, Natural History, Population, Agriculture, Manners, and Customs.* 1797. Rpt. New York, 1968.

Ingersoll, Thomas N. "'Releese us out of this Cruel Bondegg': An Appeal from Virginia in 1723." *William and Mary Quarterly* 51 (1994): 777–82.

Isani, Mukhtar Ali. "The British Reception of Wheatley's *Poems on Various Subjects.*" *Journal of Negro History* 66 (1981): 144–49.

———. "A Contemporaneous British Poem on Phillis Wheatley." *Black American Literature Forum* 24 (1990): 565–66.

———. "'Gambia on My Soul': Africa and the African in the Writings of Phillis Wheatley." *Melus* 6 (1979): 64–72.

Ito, Akiyo. "Olaudah Equiano and the New York Artisans: The First American Edition of *The Interesting Narrative of the Life of Olaudah Equiano, or Gustavus Vassa, The African.*" *Early American Literature* 32 (1997): 82–101.

Jackson, Blyden. *A History of Afro-American Literature.* Vol. 1, *The Long Beginning, 1746–1895.* Baton Rouge, 1989.

Jacobs, Donald M. "David Walker and William Lloyd Garrison: Racial Cooperation and the Shaping of Boston Abolition." In *Courage and Conscience: Black and White Abolitionists in Boston,* ed. Jacobs, 1–20. Bloomington, Ind., 1993.

Jacobs, Harriet. *Incidents in the Life of a Slave Girl.* Ed. Lydia Maria Child. 1861. Rpt. San Diego, 1973.

Jefferson, Paul. Introduction to *The Travels of William Wells Brown, including Narrative of William Wells Brown, a Fugitive Slave, and The American Fugitive in Europe: Sketches of Places and People Abroad,* ed. Jefferson. New York, 1991.

Jefferson, Thomas. *Notes on the State of Virginia.* Ed. William Peden. Chapel Hill, 1955.

Jeffrey, Julie Roy. *The Great Silent Army of Abolitionism: Ordinary Women in the Antislavery Movement.* Chapel Hill, 1998.

Johnson, Walter. *Soul by Soul: Life inside the Antebellum Slave Market.* Cambridge, Mass., 1999.

Jones, Absalom, and Richard Allen. *A Narrative of the Proceedings of the Black People During the Late Awful Calamity in Philadelphia, in the Year 1793: and a Refutation of Some Censures, Thrown Upon Them in Some Late Publications.* Philadelphia, 1794.

Jonson, Ben. "The Masques of Blackness and Beauty." In *Ben Jonson,* ed. C. H. Herford, Percy Simpson, and Evelyn Simpson, 7:161–203. 11 vols. London, 1925–52.

Jordan, Winthrop D. *White over Black: American Attitudes toward the Negro, 1550–1812.* Chapel Hill, 1968.

Works Cited

Josselyn, John. *John Josselyn, Colonial Traveler: A Critical Edition of the Two Voyages to New-England.* Ed. Paul J. Lindholdt. Hanover, N.H., 1988.

Juster, Susan. *Disorderly Women: Sexual Politics and Evangelicalism in Revolutionary New England.* Ithaca, N.Y., 1994.

Kachun, Mitch. "The Faith That the Dark Past Has Taught Us: African-American Commemorations in the North and West and the Construction of a Usable Past, 1808–1915." Ph.D. diss., Cornell University, 1997.

Kaplan, Sidney. "The Miscegenation Issue in the Election of 1864." *Journal of Negro History* 34 (1949): 274–343.

Kaplan, Sidney, and Emma Nogrody Kaplan. *The Black Presence in the American Revolution.* Rev. ed. Amherst, Mass., 1989.

Karcher, Carolyn L. *The First Woman of the Republic: A Cultural Biography of Lydia Maria Child.* Durham, N.C., 1994.

Katz, William Loren, ed. *Flight from the Devil: Six Slave Narratives.* Trenton, N.J., 1996.

Kay, Marvin L. Michael, and Lorin Lee Cary. *Slavery in North Carolina, 1748–1775.* Chapel Hill, 1995.

Kirk, Russell. *Randolph of Roanoke: A Study in Conservative Thought.* Chicago, 1951.

Kohn, Hans. *The Idea of Nationalism: A Study in Its Origins and Background.* New York, 1944.

Kraditor, Aileen S. *Means and Ends in American Abolitionism: Garrison and His Critics on Strategy and Tactics, 1834–1850.* New York, 1969.

Krise, Thomas W. "True Novel, False History: Robert Robertson's Ventriloquized Ex-Slave in *The Speech of Mr John Talbot Campo-Bell* (1736)." *Early American Literature* 30 (1995): 152–64.

Kulikoff, Allan. "Uprooted Peoples: Black Migrants in the Age of the American Revolution, 1790–1820." In *Slavery and Freedom in the Age of the American Revolution,* ed. Ira Berlin and Ronald Hoffman, 143–71. Charlottesville, 1983.

Ladd, Elizabeth. *Some Account of Lucy Cardwell, a Woman of Colour, Who departed this life on the 25th of the 3rd month, 1824 — aged 39 years.* Philadelphia, [1824].

A Lady of Boston. *Memoir of Mrs. Chloe Spear, a Native of Africa, Who Was Enslaved in Childhood, and Died in Boston, January 3, 1815 — Aged 65 Years. By a Lady of Boston.* Boston, 1832.

Lambert, Frank. "'I Saw the Book Talk': Slave Readings of the First Great Awakening." *Journal of Negro History* 77 (1992): 185–98.

Langston, J. Mercer. *The World's Anti-Slavery Movement, Its Heroes and Its Triumphs. A Lecture Delivered at Xenia, O., Aug. 2, and Cleveland, O., Aug. 3, 1858.* Oberlin, 1858.

Lapsansky, Emma Jones. "'Since They Got Those Separate Churches': Afro-Americans and Racism in Jacksonian Philadelphia." *American Quarterly* 32 (1980): 54–78.

[LaVallée, Joseph]. *The Negro Equalled by Few Europeans. Translated from the French. To Which Are Added, Poems on Various Subjects, Moral and Entertaining; by Phillis Wheatley, Negro Servant to Mr. John Wheatley, of Boston, in New-England.* 2 vols. Philadelphia, 1801.

Lehuu, Isabelle. *Carnival on the Page: Popular Print Media in Antebellum America.* Chapel Hill, 2000.

Works Cited

Le Jau, Francis. *The Carolina Chronicle of Dr. Francis Le Jau*. Ed. Frank J. Klingberg. Berkeley and Los Angeles, 1956.

Levine, Lawrence. *Black Culture and Black Consciousness: Afro-American Folk Thought from Slavery to Freedom*. New York, 1977.

Levine, Robert S. *Martin Delany, Frederick Douglass, and the Politics of Representative Identity*. Chapel Hill, 1997.

———. "*Uncle Tom's Cabin* in *Frederick Douglass' Paper*: An Analysis of Reception." *American Literature* 64 (1992): 71–93.

[Levison, William]. *Black Diamonds; or, Humor, Satire, and Sentiment, Treated Scientifically by Professor Julius Caesar Hannibal. In a Series of Burlesque Lectures, Darkly Colored*. 1857. Rpt. Upper Saddle River, N.J., 1969.

Lewis, David Levering. *W. E. B. Du Bois: Biography of a Race*. New York, 1993.

Lincoln, Abraham. *The Collected Works of Abraham Lincoln*. Ed. Roy P. Basler. 9 vols. New Brunswick, N.J., 1953.

Lindhorst, Marie. "Politics in a Box: Sarah Mapps Douglass and the Female Literary Association, 1831–33." *Pennsylvania History* 65 (1998): 263–78.

Little, Thomas. "George Liele and the Rise of Independent Black Baptist Churches in the Lower South and Jamaica." *Slavery and Abolition* 16 (1995): 188–204.

Livermore, Elizabeth D. *Zoë; or The Quadroon's Triumph. A Tale for the Times*. Cincinnati, 1855.

Lockard, Joe. Afterword to *Autobiography of a Female Slave*, by Mattie Griffith. Jackson, Miss., 1998.

Loggins, Vernon. *The Negro Author: His Development in America to 1900*. 1931. Rpt. Port Washington, N.Y., 1964.

Long, Edward. *The History of Jamaica. Or, General Surveys of the Antient and Modern State of the Island: With Reflections on Its Situation, Settlements, Inhabitants, Climate, Products, Commerce, Laws, and Government*. 3 vols. 1774. Rpt. New York, 1972.

Long, John Dixon. *Pictures of Slavery in Church and State; including Personal Reminiscences, Biographical Sketches, Anecdotes, Etc. Etc.* 1858. Rpt. New York, 1969.

Loomis, Sally. "The Evolution of Paul Cuffe's Black Nationalism." In *Black Apostles at Home and Abroad: Afro-Americans and the Christian Mission from the Revolution to Reconstruction*, ed. David W. Wills and Richard Newman, 191–202. Boston, 1982.

Lynch, Hollis R. "Pan-Negro Nationalism in the New World, before 1862." In *The Making of Black America: Essays in Negro Life and History*, ed. August Meier and Elliott Rudwick, vol. 1, *The Origins of Black America*, 42–65. New York, 1969.

Mackenzie, Anna Maria. *Slavery: or, the Times*. Dublin, 1793.

Mahar, William J. *Behind the Burnt Cork Mask: Early Blackface Minstrelsy and Antebellum American Popular Culture*. Urbana, Ill., 1999.

Markwei, Matei. "The Rev. Daniel Coker of Sierra Leone." In *Black Apostles at Home and Abroad: Afro-Americans and the Christian Mission from the Revolution to Reconstruction*, ed. David W. Wills and Richard Newman, 203–10. Boston, 1982.

Marrant, John. *A Sermon Preached on the 24th Day of June, 1789, Being the Festival of St. John the Baptist, at the Request of the Right Worshipful the Grand Master Prince Hall, and the Rest of the Brethren of the African Lodge of the Honorable Society of Free and Accepted Masons in Boston*. Boston, [1789].

Works Cited

Martin, J. Sella. *The Hero and the Slave*. Boston, 1862.

Martin, Waldo E., Jr. *The Mind of Frederick Douglass*. Chapel Hill, 1984.

Massachusetts Anti-Slavery Society. *Fifth Annual Report of the board of Managers of the Massachusetts Anti-Slavery Society, with Some Account of the Annual Meeting, January 25, 1837*. 1837. Rpt. Westport, Conn., 1968.

———. *Sixteenth Annual Report, Presented to the Massachusetts Anti-Slavery Society, by Its Board of Managers, January 26, 1848*. 1848. Rpt. Westport, Conn., 1970.

Mather, Cotton. *The Negro Christianized: An Essay to Excite and Assist that Good Work, the Instruction of Negro Servants in Christianity*. Boston, 1706.

Mathews, Donald G. *Religion in the Old South*. Chicago, 1977.

May, Samuel. *Some Recollections of Our Antislavery Conflict*. 1869. Rpt. New York, 1968.

McColley, Robert. *Slavery and Jeffersonian Virginia*. 2d ed. Urbana, Ill., 1973.

McCord, David James. "Life of a Negro Slave." *Southern Quarterly Review*, n.s., 7 (1853): 206–27.

McCord, Louisa S. *Political and Social Essays*. Ed. Richard C. Lounsbury. Charlottesville, 1995.

McCormick, Richard P. "William Whipper: Moral Reformer." *Pennsylvania History* 43 (1976): 23–46.

McCoy, Drew R. *The Elusive Republic: Political Economy in Jeffersonian Virginia*. Chapel Hill, 1980.

McFeely, William S. *Frederick Douglass*. New York, 1991.

McGraw, Marie Tyler. "The Hues and Uses of Liberia." In *The Black Imagination and the Middle Passage*, ed. Maria Diedrich, Henry Louis Gates Jr., and Carl Pederson, 191–202. New York, 1999.

———. "Richmond Free Blacks and African Colonization, 1816–1832." *Journal of American Studies* 21 (1987): 207–24.

McHenry, Elizabeth. "'Dreaded Eloquence': The Origins and Rise of African American Literary Societies and Libraries." *Harvard Library Bulletin*, n.s., 6 (1995): 32–56.

McHenry, James. "Account of a Negro Astronomer." *New-York Magazine* 2 (1791): 557–58.

McPherson, James. "The Negro: Innately Inferior or Equal?" In *Blacks in the Abolitionist Movement*, ed. John H. Bracey Jr., August Meier, and Elliott Rudwick, 79–94. Belmont, Calif., 1971.

Meade, William. *Sermons Addressed to Masters and Servants: And Published in the Year 1743 by Thomas Bacon; Now Republished with Other Tracts and Dialogues on the Same Subject, and Recommended to All Masters and Mistresses to Be Used by Their Families*. Winchester, Va., 1813.

Melish, Joanne Pope. *Disowning Slavery: Gradual Emancipation and "Race" in New England, 1780–1860*. Ithaca, N.Y., 1998.

The Merry Fellow's Companion; Being the Second Part of the American Jest Book. Philadelphia, 1789.

Mifflin, Warner. *The Defense of Warner Mifflin Against Aspersions cast on him on Account of his endeavours To promote Righteousness, Mercy and Peace, Among Mankind*. Philadelphia, 1796.

Miller, Floyd. "The Father of Black Nationalism: Another Contender." *Civil War History* 17 (1971): 310–19.

Works Cited

————. *The Search for a Black Nationality: Black Emigration and Colonization, 1787–1863.* Urbana, Ill., 1975.

Miller, William. *A Sermon on the Abolition of the Slave Trade: Delivered in the African Church, New-York, on the First of January, 1810.* New York, 1810.

Monaghan, Frank, ed. "Anti-Slavery Papers of John Jay." *Journal of Negro History* 17 (1932): 481–96.

Moore, George H. "The First Printed Protest against Slavery in America." *Pennsylvania Magazine of History and Biography* 13 (1889): 265–70.

Morgan, Philip D. "Black Life in Eighteenth-Century Charleston." *Perspectives in American History,* n.s., 1 (1984): 187–232.

Morse, Jedidiah. *A Discourse delivered at the African Meeting House, in Boston, July 14, 1808, in Grateful Celebration of the Abolition of the African Slave-Trade, by the Governments of the United States, Great Britain and Denmark.* Boston, 1808.

Moses, Wilson Jeremiah. *Black Messiahs and Uncle Toms: Social and Literary Manipulations of a Religious Myth.* University Park, Pa., 1982.

Moss, Richard J. *The Life of Jedidiah Morse: A Station of Peculiar Exposure.* Knoxville, 1995.

Mullin, Michael. *Africa in America: Slave Acculturation and Resistance in the American South and the British Caribbean, 1736–1831.* Urbana, Ill., 1992.

Murphy, Geraldine. "Olaudah Equiano, Accidental Tourist." *Eighteenth-Century Studies* 27 (1994): 551–68.

Narrative of James Williams, an American Slave, Who Was for Several Years a Driver on a Cotton Plantation in Alabama. 1838. Rpt. Philadelphia, 1969.

Nash, Gary B. *Forging Freedom: The Formation of Philadelphia's Black Community, 1720–1840.* Cambridge, Mass., 1988.

————. *Race and Revolution.* Madison, Wis., 1990.

Nash, Gary B., and Jean R. Soderlund. *Freedom by Degrees: Emancipation in Pennsylvania and Its Aftermath.* New York, 1991.

Newman, Richard. "The Transformation of American Abolitionism: Tactics, Strategies, and the Changing Meanings of Activism, 1780s–1830s." Ph.D. diss., State University of New York at Buffalo, 1998.

Newman, Richard, Patrick Rael, and Phillip Lapsansky, eds. *Pamphlets of Protest: An Anthology of Early African-American Protest Literature, 1790–1860.* New York, 2001.

News from Africa: A Collection of Facts, Relating to the Colony of Liberia, for the Information of the Free People of Colour in Maryland. Baltimore, 1832.

Newton, John. *The Journals of a Slave Trader (John Newton), 1750–54, with Newton's Thoughts upon the African Slave Trade.* Ed. Bernard Martin and Mark Spurrell. London, 1962.

Nichols, Charles H. *Many Thousand Gone: The Ex-Slaves' Accounts of Their Bondage and Freedom.* Leiden, Netherlands, 1963.

Nisbet, Richard. *Slavery Not Forbidden by Scripture.* Philadelphia, 1773.

Norris, Robert. *Memoirs of the Reign of Bossa Ah'adee, King of Dahomy, an Inland Country of Guiny.* 1789. Rpt. London, 1968.

Northup, Solomon. *Twelve Years a Slave.* Ed. Sue Eakin and Joseph Logsdon. Baton Rouge, 1968.

Works Cited

Nott, Walt. "From 'Uncultivated Barbarian' to 'Poetical Genius': The Public Presence of Phillis Wheatley." *Melus* 18 (1993): 21–32.

Oates, Stephen B. *To Purge This Land with Blood: A Biography of John Brown.* 2d ed. Amherst, Mass., 1984.

Odell, Margaretta. *Memoir of Phillis Wheatley, a Native African and a Slave. Dedicated to the Friends of the Africans.* Boston, 1834.

Olney, James. "'I Was Born': Slave Narratives, Their Status as Autobiography and as Literature." In *The Slave's Narrative*, ed. Charles T. Davis and Henry Louis Gates Jr., 148–75. New York, 1985.

Olsen, Otto H. *The Negro Question: From Slavery to Caste, 1863–1910.* New York, 1971.

Olwell, Robert. *Masters, Slaves, and Subjects: The Culture of Power in the South Carolina Low Country, 1740–1790.* Ithaca, N.Y., 1998.

O'Neale, Sondra. *Jupiter Hammon and the Biblical Beginnings of African-American Literature.* Metuchen, N.J., 1993.

Onuf, Peter S. "'To Declare Them a Free and Independent People': Race, Slavery, and National Identity in Jefferson's Thought." *Journal of the Early Republic* 18 (1998): 1–46.

Oson, Jacob. *A Search for Truth; or, An Inquiry for the Origin of the African Nation: An Address, Delivered at New-Haven in March, and at New-York in April, 1817.* New York, 1817.

Painter, Nell Irvin. "Of *Lily*, Linda Brent, and Freud: A Non-Exceptionalist Approach to Race, Class, and Gender in the Slave South." *Georgia Historical Quarterly* 76 (1992): 241–59.

Parrish, John. *Remarks on the Slavery of the Black People; Addressed to the Citizens of the United States, Particularly to Those Who Are in Legislative or Executive Stations in the General or State Governments; and also to Such Individuals as Hold Them in Bondage.* Philadelphia, 1806.

Parrott, Russell. *An Oration on the Abolition of the Slave Trade, Delivered on the First of January, 1812, at the African Church of St. Thomas.* Philadelphia, 1812.

Paul, Susan. *Memoirs of James Jackson: The Attentive and Obedient Scholar, Who Died in Boston, October 31, 1833, Aged Six Years and Eleven Months.* Ed. Lois Brown. Cambridge, Mass., 2000.

Payne, Daniel. *Recollections of Seventy Years.* 1888. Rpt. New York, 1968.

Pease, Jane H., and William H. Pease. *They Who Would Be Free: Blacks' Search for Freedom, 1830–1861.* New York, 1974.

Pease, William H., and Jane H. Pease. "Organized Negro Communities: A North American Experiment." *Journal of Negro History* 47 (1962): 19–34.

———. "Walker's *Appeal* Comes to Charleston: A Note and Documents." *Journal of Negro History* 59 (1974): 287–92.

Pennington, James W. C. *The Fugitive Blacksmith; or, Events in the History of James W. C. Pennington.* 3d ed. 1850. Rpt. Westport, Conn., 1971.

———. "To the Reader." In *Essays; Including Biographies and Miscellaneous Pieces, in Prose and Poetry*, by Ann Plato, xvii–xx. 1841. Rpt. New York, 1988.

Perlman, Daniel. "Organizations of the Free Negro in New York City, 1800–1860." *Journal of Negro History* 56 (1971): 181–97.

Works Cited

Peterson, Carla L. *"Doers of the Word": African-American Women Speakers and Writers in the North (1830–1880)*. New York, 1995.

Peterson, Thomas Virgil. *Ham and Japheth: The Mythic World of Whites in the Antebellum South*. Metuchen, N.J., 1978.

"Philanthropos." *The African Miscellanist; or, A Collection of Original Essays on the Subject of Negro Slavery*. Trenton, N.J., 1802.

Phillips, Christopher. *Freedom's Port: The African American Community of Baltimore, 1790–1860*. Urbana, Ill., 1997.

Phillips, Wendell. *Speeches, Lectures, and Letters*. 1884. Rpt. New York, 1968.

Piersen, William D. *Black Legacy: America's Hidden Heritage*. Amherst, Mass., 1993.

———. *Black Yankees: The Development of an Afro-American Subculture in Eighteenth-Century New England*. Amherst, Mass., 1988.

Pitcher, Edward W. "A 'Complaint' against 'The Petition' of Belinda, an American Slave." *Early American Literature* 31 (1996): 200–203.

Porter, Dorothy B., ed. "Early Manuscript Letters Written by Negroes." *Journal of Negro History* 24 (1939): 199–210.

———. *Early Negro Writing, 1760–1837*. Boston, 1971.

Potkay, Adam, and Sandra Burr, eds. *Black Atlantic Writers of the Eighteenth Century: Living the New Exodus in England and America*. New York, 1995.

Pratt, Mary Louise. *Imperial Eyes: Travel Writing and Transculturation*. London, 1992.

Prentiss, Benjamin F. *The Blind African Slave, or Memoirs of Boyrereau Brinch, Nicknamed Jeffrey Brace*. St. Albans, Vt., 1810.

Price, George R., and James Brewer Stewart. *To Heal the Scourge of Prejudice: The Life and Writings of Hosea Easton*. Amherst, Mass., 1999.

Price, Lawrence Marsden. *Inkle and Yarico Album*. Berkeley and Los Angeles, 1937.

Quarles, Benjamin. *Black Abolitionists*. 1969. New York, n.d.

———. *The Negro in the American Revolution*. Chapel Hill, 1961.

Raboteau, Albert J. *Slave Religion: The "Invisible Institution" in the Antebellum South*. New York, 1978.

Rankin, John. *Letters on American Slavery, Addressed to Mr. Thomas Rankin, Merchant at Middlebrook, Augusta Co., Va*. 1825. Rpt. Boston, 1833.

Raymond, Robert R. "Outline of a Man." In *Autographs for Freedom*, ed. Julia Griffiths, 1:148–60. 2 vols. 1853–54. Rpt. Miami, 1969.

Read, Hollis. *The Negro Problem Solved; or, Africa as She Was, as She Is, and as She Shall Be. Her Curse and Her Cure*. 1864. Rpt. New York, 1969.

Reid-Pharr, Robert. *Conjugal Union: The Body, the House, and the Black American*. New York, 1999.

Reidy, Joseph P. "'Negro Election Day' and Black Community Life in New England, 1750–1860." *Marxist Perspectives* 1 (1978): 102–17.

Rhodes, Jane. *Mary Ann Shadd Cary: The Black Press and Protest in the Nineteenth Century*. Bloomington, Ind., 1998.

Richards, Leonard L. *"Gentlemen of Property and Standing": Anti-Abolition Mobs in Jacksonian America*. New York, 1970.

Richards, Philip M. "Nationalist Themes in the Preaching of Jupiter Hammon." *Early American Literature* 25 (1990): 123–38.

Works Cited

————. "Phillis Wheatley and Literary Americanization." *American Quarterly* 44 (1992): 163–91.

Richardson, Marilyn. Introduction to *Maria W. Stewart: America's First Black Woman Political Writer*, ed. Richardson. Bloomington, Ind., 1987.

Richmond, M. A. *Bid the Vassal Soar: Interpretive Essays on the Life and Poetry of Phillis Wheatley (ca. 1753–1784) and George Moses Horton (ca. 1797–1883)*. Washington, D.C., 1974.

Ripley, C. Peter, ed. *The Black Abolitionist Papers*. 5 vols. Chapel Hill, 1985–92.

Rippon, John. *The Baptist Annual Register for 1790, 1791, 1792, and Part of 1793. Including Sketches of the State of Religion Among Different Denominations of Good Men at Home and Abroad*. London, 1793.

Roberts, Rita. "Patriotism and Political Criticism: The Evolution of Political Consciousness in the Mind of a Black Revolutionary Soldier." *Eighteenth-Century Studies* 27 (1994): 569–88.

Roediger, David R. *The Wages of Whiteness: Race and the Making of the American Working Class*. London, 1991.

Rollin, Frank A. *Life and Public Services of Martin R. Delany*. 1883. Rpt. New York, 1969.

Romans, Bernard. *A Concise Natural History of East and West Florida*. New York, 1775.

Roper, Moses. *A Narrative of the Adventures and Escape of Moses Roper from American Slavery*. 2d ed. 1838. Rpt. New York, 1970.

Rossbach, Jeffery. *Ambivalent Conspirators: John Brown, the Secret Six, and a Theory of Slave Violence*. Philadelphia, 1982.

The Royal African: or, Memoirs of the Young Prince of Annamaboe. London, [1753?].

Saillant, John, ed. "Circular Addressed to the Colored Brethren and Friends in America: An Unpublished Essay by Lott Cary, Sent from Liberia to Virginia, 1827." *Virginia Magazine of History and Biography* 104 (1996): 481–504.

————. "'Remarkably Emancipated from Bondage, Slavery, and Death': An African American Retelling of the Puritan Captivity Narrative." *Early American Literature* 29 (1994): 122–40.

————. "Traveling in Old and New Worlds with John Jea, the African Preacher, 1773–1816." *Journal of American Studies* 33 (1999): 473–90.

[Sansom, Joseph]. *A Poetical Epistle to the Enslaved Africans, in the Character of an Ancient Negro, Born a Slave in Pennsylvania; But Liberated Some Years since, and Instructed in useful Learning, and the Great Truths of Christianity*. Philadelphia, 1790.

Saunders, Prince. *Haytian Papers*. London, 1816.

[Saunders, Prince]. *The Sons of Africans: An Essay on Freedom, with Observations on the Origin of Slavery, by a Member of the African Society*. Boston, 1808.

Schoolcraft, Mary Howard. *The Black Gauntlet: A Tale of Plantation Life in South Carolina*. 1860. Rpt. New York, 1969.

[Schoolcraft, Mary Howard]. *Letters on the Condition of the African Race in the United States. By a Southern Lady*. 1852. Rpt. New York, 1969.

Seeman, Erik R. "'Justise Must Take Plase': Three African Americans Speak of Religion in Eighteenth-Century New England." *William and Mary Quarterly* 41 (1999): 393–414.

Works Cited

Sekora, John. "Is the Slave Narrative a Species of Autobiography?" In *Studies in Auto-biography*, ed. James Olney, 99–111. New York, 1986.

Sermon on the Present Situation of the Affairs of America and Great Britain. Written by a Black, And printed at the Request of several Persons of distinguished Characters. Philadelphia, 1782.

Sernett, Milton C. *Abolition's Axe: Beriah Green, Oneida Institute, and the Black Free-dom Struggle.* Syracuse, N.Y., 1986.

Sewall, Samuel. *The Selling of Joseph.* 1700. Rpt. New York, 1970.

Sheldon, George. *A History of Deerfield, Massachusetts.* 2 vols. 1895–96. Rpt. Deerfield, Mass., 1972.

————. "Negro Slavery in Old Deerfield." *New England Magazine*, n.s., 7 (1893): 49–60.

Sherman, Joan R. Introduction to *The Black Bard of North Carolina: George Moses Horton and His Poetry*, ed. Joan R. Sherman. Chapel Hill, 1997.

Sherwood, Henry Noble. "Early Negro Deportation Projects." *Mississippi Valley His-torical Review* 2 (1916): 484–508.

————. "Paul Cuffe." *Journal of Negro History* 8 (1923): 153–232.

Shields, David S. *Civil Tongues and Polite Letters in British America.* Chapel Hill, 1997.

Shields, John C. "Phillis Wheatley's Subversive Pastoral." *Eighteenth-Century Studies* 27 (1994): 631–47.

Short History of the African Union Meeting and School-House, erected in Providence (R.I.) in the Years 1819, '20, '21; with Rules for Its Future Government. Providence, 1821.

Silverman, Kenneth. *A Cultural History of the American Revolution: Painting, Music, Literature, and the Theatre in the Colonies and the United States from the Treaty of Paris to the Inauguration of George Washington, 1763–1789.* New York, 1976.

Simpson, J. McC. *The Emancipation Car, Being an Original Composition of Anti-Slav-ery Ballads, Composed Exclusively for the Under Ground Rail Road.* 1874. Rpt. Miami, 1969.

Smith, Cynthia J. "'To Maecenas': Phillis Wheatley's Invocation of an Idealized Reader." *Black American Literature Forum* 23 (1989): 578–92.

Smith, David. *Biography of Rev. David Smith, of the A.M.E. Church: Being a Complete History, Embracing Over Sixty Years' Labor in the Advancement of the Redeemer's Kingdom on Earth.* 1881. Rpt. Freeport, N.Y., 1971.

Smith, James McCune. *The Destiny of the People of Color, a Lecture, Delivered Before the Philomathean Society and Hamilton Lyceum, In January, 1841.* New York, 1843.

Smith, Timothy L. "Slavery and Theology: The Emergence of Black Christian Con-sciousness in Nineteenth Century America." *Church History* 41 (1972): 497–512.

[Smith, William Loughton, and Oliver Wolcott]. *The Pretension of Thomas Jefferson to the Presidency Examined, and the Charges Against John Adams Refuted.* [Phila-delphia], 1796.

Soderlund, Jean R. "Priorities and Power: The Philadelphia Female Anti-Slavery Soci-ety." In *The Abolitionist Sisterhood: Women's Political Culture in Antebellum America*, ed. Jean Fagan Yellin and John C. Van Horne, 67–88. Ithaca, N.Y., 1994.

Works Cited

Sollors, Werner. *Neither Black nor White yet Both: Thematic Explorations in Interracial Literature.* New York, 1997.

"Some Letters of Richard Allen and Absalom Jones to Dorothy Ripley." *Journal of Negro History* 1 (1916): 436–43.

Spangler, Jewel L. "Salvation Was Not Liberty: Baptists and Slavery in Revolutionary Virginia." *American Baptist Quarterly* 13 (1994): 221–36.

"The Speech of Moses Ben Sàam, a Free Negro, to the revolted Slaves in one of the Most considerable Colonies of the West Indies." *Gentleman's Magazine* 5 (1735): 21–23.

Staudenraus, P. J. *The African Colonization Movement, 1816–1865.* New York, 1961.

Stauffer, John. "Advent among the Indians: The Revolutionary Ethos of Gerrit Smith, James McCune Smith, Frederick Douglass, and John Brown." In *Antislavery Violence: Sectional, Racial, and Cultural Conflict in Antebellum America,* ed. John R. McKivigan and Stanley Harrold, 236–73. Knoxville, 1999.

Stedman, John G. *Narrative of a Five Years' Expedition Against the Revolted Negroes of Surinam.* 1796. Rpt. Amherst, Mass., 1972.

[Stedman, John G.]. *Narrative of Joanna; an Emancipated Slave of Surinam.* Boston, 1838.

Stein, Stephen J. "George Whitefield on Slavery: Some New Evidence." *Church History* 42 (1973): 243–56.

Sterling, Dorothy. *Speak Out in Thunder Tones: Letters and Other Writings by Black Northerners, 1787–1865.* Garden City, N.Y., 1973.

Steward, Austin. *Twenty-Two Years a Slave, and Forty Years a Freeman; Embracing a Correspondence of Several Years, While President of Wilberforce Colony, London, Canada West.* 1856. Rpt. New York, 1968.

Stewart, James Brewer. "The Emergence of Racial Modernity and the Rise of the White North." *Journal of the Early Republic* 18 (1998): 181–218.

———. *Wendell Phillips: Liberty's Hero.* Baton Rouge, 1986.

Stewart, Maria W. *Maria W. Stewart: America's First Black Woman Political Writer.* Ed. Marilyn Richardson. Bloomington, Ind., 1987.

Stiles, Ezra, and Samuel Hopkins. *To The Public.* Newport, R.I., 1776.

Stowe, Harriet Beecher. *Uncle Tom's Cabin.* Ed. Elizabeth Ammons. New York, 1994.

Streifford, David M. "The American Colonization Society: An Application of Republican Ideology to Early Antebellum Reform." *Journal of Southern History* 45 (1979): 201–20.

Stuckey, Sterling. *The Ideological Origins of Black Nationalism.* Boston, 1972.

Sundquist, Eric. *To Wake the Nations: Race in the Making of American Literature.* Cambridge, Mass., 1993.

Swan, Robert J. "John Teasman: African-American Educator and the Emergence of Community in Early Black New York City, 1787–1815." *Journal of the Early Republic* 12 (1992): 331–56.

Sweet, Leonard I. *Black Images of America, 1784–1870.* New York, 1976.

Swift, David E. *Black Prophets of Justice: Activist Clergy before the Civil War.* Baton Rouge, 1987.

Works Cited

Sypher, Wylie. *Guinea's Captive Kings: British Anti-Slavery Literature of the Eighteenth Century.* 1942. Rpt. New York, 1969.

Teasman, John. *An Address Delivered in the African Episcopal Church on the 25th March 1811. Before the New-York African Society for Mutual Relief; Being the First Anniversary of Its Incorporation.* New York, 1811.

Teute, Fredrika. "In 'the gloom of the evening': Margaret Bayard Smith's View in Black and White of Early Washington Society." *Proceedings of the American Antiquarian Society* 106 (1996): 37–58.

Thomas, John L. *The Liberator: William Lloyd Garrison, a Biography.* Boston, 1963.

Thomas, Lamont. *Rise to Be a People: A Biography of Paul Cuffe.* Urbana, Ill., 1986.

Tryon, Thomas. *Friendly Advice to the Gentlemen Planters of the East and West Indies.* London, 1684.

Twombley, Robert, and Robert H. Moore. "Black Puritan: The Negro in Seventeenth-Century Massachusetts." *William and Mary Quarterly* 24 (1967): 224–42.

Tyrannical Libertymen. A Discourse upon Negro-Slavery in the United States: Composed at ———, in New Hampshire; on the Late Federal Thanksgiving-Day. Hanover, N.H., 1795.

Ullman, Victor. *Martin R. Delany: The Beginnings of Black Nationalism.* Boston, 1971.

Van Deburg, William L. *Slavery and Race in American Popular Culture.* Madison, Wis., 1984.

Van Horne, John C., ed. *Religious Philanthropy and Colonial Slavery: The American Correspondence of the Associates of Dr. Bray, 1717–1777.* Urbana, Ill., 1985.

Vaughan, Alden. *The Roots of American Racism: Essays on the Colonial Experience.* New York, 1995.

Vibert, Faith. "The Society for the Propagation of the Gospel in Foreign Parts: Its Work for the Negroes in North America before 1783." *Journal of Negro History* 18 (1933): 171–212.

Views of American Slavery: Anthony Benezet and John Wesley. 1858. Rpt. New York, 1969.

Volney, C. F. *The Ruins: or, Meditations on the Revolutions of Empires and the Law of Nature.* 1802. Rpt. New York, 1926.

Wade, Richard. "The Negro in Cincinnati, 1800–1850." *Journal of Negro History* 39 (1954): 43–57.

Waldstreicher, David. *In the Midst of Perpetual Fetes: The Making of American Nationalism, 1776–1820.* Chapel Hill, 1997.

Walker, David. *David Walker's Appeal to the Colored Citizens of the World.* Ed. Peter P. Hinks. University Park, Pa., 2000.

Walvin, James. *Black and White: The Negro in English Society, 1555–1945.* London, 1973.

Ward, Samuel Ringgold. *Autobiography of a Fugitive Negro.* 1855. Rpt. New York, 1968.

Watkins, Frances Ellen. *Poems on Miscellaneous Subjects.* Boston, 1854.

Watkins, William J. *Our Rights as Men: An Address Delivered in Boston, Before the Legislative Committee on the Militia, February 24, 1853.* Boston, [1853].

Watson, Henry. *Narrative of Henry Watson, a Fugitive Slave. Written by Himself.* Boston, 1848.

Webb, Frank J. *The Garies and Their Friends.* 1857. Rpt. Baltimore, 1997.

Works Cited

Welch, Edwin. *Spiritual Pilgrim: A Reassessment of the Life of the Countess of Hunt-ingdon.* Cardiff, Wales, 1955.

Wellman, Judith. "This Side of the Border: Fugitives from Slavery in Three Central New York Communities." *New York History* 79 (1998): 359–92.

Wesley, Charles H. "The Participation of Negroes in Anti-Slavery Political Parties." *Journal of Negro History* 29 (1944): 32–74.

———. *Prince Hall: Life and Legacy.* Washington, D.C., 1977.

"What the Negro Was Thinking during the Eighteenth Century." *Journal of Negro History* 1 (1916): 49–68.

Wheatley, Phillis. *The Poems of Phillis Wheatley.* Ed. Julian D. Mason Jr. Rev. and enl. ed. Chapel Hill, 1989.

White, Shane. "'It Was a Proud Day': African Americans, Festivals, and Parades in the North, 1741–1834." *Journal of American History* 81 (1994): 13–50.

———. *Somewhat More Independent: The End of Slavery in New York City, 1770–1810.* Athens, Ga., 1990.

White, Shane, and Graham White. *Stylin': African American Expressive Culture from Its Beginnings to the Zoot Suit.* Ithaca, N.Y., 1998.

Williams, Kenny J. Introduction to *Essays; Including Biographies and Miscellaneous Pieces, in Prose and Poetry,* by Ann Plato. New York, 1988.

Williams, Peter, Jr. *A Discourse Delivered on the Death of Capt. Paul Cuffe, Before the New-York African Institution, in the African Methodist Episcopal Zion Church, October 21, 1817.* New York, 1817.

Williams, William H. *Slavery and Freedom in Delaware, 1639–1865.* Wilmington, Del., 1996.

[Willson, Joseph]. *Sketches of the Higher Classes of Colored Society in Philadelphia. By a Southerner.* 1841. Rpt. Philadelphia, 1969.

Winans, Amy Elizabeth. "Slaves and Citizens: Early African America and the Discourse of Nations, 1770–1820." Ph.D. diss., Pennsylvania State University, 1998.

Winch, Julie. *Philadelphia's Black Elite: Activism, Accommodation, and the Struggle for Autonomy, 1787–1848.* Philadelphia, 1988.

———. "'You Have Talents — Only Cultivate Them': Philadelphia's Black Female Literary Societies and the Abolitionist Crusade." In *The Abolitionist Sisterhood: Women's Political Culture in Antebellum America,* ed. Jean Fagan Yellin and John C. Van Horne, 101–18. Ithaca, N.Y., 1994.

Wood, Betty. *Women's Work, Men's Work: The Informal Slave Economies of Lowcountry Georgia.* Athens, Ga., 1995.

Wood, Gordon S. *The Radicalism of the American Revolution.* New York, 1992.

Wood, Peter. *Black Majority: Negroes in Colonial South Carolina from 1670 through the Stono Rebellion.* New York, 1974.

———. "'The Dream Deferred': Black Freedom Struggles on the Eve of White Independence." In *In Resistance: Studies in African, Caribbean, and Afro-American History,* ed. Gary Y. Okihiro, 166–87. Amherst, Mass., 1986.

Woodson, Carter G. *The Mind of the Negro as Reflected in Letters Written during the Crisis, 1800–1860.* Washington, D.C., 1926.

[Wright, Elizur]. "The Life and Adventures of a Fugitive Slave." *Quarterly Anti-Slavery Magazine* 1 (1836): 375–93.

Works Cited

Yarborough, Richard. "Strategies of Black Characterization in *Uncle Tom's Cabin* and the Early Afro-American Novel." In *New Essays on Uncle Tom's Cabin*, ed. Eric Sundquist, 45–84. Cambridge, Eng., 1986.

Yee, Shirley J. *Black Women Abolitionists: A Study in Activism, 1828–1860.* Knoxville, 1992.

Young, Robert Alexander. *The Ethiopian Manifesto, Issued in Defence of the Black Man's Rights, in the Scale of Universal Freedom.* New York, 1829.

Zafar, Rafia. *We Wear the Mask: African Americans Write American Literature, 1760–1817.* New York, 1997.

Index

Index

Allen, Richard, 72, 73, 83, 85, 97, 98, 102, 104, 126, 139–40, 156, 157, 158, 163, 178, 179, 182, 266; *A Narrative of the Proceedings of the Black People During the Late Awful Calamity in Philadelphia*, 85–86

Allen, William, 130

Allen, William G., 214, 295; *Wheatley, Banneker, and Horton*, 228, 229

"amalgamation," 138, 139, 218, 246, 294–96, 305–6. *See also* interracial marriage

American Anti-Slavery Society, 213, 221, 231, 240

American Colonization Society, 144–45, 151, 152, 156, 164, 166, 171, 174, 177, 178, 190, 192, 242; African American views of, 137–41, 155, 157, 180; African American voice in, 143, 145–46, 155, 157–61, 188–89; founding of, 134–37; images of Africans, 153–54

American Moral Reform Society, 249

American Museum, 66, 69, 74, 75, 76–77

American Peace League, 263

American Revolution, 39–40; in abolitionist thought, 221–22, 271–72, 298–99, 302; African American voices in, 49, 52–55, 57–58; antislavery impulses in, 40, 43, 44, 47–48, 57–59, 62, 120–21; ideology of, 40, 56–59, 62, 75, 96

Ames, Julius: *Legion of Liberty!*, 230

Amistad incident, 237

Amo, Anton Wilhelm, 21, 105

Anderson, Osborne, 302–3

Andrews, William L., 34, 149, 183, 240, 246, 288

Anglo-African Magazine, 269–70, 271, 306

Anti-Slavery Bugle, 261, 262

Anti-Slavery Convention of American Women, 233

antislavery fiction: conventions of, 288–96; emergence of, 287–89

Anti-Slavery Record, 230, 248

Appleton, Nathaniel, 20–21, 57, 59

Armistead, Wilson, 245

Aron, Stephen, 113

"Art of Preventing Slave Insurrections, The," 206

Asbury, Francis, 72–73

Ashmun, Jehudi, 162

Atlantic Monthly, 302, 309, 311

Attucks, Crispus, 44–45

auction block, symbolism of, 243, 248, 289

Augustine of Hippo, 12

Auld, Thomas, 241, 246

authentication, issues of, 46–47, 97, 111, 114–15, 142, 145–46, 184, 193, 248–49, 252–53; and fugitive slave narratives, 240–42, 282

Bacon, Thomas, 12, 113, 115

Ball, Charles: *Slavery in the United States*, 239–40, 242, 243, 247, 275

Baltimore, Md., 116, 144, 157–58

Banneker, Benjamin, 67–68, 69–70, 86, 105, 151, 228, 311

Baptist Church, 62

Barrett, Lindon, 244

Barton, Colonel, 218, 219

Bayley, Solomon, 189; *A Brief Account of the Colony of Liberia*, 189; *Narrative*, 149

Behn, Aphra, 24, 36, 86, 98, 119; *Oroonoko*, 24–25, 26, 27, 36, 58, 86, 119, 150

Belinda (petitioner), 65–67

"Belinda" (poet), 67

Belknap, Jeremy, 82

Bell, James Madison, 263, 271, 310, 314

Bell, Philip, 211, 251, 303, 313

Beman, Amos G., 171–72, 214, 304

Beman, Jehiel, 186

Benezet, Anthony, 19, 58–59, 68, 87, 88

Berkeley, William, 15

Berlin, Ira, 3, 116

Berry, Harrison, 275

Bethel Church (Baltimore), 157–58

Bibb, Henry, 225, 239, 241, 246–47, 256, 258, 273, 284

Bingham, Caleb: *The Columbian Orator*, 69, 89, 117, 246

Bishop, Abraham, 90, 120

Blackett, Richard, 284

"Black Whig" (writer), 53

Blake, William, 86

Blassingame, John, 226

Bledsoe, Albert Taylor, 282, 287

Index

Index

Coker, Daniel (*continued*)
155, 157, 167–68, 181; *A Dialogue Between a Virginian and an African Minister*, 116–18, 127, 143–44
Cole, Jinny, 18–19, 25, 27
Coleman, Edward Maceo, 235
Collins, John A., 225, 239; *The Anti-Slavery Picknick*, 238
Collins, Julia, 306–7
colonization, African American ideas on, 127–29, 129–34, 137–41, 155–57, 161, 177, 178, 188, 270–73. *See also* American Colonization Society
Colored American, 211, 223, 236, 237, 238, 250, 251–52, 253
Columbian Magazine, 124
Columbus, Christopher, 119
Conway, Moncure, 291, 296, 311
Cooper, Frederick, 166
Copeland, John A., 301–2
Cornish, Samuel, 163–65, 167, 175, 177, 211, 223, 230, 250, 251, 252, 253, 256
Cornish, William, 157
"Counter-Memorial proposed to be submitted to Congress on behalf of the free people of colour of the District of Columbia," 137–40, 142, 151, 155
Cowper, William, 98, 112, 204; "The Negro's Complaint," 81, 97
Cox, Virginia, 23–24
Craft, Ellen, 259, 270, 275, 276
Craft, William, 259, 270, 286, 308
Croly, David: *Miscegenation*, 305–6
Crowe, John Finley, 150, 151, 169
Crozer, Samuel, 144
Crummell, Alexander, 214
Cuffe, Paul, 129–34, 135, 136, 139–40, 141–42, 143, 144, 156, 159, 271; *A Brief Acount of the Settlement and Present Situation of the Colony of Sierra Leone*, 133–34
Cugoano, Ottabah, 63, 79, 84
Cyprian, 12, 83

Dain, Bruce, 123, 167
Dallas, George Mifflin, 274
Dartmouth, Earl of, 45
Davies, Samuel, 9, 14, 16

Davis, David Brion, 22–23
Davis, Mary Kemp, 183
Davis, Susan, 219
Day, Thomas: "The Dying Negro," 49, 57
De Bois, Oneda, 308
Declaration of Independence, The, 96, 177, 178, 181, 204
Deerfield, Massachusetts, 19, 30–31
Delany, Martin R., 211, 251, 253, 255, 269, 270–71, 274, 284, 285, 290; *Blake*, 297, 299–300, 302; *The Condition, Elevation, Emigration, and Destiny of the Colored People of the United States*, 267–68
Denon, Vivant, 123
Desrochers, Robert, 89
de Vastey, Baron, 151
dialect, use of, 49–50, 70–71, 94–95, 152, 172, 216–17, 232, 276, 277–78, 289, 290–91. *See also* minstrelsy
dialogues, literary use of, 22–24, 67–70, 116–17, 206–8, 237, 246–47, 274, 278–82
discursive communities, 29–30, 31, 32, 35, 46–47, 55–56, 72, 95, 98, 166, 194–95, 201, 208–10, 223–24, 232–34
Doctrines and Discipline of the African Methodist Episcopal Church, The, 127
Douglass, Frederick, 69, 211, 213, 222, 225, 226, 230, 231, 258, 263, 265–66, 267, 268, 271, 278, 284, 285–86, 294, 295, 300, 308, 311, 313; "The Heroic Slave," 297–99, 301; and issues of autonomy, 254–56, 266; *My Bondage and My Freedom*, 246, 259, 266; *Narrative*, 239, 241, 259, 282, 284; and William Lloyd Garrison, 221–22, 226, 254–55, 297
Douglass, Robert, 234
Douglass, Sarah, 186, 199, 201, 214, 215, 223, 234, 269
Douglass' Monthly, 269–70, 311
Dred Scott decision, 300, 301
Dumas, Alexandre, 228
Dunbar, Paul Laurence, 314
Dunmore, Lord, 39–40
Dwight, Theodore, 63, 69, 117

Earle, Eliza, 232–34
Easton, Hosea, 168, 174, 180, 193, 196, 266; *A Treatise on the Intellectual Charcter,*

Index

Harper, Charles C., 158–60

Harper, Frances Ellen Watkins. *See* Watkins, Frances Ellen

Harper, William, 280, 281

Harper's Ferry, Va., raid, 301–2, 303

Harris, Thaddeus, 148

Hartman, James, 35

Harvard University, 44, 48, 49, 57–58, 60

Haskell, Thomas, 29

Haven, Gilbert, 291, 294, 295

Hawkins, John, 2, 35, 119, 120

Hayden, Lewis, 274

Hayden, William, 240–41, 245

Haynes, Lemuel, 52–53, 72, 99–100, 148, 228; *The Nature and Importance of True Republicanism*, 99–100

Henkin, David, 219

Herald of Freedom, 218–19

Herodotus, 123, 229, 230

Heyrman, Christine, 101

Higginson, Thomas Wentworth, 259, 302

Hildreth, Richard: *Archy Moore*, 242

Hinks, Peter, 180

Hinton, Frederick, 222, 250

Hirschberg, H. Z., 122

Hodges, Graham, 151

Holgate, Jerome. *See* "Bolokitten, Oliver"

Holly, Joseph, 263, 290, 291

Hopkins, Samuel, 61, 63, 117; *A Dialogue Concerning the Slavery of Africans*, 48–49

Horton, George Moses, 169–71, 174, 230; *In Hope of Liberty*, 171; "Liberty and Slavery," 170; "Slavery," 170, 171, 200

Horton, James (slaveowner), 171

Hosmer, Hezekiah, 296; *Adela, the Octoroon*, 295

Huddleston, Eugene, 64

Hugo, Victor, 265

"Humanitas" (writer), 121

Hunt, James, 308

Huntingdon, countess of (Selina Hastings), 41–43, 46

Hutchinson, Thomas, 45

Hutchinson Family singers, 225

Ibrahima, Abd al-Rahaman, 149–50

identity, issues of, 95, 103–4, 111, 127, 249

Imlay, Gilbert: *A Topographical Description of the Western Territory of North America*, 64

"improvement," ideas of, 166, 168, 196–98, 236

"Inkle and Yarico," 26, 27, 87, 98, 292

International Statistics Conference (London), 274

interracial marriage, 4, 138, 139, 294–96, 305–307. *See also* "amalgamation"

Jackson, Blyden, 170, 303

Jacobs, Donald, 187

Jacobs, Harriet, 279, 281, 297, 312; *Incidents in the Life of a Slave Girl*, 293

Jay, John, 81

Jea, John, 103–4, 113

Jefferson, Thomas, 61, 62, 64, 67–68, 69, 78, 105, 106, 125–26, 130–31, 136, 138, 148, 151, 181–82, 276; *Notes on the State of Virginia*, 61, 64, 105, 125, 151, 181–82, 209

Job ben Solomon (Ayuba Suleiman Diallo), 26, 27, 28, 29, 65

Jobson, Richard, 35

Jocelyn, Simeon, 252

"John Koonering" (festival) 6

Johnson, Anthony, 3

"Johnson, Mr." (fugitive slave), 230–31

Johnson, Oliver, 265, 268

Johnson, Walter, 248

Jones, Absalom, 72, 73, 75, 78, 102, 105, 107–8, 109, 118, 126, 139–40, 141–42; *A Narrative of the Proceedings of the Black People During the Late Awful Calamity in Philadelphia*, 85–86

Jonson, Ben: "Masques of Blackness and Beauty," 21

Jordan, Winthrop, 2

Josephus, 125

Josselyn, John, 25

Juster, Susan, 17

Kansas, violence in, 297, 301

Kaplan, Sidney, 306

Kentucky, 93

Key, Elizabeth, 10–11

kidnapping and enslavement, accounts of, 18–20, 24, 42, 58, 98, 99, 103–4, 107, 109

Index

King, Boston, 73–74, 79
Knapp, Isaac, 237
Krise, Thomas, 27, 28

Ladd, Elizabeth: *Some Account of Lucy Cardwell, a Woman of Colour*, 149
Ladies' Anti-Slavery Society (Philadelphia), 227
Langston, John Mercer, 260, 287
Lanusse, Armand, 235
Lapsansky, Emma, 217
Latino, Juan, 21
Latrobe, John H. B., 153–54, 158–60
Latter Day Luminary, 161, 162
LaVallée, Joseph: "The Negro Equalled by Few Europeans," 68–69, 106
Leavitt, Joshua, 223, 252
Lee, Jarena, 230
Le Jau, Francis, 13, 16
"Let My People Go" (spiritual), 310
Levine, Robert, 286
Levison, William, 276–77, 284, 294
Lewis, Enoch, 165
Lewis, Robert: *Light and Truth*, 229
Liberator, 184, 185, 186, 196, 211, 212, 215, 231, 232, 233, 237, 249, 251, 254, 256, 261, 262, 267–68, 277, 278, 302, 304, 308, 311, 313; and African American literary work, 194–95, 199–206; on colonization, 188, 190–93; and discursive community, 186–88, 190–93, 209–10, 213
Liberia, 144, 153, 158, 161, 162, 163, 174, 177, 188–89
Liberia Herald, 189
Liberty Bell, 211, 229
Liberty Party, 256
Liele, George, 72, 73, 74
Lincoln, Abraham, 282, 302, 305
Lindhorst, Marie, 201
literacy, 14, 103, 114
literary achievement, significance of, 150–51, 168–69, 171, 174, 193–94, 198–99, 227–29, 234–37, 287–88, 311
literary societies, 199, 236–37
literary tradition, African American, 74, 104–9, 119–20, 128, 159–61, 228–31
Livermore, Elizabeth: *Zoë; or, The Quadroon's Triumph*, 291

Loggins, Vernon, 268
Loguen, Jermain W., 267, 268, 270, 271, 308
Long, Edward, 40, 49, 123
Long, John Dixon: *Pictures of Slavery in Church and State*, 262
Longfellow, Henry Wadsworth: "The Quadroon Girl," 292–93; "The Slave's Dream," 238
Longstreet, Augustus Baldwin, 274
L'Ouverture, Toussaint, 61–62, 90, 207–8, 230, 300, 303
Lundy, Benjamin, 147, 150, 151, 153, 158, 164, 176, 185, 186

Mackenzie, Anna Maria: *Slavery; or, the Times*, 75
Madison, James, 132
"Magawiska." *See* Forten, Sarah
Map, Thomas, 123–24
Marrant, John, 73–74, 79, 83, 84, 90–91, 102, 103, 121
Martin, J. Sella, 307
Maryland, 3, 11, 93
Mason, Julian, 42
Massachusetts, 3, 5, 11, 19, 30–31, 43, 47, 53–55, 307
Massachusetts Anti-Slavery Society, 230, 254
Massachusetts General Colored Association, 179–80
Massachusetts General Court, 43, 47, 53, 65, 82
Massachusetts Magazine, 67
Massachusetts Missionary Magazine, 112
Massachusetts Spy, 232
Mather, Cotton, 9–12, 90, 121; *The Negro Christianized*, 9
"Matilda," (poet), 64
Maverick, Samuel, 25
May, Samuel J., 218, 219, 312
McCord, David, 275, 276
McCord, Louisa, 276, 279, 282, 283
McFeely, William, 313
McGill, George, 158, 188
McGraw, Marie Tyler, 163
McHenry, Elizabeth, 199
McHenry, James, 67

Index

Index

Ohio, 93, 147
Olney, James, 243
Olwell, Richard, 40
Omar ibn Said, 150
Oneida Institute, 214, 228, 263
"On the Varieties of the Human Race,"
167
Onuf, Peter, 78
oral traditions, African American, 18–21,
29, 58, 98, 237–38, 309–10
Oson, Jacob, 124–25, 230
"Othello" (writer), 77, 83, 90, 105, 112
Otis, James, 48, 57; "Rights of the British
Colonies," 40

Pacific Appeal, 303, 305, 307, 311
Paris Peace Conference, 263–64
Parrish, John, 104–5, 110
Parrott, Russell, 108, 109, 110, 119, 143
Paul, Susan: *Memoir of James Jackson*, 238
Payne, Daniel A., 224, 235–36, 269; "The
Hour of Prayer," 235; "The Mournful
Lute," 235
Pease, Elizabeth, 254–55
Penn, William, 141–42
Pennington, James W. C., 228, 230, 234,
242, 244, 245, 246, 247, 269, 271, 308; *A
Text Book of the Origin and History,
&c. &c. of the Colored People*, 229
Pennsylvania, 13, 95–97, 216, 221
Pennsylvania Abolition Society, 80
Pennsylvania Freeman, 211, 223, 254, 262,
264, 268, 285, 287, 290
Pennsylvania Hall, 218
Peterson, Carla, 288
Peterson, Thomas Virgil, 274–75
petitions, African American, 53–55, 56, 58,
82, 127–28
Phelps, Amos, 223, 255
Philadelphia, Pa., 13, 62, 92, 106, 129, 130,
139–40, 141, 143, 156, 158–59, 178, 179,
180, 213, 214, 217, 218, 231, 271–72
Philadelphia Female Anti-Slavery Society,
213
Philadelphia Library Company of Col-
ored Persons, 236
"Philanthropos," 106, 112

Phillips, Wendell, 241, 259, 272, 285, 296,
299, 300, 305
Philomathean Society (New York), 236
Phoenix Society (New York), 236
Piersen, William D., 19
Pike, Mary: *Caste*, 295, 296
Pillsbury, Parker, 255, 306
Pinckney, William, 77
Pine and Palm, 302
"pious Negro" tradition, 74, 112, 114–15,
149, 150, 237
Plácido (Diego Gabriel de Concepción
Valdez), 228, 229, 299
Plato, Ann, 228, 230, 234, 236
Pratt, Mary Louise, 87
Prentiss, Benjamin F., 97, 98–99, 100, 103,
104, 112, 122
press, African American, 163–65, 211,
251–56, 269–70, 313
primitivism, 58–59, 65–66, 87–89, 107–
108, 120, 124, 125, 173, 231. *See also*
exoticism
proslavery opinion: African American
voice in, 71, 113–15, 116, 274–75; and
fugitive slaves, 226–27, 247–48, 275–76,
281–82
providence, ideas of, 79–81, 108, 117–19,
126–27, 130, 144–45, 167–68, 196, 223, 235
Providence Gazette, 150
Provincial Freeman, 262, 269, 285
public sphere, African Americans in, 55,
63, 65, 104, 107, 110–11, 219, 236–37
Purvis, Charles, 212; *Appeal of Forty Thousand Citizens, Threatened with Disfranchisement*, 221
Purvis, Robert, 260, 266–67, 285
Purvis family, 214
Pushkin, Aleksandr, 228

Quamine, John, 61
Quarles, Benjamin, 185
Queen of Sheba, 12, 83, 122
Quincy, Edmund, 254, 299

race, ideas of, 12, 13, 17–18, 49, 50, 57, 61,
64, 67, 74–75, 77–78, 108, 111–12, 117,
167, 169, 216

Index